IGNITE Female

Change Makers

Other IGNITE compilation books
for you to enjoy

———————

Ignite Your Life for Women

Ignite Your Female Leadership

Ignite Your Parenting

Ignite Your Life for Men

Ignite Your Life for Conscious Leaders

Ignite Your Adventurous Spirit

Ignite Your Health and Wellness

IGNITE Female Change Makers

DYNAMIC WOMEN MAKING AN
EXCEPTIONAL DIFFERENCE FOR THE
FUTURE OF WOMEN AROUND THE WORLD

FOREWORD BY **Andrea Szücs**
Actress, Therapist, Coach

INTRODUCTION BY **JB Owen**
Founder of Ignite and JBO Global Inc.

PRESENTED BY

ALEX JARVIS • ALICIA KOMIYA • ANA SOFIA OROZCO • ANANDHA RAY
ANDREA DRAJEWICZ • ANNE CATHERINE FÆRGEMANN • ARSHIYA BHAN • ASIFA AKBAR
BEEJAL COULSON • CATHERINE MALLI-DAWSON • CHARLOTTE SØEBERG
CHRISSY LEVETT • CHRISTY PARKER • CLAUDIA CHAVEZ GORDOA • CRISTINA PUJOL JENSEN
CYNTHIA VITRANO • DEBRA SCHRIEBER • DIANA BORGES • DIANA I PELAEZ • DIANA LOCKETT
ELENA HARDER • ELENA RODRÍGUEZ BLANCO • HANNA MEIRELLES • HERMIAN CHARLES
HOLLY OLP • J MEEHAN • JANNETTE ANDERSONS • JB OWEN • JENNIFER NEWTON
JENNIFER WOOTTON • JOANNE FEASTER • KARIMA NADINE STEIN • KATARINA AMADORA
LOUISE GRAHAM • MARIA EUGENIA ANÉS DRAEGERT • MARIA PAULINA MEJIA
MARNIE TARZIA • MELISSA ELEVEY • MINDY STERN • NICOLE STOKER EVANS • PRIYA LAKHI
ROSA MARIA KALLAS • ROSALYN PALMER • SIBYLLE MANI • SIMONETTA NIEDERREITER
SONIA CHOPRA • STEPHANIE BARROS • TARA PILLING • VIVIEN HUNT

PUBLISHED BY IGNITE AND PRINTED BY JBO GLOBAL INC.

Published and printed by JBO Global
5569-47th Street, Red Deer, AB
Canada, T4N6L4 1-877-677-6115

Cover design by JB Owen
Book design by Dania Zafar

Designed in Canada, Printed in China

ISBN# 978-1-7923-0671-6

First edition: April 2020

Ordering Information: Quantity sales. Special discounts are available on quantity purchases by corporations, associations, and others. For details, contact the publisher at the address above. Programs, products or services provided by the authors are found by contacting them directly. Resources named in the book are found in the resources pages at the back of the book.

Dedication

This book is dedicated to all the Female Change Makers who ride the tide of change. To those women who fight the uphill battle and go against the curve. We honor the women who look past the confines of convention and see what lies beyond. The world needs those women, those courageous souls who seek triumph not for themselves but for the benefit of everyone. They embrace change for the glorious good of the whole. Thank you, Change Makers for you make this world a better world to live in.

———————

JB Owen

TESTIMONIALS FROM AUTHORS

"What an honor to be a part of the Ignite Your Female Changemaker book! The Ignite compilation series is a process like no other. Through the art of personal storytelling nurtured in a supportive, synergistic collective space, individual authors release a powerful, constructive offering of insights and wisdom about life, as a healing balm for humanity."

~ Asifa Akbar

"My late opportunity to take part in this book was perfectly timed to capture my Ignite Moment and the changes I've made so far. It now forms a central part of my next steps to effect change, by providing a global platform to share my insights to help others. The whole Ignite team has rallied to welcome and support me in the writing and editing process. The online portal, the guidance notes for the whole process and the numerous supportive phone and video calls have all contributed to a story I'm now delighted to share, as well as improving my skills as a writer. Thank you, it's been a pleasure!"

~ Joanne Feaster

"I've been skeptical about participating in a compilation book because, in my experience, they are typically poorly written, edited, and don't hold much value for the reader. I have been so impressed with my experience with JB Owen and the entire Ignite team. They were professional, well-organized (when I wasn't), and they made me a better writer. I will actually be proud to sell this book and to be a part of it."

~ Jannette Anderson

"Writing for the Ignite Female Change Makers book was the first time I put specifics about my past out to the public. Although I initially struggled with exposing childhood traumas, I decided it was necessary so I could heal to a deeper level and help others see that transformation is possible. Writing my chapter also gave me the opportunity to start conversations with my family I had not previously approached. If you are considering participating in one of the Ignite books, I highly recommend it so you can honor your own truth and see what arises for you. The Ignite team will be there for you throughout the process."

~ Diana Borges

"It was my first Ignite author experience, writing for Female Change Makers. I knew it was time to share my story on a global platform on why and how I was contributing to raising the consciousness of the planet. The writing and editing process was thorough with great support throughout the weekly Masterminds and bi-monthly Writers' Nests. The experience led to so much personal development and growth. It highlighted to me there is so much more that I would love to share with the world. I have signed up to be part of two more Ignite books!"

~ Beejal Coulson

"I joined the Ignite for Change Female Makers book a little later than the rest of the tribe. The way that my web dashboard was organized with all videos saved made it easy for me to catch up on content. The amount of coaching, support, community, and love from the Ignite team and authors was beyond my expectations. I continue to receive support through their Mastermind weekly calls and am using that content to inform me as I now write my own personal book. The writing process was a healing journey and the editors have empowered me with confidence and enthusiasm to believe in myself as a writer. Thank you from the depths of my heart. To JB and the Ignite team, you are the real CHANGE MAKERS xo"

~ Diana Lockett

"I thoroughly enjoyed my journey to becoming an Ignite author. Most of my early career I was criticized for my writing and so I had a lot of emotional and mindset challenges to overcome. I am celebrating myself and my fellow authors for raising the collective consciousness through the courageous sharing of our most personal stories, shared with authenticity and love. Thank you for the opportunity."

~ Louise Graham

"It has been quite a self-empowering experience. "

~ María Paulina Mejía Vélez

The Code of a Change Maker

We get up early
We go to bed late
We work harder
We go farther
We keep going
We keep giving
We listen and learn
We find solutions
We see possibilities
We welcome change
We embrace newness
We know ourselves
We live in our truth
We build up others
We endlessly support
We share our wisdom
We cultivate our gifts
We give more than we take
We speak in authenticity
We love unconditionally
We honor all

My dear Change Maker, you are enough. You are more than enough. You are way more beautiful and way more powerful than you could ever imagine. And yes, you can transform the world, one person at a time, by being the most joyous, passionate and alive version of yourself. We need people who can remind us of our beauty, who inspire us to believe in life. and to follow our dreams once again. You can help others tap into their aliveness and create a ripple effect. Let's light up the world by sharing our joy, laughter, encouragement, and most importantly, our unconditional love.

~ Mellisa Elevey

Contents

Preface

What Ignite is All About

Ignite was created to Ignite others and impact humanity. Our mandate is to do more, share more, and spread conscious positive messages to as many people as possible. We believe in the human connection. We believe that power comes from being heard, being seen, and belonging to something greater. We invite people to Ignite others. To let their stories be heard, share their experiences, and find their voices. We pride ourselves in bringing people together, offering a solution, giving back, and doing something good for the planet. That is the mission and purpose behind IGNITE. There is power when one person touches the heart of another and sparks something new. Be it inspiration, love, support, encouragement, compassion or belief — each of us deserves to be Ignited and we hope these stories Ignite you.

May you have many Ignite moments that transform your
life into the amazing person you were meant to be.

— JB Owen

The World Loves Compilation Books

We know that many people read compilation books to be inspired. If you feel that your story is still unfolding or that you are still trying to figure it out, we are with you. We all have been through difficulties and go through them numerous times in our lives. Our stories show transformation *in spite of* all that. We push ourselves to go forward. We offer encouragement to rise and flourish. We support each other in as many ways as we can. The enthusiasm behind each of our authors' transformations is now behind you. We support you unconditionally and are cheering you on as you uncover your own amazing life. We extend our hands should you need a bit of support, some advice, or a friend to confide in. We offer our services should you ever want to reach out because something we said resonated with you and what we shared was exactly what you needed to hear. We are all accessible and eager to connect; please feel free to find us wherever we are in the world. We are happy to support you as you undergo your own amazing self-exploration.

We are Ignited by the idea of you turning the page and reading the many stories of Female Change Makers. We want you to be excited to read about how another woman stepped into the very essence of her fulfilling life and succeeded. Some of those stories may be filled with pain and grief. Others might be loaded with joy and accomplishment. All of them show a fierce determination to step into the next version of who they were willing to become. Their stories are a guide to the unlimited possibilities that are before you in *your* life. Soak in what they have to share and then decide to go out and do more, live more. Feel energized to venture forth with a smile beaming from your face and a spring in your step. Claim your freedom! Love your talents and embrace the dynamic change that is right around the corner.

You are a Change Maker and this book is for you!

In the pages to come, you are about to meet many women just like you. Their stories are varied and their histories are all different. They come from every corner of the planet. Some dip their toes in the sand of their home country while others live the metropolis mecca of their capital cities. Each one of these women is diverse in their nature, yet in many ways they are the same. They aspire for a better planet where we all live harmoniously. They work hard not just for success but for inner peace and personal enjoyment. They collaborate, create, and connect with others in a way that builds community, camaraderie,

and closeness. Their personal code is not just a better life ⌐
for everyone.

You are among them. Your life, desires, and dreams for the fu
with them. Your story may be different. Your home may be totall
But your heart beats in the same way their hearts do. You aspire f⌐
challenge yourself daily. And deep inside, you yearn to make a diffe
is the life of a Change Maker, the unwavering ambition to raise the ⌐
ness of the planet and create a better world where all prosper.

As you enjoy the stories in this book, you will be touched by the cand
of our authors and fired up by their words of wisdom. You will feel a se⌐
kinship with many of them. Your own change-making spirit will feel insp
to go out and be more of who you were meant to be. When that happens, w⌐
love to hear it. We want to know how this book, or one story in it, change
your life for the better. When that happens, let us know. Share how this book
or one particular story in it moved you in a new direction and *changed* your
life for the better. Your story will in turn inspire each of us.

What Makes Ignite Unique

Every word written in this book, every letter on these pages, has been meticulously crafted with fondness, encouragement, and a distinct clarity not just to
inspire you but to transform you. Many people in this book stepped up to share
their stories for the very first time. They courageously revealed the many layers
of themselves and exposed their weaknesses, fears, and discomforts as few
do. Additionally, they spoke authentically from the heart and wrote what was
true for them, infusing love, compassion, and a desire to inspire in every word.

We could have taken their stories and aimed for perfection, following every
editing rule. Instead, we chose to leave their unique and honest voices intact.
We overlooked exactness to foster individual expressions. These are their
words and sentiments. We let their personalities shine through so you would
get a deeper sense of who they are. We focused on authenticity, honesty, and
personal expression. That is what makes IGNITE. Authors serving others.
Stories igniting humanity. No filters. No desire for perfection. Just realness
between them and you.

Come turn the page and meet our authors up close and personal. We know
you're going to love them as much as we do. Enjoy!

FOREWORD BY ANDREA SZÜCS

Actress, Therapist, Coach

"As we are inspired, we inspire others."

(S)HEROES: THRICE UPON A TIME

In preparing the foreword for this inspiring book, Ignite Female Change Makers, it got me thinking about the incredible power that comes from creating change and reflecting upon the three most influential women in my life, all of whom had no idea they were my (s)heroes. Their attitudes, values, and actions personified what a woman can do when she lives her passion and follows her dreams. All three of these women influenced me as much as my mother and grandmother had before I changed my own life and left Hungary.

Once upon a time in Budapest, on a sunny September Monday in 1972, I was climbing the stairs to our 3rd-floor classroom on my first day of first grade. As I entered, 32 kids were sitting in awkward semi-silence. The school bell rang, and she entered — Ms. Margit, our 1st-grade teacher.

She was in her late 20s, wearing a plaid mini skirt and high-heeled wedges. Her blue sweater perfectly hugged her stunning figure. She had legs up to her ears, perfect hair, long lashes, and cat eyeliner — she looked like a supermodel. She was a breeze of fresh air in my heat of anxiety. Her kindness, calm, and loving energy immediately put me at ease. I trusted her. I knew I was home.

She said, "Good morning! I'm so happy to see you all! I heard this is the best class with the smartest, brightest, and most talented students in the whole district. Is that right?" How amazing for a young child to be seen by an adult and to receive such wonderful affirmation.

I couldn't take my eyes off her! I was hanging on her every word. Her confident compassion, the way she took charge of the room, and her knowledge and wit mesmerized me. She made me feel that I could do anything. A crystal clear voice in my heart said. **"That's it! I want to be an educator to help people feel good and inspire them to learn and grow while they are having the time of their lives."** She had no idea how much she influenced me.

Twice upon a time in 1982, my mom and I went to see a musical by Cy Coleman in the Vidam Theater in Budapest. My mom was coaching the lead actress during the rehearsal process, and we had two complimentary tickets for opening night. Zsuzsa (the lead actress) also invited us backstage at intermission. I was super excited! We went up the skinny stairs to her dressing room on the 2nd floor. There were costumes hanging by her make-up station with mirrors up to the ceiling. She was sitting by the window in a burgundy bathrobe, touching up her makeup.

Gosh, she was beautiful! Like a Hollywood star — a Marilyn Monroe type but lankier. My mom was sitting next to her; I was standing by the costume rack. Zsuzsa was chatting about how she loved what she did and how she was the luckiest girl on earth that her job was to sing, dance, act, and make other people happy. I couldn't take my eyes off her. She was beautiful, talented, successful, and smart with a sense of humor. I felt passion, drive, envy, and inspiration. Every cell of my body agreed: **That's it! That's it! I want to be a performer who uses her talent to make people's journeys more beautiful and to give them a break from their everyday lives while providing them with the inspiration to feel and dream again!** She didn't know how much she influenced me.

Thrice upon a time on an autumn day, I went to see the movie *Out of Africa* with my parents in Budapest in 1986. I was glued to the screen, lost in the story, admiring Meryl Streep with the fire in my belly screaming: **That's it! That's it! That's it! I want to be an actress on the screen to tell stories that may change people's lives forever all over the world.** She didn't know how much she influenced me. Some 23 years later, I was fortunate to express my deepest gratitude to Meryl Streep directly on my first day of work with her. Meryl Streep was a pivotal person in my journey that pointed me to the pathway of the performing arts which led to me pursuing acting "Out of Hungary."

After the Iron Curtain fell in 1989, I left Hungary. The world just got bigger and more complex. I lived in Vienna for six years. I moved to the USA in 1994 to follow the ultimate dream: to be an actress in America.

In retrospect, I can see that my inner purpose and passion were revealed to me very early on in life. I acknowledge and appreciate the contributions of each one of these accomplished women that I affectionately refer to as my '(s)heroes.' Each one of these women Ignited my love of teaching and performing in the theatre and on screen. I never settled for the conventional career path. I never subscribed to the notion that tells us that we have to be 'one thing' when we grow up. I always knew that my inner calling involved pursuing various roles in both: the arts and academia. I had the courage to stay true to who I was and, in doing so, I have been able to help countless other women to do the same. I can see now that I was able to Ignite positive change in my own life as I had such positive role models around me who propelled me forward to pursue my dreams with passion and perseverance.

I always say I'm so lucky that I love what I do and do what I love — although I have realized through life experience that it is less luck and more grit. Grit is the passion and perseverance one requires for the accomplishment of long-term goals. I can't remember which movie or television show I was performing in when an interviewer suggested that perhaps I had landed the role because I was just 'lucky.' I remember laughing out loud and thinking, "The harder I work, the luckier I am."

Years later, what I suspected intuitively was validated by Angela Duckworth, a MacArthur Genius who found that grit is more predictive of success than IQ or talent. In short, if you have a dream or a goal for yourself, you have to work hard by demonstrating perseverance when obstacles or challenges arise. What I know is that I had to be resilient when I was rejected. Every successful person will tell you that at some point in their career somebody in the business dismissed them telling them they were inadequate or 'not enough,' Meryl Streep included. Our success is directly proportional to the amount of perseverance we demonstrate to push through challenges. Our disappointments can motivate us. Our temporary failures are what fuel our hope. Real change comes when we embrace every obstacle and see how we can proceed differently, how we can step into the essence of who we are full-hearted, ready, and filled with newfound hope.

"Hope is the only positive emotion that needs uncertainty or negativity to be activated," says researcher Barbara Fredrickson. New studies show that we can learn to be hopeful. Positive Psychologist Dan Tomasulo, in his latest book, *Learned Hopefulness,* says that we can foster hope by seeing possibilities. Hope is the belief that we have control over our future, no matter how big or little that control is at the moment. We can learn to achieve our own inner control by cultivating positive feelings, counting our blessings, focusing on strengths, creating goals, finding purpose, cherishing relationships, and most importantly by loving change.

I often think of those who touched me the deepest. I find myself asking the question, "Who gave me hope and support?" Some were in my life for years. Some I crossed paths with for a few hours or minutes and some are still with me. Some I never came face-to-face with but rather met them as characters in a film or words in a book. The source is as varied as its influence.

So do you want the good or the bad news first? Here is the good news: **The way we make others feel makes a mark. And sometimes we don't even know it!** Here is the bad news: **The way we make others feel makes a mark. And sometimes we don't even know it!**

As an actor, therapist, coach, and educator, my passion is to inspire hope and help others to maximize their potential in order to help people become their best possible future self. How can we find ways to that voice in our hearts that motivates us to explore, elevate, envision, and engage in new possibilities? How do we Ignite the flame of getting more of what we want and less of what we don't? How do we learn from stories and trust that we can reinvent ours and help others to write the next chapter of their life? Think about it, "How many lives did YOU touch by simply being who you are?"

As we are inspired, we inspire others. Read this book with an open heart and mind and let the powerful stories of these (s)heroes influence you to Ignite positive changes in your life and the lives of others.

IGNITE Female

Change Makers

INTRODUCTION BY
JB OWEN

Founder and CEO of Ignite

"You are a Change Maker simply by being you!"

Welcome, Change Maker!

Congratulations on picking up this book and diving into the exciting power of *creating* change, *making* change, and *instilling* change.

Over the next many pages you are going to be reading and enjoying the many stories of diverse and dynamic Female Change Makers. These are the real stories — the raw stories. The Ignite moments where new learning, inner awakening, and true transformation took place. Ignite stories are the authentic stories that each and every person can relate to because they hold values we all identify with: perseverance, determination, personal growth, commitment, courage, and strength. These are universal qualities; human qualities. No matter where you live in the world, what age, color or creed you are, you feel these emotions and recognize them in other people, yet you also recognize them in yourself!

It's highly possible *you* have had numerous moments in your life where you were called upon or asked to exercise these attributes. Your path in life may have led you down a road with multiple speed bumps and various obstacles. You likely have taken your fair share of detours and, at the same time, had moments where you were happily cruising along. These unknown variables have become the interesting components of life and we all experience them collectively and in our own unique way.

Along every journey, we are learning, growing, and ultimately defining who we are. Each one of us is navigating the human experience while discovering our purpose and the impact we can make in the world. Along the way, challenges and hardships often arise. Woven between them are lessons, gifts, and a new understanding of what we need to do to become a better version of ourselves. Many individuals have found the silver lining in their Ignite stories. They have redefined their past and stepped forth renewed with both a changed mind and an awakened heart.

This book is filled with *those* stories — the ones that have a powerful way of inspiring others. Since the beginning of time, individuals have learned from and gained wisdom from the honest, life-changing stories of others. Stories that show progress. Stories that take you on a journey and allow you to intimately feel the highs and lows of the hero or heroine in the process. People love listening to and reading those moments. Through this fabulous series of pages, you, the reader, receive an in-depth and intimate viewpoint into the journey of the authors as they triumph above all limitations and emerge on the other side transformed.

It is *that* process that is so captivating. The insight into a moment that sparks a *change* and Ignites a new way of living.

This book is a collection of those magnificent moments; Ignite moments. Each one is real-life; meaning they truly happened and unfolded as the writers describe. It also means they are authentic; told in a way that is honest and from the heart. Not all the authors in this book are 'professional' writers; in fact, many are sharing their writing for the very first time. Some have written before and others are acclaimed for their writing in different ways. All of them are just like you and me — women dedicated to making a difference and improving the lives of others while improving their own lives.

What Makes a Change Maker?

I believe you have picked up this book because inside of you is the deep desire to make a change not only in yourself but for others. Somewhere along the line, your experience in this lifetime has led you to feel a deeper compassion and a greater understanding of the world around you. That moment has lit a passion, a fire, an inferno of desire to do more than ever before in your life and for those around you. Your vision includes making a bigger impact than what is currently present and it most likely involves inciting change.

Be it healing yourself, helping your community, or hugely impacting the planet, something inside of you was stirred to make a powerful change. You saw a deficiency and at the same time recognized that a solution was possible. You rose from adversity, overcame challenges, and accepted the other side of a difficult situation. Some of our Change Makers have had those same experiences in the areas of family, relationships, finances, ethics and more. Like you, they witnessed what needed transforming and did something tangible about it. They saw what was no longer working efficiently and went about implementing unique forms of change. Their devotion to their ideas pushed them to seek a new way of doing things, resulting in better solutions for many.

Change Makers love results. They love to see their efforts in action and the new outcomes that prevail. It is a quality these individuals appreciate; modification = results, alterations = solutions. They see the glass half full with plenty of options on how to fill it to the top. They push the boundaries of convention and, at the same time, push themselves. They like to cross the line to see where the line is. They test the waters by jumping right in and taking a leap of faith. It's almost a daily occurrence. Many of them go against convention and rule out 'have to's' and 'musts.' They vibrate on a different frequency — one of possibility and opportunity.

It is likely you picked up this book because, at your core, you *know* you are a Change Maker. Maybe it is because you have instilled change in yourself, your neighborhood, or on a much larger scale. Possibly Change Maker resonates in your heart because you long for a day when things are fair, equal, and accessible. You know harmony, peace, and acceptance are obtainable. You believe happiness, joy, and prosperity *are* the true way of life.

Change may have been mandatory for you. Circumstances may have been such that without change something would have been lost or perished. Such change may have been expected or it may have reached a pinnacle where it was no longer an option but a must. Change under these conditions hardened you like the pressure that produces a diamond. Friction and fusion may have happened, but it formed something rare and precious. And, like a diamond, each fragment of its composition is unique. Every facet is captivating. Every angle shimmers and reflects in a way that creates awe and wonderment in others. They are amazed at what you are doing and eagerly hungry for more. Your shining brilliance is the beauty the entire world wants to see.

Like all diamonds, it may have taken you years to arrive at this place and you may be just inching your way to the surface. Uncovering your gifts and polishing the exact parts of you that you love to give may have been a lifelong event, yet now you are ready to shine. You have found the value in yourself and want to step into the role you were designed to play. You believe you are a Change Maker and everything it represents is a perfect fit.

Similarly, each author in this book has forged themselves under pressure and needed years of fine-tuning to reach the point of being showcased on these pages. Some have obtained high standing from outward sources while others have made miraculous accomplishments working inward on themselves. *All* have made profound advances in the areas of health, happiness, personal growth, business development, finances, relationships, compassion, understanding, and connecting. Their ideas were at one point a diamond in the rough which became the jewel in their caps.

When we began this project, we wanted to spotlight Change Makers from every end of the spectrum, from changing the way we look at ourselves in the mirror to changing the way big businesses do business. Some have global initiatives that make a multi-person impact while others have made a personal metamorphosis that ripples forth from one individual outward. All change creates more change and we consciously decided that change is not measurable by numbers or facts. *Change has a life of its own. It is a living organism that moves from person to person, triggering the willingness to be motivated to adopt a new idea or concept.* Change grows more change and what we did know was from the moment a Change Maker begins their commitment to the day this book was printed, to the moment you are reading these words, a massive, exponential change could have occurred beyond any form of tracking. No one act of change trumps another. They each have a lifeforce unto their own; therefore, no amount of evaluating or comparing is possible. They all are magnificent and powerful in the changes they have evoked. They each have impacted a life and the journey that life will take. What will unfold from that journey goes beyond measuring on every level.

In the dictionary, change means: *To make different in some particular fashion. To make radically new. To give a different position, course, or direction. To replace.* All the stories in this book emulate that to a tee. Be it in their thinking, actions, or beliefs, each one of the stories has the profound concept of change as their number one objective. Your job, should you wish to take it, is to read the stories and notice the unfolding possibilities. Observe the mindset the writer underwent so as to navigate themselves through the wonderment of personal, transformative change. Track the changes and embrace the steps. See what they did differently and then see how it all can inspire you. Recognizing the changes these Change Makers made will lead you directly to recognizing the magnificent Change Maker in you.

The Gift of Change

The stories you are about to embark on are all our stories. They supersede race, culture, age, and even gender. They are the human story, the experience of being a Being on this earth. They touch at the very heart of belonging, connecting, and sharing. They are raw, real, and unrestricted— that's what makes them so amazingly engaging. They cut through all the 'stuff' we want people to see and shine a light directly on the heart of who we were born to be.

This book is particularly important to me as a woman and a Change Maker. I have spent my entire life watching my mother make strides in business and the community. She always found solutions to every problem, refused to take 'no' for an answer, and never to this day gave up, gave in, or gave any less than her best. She showed the highest example of female fortitude I ever saw. She was the Change Maker in everything she did and she did it well. Following her lead was something I took to early in life. I remember starting my first business at age nine and, from fourth grade onward, I defied all norms and rebelled against any convention forced upon me. I liked being a rebel, outspoken, fearless, and at the same time a woman pushing the boundaries of my own generation and the social condition of my time.

Like many Change Makers, I was self-taught. The school of hard knocks was my playground and using grit meant toughing it out because there wasn't any other option. I learned on the fly and 100 percent by trial and error. That in itself was a lesson — to see things differently, approach life openly, and perceive everything from a place of possibility, not constraints.

Happily, amidst my ups and downs, I have enjoyed success and triumphs. I have led the rollercoaster life of a Change Maker in times of both assuredness and uncertainty. God has gifted me with many blessings, all of which I am extremely grateful for. When I think about all the steps it took to get me to where I am, I am thankful — even for the ones that skinned my knees and caused me to trip and fall.

In writing this book, Marnie Tarzia wrote her Ignite moment about me. It was surprising to read her story and my immediate reaction was to shy away from her accolades and water down her praise. I didn't want to draw any attention to myself and discredit the impact she said I made in her life. Like many women, it is easier to see something in others and hard to see the same thing in yourself. You give praise but have trouble receiving it. A part of me wanted to keep Marnie's story out of the book, until I looked within to see why this kind of acknowledgement was so difficult for me to receive. In a beautiful sharing, Marine and I laughed, cried, and marvelled at how accomplished women feel conditioned to hide their achievements and downplay their successes. We both could relate to the feeling of staying small so as not to draw attention or outshine someone else. Our conversation moved to how many Change Makers never accept any praise for what they have created and never take in the appreciation from those whose lives they have impacted.

Together we agreed that EVERY WOMAN should know her worth, her importance, her impact, and her value... even the two of us. We vowed to do more, to shine the spotlight on *all* women who are making changes, both big and small, in their lives and the lives of others. Marnie agreed to have her story first in the book and I agreed to put mine last. We wanted our Ignite moments to bookend the others. Interestingly enough, we both write about the same moment in time, a time before we had met one another, but from two different perspectives, from equally transformative moments that resulted in not just Ignite moments but also created a beautiful friendship and a working relationship devoted to Igniting others.

We hope you enjoy our stories. Like all the stories, they show how a fragment of time... a singular moment, a gift from heaven, a phenomenon, karma, fate, fabulous sincerity, and spectacular seconds... are all intertwined in the making of a changemaking Ignite moments for Change Makers worldwide.

How This Book Will Change Your Life

True change comes from exploring every aspect of who you are and then deciding what you are going to do with that knowledge. Ultimate change comes from experiencing the pressures of life and challenging the typical responses they bring. It is about redefining the labels, overcoming the obstacles, and branching out in ways others think are impossible. It is about looking for new options and being willing to make those options a current reality. Change requires embracing what *is* and morphing it into something new. It requires strength, fortitude, and determination, for no change happens without a bit of resistance and a dose of opposing force.

This book and the stories in it show how embracing change and welcoming it can yield a plethora of delightful results. Simply exploring change can shatter old ideals and crumble a conventional approach to life. Finding new ways of doing things and uncovering other options allows flow to supersede any gridlock that was once present. Change awakens purpose, and purpose can be found on the heels of massive, emotional change. It is the heart, not the mind, that first must take the leap for all the other emotions to follow. When you change how you feel inside, you change the frequency all around you... and that, my darling, changes everything!

My wish is that when you read through these stories, you will be deeply transformed by the many other women who stepped into change and followed their deepest knowing. I hope you are Ignited by the beautiful and somewhat brazen stories of women who are blazing a brilliant new trail in their own lives. I want their conviction to kindle conviction in you. I want their passion for life to spark your passion. For each awakening they had, open your mind to a new level of self-awareness and self-belief. You will see how many of them didn't know what was possible until possibilities stood squarely in their face. They had to step right up to the edge to feel what taking a leap of faith would feel like before they actually did it. But they did it. They jumped. They let go. They surrendered. And in doing so, they began to soar.

Our authors wrote their stories so that you can personally relate to their intimate relationship with change. Each one eloquently shares how change crept into their life and germinated like a planted seed awaiting the springtime. Every word was meticulously written with the intention of inspiring a personal, explorative transformation in *your* life. They wanted to be the ones to hold your hand and be the guide as you undergo this life-changing journey. They know that change isn't easy, it's not always fun, and it is sometimes lonely. However, they also stand united in agreement that change can also be glorious, powerful, and freeing. They each offer their kindred connection and support you in your change-making process, however it unfolds.

As you dive into the upcoming pages, you will find each story starts with a *Power Quote*. It is like a self-activating, self-empowering statement. Every Female Change Maker has one and right at the top is where the authors declare theirs. It is a phrase that encourages you to do more, push back the naysayers, and hail life in your own unique way. It is what the plaque on your office wall would say or what you'd tell another woman you were graciously encouraging. Power Quotes are ideas that you can use when you need some extra confidence or when the tears are flowing down your cheeks from both life's hardships and its rewards and you're in need of a little encouragement. Every Power Quote is designed to remind you of what you have inside, what you know you can do, and how your life is your own to do whatever you wish for.

Next, you will see each author's powerful *Intention*. These are the wonderful insights and new ideas they wish to inspire in you. They are personal, heart-felt messages filled with meaning and purpose. The authors want to IGNITE YOU in living your most extraordinary life, and they share in their intentions what they hope their story of *change* will do for you.

Then, their change-making *Story* follows. It is a moving account of how they not only embraced change, but how they made the most of it. Their stories exemplify how they found change, discovered ways to change, and in the end walked up to change and welcomed it. These are their vulnerable recollections and authentic accounts of consciously awakening to the *Ignite* moment that resulted in a magnificent sequence of change. We all have *Ignite* moments in our lives that change us, define us, and set us on a new path or trajectory. These stories are those moments told in the most honest and heartfelt way. They show that we all have *life-altering* moments that not only impact us but ultimately inspire us to make radical changes.

Once you have finished each story, you will find a list of doable and enjoyable *Ignite Action Steps*. These are the tangible things our Change Makers did to overcome their challenges and rise above any fears, worries, or doubts. Each author shares her easy-to-accomplish, effective tips for you to experiment with and implement immediately. These are the processes and practices that worked in their lives. Each step is different and unique, just like you are, and each has proven to yield fabulous results when done consistently.

We all know actions speak louder than words; never is that more important than when it comes to inciting change. *You must take action for change to take root and work.* Action IS the key. To move closer to your true life purpose, we encourage you to explore each action step and then pick one you can do each day consecutively for 30 days. This book outlines many different action steps to try, so find the one that will yield the most results for you. Each one is potentially the step that could change your life forever.

The goal of this book is for something you read to *transform* you; for one of our stories to have a profound impact and catapult you in a new direction; for something to resonate so strongly within you that you just *have* to take action. This is the most important thing — that one of these stories inspires you into a new conscious realization and you feel ready to transform, ready to soar, READY TO CHANGE!

Much Love,

MARNIE TARZIA, MA

"Transform the world by transforming yourself."

I hope my story inspires you to go after the life you want with purpose, passion, and perseverance. My wish for you is that you can create the necessary change in your life to become the very best version of yourself: mind, body, heart, and spirit.

FROM EGOISM TO ALTRUISM

The Japanese have a word called *ikigai*, which translates into 'having a sense of purpose or reason for being, resulting in a feeling of well-being.' Have you ever wondered what your purpose is for being here on earth? I certainly did. I felt fulfilled in my personal life, but I felt like I was doing the wrong work. Anxious, unsettled, I could feel the stress manifesting in my body, in my back and in my knees. I felt that I had a larger purpose and I was being called to do something important, but I just didn't know what it was. I spent the first five years of my 40s searching for that purpose, for something that would give me that feeling of well-being that I hungered for.

My transformation into finding my *ikigai* began in a Zoom call with the phenomenal JB Owen. I had seen JB on the Canadian television show *The Dragon's Den*. She was seeking investment for the eco-friendly feminine hygiene product she had created, Lotus Liners, making a pitch to the 'Dragons,' who were potential investors. As I watched JB stand in front of these high-powered business folks, chin up and chest high, so graceful, charming and confident, I remember thinking, "Wow, this girl has got it." She exuded that special type of charisma that is magnetic and compelling, yet I was sure, that like a swan floating serenely on the water, underneath it all, her brain was madly churning away in an effort to move her business forward.

In her stunning well-tailored pink jacket, sporting streaks of pink within her blond pixie haircut, JB looks like she should be on the cover of Vogue magazine. But more importantly, she has an inner beauty about her that is relatable and that drew me in right away. Her poise mesmerized me. The 'Dragons' were aggressively throwing questions and challenges at her, trying to eat away at her confidence, her courage, her plans for the future, but she stood there exuding confidence and serenity as she went toe-to-toe with these people, not only holding her own but *thriving*. It was awe-inspiring. JB Owen won a whopping $150,000 deal for 35 percent equity with Calgary 'Dragon' Manjit Minhas, I was thrilled! "You go, girl!" I thought to myself.

She struck me as someone I wanted to get to know. Only the day before watching JB on TV, I had written down in my journal that I wanted to collaborate with other highly successful female leaders from all over the world. I wanted to be an agent for positive change focusing on female empowerment. Watching her, witnessing another woman going after her goals with passion and perseverance, was absolutely inspirational. Even when the 'Dragons' put JB in the hot seat, throwing complex questions at her like a firing squad, she never faltered. She was grace under pressure. It was magic to watch.

I never imagined that, six months later, I would go on to co-author a Best Selling Female Leadership book with this world-class speaker, international best-selling author, powerhouse publisher, and highly successful entrepreneur! Being intentional in my thoughts and words reminded me that the Universe is listening and will deliver your wishes to you like an unexpected FedEx™ Parcel arriving during the holiday season from a long lost friend.

In my first meeting with JB, my hands shook. My voice was a little wobbly and I might have sweated through my blouse too. Suffice it to say, I was a little intimidated, but it occurred to me to 'just be myself.'

JB, on the other hand, was picture perfect. Calm, cool, collected, confident, she was the very opposite of what I was at that moment. And there she was, standing in front of me, asking me why I wanted to publish a leadership book.

I felt like it was my turn to be in the hot seat, facing the 'Dragons' from *The Dragon's Den*, but her style was completely different. She was kind, generous, and so warm and genuine that it put me right at ease. I could sense in my heart that she wanted me to do well.

My excitement was bubbling over as I shared my idea of wanting to tell the stories of women who had stepped into their power and found their vision and voice. I pitched to her the idea of the two of us co-authoring a leadership book profiling female influencers from all around the world, sharing their success stories in the areas of health, wealth, business, relationships, and personal growth.

With every word that came out of my mouth, I could feel my purpose settling into my very bones. The nervousness went. The anxiety went. Confidence grew. In that moment as I spoke with JB, it was so clear to me that I wanted to inspire other women who felt stuck in their lives and needed traction in order to change.

I thought I could motivate women all over the world to have the courage to persevere in working to pursue their goals by showing them other women pushing through significant challenges and obstacles on their way to success.

I wanted women to feel empowered to take charge of their lives so that they, like me, could become the CEO of their own lives.

Becoming an agent for positive change was important to me. As many people do when they reach their midlife, I had evaluated where I was in my journey compared to where the younger me had hoped I would be. I engaged in a tremendous amount of introspection and study in the areas of leadership, social, emotional, and spiritual development. What I discovered in that process was that I felt compelled to pay forward to other women what I had learned. I knew I was becoming a Change Maker and I wanted to spare them the pain and highlight the lessons inherent within my journey.

Interviewing and recruiting accomplished women from all over the globe for our leadership book was phenomenal. I would end each day exhausted but happy, my head buzzing with details and my heart overflowing with gratitude and appreciation. I was in awe of these women, their openness, their bravery, and their vulnerability. As they told me their stories, they were essentially sharing some of their most vulnerable moments with a complete stranger. That takes courage!

While doing the interviews, I couldn't help but notice that the majority of the women I spoke to started the same way. With their hands clasped tightly together to hide the shaking or with a quick and easy smile that transformed almost instantly into a subconscious biting of lips, they expressed the same initial trepidation, "I'm not sure if people will be interested in reading my story. I'm not sure if I'm a really great writer." One of our greatest fundamental needs as people is to feel accepted and validated for who we are, yet so many women feel that they are not enough.

In the summer of 2019, we launched our book *Ignite Your Female*

Leadership in Pula, Croatia. It was exhilarating. As I retired to a comfy chair on the balcony of my Airbnb™, eager to relax with some music after a day spent at our pop-up bookstore in downtown Pula, and after enjoying a lovely dinner with my fellow authors at Cantina Restaurant, I heard a ping on my phone. Picking my phone up from where it lay on the small table on the balcony, I saw that I had received a text from a Canadian woman who was a friend of a friend. As I read it, a warmth swept through me and my lips curved up into a happy smile.

She told me that after reading my story via the ebook on Amazon that day, she had printed it out and put it on her bedside table to remind her to never give up on the life she wants. She described working in a high-powered and lucrative job but feeling completely unfulfilled in her life. She had forgotten her *ikigai*. When she read my story, she was reminded of her passion for painting. Inspired by my message, she decided to resurrect her art studio and start painting again.

I could hear the excitement in her voice as I read her words. Painting was her passion project and she planned to start offering workshops on weekends to see where this would take her. "Go for it, girl," I thought to myself. I thought then of my own motto, "Do what you have to do until you can get paid for what you love."

I had to smile. Three years to that day, I had resigned from a job that I had held for a decade. I had reached the top of my career ladder only to find during my mid-life review that *my ladder was up against the wrong wall.* In this moment, looking down at the text message in front of me, my heart was happy. I realized that in three short years, I had secured a job I love, working with people I adore, have two best-selling books under my belt, and I am in Pula, Croatia, launching the newest book.

As I sat on my balcony feeling the sunset warm my face, a feeling came over me like a warm blanket. I was exactly where I was supposed to be. I was reading glowing testimonials about how this book... my book... *our* book was creating positive change for women all over the globe. I pinched myself as though it was a dream. It was one of those deeply moving moments, an Ignite moment that shifted my understanding of who I was and who I intended to be.

Just then, a Shania Twain song started playing and the lyrics seemed completely fitting, "*I know that you can, then you will/get to the top of the hill/part of the fun is the climb/you just gotta make up your mind./That today is your day/and nothing can stand in your way./Today is your day/and everything's goin' your way*". Tears of joy streamed down my face.

The next day JB and her husband Peter chartered the most beautiful floating vessel, *Pirate Queen*, for us to sail around the Adriatic Sea. We talked, laughed, sang, danced and ate a fabulous lunch of fresh mackerel while enjoying the beaches and coast line. I couldn't believe that I had actively participated in getting to this moment in my life. Three years earlier, filled with insecurities and doubts, I questioned if I had made the right move to give up my day job and the only profession I had ever known. But the little voice within me would not let me settle for playing small. I felt proud of myself that I had the courage to pursue my dreams at the age of 45.

Later that day, alone with my thoughts as I relaxed in a chair on the *Pirate Queen's* deck, a conversation I had with a fellow teacher in early childhood education mere weeks before I left that profession popped into my head. I remember her telling me that she thought it was so sad when little children were afraid of the dark when the lights go out at rest time in the Kindergarten classroom. I remember vividly the expression she wore as she told me this. It was the same expression I wore when I thought of all the adults — of all the *women* — who waste away their lives by settling for mediocre, too afraid of taking risks to get to the light.

When I returned home from Pula, Croatia, I was featured in two local Canadian news sources, *The Thunder Bay Chronicle Journal* and *Women Magazine*. I was over the moon with happiness that the local media picked up on the story of our books, *Ignite Your Life for Women* and *Ignite Your Life for Female Leadership,* both promoting the importance of female empowerment. My heart hurt when I read the research that women across North America are dying of diseases of 'despair.' It makes me sad to learn that in 2020 women still don't feel like they have choices in their life. Many women reach midlife and — after caring for children, spouse, house, aging parents, and working full time — are feeling tired, not inspired. They are feeling like there is nothing in their lives for them. Women often suffer in silence which leads to depression, addicition issues, even death by suicide.

As a female Change Maker, I'm trying to do my part to change the female narrative. I'm proud of the headline I have in *Women Magazine* that reads, "Step into the Life You Want," as this should not be the exception for women in our culture, *it should be the norm*. When we hold back women, we are holding back half of our population; I'm striving to change that statistic. To pay it forward, one woman at a time.

While picking up my lunch at a local restaurant, the woman who served me asks, "Are you that author I read about in the newspaper"? I reply in the affirmative. With a shy expression, she tells me, "I recognized you from the picture in the paper. I tried ordering your book online, but I couldn't find it. Is there any other way I can buy a copy?"

Her shyness, her courage in approaching me touched my heart. I smiled and said, "I'll be right back."

I went to the trunk of my car, pulling one from the box of signed copies before returning to the restaurant to give it to her. Her eyes grew shiny and wet as she thanked me. "You made my day! I'm in a bad place right now and could use some motivation."

I gave her a hug and said, "I can tell you from personal experience that this too shall pass. I was a late bloomer and didn't start chasing my dream until I was 45. Just remember, it's never too late to live the life you want!"

I've found my *Ikigai*. Writing, speaking, and teaching on the topics of leadership and female empowerment are the things that fulfill me. What I've discovered after connecting with and speaking to women all around the world is that we need to become better leaders of ourselves first before leading others. It is not enough to just *know* our personalities; we also need to *manage* our personalities well. Leadership happens from the inside out. It is in our ability to work on ourselves that we can positively influence those around us.

Through the evolution of my own personal growth, I've come to understand that my only point of power is *me*. My competition is in the mirror. I'm just trying to be better than I was yesterday. Somehow, we have formed a self-belief that we women need *permission* to take care of ourselves *first* before caring for others.

On an airplane, they tell us to put on our own oxygen mask before helping others. I hope women can evolve to a point where we take care of ourselves first everyday and not just while flying on an airplane.

We need to be the very best versions of ourselves first before going out into the world to advance favorable conditions for others. We can't give away what we don't have. If we can take good care of ourselves and can live in harmony with ourselves, we are well positioned to live in harmony with others. If we can do that we will create peace in the world. I do not know of a more powerful way to be a Change Maker than that. When you change yourself for the better you will Ignite change in the world, one person at a time.

IGNITE ACTION STEPS

Find Your Ikigai: What are you passionate about? What do you think you came here to do? What is your reason for being? Those are big questions that will tell you who you are. The science of well-being teaches us that our first job is identifying our strengths and our second job is figuring out how we can use our strengths in service of others. When we have that information, we can set ourselves up to benefit from 'playful profitability,' which is getting paid for what we love to do.

Persevere: Once you know what your purpose is and are passionate about achieving your goals, persevere and have grit when challenges arise. Don't give up. Keep going. When there is an obstacle in your path, keep a positive mindset and work to engage in a process of positive, solution-based problem solving to overcome anything that could potentially hinder your success.

Be Resourceful: Find the people who can support you by filling any gaps you may have in your knowledge or skill set. We don't have to know everything; we just have to know what we don't know and find the people who do. Their expertise in areas that we may be lacking in can support us in bringing our goals to fruition.

Cultivate a Circle of Support: Find a small group of trustworthy and supportive people. You need a support system you can consistently network with that can help you to identify your goals and hold you accountable for achieving them.

Marnie Tarzia - Canada
Leadership Specialist, Speaker, Best Selling Author
Marnie Tarzia Consulting
marnietarzia@gmail.com

ANA SOFIA OROZCO

*"Live your values, stand up for them, and be
surprised by your power and contribution."*

**I wish that the experiences and thoughts I am sharing here serve as a
catalyst for us to acknowledge that we have the inner wisdom to live a
wonderful and meaningful life. In listening to our true values and becoming
activists to defend them, we step into the power to contribute positively to
the world we live in. When we acknowledge this, we can own the fact that
we are all Change Makers and it is through the route of spirit-inspired
contribution that we can find the substance for real fulfillment.**

EMPATH, REBEL, AND CHANGE MAKER

Trying to figure out how to live my most fulfilled and satisfying life has
been quite an interesting odyssey. I have struggled to determine what I wanted
to do professionally. I can remember I wanted to be a doctor, but just after
being accepted into medical school, my life took me in a different direction
and I switched to a business administration program. I was quite entrepreneurial and I believed being a business woman would provide more freedom
in my life. A couple of years later, I was very bored and decided to pursue a
Bachelor's degree in Philosophy. But, in the end, I graduated with a degree
in Business Administration and another in Comparative Literature. As I finished my undergraduate studies, pursuing a career in the business consulting
industry felt sexy, challenging, and exciting. I jumped right into finance and

strategic consulting and ended up getting an MBA. But I was not fulfilled at all! I felt disconnected. I was missing a more genuine connection with myself. I wanted to work at a deeper level with people. I changed gears and joined a global corporation as a consultant in organizational and human development. Yet, something still felt empty in me.

When I became a mother, I took some time away and invested it in my children's upbringing. As my babies grew into more independent kids, I started to feel a need to reconnect with my own interests and passions. I wanted to go back to work while still being able to enjoy my children and support them as they learned and grew. This was so much harder than I thought. There was no space for a woman who had been out of the workplace for years. I also realized I did not know what I wanted to do. It was difficult to acknowledge that neither my degrees nor my jobs had allowed me to exercise my full power. I knew I had so much more to give and, at the same time, I felt like a professional failure.

Gradually, I understood I had to reinvent myself. I was not aware how disconnected I was from my inner values. I wanted to allow my true wisdom to lead me, but I could not hear its voice. And I still had three kids at home who needed me. I felt very lost. Broken and powerless. It was not easy to focus on my career when I was focusing on my kids, and vice versa.

I was constantly stressed and overwhelmed. Unable to find a job that interested me and feeling pressure around the need to earn an income, I decided to start my own business consulting and coaching firm targeting small- and medium-sized companies. I managed to support a few business clients, most of whom were focused on attaining an idea of success that was not really serving them. Watching them focus on the financial lucrativeness of their work at the expense of their personal lives was very frustrating.

I decided I needed to connect with people at a deeper level and started a master's program in executive coaching and organizational behavior. I felt very proud when I received my certification as a coach, but I still did not know which way to go with my career. Uncovering my purpose on this earth was proving to be a huge challenge! I started to doubt what I was doing. I could practice as a business consultant or as an organizational/executive coach, but I was somehow tired of the lack of consciousness and spiritual depth in the business world. In looking for a more profound work, I started to consider becoming a *life* coach.

I kept on hearing that it was very important to have a clear professional goal, a specific service or product, and an understanding of your particular niche of customers, and I had none of this. I did not have this clarity and that bothered me. I was working hard to put my skills and talents into serving my community. I needed my work to be aligned with my purpose and I kept looking for my path. I wanted to manifest the power I felt in *me*. I could not identify the contribution I wanted to make, but I found support reading and learning self-development, and I started to enrich my life with conscious practices that helped me center. I learned to live more aligned with my true values and open up a space for the Universe to guide me.

I dug deep into my soul to decipher my real passions and interests. I thought about the moments when I have felt proud of my contributions to others. And I had an epiphany. I recognized that there was something special about me. *I was an empath.* I was very sensitive. I could easily relate to other people's feelings, on occasions to a point where I could get physically sick. I had never been conscious of this. At times, my family had labeled me as weak and prone to sickness, and I remember how that would make me feel like I was a problem. Today, I understand being an empath made me vulnerable. But, when I learned to manage my stress and anxiety, and how to release the tension and negative emotions around me, I started to live in full health.

As an empath, at times I ended up being a voice for others. I was known as a conciliator and an integrator of opinions and ideas. I realized how caring for others, protecting and considering them, had always been natural to me. I started to understand I needed to embrace who I was and what I could do for others. Empathy became my inspiration and I reinvented my consulting business with this value in mind. I wanted to promote empathy in families, communities, organizations, and all around the world. I had no idea what to call that professionally.

One night, catching up on work just before going to bed, I saw the words 'social entrepreneur.' I immediately felt pulled by the concept, feeling deep in my core they expressed who I wanted to be. I had been quite an entrepreneur, but it had been a while with no drive and no new projects. I fell asleep and dreamt about ways in which I could promote empathy. Ideas on how to celebrate empathetic gestures and how to generate more empathetic actions started coming my way.

After discarding lots of different options, I decided I would start with something simple: *The Empathy Match* project. I headed to a store and bought pins and hearts and decided to offer them as a gift to honor people who performed empathetic actions. I created *Empathize 2 Rise* to promote empathy around the world. I wanted to start 'The Contribution Revolution' and teach organizations and individuals how contributing to others was the best way to find success, satisfaction, and fulfillment.

I sensed something great was opening up for me and I could feel the positive energy when people received their 'Empathy Pins.' I was energized by this work and it soon grew to become an initiative reaching hundreds of people. I found lots of support and I started to find new and more effective ways to promote empathy. We printed out 'Empathy Cards' to start a chain of kindness. The cards are being passed along from person to person multiplying empathy around the globe.

Being able to instill positive change in the world felt like a blessing. Spontaneously, one sunny day, walking my dog around the neighborhood and thinking about my journey, I realized I now understood what it really meant to be a social entrepreneur. I had started an initiative around empathy, and with drive and creativity, I felt like I deserved that title. I can still feel the pride in that moment. In my excitement, I even shouted out loud in pure joy, "I *am* a social entrepreneur!"

I kept working on my projects and, during my daily meditations, I started diving even deeper into my purpose. I started studying about empaths and about empathy in general. I confirmed the beneficial effects of empathy in the quality of human relationships; I realized how being an empath had challenged me profoundly, and I discovered the power that lay in the ability to feel deeply. My sensitivity had given me the faculty to feel more intensely, to relate with others more profoundly, and to develop a stronger connection with my own sense of self.

At the same time, I acknowledged how, all throughout my life, I have had to invest energy in managing my sensitive character. I have had to learn how to keep my inner self protected and had to develop the firmness to stand up for my values and act in alignment with them.

One night I was having dinner out with a group of friends, and someone asked me what I would do in my life if I had no limitations or restrictions. For the first time, I answered spontaneously, "What I am doing right now!" My own answer surprised me. I was overcome with this feeling of purpose. After being so lost I was suddenly owning my life beautifully. Curious about what had taken me to this place, I realized it had all started working on myself. My journey to find a life purpose revealed my empathetic nature. This recognition enabled me to act with power, unfolding what I had to give and putting myself to the service of others. In other words, becoming a Change Maker.

I realized that as empathy and love were sources of great power, there was another important force that had led to this sense of empowerment and purpose. And that was courage. Realizing this was very important for me. Being able to feel profoundly was not enough. I have had to defend my true values to be able to get to the point where I was at. I have had to be a rebel and become an activist. This made me feel proud. I could go back and identify the relevance of those moments of rebellion in my life. They had allowed me to keep the connection with my essence, they had kept me aligned, and they had enabled the fulfillment of my genuine purpose.

Being a rebel played a relevant role in being able to stay true to myself. As little kids, we are able to feel clearly who we are. With time, our culture, parents, teachers, and friends start influencing our thoughts and telling us what we have to be and how we have to behave to be accepted. And because we want to be included and not isolated, we trade our true values and strengths for the safety of social acceptance. In order to keep our power, we have to be able to rebel against these imposed beliefs that threaten our freedom and our joy.

I have had to be revolutionary, genuine, brave, daring, courageous, bold, progressive, and inquisitive. I have had to be a rebel, fearless, and dashing, showing strength in so many ways, in order to stay true to myself and be able to walk this adventure. These are the moments, lessons, and learnings that defined me.

I have had to be a revolutionary to tell myself that I am not prettier or sexier when I have the slimmest body, wear high heels, or look like a doll. I remember the day in which I chose to be free from these beliefs and resigned to this idea of female beauty.

I have had to be genuine to realize that I can be feminine, kind, or generous, and powerful at the same time. I have found great relief in understanding that we can attain power even being vulnerable beings. We can be determined, resolved and commanding, while being collaborative and empathetic.

I have had to be brave to pull my kids out of the mainstream education system because I could see how the purpose of learning was being lost in heavy work and boring classes. I wanted my kids to learn from wonder. I wanted them to feel the excitement of observation, exploration, assimilation, innovation, and creativity. I have had to look for alternative education options even uncertain about the results.

I have had to be daring to break free from imposed ideas about career. I had learned to relate professional success with high income and recognition, and I had to re-teach myself that fulfillment comes from working with passion and purpose.

I have had to be courageous to take care of my health. Understanding that my body is the vehicle in which I will live, I have had to make the conscious decision of taking care of it, changing eating habits, exercising, and learning to buy products that really nourish as opposed to those modified artificially to taste good, or marketed as popular.

I have had to be bold to pick up the right health care. I have had to quit going to certain medical practices because they just treat the symptoms and not the cause of disease, and prescribe medications with no consciousness, even recommending unnecessary procedures. It has required effort to doubt the commonly used system and learn about alternative and more effective ways.

I have had to be progressive to allow my family to function within our own terms. I have found out that there are no formulas to determine a model for the perfect family. There are as many formulas as there are different types of people and of relationships between them.

I have had to be inquisitive to question the ways in which we are taking care of our environment. We have been very smart in learning to exploit our natural resources, but we have forgotten that we are affecting our whole eco-system, threatening the viability of our world.

I have had to be a rebel to learn to live more blissfully, not falling under the pressure of the fierce demands of success that today's world imposes on us. I have had to learn that we do not have to be the best in what we do, or become super humans and extraordinary. I believe we need to learn to be ourselves and embrace the power within, putting it to the service of others.

I have had to be fearless to question my culture's values, the religious beliefs I was brought up with, and even my dearest parents', educators', and leaders' teachings. This has allowed me to create beliefs that better serve me, and to live my life as a collaborative journey of exciting experiences and lessons.

I have had to be dashing to live a life inspired by love and empathy in a world where being better and more powerful than the other seems to have become the norm. Even if competitiveness is an important human trait, love and empathy are the ones who give real meaning to our lives. We evolve as we learn to understand, communicate, and connect better with others.

I realize how my life is full of acts of rebellion. And I embrace them as another strong source of power. I invite everyone to consciously work on recognizing their essence, their true values, and then find the strength to live a life in alignment.

Our ability to stay connected to our true selves, our capacity to love others and empathize, and the boldness in which we can stand up to defend our values, have been to me the doorway to finding a fun space in this world, where I can live meaningfully. This is the space where I have reconnected with my power and where I have become a source of contribution. I love seeing how my projects are changing lives each and every day and I feel blessed to have found deep alignment.

"Know your values, be rebellious to defend them, and take action; this is being a Change Maker." My story as a contributor had been that of an Empath, a Rebel, and a Change Maker. What is your Change Making story?

IGNITE ACTION STEPS

Find your own way to nourish the connection with your true self. Embrace your inner child, explore within, and acknowledge who you are.

Train your ability to love and your empathy muscle. Go do something kind for a person who is needing support. Ask them to pass it along and do the same for others. #THEMPATHYMATCH. Honor empathetic actions.

Be revolutionary, genuine, brave, daring, courageous, bold, progressive, inquisitive. Be a rebel, be fearless, and stand up to defend your true values.

With true self, love, empathy and courage, you can allow your purpose to manifest in this world. Play your part boldly and you will find your Change Maker.

Ana Sofia Orozco - United States
Transformational Coach, Social Entrepreneur, Behavioral Consultant
www.planandthrive.com

ALEX JARVIS

"Change is glorious – step into change and step out with LOVE."

My story is about the wisdom I gained on my journey of self-discovery. Stepping into my inner power and realizing 'positive' change in the smallest way increased my awareness and encouraged me to help others to have a *'voice.'* The intention through writing my story is to inspire you to take action, to feel the sense of freedom and embrace change like a 'new' friend. My wish is to motivate you into becoming one who *desires* change in the world and by gathering knowledge and resources, *makes* that change happen.

SPIRIT BIRD — YOU HAVE SEEN IT ALL BEFORE

"Why — why — am I feeling like this, so sad, so angry, so distraught?" I allowed myself to be affected so badly that it was having an influence on everything in my life and how I viewed things. That just was NOT me — the Alex who came from a space of LOVE and had been a Change Maker from a very young age. It started when I was three, my belief that I could change the world and its sadness by making people laugh and be joyful. My one wish was to see everyone happy. Now, I could feel everyone's pain and fear.

The Australian bushfires that started in 2019 were more catastrophic than any simulation of our changing climate had predicted. My intuition told me it was deeper than climate change. We needed to go back and honor our roots, our spiritual connection with the indigenous tribes and respect their gifts, their wisdom — their knowledge of how to work with fire and the land as one, using fire as a complement. The deaths of flora, fauna and humans was massive — just massive. I could feel it, smell it, and touch it all — choking on the dense SMOG-like conditions even inside the city of Sydney. Oily particles of burnt tree bark floated through the air covering everything in a red dust, traveling all the way to New Zealand. The cars in the street were coated in it, as if they had been traveling in the outback for days. It was everywhere and my guilt was huge. I felt overwhelmed and devastated. I started to regress into behaviors that didn't suit me nor anyone around me; my attitude was one of anger and dismay. My cup was definitely half empty. People disappointed me because they were getting on with their daily lives — there was judgment — judgment of myself and others. The nasty language in my head that made me feel powerless, isolated, overwhelmed — I was slipping deeper and deeper toward the point of no return.

I tried to understand my violent reaction. I felt like screaming — this was unlike me as I feel I am a positive, dynamic, empowered individual and I have always been grateful for life's blessings — aware that I create my own *dream*. I love the Persian Proverb, "He who wants a rose must respect the thorn." Life's stages take us in and out of the soft enveloping rose where we face our dark and thorny sides. I was clearly there.

There was so much negative dialogue going on in the outside world. The words, I told myself, were a reflection of the external discord. I knew I needed kindness for myself, just as we need to be kind to each other. There are times when we all slip back into old patterns. I had to remember, just don't be so hard on yourself — forgive and move forward. Look for the most simple things to do — when you meet someone face to face, set the intention that you will leave them feeling better than when you found them.

My desire to change the world as a child carried into my adult life both professionally and in my spare time. I traveled the world for over twenty years in my work with start-up Biotech companies developing medical device products with medical specialists, doctors, and surgeons. Back then, I felt empowered and could see the change and influence we had on the community — and globally. I was so in LOVE with what I did.

That inspired me to do more so I became a philanthropist, and started using my voice in numerous initiatives with non-profit organizations. Now I help others to my heart's content in the Threshold Choir, singing to the elderly, homeless, the very young, the dying, and the grieving, *anyone* on the threshold of life. It takes me out of myself, reminding me of all that is good. I work as a volunteer for Starlight Foundation, developing safe, creative spaces for children to just be children in medical-free zones within hospitals. Australia-wide — I enjoy being on many committees, acting as an ambassador for other organizations. Anyone can do the same. Small things we all do can be considered being a Change Maker.

I envision a world where all those at life's thresholds may be honored with compassion. Song, public speaking, supporting others and bringing them joy increases the vibe of positivity that spreads like fire, leaving warmth and new hope. As an ambassador of change — speaking and sharing for inclusivity, building and creating dynamic communities, it all makes my heart soar with the joy of our interconnectedness and possibility when we care for one another. Maya Angelou said, "I've learned that people will forget what you said, people will forget what you did, but people will never forget how you made them feel." If people around me go into their joy, if they're feeling that they're embraced in love, my soul mirrors their love. It's a powerful way to change.

Looking back I realize that my natural tendencies as an empathic person coupled with having a strong connection to the land — the land that was currently being ravaged by fire, devastated by flame — is what sent me on my downward spiral. My deep reverence to the earth was doubly confirmed at a Peace Prayer circle several years ago. The facilitator, a Shaman from Peru — channeled a message to us all, turning to me and saying, "I have been told to tell you all — Alex is the keeper of the land." Wow! I was somewhat surprised, but at the same time not. In my heart of hearts I knew I had been blessed with this gift. All my life I have visited places all over the globe, connecting deeply. The more I read, the more I realized nothing was by chance and I showed up at the right place and the right time to be at one with the earth's Ley Lines. Empaths need to protect themselves from such strong negativity and I had failed to do so.

I knew I had to *change* my thoughts! I was reminded of my connection to the inspiring words of Viktor Frankl, "When we are no longer able to change a situation, we are challenged to change ourselves." This felt like a resurfacing — it was like a process of sinking deep into overwhelm *then having the ability to pull myself out.* I could see that the more I evolved, the quicker I could rise out of the depths of negativity. I was the one who had to pull myself up and be the change I wanted to see.

I started to believe in myself at an early age, and by the time I was a teenager, I realized that all along I had the ability to influence a change in the world... even if it was only in the smallest ways. Through language and by giving myself permission to have a voice, I used that voice to benefit others. How could it be so simple and yet so powerful? That question kept racing through my mind. As soon as I embraced that *I* was the change — that change comes from within — the joy in my life blossomed! It was this awakening, to my many Ignite moments that gave me the courage to empower myself. I started to fine tune and develop my inner knowing, using my intuition to grow, to believe in myself, and understand that there are many different ways to influence. In gaining knowledge, loving to learn, and developing awareness, I started to shape the manner in which I viewed people and politics in very distinct ways... I believe large-scale social change could occur if enough people took the same small steps with unity and from a space of love.

They are many examples of how the power of 'peace-creating' mass meditation to decrease warfare and terrorism has been tested repeatedly. The results produced have been consistently positive with nearly immediate reductions in war deaths averaging better than 70 percent. This approach fits with the mindset of Aboriginal teachings that *we are all one*. It is time for us all to believe that we can first effect change in our minds and, with each small outward change, see massive results. I have always embraced Aboriginal teachings, believing in the interconnectedness with all life. It felt so right to my inner knowing that to be a Change Maker in the world, I needed to make the change within myself. I needed to restore balance to my life. To be the healthiest me. I focused on creating harmony with nature and found that by creating that space for health, it promoted spirituality, and by developing my spirituality, I supported my health.

I could now be the best version of myself and bring change to the community with LOVE. In the aboriginal culture, everything is about 'dreaming' — not in the sense of going to sleep and dreaming... dreaming can also be the spirit that shapes your existence, shapes the land, and shapes our connection to the land as a species because we are OF the earth and not just on earth. I believe we have lost touch with that reality — the reality that says, "We're just the same as that tree." I feel so deeply we ARE energetically connected to the earth.

I began to notice that how I spoke to myself directly influenced what would show up. It had an effect on how I experienced things in life. The more I awakened to the fact, the more I saw that if my internal self-talk was negative then there was a high chance that my external experiences would be negative as well. In such a simple, perfect way, I realized that positive internal self-talk attracted positive external experiences. I would see the 'MAGIC' in everyday life and how the unexpected could change into a mystical moment, to be in the moment, in the flow, and expect the unexpected. For me to realize how beautiful life can be and to be full of gratitude, to be aware of the little things in my surroundings. Say "Thank you," or "I receive that" when offered or gifted something.

Teaching oneself to receive requires a balance between giving and receiving. I came to this conclusion after an epic nine-year journey of health challenges, which involved having 12 major surgeries. I watched what showed up and practiced a joyful approach with a positive attitude, which helped speed up my recovery. I became at ease with my diagnosis. I decided to turn the situation into a game and have fun. To be in my joy! To make it an adventure to live in the moment, be present, and 'smell the roses.' Only positive thoughts were allowed to enter my mind. My internal self-talk was bright like a shining star — unbelievably POSITIVE. I looked for the good in everything and in everyone. I found the positive outcome of adversity — and if a contrary thought slipped into my space, I would say to myself, "Delete-Delete-Delete."

You must be the change you wish to see in the world, Mahatma Ghandi said in his famous message. His words have reverberated across the planet inspiring souls, uplifting many and invigorating the earth, air and water. Everything has a purpose, a reason and a state. We can alter our state with the smallest and simplest of words.

That was proven with water consciousness, which first gained international attention from the unconventional but groundbreaking experiments of Japanese researcher Masaru Emoto. The theory that water can understand and retain the energy of human intention. The work of Dr. Masaru Emoto and his Water Crystals has always fascinated me — the fact that, as adults, we are approximately 60% water — his research confirms we are greatly affected by the words used by ourselves and others. In the 1990s, Emoto performed a series of experiments in which water was kept in a variety of bottles, each carrying a label with a different message. The messages ranged from positive and caring (thank you, love) to negative (I hate you, I want to kill you), and then drops of water from these bottles were placed on slides and 'deep-frozen' to form snowflake-like crystals. His findings were astounding. The crystals that formed on positive messages were found to be more geometric and aesthetically pleasing, while the crystals formed by water with negative messages were chaotic and non-uniform in shape.

I have always been inspired by the world's greatest leaders and progressive thinkers. How they use the power of words to transform our emotions to help inspire others toward their vision and create actionable change is amazing. From Winston Churchill's focus on the "finest hour" to Martin Luther King, Jr's. "I have a dream." This all made me think again how evident it is that words shape our entire existence. That I have the ability to use words internally to change my life for the better — words that I believe will Ignite change, inspire action, and improve my quality of life. I have repeatedly asked myself the question,

"Can changing my words change my life?" Yes, our words are a vehicle for expressing and shaping our experiences with others. I was not always aware of the far-reaching impacts of the words I used on a daily basis. As a Change Maker, I was always bringing in new ideas and synthesizing information all around me to create change. One of the best ways that kept my mind nimble was to let myself be inspired by powerful narratives from many different authors. There will be times when we slip back into old patterns and behave in a way that is not complimentary to our existence — but there are times we *need* the shadow. The contrast can serve to remind us of our manifesting proof and power.

If I believe in something with all my heart and soul and put my intention out there in the world, it never surprises me how many incredible people and opportunities are drawn to it. I am you — you are me — we are LOVE. *We are all Change Makers and it can be as easy as changing your vocabulary in how you speak to yourself and others.*

A rose in a desert can only survive on its strength, not its beauty. Pretty words without any movement will not survive, let alone guide and inspire change. We must be passionate and instill strength in our words, followed up with action. My message to you is simple… "Set out in search of your treasure." Change is glorious — step into change and step out with LOVE.

Spirit Bird... *The sweet words of Xavier Rudd, Aboriginal singer songwriter*

Give it time and we wonder why
Do what we can, laugh and we cry
And we sleep in your dust because we've seen this all before
Culture fades with tears and grace,
Leaving us stunned hollow with shame

We have seen this all, seen this all before…

Ignite Action Steps

Changing your words can change your life. How you speak to yourself directly influences how you experience things in life. If your internal self-talk is negative, chances are that your external experiences will also show up that way. Use words that will Ignite change, inspire action and improve your quality of life. It is important to watch what shows up in your life and observe your inner voice. Start a daily practice of using positive words to express your intentions

The power of transformational vocabulary is its simplicity

Step 1: Check yourself: be aware of the words used habitually to describe unhappy feelings and replace them with words that will have less of an impact.

Step 2: Identify six negative words you use and come up with alternatives.

Step 3: Find six positive words — and amplify them. Use and own these words.

Step 4: Pick three 'accountability' partners to support you and keep you on track.

Listen: To interviews with Change Makers, entrepreneurs, scientists, and people just like you who are growing awareness in their communities.

Learn: From everyone around you — in the coffee shop — local library — any connection. Set the intention you want to leave that person with... a feeling of inspiration and being uplifted — a sense of love for each other. Be somebody who is interested in learning more about how we as a community support each other.

Be passionate about reading: Keep updated on what's happening in the world — what's good, what's not, and what people are doing to grow solutions in their communities.

Love to embrace the art of storytelling: Through public speaking, films, short documentaries or animated clips, podcasts, books, magazines articles and blog posts — all are places to develop a narrative about who you are and to spread your message.

Messages from the heart: Share on Instagram, Twitter, or Facebook with a positive hashtag. Messages 'trend' and receive more attention that highlight inspiring news.

A picture says a thousand words: Sharing images on Facebook and other social networks are good places to share the 'me' you want others to see and the message you want them to know.

Alex Jarvis - Australia
Interior Designer, Rose Alchemist, Speaker, Author, CEO
www.jarvisinteriors.com.au

CHRISSY LEVETT

"From a place of despair can come our greatest learnings."

We can all change the world; we can all be 'Change Makers.' This story is a testament to that. Anything is possible, often from places of discomfort, despair or frustration comes awakening. We can change things with simple choices and conscious actions. We can safeguard our future and for generations to come, one *person*, one *step*, one *action* at a time.

FROM A PLACE OF DESPAIR TO PURPOSE.

As I stared into the garbage bin beside my desk, I knew what I was doing was meaningless: discarded packs, designed for the trash. Beautifully crafted tins and cardboard boxes, rubbish destined for the landfill every single day. I felt dismay in my heart. Our planet is dying and we are killing it, one object at a time. What saddened me was knowing that my job was to create beautifully crafted trash for pointless, even destructive products. Years before I'd been able to use 'design' to save lives but now I was using it to destroy.

I feel scared and frustrated for our future; I've awakened from Armageddon-style dreams with visuals to match. Despite these nightmares, I'd like you to imagine a world, a world where every single thing that we make, that we create, that we build, and even what we manufacture, serves humanity and our planet. I'd like you to close your eyes just for a second, pause and imagine that world…

Now, that would be a very different place, don't you agree? It would be a fairer, healthier, and more sustainable existence. And it is possible because there are businesses and organizations that put people and our planet first, and they are thriving, and successful.

My story starts around 10 years ago; I was working as a creative director. I was also the first and only female member on the board of directors for a creative agency in London. Many would say, successful; well, on paper at least.

My job was with a medium-sized design and branding agency, maybe 50-odd people housed centrally in a fancy studio, a converted warehouse space with huge double-height ceilings and loads of light. A massive space, way more than we needed, partitioned by trendy glass walls. A library full of inspirational books, glossy pictures featuring great designs. Next door, we had a gigantic open plan studio, where we, the 'creatives,' drew up concepts and ideas, aided by the latest digital equipment.

I was fortunate, privileged. I had four design directors, lovely and talented; each had teams of younger designers in their charge. There was a real family feel and it was a great place to work. The role was wonderful, in some ways a perfect fit for me, in terms of creativity. We designed brands and developed new products; we had teams for strategy, client services, production and new business. It was the place to be; I was blessed externally but it wasn't sitting well within me.

We worked largely on luxury products: lots of booze and chocolate. My team and I did beautifully crafted work. We built brands with lasting ideas, bespoke glass bottles with granite inlays, quality print using foil blocked, embossed, varnished technical printing. We won international design awards given by our industry and related businesses. The only thing was, we were creating, designing, and producing quality work that would be consumed and later thrown out. It was 'award-winning rubbish.' I used to joke with people I met that "We design for the bin!" Not funny, but it was true. I had known deep down for a long time that my job was meaningless, but as I learned more about our world, I started to understand that it was also destructive.

It was springtime; we had just won a new client and much excitement moved through the studio. With a new job came new creative ideas, a completely new brand, an opportunity, everything from scratch. The client was investing in a new production line, tooling… machines… the lot. Thousands, if not millions of euros. The client was a European dairy manufacturer. I now know many unpleasant things about that industry, but I was naive back then and excited to start the project. I believed we could make a difference, be 'game changers,' even lead the way! It was a rare opportunity to be at the start of a completely new product and expectations were high. We could design consciously, for the future, and the future of generations to come.

The brief was set, research and creative concepts crafted. We dived deep into structural ideas. Ten years ago, 'plastics' were not on mainstream agendas. There was no Sir David Attenborough on the BBC showing their devastating effects on the planet. There were no images of turtles caught in nylon nets or of ocean birds split open to reveal guts of colored plastic. Even so, I knew some things. I was naive, but not blind. I knew single-use plastics were not good for the planet, and that we, as designers, had in our hands an opportunity to make a difference; wasn't that our responsibility after all?

The time came to 'wow' the client and pitch the concepts. I'm not entirely sure how many of us flew to Denmark, but I do remember it was a clear day in the late spring. Stunning cool blue skies. The flight was short and smooth. I don't recall much else about the journey as we attended many such meetings in this part of the world, but I do remember the room. It was large and rectangular with a beautiful wooden table dominating the center of the space. A stunning piece of Danish design. Stylishly simple. The Danes use wood like few others and I remember being enchanted by this piece. As I took my seat at the table, I touched its texture; it was seductive and moreish. I was excited to share our innovative concepts.

We presented the branding with digital visuals shown on a TV screen mounted on the wall. Our work seemed well received, although it was always tricky to know what our Nordic clients thought. They would always remain unemotional and quiet in presentations, not a part of the world where gushing expressions live. Unlike our Italian clients who would arm-wave with passion and excitement, the same was not so with our Nordic friends. They were, however, a joy to work with: pragmatic, honorable, and fair.

The screen went blank, some comments were noted, and it was time to present our structural work. We would show this on a large scroll of paper strewn lengthwise across the naturally-buffed wood. It looked great. Standing at the head of the table, feeling confident, I leaned forward and began speaking with pride.

"What would it take," I said, "to build a structural product that would not only be a sustainable piece of innovative design but would leave your competitors behind and safeguard all our futures?" The room remained silent. I continued, "As businesses — as brands — we have a responsibility to create, design, build and even manufacture products that help people and sustain this beautiful planet."

There was still not a word from the client's team. I started to feel the silence for the first time. "We have an amazing opportunity here; there are now materials available — biodegradable, safe, non-toxic materials." *Still only silence.* Unphased, I continued, "Sustainable packaging exists that could make your business *leaders* and pioneers for change… and for the right reasons." *Still no feedback.* It was normal, as expected, a sea of stony Nordic faces staring back at me. A tumbleweed moment. Time started to feel sticky and slow. I noticed the sound of the ticking wall clock. I became aware of bottoms moving awkwardly on seats, the rustle of papers noisily coming from our side of the room.

Before I could continue, a nervous, squeaky interruption suddenly broke the audience's attention. My colleague at the far end of the table, one of our client services team, jumped up and started babbling nervously, killing the flow and train of thought. I'm not sure what it was she said, I really don't recall, but I do remember in that moment feeling incredibly sad, let down, and deflated.

We continued with the presentation, leaving their offices with smiles and thank-you's. I felt there was no problem. The following morning, however, I was called into the managing director's glass-like box, his office. He told me that I should never again ask clients such questions, that it wasn't my place and it was inappropriate. I didn't understand. As designers, how was it 'not our place' to ask questions, to open up new possibilities? Whose place was it then? Something needed to change. Most poignantly, I later learned that these comments had not come from our client, who was happy with the work, *but from our very own client services team.* They had come from a place of fear, and fear stops us from being great. Imagine what that business could have designed, owned, *built* if we had been allowed to carry on the conversation. Imagine the thousands, if not *millions* they could've saved in investment, especially now as much-needed legislation arrives around the production of single-use plastics. Imagine the power of brands that innovate and build for a future — putting people and planet first. The idea of doing anything less — of INTENTIONALLY doing anything less — sent nausea roiling through me; it's bitter, sour taste lingered in my mouth. It was then that I knew I was working, really working, in a broken, fearful system. This was my Ignite moment.

I'd been tasked by 'the board' to get our agency in the press and had reached out to a number of design journalists. The response was the same: unless we were doing something different, which we weren't, no one was going to write about us. At the next quarterly meeting when the 'bosses' asked, "How are you getting on with our media profile?" I explained the uninterested responses but offered up a potential solution. I told them about an external community project I was working on called Creative Conscience: a digital platform to engage, inspire and reward creative thinkers to use their talent for social and environmental impact. The idea for the project had come about as the result of a self-expression and leadership course undertaken in my own time for the purpose of instigating change in our industry. I offered this up to the business as a way for us to be 'different.' Gently pitching the 'why' and 'how.' Morally, it had appeal to the board, but they deemed there was 'no return on investment.' I was not surprised really, given the culture I was working in.

I didn't feel despair; after all, I'd merely mentioned it as a way of supporting the agency in its aim for recognition. It wasn't going to stop Creative Conscience; it was already being built. We had established a small community of creatives and were working on the network, branding and vision. Working tirelessly outside of the office, it grew and it felt *easy* to me. It soon became a passion project for all of us, and that passion started generating positive impact.

Working on this finally felt rewarding. Yet outside of work, I felt my own sense of despair. I was newly single after ending an abusive relationship so building something positive, fun and full of 'change making' potential was a form of healing, a wonderful distraction. I'd write, ask, and plan at night, once my two boys were in bed. It was therapeutic. A distraction from the questions I had around my personal situation. Instead, I felt a renewed passion for the possible impact I could make. The Change Maker in me was coming alive.

Three months passed and I was sitting in the agency's quarterly board meeting, oh joy! It was figures, forecasts, finance, business as usual until at the end someone asked about 'my little project,' the side hustle. With glee, I reeled off a list of names, those who we'd reached out to, all well known in the world of design and our creative industries: Zaha Hadid, Dame Vivian Westwood, Sebastian Conran, Sir Quentin Blake, Professor Helen Storey MBE, Thomas Heatherwick... the list went on. Sir Jonathan Porritt, world-famous environmentalist, was 'in' as were the head of design at Jaguar/Land Rover, the CEO of the Design Council and more. I looked around the table and watched the jaws drop while wearing a Cheshire cat smile on my face. The little side hustle was indeed impressive. It was at that moment that everything changed. The big 'bosses' finally got it. With the board's approval, Creative Conscience took off. We as an agency had the internal resources to build the first platform. Interns and juniors could work on it during quiet moments. We continued to reach out to our creative community and, in 2012, we launched our first annual award initiative. Creative Conscience had come to life, bold and full of possibilities.

Back then our industry, as I learned in Denmark, wasn't ready to be brave, to lead clients on social and environmental issues. But the next generation could. Nelson Mandela said, "Education is the most powerful weapon which you can use to change our world." So that's where we started. In art schools and universities, it was free and open to any student or recent graduate from any country, from any design or creative discipline. Filmmakers, photographers, fashion-textile designers, animators, motion graphics designers, architects, product designers, interiors, anyone and everyone; they started to send us their concepts. We did zero marketing; we simply built the platform and it took off.

Since launching in 2012, Creative Conscience has gone from strength to strength. A community-built organization, we've inspired more than 4000 projects sent by creative thinkers and global citizens, from more than 70 nations. At the heart, the core of every single project is creative thinking focused purely on social and environmental impact. We've developed tools, workshops and systems to help people change our world. And we're getting this type of thinking into education systems globally. That fills me with hope and purpose.

So many projects, so many back stories, so much change. Elena, a Romanian illustrator, created a stunning 166-page graphic novel about bullying and teenage suicide for our platform. After winning an award, it went on to touch the lives of millions. Elena received hundreds of messages from young people around the world telling her that her project had saved lives and stopped negative behaviors like self harm. Fatma created a campaign on the issue of female genital mutilation after living in fear of being cut herself. Scott designed powerful creative concepts for men's mental health after losing his father to suicide during his second year at university. Rob and Rowan designed a new non-toxic building material made from waste potato peelings, a project now funded and in production thanks to the Creative Conscience community. Hundreds and thousands of stories and solutions for things that simply aren't working for humanity and our world. Creative Change Makers, each and every one of them.

This Ignite story may have started in a meeting room in Denmark, but it also came from a place of personal despair. I now understand that fear stops us from being great, from making a difference. I know that every single one of us can positively change our world. Each action we choose to take impacts our future and each choice we make is a choice not only for ourselves but for the future of generations to come. We can all change our world. We are all potential Change Makers, if we decide to be one.

IGNITE ACTION STEPS

What can we do to create change? How can we all be part of the solution? There are so many opportunities for us to help safeguard our future and our beautiful planet. Challenge yourself; set a goal for a social and/or sustainable action that would lighten the burden on your soul, the planet, and then do it for a week, a month, or even for the rest of your life. Try not to consume new products for a month. The products and packaging you buy are intentionally designed to attract you. Resist. There is so much that we do not need to use. Be conscious about what you buy, eat, how we consume and from whom. You as a consumer have the power to incite change in organizations, companies, and brands so they will support the planet in flourishing.

We have research and data that proves being involved with this way of thinking i.e., being in service to others, helps mental well-being; so why not try it? It's magical.

Paul Hawken (Drawdown) says, "If what we tell ourselves is that we're screwed, it destroys our imagination, our creativity and innovation for solutions." Please don't believe our media. We need hope and action to be Change Makers. Join in. Let's build a future that safeguards not destroys, a shared vision of a fairer, healthier and more sustainable world.

Chrissy Levett - United Kingdom
Founder Creative Conscience
www.creative-conscience.org.uk

PRIYA LAKHI

*"We have no choice but to change, as change is
the only stable ground to stand on."*

**I want to empower you to awaken to your magnificence. I urge you to bring
forth the wisdom that there is no 'should' and no 'right way.' Don't worry
about having it all figured out. Remember that pain can spill into clarity and
discomfort can be the greatest gift. Your soul is rooting for you. I want to
Ignite you to break down the cage and become untamed. Don't play by the
rules. Reclaim your inner authority and enjoy the adventure of being alive!**

THE WILD ART OF UNBECOMING

I'll never forget the first time I walked into the prison. As I entered the
security area, the guard shouted as if he had said this a thousand times before,
"Bag here, shoes there, and spread your legs." The next thing I knew, I was
being roughly patted down and semi-strip searched by an unhappy and stoic
female security guard. Big, heavy prison doors banged closed behind me.

Taking in my last breaths of fresh air, I exhaled. Navigating the maze of
hallways filled with fluorescent lights, I could feel my palms sweating and my
heart beating. I opened the door and took a seat on the cold metal chair facing
a wide expanse of table. Taking a gulp, I hesitantly started speaking.

"My name is Priya and I will be your attorney." Across from me sat my first
client. The gleam of his wedding ring caught my eye and he reached out his
hand to shake mine.

I didn't know I wanted to be a lawyer. It was part of the expectation that was placed on me. While in law school, I loved criminal law. I had a passion for it. It felt like a deep calling. You can't practice criminal defense unless you truly believe in justice, and I believed.

In my final year of law school, I landed my dream job working on social justice issues in Atlanta, in the heart of the southern United States. I wanted to make a real difference and be a Change Maker.

When I left for my first lawyer job, my father refused to speak to me. He had the same fears, worries, and doubts as any parent, except he didn't know how to navigate a world where his daughter was independent enough to not 'need him.' A good East Indian girl doesn't leave her parents' house until she is married. A proper Indian girl doesn't disobey her family. An obedient Indian girl doesn't live a life outside of the box. Moving to Atlanta was my first big step to saying 'No.' For most of my life until that point, I had suffered in silence in this crazy world where I wasn't Indian enough or American enough. I struggled with the pressure of an immigrant culture where South Asian girls don't do what those 'American girls' do. I learned early on how to pretend to be small and not have an opinion, just to make everyone happy. I became a people pleaser. This trait carried into my adult life.

I had come from a long line of women not feeling seen or heard.

When I was 5 years old, my family moved to the United States from Mumbai, India. My mother had married my father in an arranged marriage. She had wanted to become a doctor, but her father had said no. Most households in India teach girls to accept what family members tell them to do, and she did. As a teenager, noticing the freedom that my American friends had, the thought of this lack of independence distressed me. I believe it also distressed my grandmother. My grandmother is the silver lining in my parents' story. After my parents got married, she was the one who strongly encouraged my mother to go to college. And, she did.

My grandmother was also the one who encouraged my parents to change. She pushed them to the United States to pursue the dream of opportunity. While this move was one of the best decisions they ever made, it also introduced major conflict about how to adapt to the American culture while preserving our Indian heritage. Like most immigrants, my parents, both with college degrees, had to settle — unhappily — for low-paying jobs when they first moved to the US. All of this contributed to my childhood. I was always sensitive to the needs of those around me. I knew in my bones when life was hard.

Growing up in white suburban Ohio, I was the only brown kid in school. Looking different led to constant name-calling and, in elementary school, taught me that my Indian heritage brought ridicule. No one could pronounce my name and my entire identity felt shameful. By middle school, I knew that in order to survive socially, I needed to distance myself as far as possible from anything Indian. I chose to assimilate as culturally white as possible.

My parents struggled with the realization that their children were adapting to the American way of life, feeling we were becoming 'too Americanized.' Throughout my teenage years, I had to hide my 'American side' from my Indian parents. I was living a double life. We all were. We were all caught between two worlds.

Then came adulthood. For the first time in my life, I had a degree and a job, and I did not need my parents' approval. They had lost their control and I had gained some level of freedom, even though I was guilt-ridden about it. It was most surreal. There seemed to be only one 'right way' for success. Be a lawyer. Get an arranged marriage. Have kids. Smile. Live happily ever after. But someone else's box never felt 'right.'

When I walked in to see that first client behind the prison gates, I felt like I had moved mountains to be there. I was determined to be successful and independent! Making my own money, enjoying a boyfriend and a life full of fun... my dream had become reality. Except I wasn't entirely sure whose dream it was. Mine? My parents'? Society's?

A few years into my career, I started having bouts of anxiety and depression. I would get restless wondering if life was only about: eat, sleep, work, repeat. Like most of us, I defined myself by my career. I easily ignored all my internal conflict. It had been such a long road to achieve liberation and I sure as hell wasn't going to question it now.

The Universe was, as it does, nudging me to Ignite change. And that nudge was starting to get louder. I had checked all the boxes society told me to check to be happy, and yet I wasn't. I was on autopilot. I didn't have the life I loved. When I asked others about the meaning of life, I was met with a look of surprise. No one had an answer. I kept resisting the small voice within. I led a life on the outside that would make anyone think I was on top of the world, but I was playing hide and seek with my fears of unfulfillment.

Finally the Universe started to take drastic measures to get my attention and Ignite change. As I soared past each societal milestone, wanting to be filled with joy, I was confused by the emptiness I felt inside. I woke up everyday thinking, "What's the worst thing that is going to happen today?" I was spiraling into a hole of self-destruction. I felt my deepest fears of insignificance erupting; my soul was starving for wholeness and I couldn't feed it.

The hard crash to rock bottom was painful in every way. The thing is, nobody ever tells you how to deal with extreme pain or failure in life. My family knew I needed help, but I knew nobody could pull me out of that tailspin. I had no choice but to face myself... brutally, painfully, and honestly. Pain was spilling into clarity and I looked my own darkness in the eyes. Although I was adept at advocating for my clients and being their comrade in fighting for hope, I had no idea how to empower myself.

It was in this heaviness that I found my answer. A whisper to visit the motherland — India — to break the compounding darkness. The last place I wanted to go was India! India was the land of painful childhood memories. A place that I had a love/hate relationship with. My entire being rebelled at the thought. The hair on my arms stood up, my shoulders grew tight, my breathing sped up. It was a resistance. It felt like the whole pressure of my parents again. But that whisper was unrelenting. The voice of God speaking right to me and telling me to go. I lay on the bathroom floor, piles of crumpled tissues around me, knowing against all rational thought that India was calling and I had to leave.

I now know that I was knee deep in the spiritual concept called 'the dark night of the soul.' The Dark Night is a kind of initiation, taking you from one phase of life into another. We do NOT choose it willingly. It is the sign of a *High Calling*. It is a threshold we cross. We have no choice but to change as change is the only stable ground to stand on.

My plane landed in Mumbai and I went straight to my aunt, a yoga teacher and an energy healer. I had nothing else figured out. For the first time in my life, all I wanted to explore were the questions "Who am I? Why are we here? What does it all mean? Is there really a God?" I was aching for answers.

One look at me, and my aunt knew exactly what to do. She fed me, she healed me, she looked into my eyes with kindness, and she loved me fiercely.

Bathed in her unconditional acceptance, I started to feel small bits of joy in my day. I looked forward to waking up. The Dark Night was very slowly revealing its Light. By this time, I had made significant changes. I took a sabbatical after 15 years as a lawyer who had worked all over the world, I broke up with my boyfriend, and gave up my duties as a law school professor.

One day, my aunt asked me if I wanted to learn Reiki. As I walked into that first spiritual class, I was still weak in spirit and body, and I knew my life depended on that moment. I gave myself the power to create a life I love.

It would be a year before I would leave India to come back to the United States. A year where I traveled mostly alone. A year where feelings that had been suppressed for decades were peeled back, layer by layer, then microscopically examined.

Mother India brought me to my knees.

I changed what no longer served me. My teachers pushed me forward into destruction, allowing for a rebirth. The world as I knew it was gone. In its place, I had unbecome everything I had thought was me.

Along this journey, I met with healers, shamans, yogis, and teachers and started trusting my intuition. The lawyer in me was always looking for proof — proof that the Universe does have my back. I couldn't deny my experiences while the unseeable forces of the Universe were happening daily. My hunger for spiritual knowledge was awakening. I started exploring my own inner wisdom and living in a world where I was fully in sync with my mystical gifts. It was so evident that my next evolution was to fully Ignite my spiritual side. To integrate my intuition with my intelligence, and to use this gift to be of service to other women. To continue my journey as a Change Maker.

I look back with immense gratitude for the incredible gifts that India bestowed upon me. It instilled in me a deep trust with myself. I'd do it all again, in a heartbeat, for the extraordinary insights and growth I gained through what were most definitely my darkest hours.

India was preparing me to fulfill my destiny. It was time to stop settling for the status quo. I learned that what we are hungry for can never be met by something outside of us, be it a job, a spouse, or money. We yearn for a deep connection with the Divine within us... a fierce knowing of our power... a gentle embrace with our own soul... a connection so grounded that we are able to effortlessly rise to meet our full potential.

When I came back 'home,' I was elated. The goddess Kali teaches that to create, we must first destroy. I felt like I had slayed my dragons and won. I had unbecome the old me, and created the new me. I couldn't wait to figure out how to start my new business as a healer. I had awakened my magnificence and I was so much closer to being the woman of my dreams.

The reality of being back in Atlanta slapped me in the face. While I felt like an entirely changed person, many people in my life were the same. The new me was met with a lot of resistance and I almost questioned if India had been real. There I was, 42 years old, and the new me knew nothing had the power to stop me. The Phoenix had risen.

Two months after returning from India, my company, Awaken Ananda, was born. A-nan-da is a Sanskrit word meaning 'your highest potential where all possibilities can blossom.' I learned the magical thing about sharing your gift is that it will connect you to the world again. Everyday, I celebrate and honor the birth of this new incarnation. I am in awe of where my curious untamed woman has brought me. I will always protect my soulful life. I cherish the sweet 'good girl' I was, the powerful lawyer I became, and I passionately embrace the Change Maker I have become.

I want to empower you to awaken to your magnificence. You can prevent your life from being silenced by the beat of someone else's drums. Instead, you can dance your own dance. Orchestrate your own existence. It begins by questioning everything. Allowing yourself to be seen and heard to get to the heart of the matter. With breathtaking boldness, I say this: Ignite your Truth so you can CHANGE YOUR LIFE. The amount of joy you will experience will transform you.

IGNITE ACTION STEPS

The timing may not be yours; choose to be ready. The most important thing I can tell you about the timing of your rising is this: when it's time, it's time. Even if you are not ready. Even if things are undone. Not because today is a good day. Not because life is all nice and uncomplicated. No, you rise because it is time and therefore you must.

Choose to make changes, not excuses. It takes an incredible amount of courage to even decide to change — not to mention energy. Most don't choose to as a result. As you look in the mirror, know you are wise, loving, and free. Today and every day, intentionally Ignite your change.

Live by choice, not by chance. Ask yourself sincerely, "What do I want and what do I really need to be happy? How does this apply to my work, motherhood, friendships, partnerships, and self-care? How can I fulfill this need?"

Be courageous and look deep within the shadow of you. Choose to pay attention to negative habits, addictions, or problems that keep arising. These hold a message for you. Be brave. Let them teach you about yourself. Confront your life head-on in all its glorious messiness.

Choose radical self-compassion. Be your own best friend. Spend time hearing, really hearing, your intuition and the magic of the Universe. Express gratitude, for real. Everything on this Earth school is here to teach you, guide you, evolve you.

Choose to be connected. We are not meant to walk the Path alone. Isolating yourself in vicious independence does not serve you. Find a teacher, a mentor, a coach, a healer. Our human brain is evolved for relationships. There is something very right with you when you need emotional safety and support.

Today, choose to no longer live the confiscated life. You are worthy of change. It is time to come home to yourself. You are of the Earth and of the stars. Give yourself the power to IGNITE a life you love. May you grow to know the Change Maker that you are.

Priya Lakhi - United States
Healer, Master Coach, Hypnotherapy,
Spiritual Teacher, Speaker, Author Founder
www.awakenananda.com

Jannette Anderson

"The first step to lasting change is momentary courage."

Have you been called to step into playing a bigger game? Whether that's at the level of being a better parent, growing your business, or leading a global movement. We've all got 'reasons' why we haven't fully stepped into the change we want to be in the world. My intention is to share tools I've found that can overcome the B.S. stories that limit us and create procrastination, spinning, and playing small! The world doesn't have time for us to withhold our gifts. That's why I'm so excited to share the five strategies that took me from being a resistant rebel to a committed Change Maker!

Call Waiting Was Never Meant for Dreams

I was quivering on a platform nestled in the tree-top canopy, 900 feet high with a webbed harness digging painfully into my thighs and gut. The thought kept running through my head over and over, "Who's stupid idea was this?!?!?!" but it was drowned out by the loud knocking of my knees. Javier, a wickedly-handsome Costa Rican, almost a foot shorter and two decades younger than me asked, "Are you ready, Jannette?"

"HELL NO! I am not ready to die!" Because I was 100 percent convinced that the thin wire would never hold my considerable body weight. I was envisioning the wire snapping and my body twisting and turning as it plummeted through the air to the jungle floor nine stories below me. "Let's get you on the wire!" he said with what I was pretty sure was maniacal glee.

It was a turning point... a point where I needed to choose in — or out — of an experience. In or out of my commitment to me. In or out of life really... in fact perhaps literally. I had decided I was going to overcome my abject fear of heights, and so on my seven-month solo journey throughout Central and South America, I had committed to doing a bunch of things that scared the bejeezus out of me like ziplining in Costa Rica, paraponting in Ecuador (jumping off the side of a mountain and sitting in an armchair in the sky), and traversing a high ropes courses through the cloud forest in Nicaragua to name a few. At the time they made sense.

As the line of people behind me grew impatient and the zipline chasm in front of me grew even more intimidating, I reminded myself of why I was doing this. I HATE being constrained by limits. Even, perhaps especially, self-imposed limitations. If it scares me... if it stops me... if I have the words "I can't" running through my head and heart... it frankly pisses me off. Always has. But not just because I am a rebellious bad-ass; unfortunately, because of the opposite.

It bugs me because it pokes that bruised place that lives in the shadow of my soul. That part of me that agrees with the limiting belief, "It is true. I can't." That quiet, insidious voice that whispers — and sometimes shouts — "You ARE not good enough... you'll never succeed."

It's ironic really because, based on results, I have succeeded wildly. I have traveled to 29 countries so far, as well as every province in Canada and every state in the USA. I've swum with great white sharks, jumped out of perfectly good airplanes, survived seven near-death experiences, and hung with shamen in the jungles of the Amazon. I've been a white water rafting guide and a VP in a Fortune 500 company. So far I have built four of my own businesses that have helped thousands of entrepreneurs profit from their purpose and passion. You could say that I've been driven to suck the marrow out of life because I grew up with so many "No's." I vowed early on to live a "Yes" life!

You see, I survived a childhood that many wouldn't have. It included a lot of abuse, multiple incestuous relationships, foster homes, five 'fathers' before the age of eight, incredible amounts of violence, a year and a half in the hospital for seven operations before I was six, 27 moves in my first 29 years, and an alcoholic single mother with a borderline-personality disorder, to name just a few of the challenges.

I grew up steeped in scarcity and instability. Although I think Mom sought security in all of her marriages, she consciously married for money the fourth time around. Howard looked exactly like Santa Claus and was a pillar of the community. So people never suspected that he would often drag Mom into his meditation room by her hair to beat her bloody in front of his picture of the Maharishi. We lived with isolation and violence for almost two years until one morning I found her more dead than alive and risked telling my first grade teacher, who sent the police. What happened next was a blur, but I do remember wearing the same blue t-shirt every day for the next week. Once Mom was out of hospital, we found our way to a shelter. We had nothing, but we were alive.

When I look back at my younger self, it made sense that the story she told about life was that it was not safe to rely on others and you have to pay a big price for having what you want. There was always some version of *not enough* going on. Scarcity infects us with an insidious inclination to settle. To not ask for too much, not expect too much, and definitely not demand too much… of yourself or of life.

Mom wasn't evil. She grew up during the depression with a mother who also had mental health issues. Although she loved me fiercely, she battled with wanting more for me — as all parents do — and with not wanting to be surpassed. When she kept me small, she thought she was keeping me safe.

I remember driving down Ninth Avenue in Calgary, Canada in Moms' car, a 12-year-old Pontiac, and seeing a sleek, sexy, midnight blue Jaguar XJS in front of us. I confidently said to her, "I'm going to have one of those one day!" She turned to me and said in all sincerity, "Why do you need *that,*" pointing at the Jaguar, "when *that,*" pointing at a rusty Chevy Nova beside us on the road, "will get you where you are going just as well?" This is another track that runs on the 'play small' record for many of us: "Who do you think you are to want so much?"

The rebel in me pushed hard against these tracks and was determined to take control and create a vastly different life to the one that most of my family experienced. I always saw freedom and choice as an option. I stand proudly on the foundation of these experiences and bless my mother and my childhood for creating a tremendous capacity in me! All of it helped shape the Change Maker I have become.

Pushing back and changing the story, it turns out, is what I'm best at. In fact, learning to tell better stories has become a lifetime passion. It's what I learned to do when I became a personal development facilitator. It's what I've been doing as a coach for 30 plus years and in all of the business growth training and consulting I do. A wise and inspiring mentor of mine, Chung Gu Park, once said, "Cha! You must live a story life! A story life!!" So, that's why I was in the Costa Rican jungle on the edge of a rickety platform. I was creating new, better stories about who I am and what I was capable of!

When Javier asked me if I was ready, I thought about why I wanted to do this in the first place. Oh ya, I wanted to overcome my fear. He asked me to come to the edge of the platform so I could be hooked onto the wire. "Oh Javier, you are definitely going to need reinforcements!" I pointed out. His Latin male pride was a bit wounded, but he did call over Miguel and Alex to help. Between me hopping around like a demented kangaroo and the three of them trying to hoist me awkwardly onto the carabiner, I was finally attached. As I looked at the 500-foot expanse stretching in front of me, Javier kindly reminded me to breathe. I guess blue wasn't my best color.

He repeated what I was to do: not to hold on too tight or I would stop myself and someone would have to crawl out to rescue me (a challenging situation for everyone), and not to let go entirely because I was responsible for my speed coming into the other platform. While the tree across the chasm did have a mattress wrapped around it, a feature that was both reassuring and alarming, I knew that it would not be a soft landing if I wasn't taking some control. The metaphors for life were not lost on me even in my semi-panicked state.

That was when Javier asked me a truly stupid question, "Are you ready, Jannette?"

No. Nope I wasn't. No, I wasn't ready to potentially die. I wasn't ready to pee myself in public — which was pretty much a given! I wasn't ready... but I dug down and reminded myself of my commitment, and of the potential for a breakthrough. I wasn't ready, but I was *willing*. I swallowed the lump of fear the size of a grapefruit and said with far more bravado than I was feeling, "OK, let's do this." All that was left was to make the leap. To take that step into the abyss. To trust. I inched forward. And I jumped!

For the first few moments, my eyes were squeezed shut. My mouth was wide open, shrieking and I had a death grip on the harness. When I realized I wasn't plummeting to the jungle floor, I peeked out to see the beautiful emerald blur of the canopy whizzing past me. I heard the chirps and caws of a jungle symphony and smelled the verdant green aliveness surrounding me. I was flying in full-blown awe-mode.

All at once, the canopy that had cocooned me dropped away and I emerged from the tunnel of green like shooting out of a womb into the bright sunny world. The vast valley opened up right and left for miles. It was literally breathtaking.

I felt the wind whipping at my sweat-soaked clothes and the heat of the wire screaming through my gloved hand. For a brief moment, hanging suspended over the earth, I relaxed. I surrendered. Peace, joy, and oneness washed over me as I flew. There was a lifetime in that moment.

Suddenly, the once distant platform was rushing at me way too fast. I frantically squeezed to slow myself, shredding the leather on my gloves, and landed with a thump! Yay! I was still alive. In fact, vibrantly alive! I learned much from that one brave leap.

Three years later, back home in Canada with my jungle adventures a distant memory, I was called to make another leap... It was during a meditation that a vision unfolded in front of me in glorious detail. It spilled onto twelve pages in my journal. Afterwards, I read what I had written and literally slammed the book closed. *"What are you thinking God — I'm not a feminist. I don't even really like women — you've got the wrong person!"* I was being called to lead a tribe of women committed to 'Shifting our world from fear to love one happy woman at a time.' It was about inspiring them to be bodaciously bold! But I hung up the phone! At the time, I hadn't worked with women a lot and frankly mistrusted 'sisterhood.' A LOT has profoundly changed since, but back then, I thought, "You've got the wrong number God... find someone else!" I literally put the dream on hold!

About every six months from then on, I'd receive a little reminder. A nudge. Sometimes a direct 2x4 upside the head saying, "This is yours to do!" But I never had a shortage of excuses why I couldn't...

"It's been done... there are LOTS of women's groups!"
"I'm not the right leader. I'm a lone wolf."
"I'm busy. I just got a new contract doing someone else's meaningful work."

And more, but you get the idea.

A surprisingly persistent and patient Universe kept asking me, with increasing urgency, "Are you ready Jannette?" **Finally** I heard the question but in Javier's voice. Oh... I am being asked to leap! Why didn't you say so?

I'd like to say I graciously surrendered and stepped right up. But I'd be lying. It was more like, "Alright I'll do it, stop &%*#ing bugging me!!" I started to build *Bodacity* with hesitancy, resistance, enthusiasm, focus, and avoidance. I'd also like to say that it was clear sailing right from the outset and the path was smooth... but that's not true either.

My dance of resistance went on for eight long years, causing me tremendous frustration, shame, and guilt. I did workshops and started to build a community, but mostly I planned and planned and revised the plans and the branding and the positioning... and then I'd start over. If this sounds at all familiar, I urge you to stop 'drowning in the shallow end of the pool!' — dive in or get out! This passion as a passtime vs. a purposeful business is *draining*. Even though there was a spark within me, I was letting my fear smother what was waiting to be Ignited. I finally reached what I call my "F-It" point. The pain of avoidance and not doing what I was called to outweighed the fear and inertia. I got tired of my own stories, I turned up the volume on why this mattered, I called in more support, and I leapt!

I quit the contract where I was building someone else's dream, tribe, and business. I committed to finding the keys to breaking through my wall of fear on an ongoing basis. And I focused on what I did want and who I was choosing to be in the world. But bringing my life into alignment so I could walk my talk called for a number of changes.

I sold my house and most of what I owned, downsizing my 2400 sq. ft of belongings to only what fits in a 10x10' storage unit. Less encumbered I could live the mobile lifestyle I've always longed for. Now I get to work with amazing clients and leaders who live all around the globe from anywhere I choose to be in the world. I have the honor of leading a beautiful and brave tribe of women who are committed to building their *Bold Life and Bold Business!*

Bodacity.ca is a mindset, a community, and a global movement committed to reinventing how we do business and life! I believe that women need to accelerate and *lead* the move from fear to love if we are to survive and to thrive as a species.

I may be an unlikely leader. You may be too; but just like getting off the platform, all that's needed from any of us is willingness. Willingness to take the leap and say Yes!

For four decades, I have loved coaching entrepreneurs on how to successfully turn their passion into practical contribution and profit. I am excited when I get on stages to share my call to women to step up and go ALL IN so we can ALL WIN! You have a gift, we all do, and *every one* of our unique gifts are needed to make the changes that we know need to happen — now. So, I invite you to take your dreams off hold, grab life by the ovaries, and say, "Let's do this!"

IGNITE ACTION STEPS

- **Be Willing.** I wasn't ready. We seldom are. I didn't even want to do it… we often don't. I didn't feel prepared, or knowledgeable, or equipped to make that leap. What I was… was *willing*. Courage is not the absence of fear but the choice to act in spite of it. And as far as being equipped enough — I really love this quote: "God does not call those who are equipped. She equips those whom she has called."

- **Ask Yourself 'Why.'** I had a cause, a bigger reason for stepping through my fears. What are the big juicy carrots that call you forward?

- **Clarify Your Price For Playing Small.** This is where you bring in the stick to motivate yourself. What is the price you pay for NOT taking action?

- **Create a Community of Support.** I could not have zip-lined without Javier's encouragement. My friends, family, coaches, and mastermind groups have supported me in many, many other leaps. Find your community of support. The biggest block to being a successful Change Maker is trying to do it alone.

- **Commit!** You cannot cross a chasm one step at a time — you need to leap!

Jannette Anderson - Canada
The Why Whisperer
www.bodacity.ca

CATHERINE
MALLI-DAWSON

"Find the quiet place within so you can manage the chaos without."

My intention in sharing this story with you is to let you know that you are not alone in your struggles, and there is a way forward that enables you to live your most extraordinary life on your own terms and in alignment with your life's purpose.

SIX ELEMENTS OF LIVING AN EXTRAORDINARY LIFE

Sitting at my desk in the little cramped office space tucked away at the top of the stairs, I stared at my hands as they shook uncontrollably. I could feel my heart racing in my chest and my lungs tightening as my breathing became shallower and more labored. There was a rushing, pounding freight train racing past my ears as the blood pumped through my veins past my eardrums. I was 35 years old, home alone, and had no idea what was happening. Confused and more than a little scared, I wondered whether I needed to phone an ambulance, my fiancé, or just lie down.

I forced myself to sit back in my chair, took several deep breaths and made my way to my bedroom where I laid down to rest. I fell asleep for a few hours and when I woke up I had reclaimed a sense of calm. I realized what I had experienced was a panic attack. I had no idea what had caused it. There was no specific trigger. No conversation or conflict. And this was *not* something I had ever experienced before in my life. I had come face to face with a feeling I would label 'overwhelm.' I was caught in the trap of taking care of everyone and everything and never myself.

Scared and unsure about who I was and what I was doing, I knew I was physically making myself sick. My body was trying to send me a strong message and if I didn't listen, it was going to take drastic actions: shaking hands, racing heartbeat, sweating palms, and shallow breathing. "What was next?" I asked myself. But I didn't really want to know the answer. I was your classic high-powered executive, climbing the corporate ladder, making my mark on the world while simultaneously taking care of my family, finishing my Master's degree and preparing for my wedding. Yet above all of that, I felt like a fraud, a failure, a fake. I feared that *they* would find out at any minute. I'm not sure who *they* were, but I knew I couldn't hide from them any longer.

I had worked so hard to get to where I was in life. I was a single mother who traveled half-way around the world to grow my career. I had an *au pair* to care for my son when I traveled. I was completing my Masters degree (the first in my family) and I was in love and planning my wedding. And yet, I felt like such a complete failure.

I had a choice to make. I could continue on this path hiding behind my carefully crafted persona of the high-powered executive or I could choose to change my life. I needed to step back, take a moment to figure this all out. I decided I *had* to take time out for myself. For the first time in my life, I booked into a health spa and allowed myself to disconnect and relax. This one seemingly simple decision set me on a path that changed my life radically. I spent the hours lounging, relaxing, and being nurtured over three miraculous days.

As I drove home, I gazed at my beautifully manicured nails with the glossy, red polish and realized I had never taken time out for myself before. All my friends had spa days regularly. There I was, living in England, in my mid thirties and I had never taken the time to fully allow myself to be cared for. I decided at that moment that if I didn't change, if I didn't start putting myself first, I was likely to die a broken and miserable woman. The panic attack had triggered fears of poor health and proof of the stress and anxiety I was living with. I knew I couldn't continue on the corporate path and I needed to figure out how to move myself out of it without destroying my life and my family.

More importantly, I needed to figure out what it was I wanted to do next. If not the corporate hamster wheel, then what? I had already defied all stereotypes of a trailer-trash brat, high school drop-out, and single mom. Why was I now feeling so scared and uncertain about what I wanted in life?

I've always operated from a holistic mind-body-spirit point of view, so now, needing to understand and reconnect with myself, I chose to explore meditation and metaphysical teachings. I spent the next few years healing my inner child, learning Reiki, astrology, and meditation. I continued to work in my corporate role, however, I stepped back and didn't put myself forward as often as before. I allowed others to take the lead while I migrated into a supporting role. In my personal time, I attended every mind, body, soul exposition within a drivable distance. I listened to guided meditations and connected with a higher power, allowing intuition to guide my actions and behaviors.

As life unfolded, I grew less defined by my career and more connected to my family and myself. Ultimately, I learned what I *didn't* want and how I *didn't* want to live my life. I got married, eventually negotiated a redundancy package, effectively making myself obsolete. I drifted for a while, helping budding entrepreneurs in the holistic therapy field figure out how to market themselves and build their businesses. Then I convinced my husband it was a great idea to start our own business. Be our own bosses.

We talked about coffee shops and juice bars, unique craft shops and bookstores. We scouted locations and met with real estate agents. We were on a treasure hunt for the right location and the ideal business. We spent hours researching business models and legal implications of our various ideas. By pure chance, we came across a boutique health and beauty center in the crossroads of a little village called Minchinhampton, in southwest England. The owner was closing down due to the sudden loss of their partner. Located in South Cotswolds, it was like something out of a story book. The narrow one-way cobbled streets were lined with centuries-old stone cottages, many of them leaning in precarious directions. The local cattle farmers would graze their cattle on the common land surrounding the village. When the herds wandered into the village center, little old women would bat them with their canes as they munched the flowers in the window baskets and doorsteps along the street. After the realization I had about my inability to put myself first, I felt it was an amazing opportunity for me to explore a more caring, nurturing way of life. We negotiated a fair exchange and set about establishing ourselves as The Village Sanctuary.

We offered therapies, beauty treatments, and accommodation. We even had a storefront filled with beautiful products, gifts, and books. I learned the local pastor had taken offense to our name, claiming, "The only *sanctuary* in this village is mine." However, I eventually won him over and his wife would frequent our shop and enjoyed the therapies. There was one family who often knocked on our door late in the evening looking for a last minute gift for their daughters. They said they always knew they could find something in our shop that would suit their needs and we were always happy to open up for their private shopping experience.

Ironically, this choice of business meant I was again taking care of others. The difference this time was that I was also taking care of myself and I loved what I was doing. I was making a difference in people's lives. It felt good when our guests showed up with the weight of the world on their shoulders and left with a lightness in their steps and a smile on their faces. I was working harder than I had ever worked in my life, yet I was enjoying every minute of it.

We settled into village life and became central participants in all the village activities. Whether it was a competition for the best flower boxes, a gnome hunt, a leading role in the local theatre troupe, a late night at the local pub or a visit with royalty, we got involved and became an integral part of the community. We were connected. We were part of something bigger than ourselves and we were working seven days a week. We tried to close over the holidays and found there was always someone who needed to rest and restore themselves, so we invited them in and cared for them.

It was a beautiful time and a trying time. We argued and we laughed. We celebrated and we cried. Most of all we lived and we served. We built a successful business over the next three years and became the go-to boutique spa in the Cotswolds.

Then my mother's health began to fail. She lived in the USA with my disabled sister. I, being the youngest and the caregiver in the family, would fly home every few months to help them and generally make sure they were okay. This went on for over a year while we continued to grow our spa business until one day I finally had to make the decision to let go of my dream and return to the States permanently so I could care for them more directly. I was crushed and a little relieved. The business was busier than ever and we had added additional services that meant we were open later in the evenings. I was finding it more labor than love. Of course, the frequent trips back to the States only compounded the situation.

When I raised the prospect of moving to the States, I didn't get much argument from my husband. He was also eager to relieve himself of the burden of the business and was excited about moving to the States. I relocated first to get everything established and found a job back in a corporate role where I easily stepped onto the hamster wheel and started pedaling. I moved my mother and sister in with me so I could give them the care they needed. My husband stayed in the UK for another 18 months while his green card was being processed. We still joke to this day that if we can survive a forced 18-month separation, then we can survive anything.

When he finally joined me, I was well established again in the corporate grind. Working long hours, traveling and generally making my mark once again. Returning to the States gave me an opportunity to evaluate in what industry I wanted to work. I explored the utility, finance, manufacturing and healthcare industries. I looked at each one and determined that healthcare seemed to be the most exciting and had the most potential for growth. My skills in telecommunications management easily transferred to becoming a healthcare information technology project manager. It was an easy fit and I enjoyed learning a new industry.

It wasn't long before I started recognizing the same symptoms I had experienced previously. Shaky hands (probably too much caffeine), shortness of breath (not enough exercise), poor sleep (busy reviewing my to-do list), forgetfulness (multi-tasking), lack of focus (more sleep needed), irritability (again too much caffeine), and digestion issues (too many trips through fast food drive-thrus). I was a walking advertisement for any number of medications. I think the only thing that kept me going was my daily supply of aspirin and Starbucks lattes. I had let go of my meditation practices. I had forgotten all my self-care treatments. I had forgotten myself – again!

Living in Arizona, the land of vacation resorts, golf clubs and luxury spas, I had no excuse for not visiting a spa and taking some time out for myself. So I booked a retreat weekend in Sedona and began the process of reconnecting with what was meaningful in my life. I meditated, got a massage, did yoga, went for a hike to an energy vortex and had an amazing time caring for myself and allowing others to care for me. When I returned home I was calmer, more centered and grounded. And, I again realized, I needed to make a change. While I enjoyed what I was doing, I didn't like *how* I was doing it. I recognized I had slipped back into the bad behaviors from before and I needed to re-evaluate what was driving me and *why* I felt compelled to be everything for everyone, except myself.

Change began... I restarted my meditation practice and made regular self-care dates. I scheduled manicures and pedicures (allowing myself to be pampered), started getting monthly massages (relaxing and letting go) and taking the dog for morning walks (connecting with nature)... I stopped feeling guilty if I chose to read a book instead of cleaning. This allowed me to take the necessary time out to relax, regroup, and reconnect with myself. I also realized that I had become so absorbed in my job that I didn't have any friends outside of my work colleagues. I made a conscious decision to meet new people and connect in different ways. I became more involved in my community. I helped my mother and sister move into an assisted living home where they *too* could make new friends and have others care for them. I spent more quality time with my husband and son. And most importantly, I took time out to be with myself.

Along the way of my life's journey, I learned that to be truly loving, you have to first love yourself. I had to change my perspective to discover my life's purpose — to live the most amazing life possible on my own terms. I learned that in order to grow, I need a solid foundation. If I want to be connected with others, I need to first connect with myself. I recognized that communication internally is as important, if not more important, than externally. I learned, nothing is going to happen if I don't take action and make the hard choices. And most importantly, I learned to celebrate. Celebrate the wins, learn from the losses, and not let either define me.

Those lessons led me to develop key elements of living an extraordinary life. By paying attention to the signals and messages my body sends me, I am able to step back and evaluate my situation. This has enabled me to become aware of who I am and, in turn, helps me establish what I want and why I exist. I connect to my purpose and my 'why.' This internal compass now directs me in everything I do. With attention and awareness, I am guided to live in alignment with my purpose. When I have a decision to make, I first ask myself which choice will maintain my alignment with my 'why.' Which action, decision or thought keeps me moving forward. While I am excited about where my life is taking me, I'm allowing everything to unfold and I live in gratitude every day.

I now empower others to reconnect with themselves, listen to the messages their bodies are sending them, and to find their 'why' that influences their every action and decision. My mission is to inspire people to become aware of who they are, why they exist, and how they want to show up in the world. I encourage them to build the foundation of daily practices that will help them stay in alignment with their core purpose. And finally, I give them permission to allow their lives to unfold without attachment to the outcome.

By following the six elements I've outlined in the action steps below, you can live an extraordinary life. It doesn't matter if you're a stay-at-home mom, a high-powered executive or a budding entrepreneur, these elements will change your perspective and empower YOU to live an extraordinary life on YOUR own terms.

IGNITE ACTION STEPS

The Six Elements of Living an Extraordinary Life

Purpose: Figure out what gets you excited. What makes you feel alive? What makes you want to jump out of bed in the morning? That is what you should be focusing your energy on. Ask yourself the four soul questions daily with no judgment. Let the answers come up and release them:

- Who am I?
- What do I want?
- What is my purpose?
- What am I grateful for?

Foundation: Build a solid foundation of daily practices that allow you to take time out for yourself to ground, re-center, and connect with yourself. Incorporate daily meditation, exercise regularly, provide your body with healthy nutrition and drink plenty of water to sustain hydration.

Communication: Pay attention to your inner and outer dialogue. The inner dialogue often dictates how your outer dialogue is delivered and received. For inner dialogue, try journaling every morning. For external dialogue, become the observer. Pay attention to the emotions that arise when you're in conversation with others.

Community: Build a rich community who you love to hang out with and can trust to be there for you when needed. A tribe where you can nurture others and know that you will be nurtured and cared for in return. Join a local book club, volunteer at a nursing home or local school, organize a get together with your colleagues at work. Anything to connect to other humans in meaningful ways.

Performance: Commit to following your daily practices. Integrate the first four elements into your life activities and ensure you are aligned to your purpose. Track your progress and watch your growth. Connect with an accountability partner or coach to help you stay in alignment.

Celebration: Celebrate your wins, learn from your losses and, most importantly, allow your life to unfold in the beautiful way the Universe guides you. Part of celebrating is also learning to let go. When you've achieved something or learned a lesson, integrate the lessons and allow yourself to be open to what comes next.

Catherine Malli-Dawson - United States
Founder, CEO
www.lifewhysllc.com

Tara Pilling

*"Real change is an inside job! Change the inside
and the world will follow your lead."*

**My wish for you in reading my story is that I will inspire you to do your
inner work. YOUR inner work is where the magic and miracles happen!
The world you see is only an expression of the world within. Everything
is created twice, first in thought and then in form. It's all by Law! If you
are not happy with your results and life, if you don't like what you see
happening in the world around you, go within and start with the divine
work, the big work. Be a Change Maker!**

Change is inevitable, Personal Growth is a choice!

Since I can remember, I dreamt of changing the world around me.

As a child, like all children, I was a dreamer, often in a make-believe world
of my own. It looked and felt like heaven on earth, a dreamscape far from the
world I was presently living in. In my imagination, the world I created was safe,
peaceful, and joyful. In that unseen world, I had healthy and happy parents. The
people around me were calm and peaceful, always kind to each other, every
action taken from a space of love and tranquility. All the beings of the earth,
animal friends included, lived in peace and harmony and were safe from all
hurt and harm. But slowly, like all children, I quit dreaming.

From the perspective of a young child, the world I lived in was terrifying, loud, and hurtful. I never knew what was going to happen next. I recall the dominant thoughts of my young mind being consumed by fear, worry, and feeling responsible for the well-being of my parents and siblings. I was constantly on alert, waiting for what could happen. Four-year-old me often wished my parents would stop yelling and hurting each other. Like all children of alcoholics, the world around me was scary, chaotic, and confusing. As a result, I spent most of my life in a 'fight or flight' response.

As an adult, I now know that both my parents struggled with addiction, lacked self-control, had little to no self-confidence, and acted out of dysfunctional genetic and environmental programming. They did the best they could with what they had. Unfortunately, this was a disaster from the beginning: four young children, dysfunctional patterns, and a history of hurt and trauma. It wasn't until later in my life that I would discover this, when *my* health, well-being, and relationships suffered greatly because of it. You've probably heard the saying, "Old habits die hard." — True story: Even today this is something I have to be aware of.

"Give me a child until he is 7 and I will show you the man [woman]." —Dr. Bruce Lipton often shares this Aristotle quote.

As a child, I picked up some distorted beliefs that kept me stuck and unhappy for a long time. The biggest lie I told myself was that I was responsible for those around me. It became an incredible weight on my shoulders and only reinforced how unlovable and bad I was when I couldn't help or save the people I loved the most. The negative thoughts and feelings that went along with these beliefs consumed my being from waking until the wee hours of the morning when, with my hand unconsciously applying pressure to the stress points in my forehead, I'd finally fall asleep due to exhaustion.

As a child, I remember many nights were spent looking through the keyhole in my siblings' bedroom door. It was the only bedroom door in our home that had a lock on it. My parents would put me in this room when they were out at the bar and would come back with friends. And, as usual, things would get out of control. I remember looking through that keyhole as if I was being tortured. I'd stay quiet for a while, listening, then as the atmosphere became violent and chaotic, I had the feeling that someone was going to die and I would not be able to save them. A foreboding fear would rise in my throat and choke out my breath, I'd cry and scream and beg them to stop fighting, to stop beating up one another.

Of course things always started out good: laughter, beers, and Elvis Presley music playing in the background. I learned quickly that there was a pattern and

I made sure to stay up for it all, as if by staying up I could help make things better and change what was happening. Yet, I was powerless. No matter how I dreamed of changing what was going on, I couldn't.

On a few of these nights, I'd get so worked up that I'd pass out completely and need to be rushed to the hospital a few towns over. I was born with a heart problem so my mom would take these episodes seriously. I remember being relieved when it was all over. The fighting must have stopped. I'd wake up in the hospital. I always felt the safest there. It was calm and quiet. I could rest and feel at ease.

When I was six, Mom grabbed us and ran, leaving Dad, but things didn't change much. Mom continued to get into dysfunctional abusive relationships with men and continued self-sabotaging and hurtful patterns toward herself, which affected us kids.

Growing up in this environment was an incredibly heavy burden to carry. It kept me locked in survival mode for a huge part of my life. Around 10, we started uncontrolled screaming matches. These incidents often ended in tears on both sides. I can't count the number of times we ended up in this cycle of dysfunction. The adult in me now knows neither one of us could step out of our programming.

Due to the heavy responsibilities that fell to me and I took on, I felt like I was ten going on forty. I didn't have the ability to know how to show up for Mom, and she continued to drink and welcome unhealthy men into our lives and home. I was frustrated and hurt, so I reacted out of anger toward her. Before my grade 12 graduation, I moved out to live on my own, working at a fast food restaurant. In all fairness, Mom was trying at this time to get better, but I reacted out of years of hurt and anger that was so deep. Lost and confused, I remained stuck in those negative feelings for some time.

Sitting on the floor of my room one day after yet another fight, furious with the choices she was making, I made a decision that I would *never ever, ever* be like my mother or father. That I would create a much better life. I'd go to school, be healthy, happy, and make something of myself, and that is what I did... in a kinda, sorta way. Because the patterns and programming followed me, as they always do.

Life on my own seemed good. I was living the dream, living life on my own terms. Proving to Mom and Dad and the world that I wouldn't repeat these dysfunctional patterns and that I would make something of myself and help change the world.

Once I moved out, things between Mom and I changed. We spent many years finally becoming close. To my surprise, I found out she had been struggling for years with mental illness and, in an astonishingly beautiful growing vulnerability, she invited me to attend her psychology appointments, which gave me a whole new perspective of the struggles she was having with herself. I had no idea she had been living in such inner torment and fear. Years of drinking was her way of self-medicating.

Many years later, on the night before New Year's Eve, my dad called. I picked up the receiver and he announced the devastating news: Mom was dead. She had died in an uncontrollable house fire at her home. I had spoken to her earlier that night. She had relapsed and was drinking. I told her to call me once she was sober. I was angry and hurt, upset that she had done that to herself, *again*! In my disappointment, I cut Mom off. Sadly, that was our last conversation; the alcohol had taken over and she didn't wake up, she was gone. In that heartbreaking moment, I went back to the four-year-old me, lost, scared, and confused. I should have been taking care of her. She was my responsibility and I had let her down.

I spent the next twenty years searching for a way to feel better, a way that conventional medicine couldn't give me. I knew an antidepressant or sleeping pill wasn't going to fix the problem. It didn't work for my mom, and I knew what that would look like long term. I did 'cope' on and off in unhealthy patterns of also drinking too much at times.

However, I also embraced healthier coping mechanisms, burying myself in studying, practicing yoga and intense energetic healing, traveling overseas for many years to study with the best health and wellness teachers I could find. My life started to change. I became my own Change Maker. In many ways, this saved my life. I am forever grateful to the unseen guides who nudged me forward when I didn't feel like it. Isn't it amazing how when you start asking the Universe for something, the teacher always appears? During this time, I prayed a lot, and asked for help every day, sometimes every moment. I learned to trust my inner wisdom and I got comfortable with what was uncomfortable.

Through my years of studying I've come to understand 'it is not my fault'. Our thoughts, feelings, and actions are a result of our childhood imprinting. We are genetically and environmentally programmed and the results we get in life are a direct reflection of our conditioning. The way we learned to cope as children is deeply embedded in our mental subconscious mind and if we don't understand how our mind works, we will continue to get the same results. We may get better by focusing on our health and wellness practice but not the lasting change we want if we don't do the deeper work. This is what happened to me. I didn't understand how my mind worked and why I did the things I did, therefore I continued to get the same results. Through many years of intense study and practice, I have learned that it takes effort to understand our minds. If one doesn't understand their mind, how do they work with something they don't understand? I have learned much about the mind over the years but it was the material that my mentor, Bob Proctor teaches, that helped me truly understand my thinking and do the necessary inner work to *change* it.

James Allen, in his classic book, As a Man Thinketh says, "Mind is the Master... Man takes the tool of Thought... he thinks in secret, and it comes to pass: environment is but his looking-glass."

By virtue of your thoughts, feelings, and actions in which you choose, you create the world you live in. I've learned from my study of Allen's work, the mind is the master weaver, both of the inner garment of character and the outer garment of circumstances. The world around us is merely a reflection of what is going on inside of us. The first step is to accept responsibility and take accountability to do what is necessary.

In my wellness journey, I was introduced to incredible teachers, healers, and mentors, Bob Proctor being one of them. Years into my healing journey, through Bob's vision of our 'potentiality,' I uncovered what was holding me back — it was my programming. I had let my childhood fear disempower me. That was my past and now it is my responsibility to decide my future. It's truly been an incredible journey and it continues to get better and better. Bob is my personal mentor and today I teach and mentor others with him, working with individuals and corporations on how to *change* their mindset and get the results they want. Your mind is your greatest gift or it becomes your greatest enemy — you choose!

The way to make it your greatest gift is to be a continual learner. "In times of change learners inherit the earth; while the learned find themselves beautifully equipped to deal with a world that no longer exists."

Eric Hoffer

Historically, learners have possessed certain attributes. They anticipate and respond rather than react to change. They become essential facilitators within their altered environment. They are effective advocates and understand their minds, and know how to use their minds instead of the other way around. They skillfully communicate, do the work, and take action. They are the Change Makers.

In the past, I spent a lot of my time focusing on everything and everyone around me. My limited thinking was in control. I lived in ignorance and fear and I couldn't see that the real problem *was* me. I was programmed to react. My focus was on what wasn't right in my life and in the world. I was told to live the 'victim' story, to be sick, to bring dis-ease into my mind and body. It was my conditioning. I couldn't see that *the only problem* and *the only solution* was me. Change became inevitable. Personal growth became my choice!

Change Makers own their minds. They develop their mindset and themselves to such a degree that nothing can shake their bigger desires and dreams to show up in their lives and in the world. There is an internal pull, a desire to be and do more. To show up!

The simple desire to 'feel better' led me into coaching and mentorship, which are now my path to show up as a Change Maker in the world. I still recall the day I made a clear decision, "The buck stops with me!" Two things became non-negotiable for me, receiving coaching and mentorship and giving it to others. This clear intention became a burning desire once I had my own children, and I will continue to study and do the necessary inner work everyday for the rest of my life. Why? Because when I do, my results and my life just get better.

I initially started my journey in physical therapy, fitness, and nutrition, but I have since worked with incredible health and healing mentors. This gave me the ability to heal my own body and mind and serve hundreds of clients around me. I studied for over 20 years with the best teachers in vibrational and energy-based healing and continue to use that training in my life to help my clients and those around me. I am grateful as this devotion has gifted me into my 40s, truly a miracle! The 'kid' in me is skipping with joy.

As a Change Maker, I teach people how to reprogram and heal themselves and therefore transform their lives. I mentor others all over the world so they can get the results they want and be the solution to the current challenges our planet is facing. They go out into the world empowered and they become Change Makers! You can do this also. I don't believe in coincidences. You are reading this book and these words for a reason. *You are ready.* Get interested! Find a good mentor who understands the mind and do everything you can to welcome change. You are a Change Maker in your own right and lasting change comes from within! Change what is inside yourself and the world will follow your lead.

Ignite Action Steps

Most people are stuck in 'not knowing' the gifts their mind can give them. They don't feel good, they are not at ease, and they're not getting the results you want. Many of us can be controlled by outside circumstances and events; putting out a lot of reactive energy in the wrong direction.

Change comes from knowledge and study. Ignorance comes from lack of understanding which leads to worry, doubt, and anxiety. Anxiety can become suppressed over time, which becomes depression that turns into dis-ease (lack of ease). The opposite of all of those low vibrating emotions is KNOWLEDGE and study which lead to understanding which becomes *FAITH*. Faith is inner well-being and when expressed, becomes acceleration which becomes At-Ease and this becomes *CREATION and CHANGE.*

Action is key; without action, nothing changes! If there was one action step out of all the hundred I could list here for you, it would be to find yourself an incredible coach — a mentor who inspires you, who is getting the results and living the life you want to create. If you're reading these words I believe there is something inside of you that is ready! Listen up! Don't ignore the pull you feel to do something about it. **Take action!**

Sometimes pain and suffering will be the motivation that inspires you, and reaching out for help will take a lot of courage. You can do it! The good news is: change is inevitable, personal growth is a choice! There is a saying, "You have to do it by yourself and you can't do it alone." So true! As you read this book, if you find yourself resonating with myself or any of the authors, reach out! It takes courage, real 'guts' to reach out and ask for help. The one thing that all successful people know is that having a good coach and mentor is key in reaching their goals and dreams. **Reach out!**

Tara Pilling - Canada
Certified Proctor and Gallagher Consultant, Holistic Results Coach,
Ayurveda and Yoga (E-500RYT)
www.tarapilling.com

DEBBIE SCHRIEBER

"Within every CHAlleNGE, one must learn, love, and embrace change."

My story is designed to show the power a person has to inspire others. Unconditional belief in someone is a gift. It only takes one person to believe in you more than you believe in yourself; they will keep you accountable and be by your side. Find that inspirational person or be open to them finding you.

BE THE CHANGE

Life is a game; no matter how it's played, it will always throw you challenges. How you address those challenges is what's most important. You don't have to be the smartest, tallest, fastest, most skilled, or most experienced; you just need to be the one with the most heart and a vision for success. How does one get past the excuse of "I'm not good enough?" The challenge is to change your mindset. One of my favorite quotes is "You can't spell CHALLENGE without CHANGE!"

— Unknown author

I played every sport I could growing up. I just had to give it a try. Was it a challenge? Most definitely! Athletes have an image of being tall and powerful, yet I was always the smallest and shortest. In the process of testing the waters in many different sports, I fell in love with two team sports: volleyball and softball. I didn't know at the time how much both of those sports would provide so much guidance for where I am today.

The young, petite girl I was just wanted to play and be in the game. I knew that if I made the team, I would give it my all and do my best to get as much playing time as possible. Being coachable and willing to learn always earned me a spot on the team!

For years, I put in the work, did everything asked of me, and a little more. I would look for a coach or assistant coach who was willing to stay after practice and pound balls at me 'til my arms were red just so I could work on technique to push to be better.

An opportunity to play on a travel team was presented to me and I was so excited. Unfortunately, when I asked my parents if I could participate, they just didn't have the extra funds. Knowing my love for the game, they recommended I ask to borrow the money from a sponsor. I will never forget the fear of asking for money. I was an extremely shy kid and playing sports was the only time that I was outgoing. Asking for financial help, needing someone to make this all possible, was contrary to my nature and I was terrified I would be told, "No." When my sponsor said, "Yes," my whole body sagged with relief. They believed in me enough to give me the money, and that escalated my confidence in myself. It also solidified in my mind that I wouldn't let them down; I knew I had to do justice to their belief in me.

After two years of travel teams, I switched to a stronger, more competitive club. Little did I know that being asked to be team captain would become the norm for me from this point on. I was still the smallest one. I was never the most physically talented and I chose sports where the standouts on the team were tall and powerful. Most of the time I was one of the younger players. So why me? Why did coach after coach ask me to be the captain? It wasn't until a few years later I had the 'aha' moment. Sports, business, life, no matter what, it all comes down to one thing. Who has the most heart? Who has the 'whatever it takes' mentality? I was the one willing to do a little more and they recognized that. During practice and games, I always cheered on my teammates, giving them high fives or offering encouraging words. We all did, it was a 'team thing,' and it became so natural for me the more my love for the game and for my team grew. As T. Harv Eker says, "How you do anything is how you do everything."

I had no idea at the time that I was being taught to effect change through inspiration, and in the most subtle of ways. The biggest, most important message was being ingrained into me and I had no clue. Looking back, it all makes sense.

We were being taught to support each other, to help each other through rough spots, inspire each other, and celebrate everything, both big and small. I found myself becoming a mentor to my teammates, and finding my own mentors in my coaches. And what I learned was: we need supporters. We need mentors, someone who pulls that little extra out of you when you don't know you need it or don't think you have it in you.

My biggest supporters were my parents. At least one of them was at every game I played in junior high, high school, and college. One of my favorite memories was my dad riding with our team on the school bus to a game just so he could watch me play and see my team bring home the win. School games had more consistency and were local, but it was my club volleyball team that traveled most weekends where not only was it a commitment by me, but also my mom who made sure I never missed a game. My family saw my passion. They saw how much heart I threw into it. They saw my absolute commitment and they did everything they could to support it and help me succeed.

You never know who is watching. You never know who sees what you are capable of, even before you see it in yourself. A shy, young girl, my dream to be included on a team became so much more. My coaches gave me a challenge — a challenge I accepted year after year. Sports was my first taste of teamwork and success. It was my first memory of an opportunity to make a change in myself, but more importantly, a change in the lives of others. My role was to lead the team, inspire each of them to do their best and to encourage each other too. Like anyone, especially a competitive teenager, I wanted to win. I always wanted to win, and to this day, everything I do, I want to win. But when I think about winning, I see it as a shared challenge. I learned during my teenage years that when we step on the court and face the challenge of our opponents, we would need to work together, play with heart, and adapt our strategy to be successful. We had winning seasons year after year, but losses were just as much of a win because they became our biggest opportunities to learn.

Volleyball was 'my life,' the sport I committed to most and where my biggest lessons are pulled from, but the same lessons are applied equally no matter the team, be it sports, an orchestra, a family, or a work team. Being placed in a leadership role was just what I needed to rise up, know my value, trust myself, and create the change I want in any situation.

I loved the game and I knew every opportunity to play would make me happy. I always gave it my all and, as we say, I'd 'leave it on the court.' I showed up for me and my team, to improve my skills, cheer on my teammates, and most importantly, have fun. One day, after a full day of playing a volley-ball tournament, my mom told me a local college coach came up to her after watching me play. He had no idea it was my mom but was asking her questions about me, complimenting how I played and seeing if she knew my college plans yet. On our ride home, my mom told me about this story. I had a huge smile on my face. Like I said before, you never know who is watching. I am so happy I didn't know college scouts were there that day because it gave me the opportunity to shine with no expectations. I showed up, played my best, worked together with my team, and we made adjustments in our game as needed. Change happened easily for us throughout the day as we knew what we had to do to accomplish our goal.

Losing a game is never easy, but it happens, and this is where the biggest lessons are learned. What went wrong? What can we change? Communication is key. This is where our coaches would take the lead. They let us know it just wasn't our day to win, but we are still winners in their eyes. We always showed up, gave it our all, and were capable of winning. You can't win one hundred percent of the time. I consider it a personal win if I gave it my all in that moment, and a team win, if everyone gave their full effort too.

After a loss, you start thinking to yourself, "Was it me? Did I cause us to lose the game? Was there something I could have done differently?" What the coaches say to the team at that moment is key. A good coach, an effective leader, communicates clearly, always reminding us to remember we are a *team*. No one is perfect and no *one* caused us to be less than victorious. We re-group and go out to win the next game... as a team.

These lessons have been invaluable. In junior high where we were all equal, everyone was learning together. By high school, those tall and natu-rally athletic teammates had an advantage and I had to find a way to play at their level. What did I need to do? How could I be just as good in my own way? My high school team was an environment in which I learned so much. I had amazing coaches and teammates. I was far from the star, but that was perfectly fine for me.

Knowing I was in a leadership position on my travel club team, I could change my way of thinking at school and embrace the opportunity to learn from the best around me and support them in a different role. The best leaders are the best learners. We were champions season after season and we couldn't have done it without each other. These lessons have stayed with me and, as an adult, I would choose working with a team any day on any project over doing it all myself.

Sometimes you get to choose your team and other times you don't. I've been part of both and I have learned to love them equally. You can't change a person, but sharing your unconditional belief in the team, you can motivate them to make changes in themselves. Watching that unfold is priceless.

To me, everything in life is a game. I love team sports, team business, team anything. There is power in a team. Working together toward a goal, overcoming challenges, learning and growing together is *so much more powerful* than any one person is capable of on their own. I am always motivated by one of my favorite quotes by Mahatma Gandhi who said, "Be the change you want to see in the world!"

You've heard the saying over and over again… "If I can do it, anybody can do it." Have you ever thought, "If they can, of course I can," but then the moment of power and belief in yourself wears off and you start thinking, "But how?" We all have been there!

Throughout my entire sports career, I was put in the position to create change around me, to motivate my teams, to lead us to success, and that has led me to where I am today.

There is no 'I' in team, and that is as true in a marriage as it is on the court. Now, married, my husband and I work hard to create the future we desire. We are real estate investors who have built a solid team around us. We make changes to our plan constantly as we adapt to the current market conditions. I live my life like I am still out on the court with my teammates and those values still hold true.

In business, my team consists of those better than me, smarter than me and who motivate me to be even stronger. I've realized I enjoy being a leader. I found my role. I look at it the same way I did when I was chosen as team captain. Today I choose to be the team captain. I fell in love with the idea, feeling, and challenge of motivating others. My mentors always remind me to surround yourself with the people who inspire you. "You are the average of the five people you spend the most time with." —*Jim Rohn.*

I love my circle and am always looking to expand it as I know there are so many amazing people in this world I have yet to meet. I have carried this feeling with me for the majority of my life. I love being creative and challenged. I know I grow most when I step out of my comfort zone. Whether personal or business, it is all the same to me. If I am asked to take the lead on something, I almost always say yes. If I don't quite know how, that's when I remind myself to be the change I want to see in others. As an entrepreneur and Change Maker at heart, I always find a way.

Now, 20 years later, I try to embody what I learned on that court as a teenager. Teams consist of many moving parts. Although you have an end goal, all parts must work together to get there. Every team I lead, I start with writing down our end goal. I make a list of what needs to be done and by when, who I want on the team, and what I expect from each person. I take our end goal and work backwards setting timelines and deadlines. I have yet to be part of any team where things are exactly as I planned. That is where the team works together to make the necessary changes to succeed. As a leader, I am the biggest support to them individually and to the team as a whole.

Leading a team and being part of a team are equally important. If you have ever played a sport, musical instrument or worked a job with others, I hope you can relate. Change your mindset from 'I' have to be the best to 'we' have to be the best. Success feels better as a team. Ask yourself, "Are your top five team members elevating your game?"

Applying these lessons, I get to do more of what I love. In business, a team is a must as we all only have so much time in a day and can't do everything ourselves, even if we think we can. When I'm not working, I manage one of my softball teams, I travel as often as possible (visiting 32 countries and all 50 US states so far) and I take way too many pictures, but it makes me happy. Recently, I took on the role of captain for our Ragnar running team which has multiple layers of coordination, planning, and creativity among other leadership roles in my daily life. If it needs to get done, I do it! It's not always easy, but in the end it's worth it.

I share my story because I am just 'that girl,' the one who didn't know (and sometimes still doesn't know) what she wants to do. I am that same woman who learned to believe I can do anything from that one volleyball coach who believed in me before I believed in myself. Change is inevitable and I know I can do it; more importantly, I know you can too!

Change Makers look at tasks through a different lens. As a Change Maker, you reach goals and effect change in those around you. You may make a difference in your community and everyone knows you for those changes. Or you may lead a more quiet movement. No matter which path you take, the change you are making is powerful. It takes one person to believe in you and for you to believe in one person to make a change toward something great. Accept every challenge and make the change! That's how you win the game.

Ignite Action Steps

Everyone needs a coach, a mentor, a cheerleader. Find someone who inspires you and pushes you to reach past your goals. Find your accountability partner.

Write down your goals. Break each one down so it is simple and achievable. For each goal, write at least one thing you need to Change to make it happen. Give yourself deadlines. More importantly, give yourself rewards.

Evaluate your circle, the five-ish people you are around most. Do they inspire you to be better? If not, who do you need in your close circle?

Find a person you can help, coach and inspire. This is an invaluable gift that you can give someone. Pay it forward!

Debbie Schrieber - United States
Entrepreneur, RE Broker and Investor, Photographer
debbie@mightymouseleadership.com

HANNA MEIRELLES

"What changes your life can change the world."

I hope my story will help you find the answer to *What drives you?* What is it that makes you wake up in the morning? What makes you get up with energy because you know what you are going to do will make a positive change in the world? Live life believing everything you do has an impactful result: it is your choice to make it powerful.

TURNING *NO*s INTO *WIN*s

Recently, I had the opportunity to facilitate a meeting with my clients in a large auditorium-style space. The room was filled mostly with men and the discussion was lively. The topic was the recruiting and onboarding of new employees. I heard one of them say, "It is so good we are recruiting more women to work with us. This way, our environment is going to be more flowery and beautiful."

Almost immediately, his boss replied, "This is not the reason why we are bringing women into the business. If we want a more flowery place, we should plant more trees."

That answer shocked most of the male audience. The few women present were celebrating, smiling timidly in awe of the courageous leader who indirectly made the point that women have a lot more to offer beyond their natural beauty.

A few years ago, that conversation was unimaginable. The first gentleman would have said exactly the same thing and every man around would have agreed with him, adding a couple of sentences like, "Finally! Even the smell of this place is going to be better!" The women would have smiled politely, but those sentences would not have resonated with them. They knew that their looks and smell were not the reason why they should be in a working environment side-by-side with male colleagues. They also knew they had a valuable contribution to make in the business world. They always sensed that besides bringing life into this planet, they could also bring peace to the world through equality.

During my career, I have heard a lot of men make statements like these. Most women I work with felt that something had to change, but not all were brave enough to initiate it. "How many women have been exposed to as many opportunities as men?" I questioned. How many women have felt they could express themselves clearly about what they wanted professionally? Or, how many have thought about *if* and *how* they wanted to participate in the economy, despite what limitations had been placed upon them?

When I told some relatives and friends I was going to study Business Administration after high school, they said, "Are you crazy?" Being an A student for 12 years of my life raised the expectations of everyone around me. They thought I had to become an engineer, a doctor, or a lawyer. Anything else would be a 'waste of my talent.' The great thing was, for my generation, women could choose careers that during my mother's time were not available to them.

I had no idea of what Business meant as a career. I first considered it because my best friend told me, "I saw this profession in a magazine and I think it just looks like you."

As a child, I liked being the different one. Being the oldest daughter, I cannot say I was a rebel as I had *Responsibility* as one of my strongest characteristics. But since a young age, something drove me to not be like everybody else, to not fit in to the conventional societal norms. As far as I remember, I have had this internal urge to push boundaries, to come up with different ways, to defy rules, to influence positively, and to demonstrate that there were more possibilities than we could ever imagine for everything in our lives. If ever somebody said *NO* to me, I would find a way to turn that into a *YES*, or a *WIN*.

One of the times I turned a *NO* into a positive answer was when I was ten years old. My friends and I were going back to school by bus after a trip to a theater. I was sitting near the back of the bus. I noticed one of my friends starting to walk slowly from the front all the way to the back, distributing birthday party invitations. As she came walking toward us, my friends and I got more and more excited! You know… going to a party with my school mates, "What am I gonna wear? Would there be dancing? I love dancing! What if my mother does not allow me to go?"… All of this was going through my mind. After she handed the invitations to all the friends in front of me, it was finally my turn. When she faced me, she said, "Hanna, I cannot invite you." And I asked her, "Why?" She replied, "Because you are poor."

I felt devastated, as if somebody had cut my stomach in half. To be excluded from a gathering of all your friends because your family doesn't have the means… For days, I wanted to throw myself into a hole every time I saw her. I was somehow able to put together the following thought: I did not want anybody, ever, to go through that same pain I went through. Because I felt excluded, I decided that I would instead include everybody… *always*. No matter if they were poor or rich, black or white, men or women, from this country or that country… I wanted to include all the diversity around me, play, study, work, and be friends with absolutely everybody.

Later in life, I had the clarity that all that desire for inclusion was part of my mission, which is to inspire and empower people to be free, to have freedom of choice so they can develop their own potential while respecting diversity.

Throughout my childhood and teenage years, I kept that drive to be unique and challenging, but at the same time, wished to be accepted and included and did everything I could to show others that there were alternative ways to get what we desire. It took a lot of confidence to do this.

I learned how to be confident with my parents. My father was a salesman and an entrepreneur. He inspired me with his amazing ideas and the businesses he created throughout his life. Eventually, all those businesses failed, leaving our family constantly in financial difficulties. But even today, his tenacity, willingness to start over, and never giving up still impresses me. My mother was a teacher and she was excellent in the art of influencing. Her students loved her, and she inspired me to start teaching when I was 11. My mother kept encouraging me in this, as she saw I loved what I was doing.

It felt natural to me to have an unshakable faith in myself, in others, in humanity, and in the world. I couldn't articulate this at that age, but I always had the belief that life was really good to me. Positivity was my constant companion, even against the odds.

During my teenage years, I was a rhythmic gymnast. In a school competition, our coach split our class of 20 girls into five groups. My group was considered the weakest of all. We were by far the least flexible ones. Three of us were a little overweight in contrast to our slim co-competitors. Exercises which required more effort would take our breath away completely. Standing beside my three teammates, I was too tall, which visually could compromise the judges' evaluation in that type of gymnastics. We were clearly the underdogs. Everybody was absolutely sure we would be in the last place in the competition. That idea was verbalized many times. During training, the other groups would make sure they would mock us every time we would fall or make a mistake. We had four months until the tournament.

In the beginning of the training process, I had a conversation with my teammates. I told them that I really believed we could win, but we would have to train very hard. Harder than any other team. Harder than we had ever trained before for anything else in our lives. If we wanted to win, we would have to do something different. So, we agreed that while the other teams trained twice a week, we would train for five days, arriving earlier and leaving hours later, so we could benefit from the gymnasium, equipment, and the extra coaching.

We gave it our everything: during the training and during the tournament. We trained so diligently that not only did we win first place, but we turned everyone's previous rejection and misbeliefs into respect and admiration. Today, I look back to that *NO* and ask myself, "How did we do that? How did we make that into a *YES* for us and a *WIN* for life?" It was a combination of positivity, passion, determination, and incredible effort.

I had the pleasure of these kinds of experiences *before* becoming an adult. They shaped my mind, my heart, and my spirit. They made me believe that, no matter what other people say, no matter if I was a woman or man, no matter what society had apparently written in the 'destiny book' for me, I could always choose differently if I wanted to.

I did choose differently. I chose to go against most people's perceptions about what I should study at the university, choosing Business without really knowing what was waiting for me in the years ahead.

On my very first day, I was surprised by a presentation from an organization called AIESEC. It was the largest non-profit student-run organization in the world. They were developing young leaders through international exchange programs. Their mission was to strive for peace and fulfillment of humankind's potential. That resonated strongly with me and I was hooked! I not only wanted to go on an exchange program myself, I wanted to change the world with them. Intellectually, I knew it would develop my leadership and business skills, but my Spirit knew if there was already a group of change agents out there, I wanted to become a part of it!

I applied to work with them, aware that the next *NO* was just in front of me: in the selection process. One of the requirements was to speak English fluently, which I didn't. I was a Brazilian who was educated in Portuguese and came from a family that couldn't afford extra language courses. But I didn't let that stop me.

In my core, I sensed that opportunity would allow me to learn, to shine, to thrive, to belong, and to serve the world in ways I had never experienced. It was the right context for me: a global and respectful mindset coupled with a diverse environment where differences were not only allowed but encouraged. They were growing themselves through self-awareness, and through generating and implementing ideas to solve many of the global problems, such as wars, inequality and lack of education, among others. They had a genuine concern with the planet's sustainability when nobody else was talking about it. Living a legacy was a common theme in their vocabulary. My wish to be part of them was so huge that with all my grit I persisted throughout the different tests, group dynamics, and interviews. Somehow, they were convinced. Despite the language barrier, I was chosen to be part of their team; one more *NO* that turned into a *WIN*.

I LOVED working there. Although it was totally volunteer, those were the happiest and the most rewarding times of my young life. Over and over, I saw we were *changing* the world one step at a time through the work we were doing.

It was with them that I heard for the first time Mahatma Gandhi's famous quote, "Be the change you want to see in the world." Motivated by that, I decided to put my name up as a candidate for the election process to become one of the vice presidents of our local office. The *NO* came easily. I lost that election but quickly understood it was the best thing for our office at that moment. It also gave me the opportunity to explore new areas, and acquire new knowledge and abilities. As Nelson Mandela said, "I never lose. I either win or learn."

A year later, my passion and persistence surfaced again. I was fascinated by what leadership really meant in the world. I was also intrigued by the fact that the management team were predominantly men, although there was a gender balance overall in the office. I wondered why so few women stepped up into leadership positions. I decided to be a candidate in the next election and subsequently became the first female president since our local office was created nine years before.

I had to face a lot more *NOs* along the way. I had to change the perception of people who thought I was not capable or competent. I heard countless people saying, "You shouldn't be doing this, you can't do that, you are not good enough." But I didn't listen. I kept advancing to other leadership positions.

Deep down, I knew what my mission was. I knew the legacy I wanted to leave.

Two years later, empowered by my knowing of what I wanted as my next steps in life, I met up with a mentor who said, "So, you are going to be the next national AIESEC president. Am I right?" I took a deep breath in and the *NO* came quite easily from my own mouth. I didn't aspire for that particular position, but I wanted to continue to lead, to make a difference and to empower other women. I wanted to get new skills through a different path by experimenting through other avenues. I knew there were so many ways I could positively influence and impact the world. With his compassionate heart, he said, "I know you are going to change lives in whatever you choose to do."

At that moment, my mind was totally blown away. I realized he saw much more in me than what I saw in myself. I had figured out my calling, but I was playing too small. There was a massive potential for something bigger, and it was all in my hands. It has always been. I realized I had choices. I chose my profession, my careers. I chose where to work, where to live, who to be friends and colleagues with. I chose my next steps. Turning the *NOs* I have received into *WINs* for myself was a *choice*. But I knew that not all women had the same opportunities to choose as I did, in this world full of biases.

I chose to work in male-dominated industries all over the world and, for many years, I was the only woman in my team. I was paving the way without consciously noticing it. Taking leadership positions, I could demonstrate to all those men that there were a lot of women out there ready for challenges. I started to teach them how to develop Female Change Makers who would not only work effectively but would bring sustainable solutions for most of their business problems. I encouraged them to take steps to be educated in gender equity in ways that, otherwise, they would never be exposed to.

I could have given up so many times, but I didn't. There were many more people who disagreed with my opinions, abilities, and competence than ones who offered unconditional support. Despite this, I persisted. And I still persist. I feel it is my responsibility to be empowered and to empower other women to offer their gifts to the world. When we women take responsibility in our role as Change Makers, our collaborative spirits end wars and bring peace. When we are out there actively participating in the community, the entire society benefits from it. This is why we have to be involved in businesses of any nature: to make them sustainable for the planet and leave a contribution for future generations.

When you leap out of bed tomorrow feeling energized and wanting to contribute to a better world, you only have to take one small step to make a positive change. What step will you take?

IGNITE ACTION STEPS

How do you become a Change Maker? How do you turn the *NOs* into *YESes* and *WINs*?

Have faith and grit: Don't give up easily. You know what to do in your heart. Listen to it.

Stand up for something: What is your cause? What do you fight for?

Be a pioneer: Start something where others haven't done so yet. Be the first in your family or in your company to do something completely different. Break through your own fears, opening a path for others to become extraordinary like you.

Find mentors: Inspiring people will guide you through the path of change, with meaningful questions that will allow you to grow.

Understand the biases: When you experience something that doesn't sound respectful toward women, open up a dialogue! Educate others about the changes we have to make in our vocabulary, in our actions, and in our hearts. Make positivity your constant companion.

Hanna Meirelles - Brazil
Global Trainer and Development Facilitator,
Leadership Specialist and Founder of Life Level 10
www.hannameirelles.com
🞅 *lifelevel10byhannameirelles*

SIMONETTA NIEDEREITER

"Unleash your true potential as a badass Change Maker."

This is a story that documents how I reclaimed my true self, retained my dignity, and, with resilience, went beyond being self-actualized to paying it forward as a conscious Change Maker. I want you to know you have this power in you also. No matter where you are coming from in life, you can get through any challenging times, just as I did, without sacrificing yourself on the altar of ego.

YOU CAN DO THIS

Growing up in a family of strong personalities, for me, meant staying small. If someone had told me then that I would grow up to become an entrepreneur and a Change Maker, I would have never believed it. It was unthinkable. Unachievable. Crazy. It would have scared the crap out of me. But... here I am.

The road to being a conscious Change Maker was neither easy nor straight forward. Not only was it meandering and often hazardous, but I trod this road for many years with no sense of direction. I had neither a map nor a compass, nor any specific destination. Being a mother of two grown-up sons, I knew the last thing I wanted was to have my children associate me with defeat or remember me as a demonstration of someone who gave up in life. I was determined to show them that no matter what challenges life presents you with, you can face up to them. If it was the last thing I was going to teach my boys, it would be how to be courageous and step up. And they in turn would eventually pass that inner strength, that conviction, on to their children. I owed it to them, to the ones I love, to the people around me who believed in me… and I owed it to myself.

It took me some years to debunk my old habits and beliefs. I thought that I should be the compliant one, the silent one, the behaved one. But when it came down to the wire, when it was time to take responsibility, make decisions, and accept the consequences thereof, I knew I only had two choices: to give up, declare defeat, let myself go, and dive into a state of self-pity; or to stand up, face the dragon, and fight.

I struggled at that time, playing a number of roles I had been previously cast into but had not auditioned for. Through complex circumstances, I took over a major business and had to change its fortunes. Thanks to my family, my sons who believed in me and stood by my side throughout the difficulties, I was able to face all the challenges that looked insurmountable. I was terrified about having to make all these changes and decisions, but I had no choice. I came to realize if I wanted to change anything, I had to change from within. To become the boss of myself. To become self-reliant, making many tough decisions and owning their consequences. To be the captain of the ship called *My Life*.

It took both external and internal forces to bring me through this painful and scary time.

I knew that I needed to get all stress and pressure out of my system. I started going to therapy, which was a blessing because I knew I could spill my heart out once a week and talk through anything . She was a professional, she was patient, she got paid to listen to all that I needed to say and it prevented me from dumping my frustrations, worries, fears, and even anger at times, on the people closest to me. This made everyday life slightly more bearable, but most of all, I felt lighter and freer to be present with my loved ones.

I made sure that the times spent with the people I love were precious. I wanted to be inspiring instead of draining. I learned that, when I was taking care of and being of service to others, I forgot the difficulties I was facing, and the 'climb' to freedom and to conscious living became easier.

I was determined not to become a burden for my family, so in case my efforts in the company were going to fail, I devised a Plan B. I started studying again and became a certified clinical hypnotherapist in the RTT method of Marisa Peer. I decided I would create this new business and make it work somehow. I had no idea how big an impact this decision would have. It was life-changing and transformative.

Hypnotherapy opened a whole new world and triggered the next step in my development. I learned meditation and started doing so every morning, including a gratitude meditation for even the most simple things like waking up in a warm comfortable bed. Continuing my self-development journey, I got myself a coach who helped me recognize the patterns I was repeating. A friend and I created a drawing group where, to this day, we encourage each other to draw daily as a gift to ourselves. This gave me the opportunity to lose myself in art for an hour every day and stay connected to my creative self.

I immersed myself in quality time with my loved ones, making every moment a treasure. I continue this even today. Time spent with my grandchildren is most precious — these little people live in the NOW — they are true and unique — the tenderness of their hearts is a true gift — they are my greatest teachers.

What I didn't realize at first was that this inner work, which I thought was just a way of keeping me sane and balanced, actually created the strength and grounding within me to give me the courage to deal with the business I was running and all the difficulties I was facing.

Growing up in different countries during my childhood and teens, I soon had to learn that flexibility was a vital requirement for survival. Complaints, wishes, opinions or needs were not qualities that were either encouraged or accepted. Expressing those opinions meant I was regarded as cheeky, misbehaved, and obnoxious. I was expected to be quiet and behave, and others were entitled to make decisions that determined my life. Daring to wish to go out in my teens was an outrageous act that made me feel guilty of even having such a wish. The lesson was, "There is always something or someone more important than me, my wishes or needs." There was no time for me and I always felt left behind, forgotten, and not entitled to anything. It was as if I were part of the furniture.

We had a wonderful house in West Africa with a lot of space and a large terrace facing an endless garden, verdant and lush, full of palm trees. As children, we would watch the gardener recover coconuts by climbing the trunk with a special rope. Once he descended, he would treat us with a taste of the coconut water. We enjoyed freshly-cooked yam and palm oil from the locals — that was yummy. The beautiful Jacaranda plants adorned our terrace and we took it for granted that it would bloom forever with its beautiful fuchsia red. Sunshine was an everyday given, just like cockroaches, snakes, and malaria. They were all part of our everyday life.

My father took a leap of faith and created a thriving business. It was only then that we were blessed with material comforts. My mom no longer needed to work or struggle to shop for bargains to buy cheap. Baskets full of exotic fruit graced our table every morning, the scent of which still lingers in my nostrils sometimes even today. We traveled to Europe more often and my parents started giving important dinners where my mom hired a cook to help her out. Our life from the outside looked perfect and plentiful, but on the inside it often felt empty and very lonely.

In those days, my imprint belief was to be a good girl — and I really wanted to be that girl. I believed the more compliant and obedient I was, the more I stood a chance to be loved. My belief was that love is something you have to work hard for — you have to earn it. Nothing is guaranteed. This was reinforced to such an extent that I carried it on for many years. However, thankfully today, in my best moments, I recognize these patterns for what they are and uninstall them at the deepest level of my subconscious. It was a hard pattern to break and, even today, I still have to be on alert and pull back when it occurs.

When my parents moved to London, my world in Africa abruptly came to an end. Our sun-soaked everyday life was replaced with cold, rainy weather. Everything was different and unfamiliar, and our lives started to crumble as my parents drifted apart and eventually got divorced. It was tough times for mum and dad and we, the kids, were left in the middle, trying to figure out what was happening to us. Circumstances were so harsh that I constantly felt in a state of alert; it was like being at war never knowing what we would have to face from day to day.

At 16, I found myself having to take care of my siblings and the household while going to school. I was in a new location, new friends, new culture, new rules. There was no instruction manual on how this new world worked. The first time I had to take the Underground alone, what an alien world that was! People were rushing past me, all seemingly knowing what they were doing, and it made me feel scared and odd. I had to take exams and be supportive at home.

The vibrancy and color of London in the punk and rock and roll era took place behind a closed glass window for me. I could walk amongst it and see it unfold, but I did not have permission to be at one with it and live it. The fact that I was so young did not occur to anyone and so my teens went by unlived and unhappened. My youth slipped away, taking with it so many of the sweet dreams I sometimes dared to dream and cherished in my heart.

Reflecting back, I realize that we are the imprint of what our parents and caregivers have passed on to us, and in turn, *they* are what *their* parents passed on to them. It is an unconscious circling, this passing on beliefs and behaviors onto the next generations, and we all receive this unconscious programming. It is our inheritance. We make it a part of us because it has been instilled in us from even before we were born. Sadly, at that time, I didn't have this knowledge and did not know I could even question it — it felt like the world I wanted to be a part of was not available to me. I often felt trapped as if being rolled up in a tuna tin can, unable to get out.

We play the game of 'whispers' with our ancestors. In the end, each one of us has our beliefs that we have created for ourselves and we are driven by them. We make up our own conclusions and our own truth. They are the whispers changing and morphing into something new as we grow up, interpreting our environment and the situations we face as life goes on. Sadly, our subconscious makes sure we don't forget the experiences we had to go through to create those beliefs. It makes sure we stay in what is familiar.

Sometimes, we realize that we need to change the path we are walking... and we shift. Many of us get a wake up call, if we are lucky. This can be devastating, scary, disruptive, and challenging. It can take the form of health issues, losing someone we love, or the security we had. My wake up call, my chance to grow, came many years later as I had to take over the family company and step up to being a leader.

Our company was on the verge of bankruptcy for 5 years and it was becoming more difficult to keep it afloat with every passing day. The banks were unsupportive. I didn't know how to pay the bills and had to ask my children to lend me money so I could pay our staff.

I had to lead the company and project an image of it being 'business as usual' despite the difficulties so no one would be alarmed. It was like a living nightmare. I thought I had reached my end and was facing the edge of a cliff. I remember sitting on the floor, crying desperately one night, not knowing how to proceed, or what to do next. At that moment, a voice in my head said, "You can do this! Go and make this OK." Suddenly, I felt this incredible energy inside me and my heart filled with courage and the strength to face up to this nightmare.

I started to work with Rosalyn Palmer, an RTT therapist and coach, who had been through adversity herself and knew what it felt like to have to *reset* yourself and come through the tough times. The new voice in my head was, "I can do this!"

Taking little steps every day, I stopped feeling sorry for myself, replacing those thoughts with the idea that if there was a way into this labyrinth, there had to be a way out too. I told myself, "I will make it one step at a time." When I stumbled and took a step back, I still kept a sense of perspective about how I was always going forward, even though it was a struggle. With this perspective, I slowly started turning things around. I dealt with difficult people with a new courage and clarity. I had learned to be fair to myself first, that I could be daring and that I mattered, along with my team and my customers. This made me resilient. I had taken off my blindfold and come out of the jungle.

I realized I needed to take control of what the company was doing, its vision and purpose. I got rid of the people not aligned with my intention. I had to be daring. Making bold decisions, making and embracing all the responsibilities of my company. I pushed through the fear and created a win/win situation by being vulnerable, honest, and open with those who wanted to work with me. I had to make changes, take new steps, raise the standards, and lead by example. I proved to myself and everyone I worked with that I was willing to stand in my vulnerability and truth. That was the change I needed to make. I stopped doing what I was told and did what was best for everyone in the company. I had to step up and do what was required, no longer trying to be the good girl, but instead the one inciting success. It wasn't easy, but I am truly grateful for it. Through it, I have unlocked my true potential and discovered my resilience.

If my story provides inspiration for courage, resilience, and hope, even for just one person who reads it, then every painful step of the way will have been worth it. You can stand up, make a change and design your own unique blueprint for your work and courageous life. Discovering the Universe within me enabled me to do it all. Your journey is to discover your powerful Universe. To overcome fear and doubt and step into your vulnerable truth so that you can unleash YOUR true potential as a badass Change Maker.

IGNITE ACTION STEPS

Your inner Universe can be reached through meditation and therapy-based self-development. Knowing that you are enough is key. I had to learn to tap into it due to necessity, but everyone can choose this path and can take inspiration and reassurance from my story. Anyone can do it; we are all geniuses and strong, resilient human beings. We have endless power within us. If we learn to connect to it, then we can heal ourselves and be an inspiration for the world around us.

Meditation was one of the key tools that helped me. Create a comfortable cozy place where you can meditate. Make it special and friendly, a place you like to go to. Wake up a half hour earlier at first; you can slowly increase the time as you get into it. Make sure you sit up straight so you prevent falling asleep again. Then, use any type of meditation technique you like to go within and listen to your inner chatter and hear what you say to yourself. Stay there and quiet it by breathing in and out. Concentrate on the words in and out and interrupt the chatter, eventually reducing it.

Praise yourself even for the tiny little steps you've made. We all tend to see the negatives long before we accept the positive. Recall the things you have achieved and mastered every day and praise yourself for having achieved them. Every single little step counts and is precious. Make small rituals where you do something good for yourself — take a bath, go for a walk or a facial — do yourself some good.

Create distance from toxic people even if it hurts. At the same time, you need to forgive them without taking on their toxicity, or accepting it. Learn to forgive, then move on.

Remind yourself of the good things you have in life, even the smallest ones. Notice and be grateful for the beauty around you. Do this every day and every time you stand waiting — at the grocery store, at a red light for example — and before going to bed.

Friends and loved ones are tremendously important in our lives - you don't need many. Surround yourself with people who genuinely love you. Do not criticize others when you are with someone else or on your own. Train yourself so that you would not blush if anyone should hear your thoughts. Make your thoughts crystal clear so you can be in the present. The present is a present to yourself.

Simonetta Niedereiter - Austria
CEO of SINI-MEDIK Niederreiter GmbH, Certified Qualified Nurse
and Clinical Hypnotherapist.
www.sini-medk.com

J Meehan

"Peace begins with unplugging, then, when inspired to plug in again, take action with absolute determination."

It's my intention to inspire you to be willing to risk everything in order for you to have deep and meaningful connections with yourself and others. My story shows how it is possible to go from severe depression and self-hate to living a life brimming with self-love, joy, peace, and grace. You are not alone, and every human being, including you, is worthy of feeling inner bliss.

Changing the Love Within

For years, I wrestled with severe depression. It was my dirty little secret that every morning I would wake up and will myself out of bed, will myself to my kids' activities and parent meetings, will myself to make the calls for my business, and mostly will myself to look as normal as possible. Long after the daily suicidal thoughts were gone, I was left with an invisible feeling of crippling anxiety. Deep insecurity plagued my body as I went through each day of my life trying to look normal. Trying to be normal. You could not see it in my social media pictures or at the network meetings, but my deep feelings of angst were always there.

Insecurity comes at a cost. I had no Idea that the life I built, the choices I made, the decisions I made daily, the people I kept in my life, and the way I spent my money, time or energy were all protecting and keeping me safe from dealing with this insecurity. That cost was insurmountable. It was the cost of my freedom.

I felt worthless. I felt not worthy of breathing air. I felt unwanted and unloved. I believed at an elusive level that I ruined my mother's life, my father's life, and my grandparents' lives just by being born. I was full of guilt and anguish. I was a tortured soul in an unwanted body. I was trying to raise my children with love and consciousness, trying to run my businesses the same way, and feeling like I had been a failure from the very moment of conception.

My mother and father married young, very young, and I was conceived shortly after. They were a toxic match and they knew it, and when they found out she was pregnant, my father left my mother. When I was six months old, my mother left me with her parents so she could finish college and find a way to support us. Circumstances led to me living full time and being raised by my retired grandparents.

My mother couldn't find a good fit with a company and eventually returned to my grandparents' home, defeated. I could feel her sadness and her own feeling of worthlessness and my six-year-old self believed that it was all because I was born. The fighting between my mother and grandparents added to the toxicity of the home. I felt like a burden. If I asked what was wrong, my grandparents said nothing, but I could feel they were not telling me the truth.

The little girl I was created a belief within herself that her existence was the problem. She hated herself. She would hurt herself and act out, not only to punish herself, but to punish the grownups around her also. It was a perpetual cycle of guilt, anger, pain, wanting to be loved, and needing attention. It was at this time that I had my first thoughts of suicide. I was in the second grade.

I felt like a victim. I *was* a victim… a victim of my own hand.

I met my ex-husband when I was 15. I was beautiful, rebellious, full of insecurity, and self-loathing… and looking for someone to love me. He was the first person ever to see the real me. To see something that was deeply buried under the shell of protection I created. He loved me unconditionally and I was crazy about him because of it. We married at 18 after high school. He would say, "Life with you is like loving a porcupine while riding a wild mustang. Adventurous, fun, painful, intense, and fast." We purchased our first house at 18, a second house at 23. We started our first business at 24, had three children by 27, and made our first million dollars before we were 30.

We were out of the gate at neck-breaking speeds, driven by my need to prove my worth as a human, feel valuable and loved — all to cover up my deep insecurity. I intertwined my safety and security with my husband, like the roots of two trees growing together. If we were moving in the same direction, it felt like anything was possible. I was always running after success, always on a treadmill. I could see it, but not touch it. I was never content nor satisfied.

I lost myself after my husband and I were fired from our own company. I had put everything into it. Everything. Yet, our business partners wanted us out. I had spent years missing my kids' soccer games, missing out on their daily life as the nanny cared for them. Our company held my entire self-worth. We immediately started to rebuild another. Looking back, I wasn't hearing the messages or reading the signs from the Universe that wanted to help me out of my internal misery. Then, as I hit my lowest point and felt I couldn't feel unhappier, I was drugged and sexually assaulted while at a bar.

I was shattered. I hid in my bathroom closet for months. We all spent Mother's Day on the floor in my closet because I felt ugly, broken, and worthless… and I felt everyone could see it, even strangers at the grocery store. My husband set up a trailer in the woods, miles from everything, and my two oldest kids and I ran away to that sanctuary for a few months to find peace. My kids saved me.

This triggered a journey of inner work, a delving into the deep dark night of the soul. I realized that I had a purpose and that I wanted to live. I wanted to be a mom to my children. I wanted to help others understand how to take responsibility for their feelings as a way to internal peace. Slowly, the daily thoughts about killing myself faded away and I felt a resounding dedication to my soul's work in their place.

At the time, this felt hugely transformative, but, little did I know, there was a bigger transformation to come and that began with my grandparents' passing.

A happy couple on the outside, my grandparents had been miserable for many years. In fact, on my grandmother's deathbed, she declared to me she seriously wanted a divorce from my grandfather. She was plagued with guilt and anger over her decisions in her life, many filled with manipulation and control. She martyred herself to the grave. During her dying months I spent time caring for her; the results of her martyrdom changed me profoundly.

Sitting by her bedside, witnessing her utter unhappiness, my entire body rejected it. I could feel the nausea rising in my throat. I felt the acid churning in my stomach. And then I ran for the toilet, vomiting up all the pain, sadness and grief that I had absorbed from her as she died. I decided then and there I would live my life to the fullest and be satisfied, peaceful, and grateful. On my deathbed, I wanted those to know I had lived joyful and free. I didn't realize that I needed to totally upend, fillet, and shatter my beliefs, habits, relationships — and ultimately my world as I knew it — for this to happen.

I looked at my life as it was then. I was over 230 pounds and with constant back pain. I asked my husband to be my partner in starting a business and he refused to join me. My relationships with my children had become disconnected. I was lonely living in a house full of people. I decided to write down my perfect life. I wrote about what I wanted in a business partner, and what I wanted my relationships to feel like and look like with my children and my friends. What kind of car and clothes I wanted to fit into. What my body felt and looked like. What I wanted in my life partner. Then, I thought about everything *that* partner would want in *his* life partner... and started creating that version of myself.

I searched out inspirational and action-based programs to help me with my inner belief systems and would listen to them as I rode my beach cruiser around the lake. I added more daily whole food nutrition and found a chiropractor/physical therapist who used different techniques to work with my body so it could heal and be naturally aligned and pain free. I joined a global leadership program and took speaking classes. It was uncomfortable to be around people who were working on themselves just as devotedly. It was *hard* to be myself in front of people. To be exposed. I had been thinking about attending a conference in Tallinn, Estonia, where a group of a thousand like-minded people were gathering for a month, but kept shying away, not wanting to make myself quite that vulnerable. One night, when I was longing for a deep heart connection, I heard my inner voice say, "How will he ever notice you if you are not willing to stand up and fully be yourself?" Hearing that, I booked my ticket to Tallinn right then and there.

I was scared to death! But under the fear, there was a force pulling me there. By listening to my intuition and the sensations I felt in my body, I ended up in Estonia having the most amazing conversations with incredible people who were just as scared as me and yet were doing very impactful things on the planet anyway. I learned so much about myself. I could see my value and how I actually had something to offer others. I could also see the things that I wanted to change about myself. Being able to alter my daily perspective and location on the planet for a month was... priceless.

After returning home from Tallinn, it was clear that my relationship with my husband of 25 years was no longer serving each of us. We were unfortunately misaligned in our wants, desires, and beliefs. With that realization, we separated.

What followed was a year of exploration and adventure! I made plenty of time to connect and heal the relationships with myself and children. I traveled 118,000 miles that year to be with them and do more healing work. That opened an opportunity for me to work with an international transformation company that valued my expertise to make an impact. I took the job and then took one of their week-long immersive programs that went deep into the trauma that I experienced in childhood. I decided to use this opportunity to clear anything else that was hindering me from attracting a life partner with the same desires, beliefs, and wants. I jumped in and played full out.

I was rewarded with a full body experience of knowing that I *am* wanted and that I *am* loved. It anchored into every cell of my being. That childhood belief of being unwanted from birth melted away. I remember waking up the day after and for the first time in my life the daily low-level anxiety that plagued me was gone! This powerful heart opening allowed me to experience a transcendent vision of who I really *am* and how One we truly are.

Shortly after that profound awakening, I flew to Norway where I would be staying with one of the company owners. Her friend picked us up at the airport in the tiny city of Stavanger and drove us two and a half hours to the beautiful green countryside of Lyngdal. He gave me a hug in the airport and as soon as my body brushed up against his, an intense connected energy began running from my nose to toes. My whole body was magnetized. Throughout the entire drive that feeling continued. All through dinner and the group conversations that ensued that feeling amplified. As the group drifted apart, filing up the tiny, narrow cottage stairs to our beds, he commented on feeling a connection and my heart jumped, going right to my throat. *He felt it too.*

We decided to spend time on the weekends exploring and investigating what this could be. I was both nervous and excited to jump into something new. Each time we got together, we went deeper and deeper, not wanting to jump into sex but just spending time walking, listening to music, and talking for hours. We were willing to risk everything, but slowly, intentionally. It took us weeks to even kiss. I felt like I was a teenager again! The transcendent experiences were plentiful and the epiphanies mind blowing.

On the day I was leaving for my home in San Diego, an incredible thing happened to me. We were connecting, and the energy was so magnetic it felt like I was being held by God. We had realized that our integrity and our compassion were the same, and that we had never experienced anyone who could hold people to that degree of understanding and love. I lay in his arms and started to feel and see through my mind's eye. I felt myself becoming green, only to realize I had become the leaves on the lilac bush outside the window. Purple came next as I became the lilac and that favorite fragrance of mine. Then I became a rabbit, feeling my heart beating fast... jumping... sensing my legs and how strong they were... experiencing what it was to be a rabbit. I then became a bird soaring over the water and felt the freedom of flying and the pressure of the air moving through my feathers. I looked down at the vast endless ocean and became it too, surrendering myself to the ebb and flow and all the creatures moving through me. I knew then the love that the water feels for its inhabitants. I felt myself crash onto the sand and become the sand, then the woman sitting on the sand. Sinking into the sand, I embraced the solidity of the tiny grains supporting me and the warmth of the sun kissing my shoulders.

That's when it happened. That's when I realized how amazing my body is. How wonderful it is to have the ability to feel and create and love. How I wanted to live not just to fulfill my purpose but to experience every aspect of life… to make love to every moment.

I realized I wanted to move my body and dance with reckless abandon. To eat delicious food and fall in love with everything I put in my mouth. To connect deeply, truly, and with vulnerability to everyone around me. For the first time ever, I wanted to be human and fully LIVE on this planet.

Leaving him that day was one of the hardest things I have done. I missed my children, their love, their endless support, their chaos and noise and neediness. At the same time, I was wanting to stay in that moment of peace, love, bliss, and deep connection. I was the last off the airplane at LAX. As I was sitting on the airplane before rising from my seat to gather my things, I felt paralyzed. I just could not move. I knew it was time to play full out in every aspect of my life. I needed to get back to writing. I needed to speak when compelled, to move when motivated. To Love. To *live*.

After this encounter, my relationship with myself and with my friends deepened. The more love and acceptance I experienced for myself, the more I received from others. I let go of the people who weren't willing to follow me into this new space of vulnerability. I had lost my taste for many of my relationships and activities and they gracefully fell away. For years before this, I had been consumed with looking for my shadow parts, my unhealthy ego and its pattern, and that's what was reflected back to me through my relationships. It's how I grew, evolved, and learned about myself. This new place, this new way of being was the first time my exterior world was so loud with resounding love and acceptance… my life had changed! It was amazing and full of synchronicity. Even my mother called me for the first time since my grandparents passed to reconnect.

Change is powerful. How we accept ourselves is truly reflected back to us through our exterior relationships and experiences. You can shift, *change*, and create your own personal reality. Take time to quietly sit with yourself. Don't feel compelled to always be moving or 'doing.' Just listen. In the stillness, you'll have this thought or urge... it comes from your gut, your heart, from deeper within you. And then it almost consumes you. It's wanting to manifest. It just keeps pestering you until you do something about it. So do something about it! When you feel the pull from within... follow it wherever it may lead. Follow the next urge... and the next... and *live*.

Ignite Action Steps

The most impactful thing you can do is your own energy audit. This is where you look at what things are draining your energy and throwing you off. The best place to do this is when you are feeling exhausted, or out of money, or out of time. Put yourself in the observer position. Ask yourself, "What am I spending my money on? And why?" "What am I spending my time on? And why?" "What activities am I devoting my energy to? And why?" The question that comes after that is, "Am I doing these things from a place of fear? Or is it motivated from a place of love? Am I doing this out of obligation, or am I doing this from my heart? Am I compromising my own integrity to make someone else feel better? Am I doing this to look good?"

What it boils down to: "Is this intention spawned from love?" That right there will unravel and begin to change your whole life!

J Meehan - United States
Business Expansion Coach
www.ExpandLWP.com

Alicia Komiya

"Determination outlasts prejudice."

My story is the sum of my experiences. My wish is to remind you that in the face of adversity, the fear that traps us can be transformed by a positive attitude followed by determination. Determination to face challenges, confront your fears, and be open to learning about new cultures.

The Action That Reflects Transformation

I am a very determined person, but I did not start out that way. Holding myself accountable for my actions and living with the mental freedom to make my own decisions without expecting permission from others, led me to be myself and find my true identity.

Just days before graduating from the university in my hometown, the crowded, modern city of Bogota, Colombia, an employment offer by one of my professors turned out to be the best thing that could have happened to me. His offer to work as a reporter at the local television station ignited the dream of being an independent woman. The thought of fending for myself released me from depending on my parents for my livelihood.

My father was an exemplary hard worker. He was an optimist and was determined to provide only the best for his family. He was known as an authoritarian and well-respected in his work; nevertheless, he was a disciplinarian at home, instilling fear in my brothers and I. My mother, on the other hand, was caring but submissive, and clung to her religious beliefs and norms. She was (and remains) my best friend.

As customary in my culture, I was educated in a religious school and taught by nuns. Thus, religious values, the expectation to do as I was told, to never to be in disagreement with the basic principles of family hierarchy were instilled in me early. Opinions were not to be expressed or argued. Similar to norms in other countries during those years, 'children were to be seen but not heard' was very true in our family.

I can vividly remember our family vacations in my youth. We would stay at a big, beautiful house my father had built for us two hours from the big city. There were several bedrooms for all of us and a large swimming pool we enjoyed playing in during the hot days that were so different from Bogota's cooler weather. We would all sit around the dinner table to eat delicious meals prepared by my mom and the maids. These dinners many times took place in total silence. Father dominated the conversation and we meekly listened. Only on rare occasions did any of us attempt to express an opinion of our own. And, if we did, we did so in fear, hoping to avoid any discord. To a certain extent, I always felt protected but not safe, no matter how small my decisions with personal matters. I surrendered to the fear and limitations of my environment. These restrictions, to me, were manipulation and emotional restraints holding me in fear of committing an error.

My disciplinarian upbringing molded me into an organized and structured person in both my activities and my work ethic; however, each step of the way, I always sought the approval of others. My new life as a reporter was an opportunity not to be missed. Each day began with a sense of pride and accomplishment as I said goodbye to my parents and was off to work. However, my father strictly monitored my schedule. He was concerned for my safety, but he also needed to feel in control.

As my skills and proficiency grew at work, opportunities for advancement followed. My senior colleagues motivated me and provided the path for growth and development. Most were older than I and had years of experience in the field. One day, after a successful event, we all wanted to celebrate our achievements and so we went out to dinner. Before doing so, I called my mother and provided the details of who was with me and where we would be dining. After the dinner engagement, several offered to take me home. There, in front of our house, my colleagues patiently waited to ensure I entered safely. When my father opened the door, he was upset. I was late and had disrespected his schedule. Angrily, he reprimanded me in front of everyone. I shrank in fear, emotionally torn, not understanding his enraged reaction. I ran upstairs to my room as fast as I could, feeling my mother's surprised gaze following me. I felt trapped. I knew I had to do something to remove myself from his control.

Obviously, as an apprentice, my salary was not abundant, and this tied me to continue living with my family. Society expected that young ladies would marry before leaving their homes, but I was not interested in marriage. I was conflicted about returning to work, but mostly embarrassed to have to face my colleagues. And I wondered, if my father loved me then why did I fear him so much? I questioned the difference between respect and fear, finally concluding that the only solution would be to sever my dependency on my family and leave.

Soon afterwards, I quit my job, gathered my passport, bought airline tickets, and headed to Spain. The night before my departure, as I was packing, my father came to my bedroom and laughed at me, asking, "So, do you have a lot of money for this trip?" My response was one single word, "No." I told him how grateful I was for everything he had done for me up until then, but how from that day forward I would be financially responsible for myself. My mother, my biggest supporter, was heartbroken. Her 'innocent child,' the 'dependent and quiet one,' was now full of anxiety and had no idea what was to follow. I was living with nothing except my independence.

And that was *everything* for me.

The freedom to decide for myself, without imposition from anyone… with the right to voice my opinion and my thoughts… encouraged me to take on the risks and challenges ahead of me, and accept the consequences of my decisions; it made me even more determined to achieve my goals *my way*. Ironically, my father's words filled my thoughts a multitude of times throughout my life, "The young one thinks she's a General." I had laughed at the time, but in retrospect, those words made me determined to stay true to my goals and not give up.

The challenge before me was how to confront these new paths ahead of me. I used faith, determination, and positivity as my guides. I chose to look ahead, to be firm with my decisions, to follow orders without losing myself, and that fueled the will to succeed. Feeling misplaced, I buried myself in academia, applying at the university to complete my graduate studies. This opened opportunities to meet people, which led to my discovery that my happiness depended on my own positive attitude in any situation. I came to realize only I could control my feelings and circumstances; no one else.

I saved all my money so I could study at the University in Spain. One day, while in the library, my professors approached me to tell me some people were looking for me. Much to my surprise, they were my parents. They were accompanied by a young Japanese man whom I had interviewed during my apprenticeship as a reporter back in Colombia. My father embraced me tightly, my mother cried with emotion, and the Japanese man excitedly explained we were 'all' going to Japan to visit his family. Everything had already been planned. Overwhelmed by the unexpected visit and surprise news of going to Japan, I was a little apprehensive.

Meanwhile, my colleagues eventually convinced me to seize the opportunity to go to a different continent, to complete my degree, and to accept this change of plans. Soon afterwards, my mother divulged how often the Japanese man had been visiting them during my absence. He spent many weekends befriending my father and family. For me, returning home as a newly-empowered person made me feel self-confident. This confidence in turn allowed me the perspective to gain a better understanding of my father's intentions for our family's success and welfare. With this new understanding, our relationship changed into something more harmonious.

Over time, I enjoyed new profound conversations with my father. Eventually, I expressed my true sentiments and past experiences without fear of retaliation. And be my father openly demonstrated his pride and respect for my accomplishments as a woman and a professional. Each of us are a result of our beliefs, traditions, and the cultural norms of the moment. We do have the choice, though, to identify our weaknesses and develop our strengths to achieve our goals.

As my relationship with my father grew, so did my friendship with the Japanese man. And that friendship with him eventually turned into marriage. Our interracial marriage gave me a rare perspective on the world and opened up my potential to recognize that all cultures have distinctive values rooted in a variety of elements. A bi-racial marriage was almost unheard of 38 years ago. Bi-racial marriages were predisposed to prejudices and broke with family traditions. But for us, two people from distinctly opposite cultures united, forming what today is a successful long-term marriage. That Japanese man whom I interviewed in my youth is the son of a conservative family. He is an optimist, highly educated, and a very generous man. I fell in love with the orator, the entrepreneur, and his impressive ease with numbers. But alongside all of these wonderful qualities also came the challenges of our different cultures. It took time, but eventually my father grew to appreciate my husband and our life together.

A few years into our marriage, we relocated to Japan. Soon after we moved, I realized I needed to make a big effort to adapt to this new culture if I wanted things to work out. Japanese culture expected me to address my husband as 'Sir.' I was expected to not be too close to my husband in public, and always walk behind him. As a Latin woman, I was used to using a passionate tone of voice. In Japan, I was to speak softly and only when asked. I was absolutely appalled with these new social rules. I felt distraught and helpless, and even more challenged by my inability to communicate in Japanese. It all seemed as if life was repeating itself. I had flown from a confined family environment with an authoritarian father... and I had landed into an even stricter set of rules.

Even though I struggled, I also knew I had to try to change my ways. I invested all my energy and efforts in trying to understand this new culture and its societal norms, as well as the weather. It all felt too cold. The winter months were freezing to a point that sushi was no longer as appetizing that cold! With time, I started to acknowledge that I was responsible for making the best out of this. I began to pay attention to the beauty of new flavors, scents, and cultural manifestations. I decided that I would need to learn Japanese. I developed new interests and started discovering wonderful things.

Struggling to remain optimistic and accepting of my new surroundings, I was tested with the repeated visions of my mother-in-law kneeling on the floor bowing to her husband — her *Otosan* as a sign of respect at each departure and return from work. It shocked me how she rushed to ensure his clothes and shoes were ready for him, how she was always ready to receive and hang his coat; she meticulously prepared his meals, calculating his arrival precisely. She prepared his evening bath before retiring. All the while, she cared daily for her mother-in-law who had been bed-ridden years before. It was an exhaustive schedule, causing me to ask myself, "When does this woman rest?"

Our deep appreciation, trust, and admiration for each other grew stronger as she allowed me to help her. She, in turn, taught me how to navigate in the traditions and customs of her world. At first, everything seemed arduous and complex. I had to overcome the fact that every country and family has their own rituals and patterns.

Meal time once again was eaten in silence, this time kneeling for what felt like an eternity. Even when exhausted, we had to stay kneeling until the elder had finished their meal and left the table. Only then could my father-in-law rise, and then the rest of us in order of position, me being the last one to get up. I questioned myself repeatedly, "Why had I accepted to marry into this culture?" To appease myself, I would remind myself that I was there because of love. I needed to be strong, to learn about new things to find happiness, to think positively, to not forget that I had to assume the consequences of my actions for my own good. I reminded myself that it was my duty to keep the light burning for my husband's love and the survival of my marriage.

Learning to accept that we are all different and that we cannot change people's mental attitudes was not easy. Learning to respect cultures and their differences is a difficult process, but not impossible. With patience and perseverance, I started to feel integrated into my new lifestyle without converting myself into a victim of circumstances.

I was determined to find beauty in my surroundings, bring balance to my routines and work, and slowly broaden my possibilities. Communicating became easier and it facilitated improved relationships. I took advantage of all opportunities presented to me. In other words, assimilate into the new cultures, customs and traditions, integrate yourself — be a part of the whole. Often my husband would say, "Just like I did in your country, I learned your language and to enjoy your culture; you can do the same."

My faithful teacher in adapting and fitting in was my mother-in-law. She helped me understand that no culture is better than the other; each has its differences in their essence, some more strict than others. Just as we have differences in personalities, some are more complicated than others. We learn something new each and every day... especially that none of us are perfect. Although I may not be in agreement with all practices and protocols, I have learned to respect and admire them for what they were.

Accepting customs with which I don't agree with a positive attitude has made my life more pleasant. If asked, "What can I contribute from my experiences to women in interracial marriages?" My response would be, "A lot!" My life has been so enriched by the sum of both cultures. My knowledge has grown exponentially. I have learned a language that has expanded my horizons not only from my appreciation and understanding, but socially, politically, and culturally. I have learned to be more tolerant, to accept more readily, to not be so judgmental, and to not stereotype people.

As a woman, I learned to be determined in my decisions. I also learned to find balance among being a wife, mother, and professional. The unconditional support that my husband has given me contributed in making my projects a reality, bringing them to life. Mastering my attitude, choosing to be who I want to be... only I can own that. To persist and appreciate the opportunities presented in life, the curiosity to learn, to enrich my knowledge... it captivates me. After having my third child, I decided to get my Master's Degree in International Relations, graduating alongside my two other grown children. In studying Japanese culture, I developed a deep appreciation for it. And, I discovered a love of art, a new aspect of myself. I found an audience for the books I have published on Japanese art. Through it all, I take full advantage of each moment, taking no time for complaining, and appreciate everything around me. To see the positive, ignore the negative, and remain determined enriched my life profoundly. Having unearthed my artistic side catapulted me in a closed society that today appreciates my work.

Barriers of communication are part of the past. The ability to communicate empowers us all to integrate into a societal community. Understanding our differences and having eagerness to learn, then contributes, allows us to change social stigma. We have to learn from each other, enrich all cultures, see the good in everyone. Determination to learn about others and change our opinions inspires us to improve ourselves.

IGNITE ACTIONS STEPS

Persist in being an excellent human being. Leave a fingerprint of positive for the new generations. Having a better sense of self (thoughts, feeling, emotions, and fears) allows you to understand your own mind on a profound level and affects how you perceive others. Put aside racial and cultural criticism. Leave no time for complaining; focus on using your efforts to increase your knowledge and understanding. Being determined to make tough decisions allows you to take control of your transformative experiences as well as your mental and emotional approach to all that life has to offer.

Alicia Komiya - United States & Japan
Journalist, Author, Masters Degree Political Science -
International Relations
Komiyalix@gmail.com

Mindy Stern

*"Responsibility is something that you consciously
'take', not something that you're given."*

**My wish for you is that you come to see that you can have a great and
empowering relationship with money no matter what your financial situation is. You can always turn it around and make it not only better but
really great! Money is a resource and if you use it well... you can make
all your dreams come true.**

I'll show them who's irresponsible!

Magical Transformation

I used to think that the best profession in the entire world was being a hairdresser... When I would go to the beauty salon, I would look at the women as
they came in. They looked tired. They had low energy. Sometimes it appeared as
if they had the weight of the world sitting on their shoulders. However, during
their time in the salon, they were magically transformed!

When the hairdresser was finished with them, they seemed to be a few
inches taller, light on their feet, and with smiles from ear to ear. Their whole
persona changed. I saw it in them and I felt it in myself, standing straighter,
more confident, glowing. I would tell my hairdresser how lucky he was to
have a profession that made people so happy and made them feel good about
themselves. It was a gift.

Little did I know then that I, too, would have a profession that would transform people's lives and create such a positive effect, making them feel satisfied and fulfilled.

My Calling

Just before a meeting with a new client, I sit and wait at my desk in my office anticipating their arrival. I have my notebook and pen at the ready, and also a box of tissues. I'm full of anticipation… wondering what is going to unfold, where the process is going to take them. Sometimes my client is a divorced mother or perhaps widowed. Other times it's a married couple. They are always parents… people who want to give their families the best life possible.

They usually show up for the first meeting tense, stressed out, and kind of bent over, weighted down. Many times, they speak in short sentences. They seem confused. They lack confidence. Then, meeting after meeting, you can see their posture change. They stand up straighter. There are extra and added smiles. And by the fourth or fifth meeting, they walk into my office smiling from ear to ear, glowing, laughing, and feeling like a million dollars. Every time I see this transformation take place, I think about my hairdresser and say to myself how lucky I am to have a profession that can make people so happy. A profession that changes people's lives forever.

No, I am not a psychologist. Not a massage therapist. No, I am not a plastic surgeon… I am a financial empowerment coach. I help families who are struggling with money create a whole new relationship with it. It thrills me to create with them an empowering money mindset. I love teaching them how to use easy tools to control their finances. Together, we go through the coaching process in an encouraging and positive way, focusing on what they have, on their successes, so that we can find the right way for them. My clients are smart and capable people, and I support them to see that. I show them how to leverage their skills to ensure that their money supports them and that they have enough for everything that is important to them today and in the future. I empower people to create a life of abundance where all their dreams can come true.

What I do is more than a profession; it's a calling. I did not choose it. It chose me.

Making Good Money

Since I was a child, I have always been interested in business. When I was in high school, I had a good friend who was into clothes, shoes, and fashion. I was not. I was fascinated by stocks and news about business and the markets. For my sixteenth birthday, I thought my friend was going to buy me — makeup or the latest jeans. No!! She knew me better than that. She bought me a subscription to the Wall Street Journal. It was the perfect gift.

I used to pour over every issue of the WSJ that came in, losing myself in the news, following every up and down of the market. After high school, I continued that love into university, doing my Master's in Business and then I spent the next 20 years in marketing and business development in the corporate world. I loved what I did and was fantastic at it. I had great positions and I made good money… really wonderful money.

Just as the money flowed in, it flowed right back out! In fact, more money flowed out than flowed in. It was frustrating. I saw myself as an educated, professional person, and I wanted to live the kind of lifestyle that was associated with that 'type' of person. After all, why did I invest so much time and money going to university and getting a good job if not to have that grand lifestyle society told me I would achieve? It was a promise of happiness and I wanted it. Or at least I thought I did.

To live the dream.

I didn't live an extravagant lifestyle, but I did have an apartment in a nice neighborhood. My kids had the best toys and went to numerous after-school programs. I have pictures of my daughter that follow her through her years of dance classes — the little pink tutu she was so thrilled to wear at age three slowly changing into edgier and more grown-up costumes as she got older. I likewise have pictures of my son on the soccer field from the time he was barely able to kick the ball without falling over to later when he dominated the field, me standing proudly on the sidelines and cheering him on every step of the way. I took the kids hiking and touring on the weekends; we ate out from time to time and went to visit my family abroad once a year. Normal stuff for a middle class family. I made a good living, so why not?

I did not understand at the time that in order to maintain such a lifestyle, I needed to actually *manage* my money. I needed to plan how to use it and how to make it work for me. My parents never discussed money with me and I did not learn anything about it in school, so I just took it for granted that if I earned enough, everything would work itself out. But it was not that easy. I may have been living the 'normal' lifestyle that I was used to and felt I deserved, but I spent a lot of time working very hard to earn that good living. Unfortunately, it only resulted in anxiety — sweating bullets every time I had to pay for something, wondering if we were going to be okay.

My worries were not unfounded. The more money I made, the more debt

I had! The more debt I had, the greater my worry and anxiety about money became. Sound familiar? (80 percent of adults in Western society are living in debt!)

Being a Responsible Adult

Every now and again, I would reluctantly sit down at my computer and log into my bank account. That's what responsible adults do, right? But the idea of logging in filled me with dread. I would drag my feet and do *anything* other than face what I was going to see there. I hated it because each time I did, I saw that my debt was getting bigger and bigger, and I knew that there was no easy way to deal with it. I would stress out and use some savings to lower it (painful), or I would try to completely stop any kind of spending (even more painful), or I would take a loan (which felt like an easy solution but was actually the most detrimental thing I could do), then as a last resort, I would consolidate old loans and sign away my financial future.

When things started getting really tough financially, I can remember going to the mall with the intention of getting just a few things for my kids and coming out with bags and bags of 'necessary' stuff. Even before I got the bags in the trunk of my car, I can remember standing there sweating, thinking, "How am I going to pay for all this?" Head in the sand, unsure of what my bank balance actually held, I would hope and pray that somehow it would all work out. Because of this, my financial situation just got worse.

Grand Theft

The straw that broke the camel's back was when I logged into my bank account one day and realized that there was nothing left. I had no money. I sat there staring at the numbers on the screen, wondering what had happened. I was hardly spending anything by this point — no clothes or shopping trips, no unnecessary haircuts, no movies or toys for my kids — I was just paying the bills. My body was trembling and I was on the verge of tears. It was unfathomable. Where had all my money gone?

There was only one person to blame! I stormed into my bank manager's office with six months' worth of bank statements and accused him, the bank, of stealing from me. I knocked on the door and insisted that he see me immediately. I shoved the paperwork right under his nose and told him emphatically that I was not leaving until we combed all the paperwork and found out exactly how that bank was stealing from me!

Seriously!

Today I can laugh about the ridiculousness of it, but when I went there, I was dead serious. I felt like I was not spending money at all, nothing, nada, but my debt was increasing anyway. The math just did not add up!

The bank manager was very kind and patient with me. He invited me in and offered me a chair. He sat behind his desk, legs crossed at the ankles as he listened to me rant about my missing money. In the face of my extreme upset, he exuded calm and peaceful listening. Once I stopped to take a breath, exhausted by my ravings, he said very politely, "Mindy, the bank is not stealing from you. You are simply being irresponsible with your money." It was as if a sledgehammer hit me in the stomach! I could not breathe. I could not speak!

ME?! Irresponsible?!

I had no comeback for him. I had no words. There was no smart thing that I could say to him to prove that I was responsible. I am probably the most responsible person I have ever met! I was at a complete and utter loss for what to do next. Holding back, I thanked him for his patience and walked out as calmly as I could, but the little voice in my head was shouting angrily, "I'm going to show him who's irresponsible!"

A few days later, even though I didn't have any money to spare, I invested in my financial education and took a course on how to manage my money. And guess what I learned... I learned that I was irresponsible! Not because I was an irresponsible person but because I never *took* responsibility for my money. I took it for granted and never learned how to use it. I never learned how to make money work for me.

Within three months of starting the course, I was totally out of debt and in control of my finances. I knew exactly how much I had and what I wanted to use it for. I felt empowered! A huge weight had lifted from my shoulders. Getting control of my money gave me freedom — the freedom to choose how I wanted to live my life.

Freedom

Suddenly, I didn't feel so scared, dependent, or stuck. I knew that no matter what I would be able to pay my expenses and maintain my home and my family. For the first time since I was a young adult, I felt like I had choices and opportunities! I could create a life that is so much better and so much more in alignment with who I was becoming.

At the time, I was in my early forties, divorced, with two kids who were becoming more and more independent. I felt like I was entering an era of personal liberation. Maybe it was my age. Possibly it was because of my new financial status. Most likely it was the combination of both. Whatever it was, I was ready for a change.

I was tired of the corporate world, of the competition, of the pace of it. I wanted to work in a more intimate environment, to help individuals, not big businesses. I wanted to be able to spend more time with my children. Getting clarity about my money situation and having a solid financial plan freed up my mind to explore a new kind of lifestyle and start meeting some of those deeper desires.

Going through my transformation, I couldn't let go of the idea that I wanted others to feel the same freedom I had discovered. It was like I had found a secret machine that knows how to make life so much easier and I felt passionate about sharing it. Getting control of my money gave me freedom and empowered me. Helping others get out of the same yucky place that I had been… it felt like my calling. I wanted to help other people make the same transformation I had. People suffer so much because of their lack of education around money. It would be a crime to keep the 'solution' a secret.

I was already studying Life Coaching in the evenings and decided that I would become a professional Financial Coach. I started to plan my 'exit' from the corporate world. Two years later, after successfully coaching others on the side, I left my job in corporate and days after my forty-fourth birthday, I founded, together with my business partner, **Healthy Finances**. My calling had chosen me.

Healthy Finances

We named our business **Healthy Finances** because we both wanted full and healthy lives for ourselves and for our clients. When you manage your money and use it well, you improve your physical and mental health and you create a healthy environment.

Our mission is to reverse the debilitating financial statistics that almost 80 percent of all Western adults are in consumer debt and 70 percent of divorces are caused by financial disagreements. It is a big mission, but I am confident that if I can change my financial reality then anyone can! And I am committed to helping everyone who is willing to take responsibility and has the courage to step up.

Since that first course in money management, I changed my relationship with money. I continue to invest in my financial education and travel around the world to learn from the best in the financial world. What resonates with me, I implement in my life. If it works for me, I share it with my coaches and my clients and we all spread the word to create a financial ripple effect. It is interesting that the tools that have the biggest effect are the ones that deal with changing mindset, not the ones that deal with numbers...

Financial Freedom

Twelve years after that first course in money management and ten years after I started Healthy Finances, I became a Change Maker in other people's lives. My business not only helps families across the globe create a life of abundance, where all their dreams can come true, but also increases the mental mindset, leading to emotional freedom. Learning to have money is not about how to *make* money. It is about understanding how to use money as a resource to live how *you* want. That is empowering. If you are in control of your money, then you can funnel all your resources — time, money and energy — into living the life you desire *and* deserve.

Ignite Action Steps

How can you change your financial reality?

The first thing you should do is see what you have. Connect with the money that you *do* have. Next, make a list of your goals. Start by defining the life you want. Forget how you *are* living your life. Think about how you *want* to live your life. What's important to you? What are your values? What wonderful things do you want to bring into your life?

Then look at your spending. Make sure that your money is going toward the things that are important to you. It doesn't have to be in a big way — but it's vital to do the things that make you happy. This will have a huge effect on your sense of abundance.

Money should make you happy. Make sure you're tasting that happiness all the time.

Mindy Stern - Israel
Founder & CEO, Healthy Finances, Financial Empowerment Coaching
www.healthyfinancesglobal.com

Elena Harder

"It is only by sharing our stories that we can truly be healed."

I want to make sure no one ever feels ashamed or alone in the worst moments of their lives. In sharing my story, I want you to know that no matter how bad it is, no matter how hopeless it seems, you can find a way to make a change and be the mother you desire to be.

The Deep End of Mom Guilt

The birds giggle in the trees, the sky a brilliant blue, wind skitters through the palm branches. It seems like paradise, but I'm too busy to notice as my thoughts whirl around in my endless to-do lists, how lonely I am, money worries, and suffocating mom guilt.

My son is splashing, giggling, and playing in the pool. He waves, "Mom, come play!" I shake my head no pointing at my phone. "Mommy has work to do." I look guiltily at the screen, it's not work, it's Facebook. "More like avoidant distraction," I mumble to myself. My soul is so tired, these days I only move if my son is hungry or in danger.

"Mom! Pancakes?" His voice cuts through like the last strike of an axe felling a tree. I manage a half smile. "Let's go make pancakes." My mood lifts briefly as his little hand slips into mine, his feet clumsy over the cobblestone as we move in slow motion toward the house. All he wants is my attention, but I am too preoccupied with panic over how to pay the bills to give it to him. I am constantly searching for escape plans. It's been brutally hard since 'the ex' left and my dream of 'our happy family' was shattered. My thoughts of suicide are getting louder than they've ever been. But I can't tell anyone my thoughts, surely they will take my son away from me. I need help. I'm watching the free and independent woman I used to be drown under the daily demands of single mothering.

I never wanted to be a parent. Now I want to die, but I can't abandon my son. Often I think maybe we could both 'accidentally' fall off something deathly high at the same time. My mind hurls itself away from that thought. What kind of mother thinks such things? He tugs on my hand again, "Pancakes?" Even though I've agreed, I know that's the last thing we need. I remember us binge eating pancakes last week, then him yelling "You're stupid!!!" at me over and over again. I went into a screaming rage, unable to control my emotions. I can't stop thinking about what a friend shared about mood instability caused by neuro-inflammation from wheat, and sugar... basically pancakes.

Yet here I am again, feeling guilty and still making them. I know we both need to stop, but it's one of the only meals he will reliably eat. So I grumble over this while I wash the pan, crack the eggs, mix, and pour, wait... flip... wait... flip... He picks one up with his chubby and uncomfortably grubby little hand and smushes it into his face. "Yucky! No!" he spits them out as two-year-olds often do. Does he have ANY IDEA the strength I've summoned just to make them? No actually, clearly he doesn't care, he's two. I reach over and lift the top pancake, flapping it like a mouth. "Come eat us, we were made JUST for you..."

"No!" He barks and the remaining slivers of my 'caring mother' are destroyed. Another part of me screams, "Eat your fucking pancake, you little shit!!!" but you can't say such things to a child. A strikingly clear visual of shaking him so hard he doesn't come back flashes through my mind. I didn't mean it and I'm horrified at the graphic and violent nature of these thoughts. "What kind of mother am I? Obviously terrible, I deserve to die." I take a deep breath and stuff that thought in the bag with all the other thoughts I'm not supposed to think. After 26 months, 8 days, and 20 minutes of being a mom, the bag is overflowing.

That afternoon at the playground another mom asks me, "Did you hear about the boy?" She whispers and I see her wanting to connect. She seems horrified and is asking for support, but all I feel is numb, even her face seems blurry to me. "What boy?" I ask dutifully, I must at all costs keep up the facade of 'fine and normal.' She shares with me, "A family with a little boy, only two and a half. The babysitter wasn't watching, he drowned while she was on Facebook."

I scoff inside, thinking "That's not so bad, I daydream worse ways for me and my son to die every day."

Her voice barely audible, she continues, "But the boy didn't actually die in the pool. I heard the babysitter's boyfriend got high on crystal meth. He locked the older brother in the bathroom, then raped and killed the younger boy. The parents came home from their dinner to find their children, one horridly dead, the other locked up and still sobbing." Her voice breaks and she looks at me, eyes pleading for understanding.

For the first time in a long time, something pierces the numbness and a surge of fear rises within me. The story is *way too familiar.* It's the culmination of ALL the worst fears I've had: babysitter might betray us, Facebook, the pool, strange men might hurt him, finding out meth addicts were sharing our hangout spot last month, homicide. All of it. My reality, right now.

I remember just the day before, hearing an otherworldly scream. One of utter anguish, unreal, wretched and torn. Something far beyond what I had imagined a voice could create. I understand now, it was the sound only a mother's shattered heart could make.

A new truth floods every cell of my being, a wave of clarity shakes loose all the thoughts of death. "You think you're stuck with your son forever? Wrong. You are the powerful creator of your life and you can manifest him dead. *If you want…* he could be gone, and you could be free. This is your warning shot."

I see the true power of my terrible thoughts and the Law of Attraction. "Do I truly want him dead?" My body quivers with the memory of her scream as if I'm inside of her.

"No, NO! Not dead. Anything but dead."

Suddenly, the anguish I've been experiencing seems like *nothing.* Life would certainly be worse with the permanent trauma of my son dead. I imagine how my own mother would feel if she lost us both. A mother's heart is not made to outlive her child. Death is no longer an option, no matter what challenges I'm facing right now, I am now determined to live. For him, for myself, and for my family. I must.

While the end of the day finds me exhausted as always, I also feel an inner vigor that wasn't there before. With my son asleep, I slump into my favorite chair. I can feel the stinging behind my eyes from the tears I've been holding back. I've lived terrified of what might happen if I let those feelings out, but living with them has been a nightmare. Years of tears and anger I've stuffed and never let myself feel. Now there's no holding back.

All the memories of my emotional absence to my son's requests, my frozen heart, my blatant neglect of his deepest needs, all the guilt comes pouring through me. Instead of stuffing, I let go and surrender, finally feeling it all. I have no excuses right now, there's nothing else to do, no distractions. Only me with my tears. Crying out the entire ocean of self-loathing I'd built around myself.

I feel another sensation rising. It begins as a whisper of awareness, then swells all around me. A feeling way bigger than me moves me into surrender. A peaceful warm sensation, it carries the feeling of forgiveness and love like a sweet mother rocking her unsettled baby to sleep. The hollow sounds of my crying seem to become less about what happened... more about how unworthy I now feel of the grand love that holds me at this moment. For the first time, my sadness feels healing instead of dangerous.

Later, still held in the sweet arms of this divine forgiveness, I return to my son sleeping quietly on our bed. No endless toddler requests, only sweetness. He looks different than I've ever seen him before. I lay down, my body curved close around his tiny one. My heart is warm, a strange new sensation. Is this what it feels like to be a loving mother? Suddenly, it occurs to me: "He didn't mean to hurt me; he's only a child. Nothing he's done — nothing I've done — can't be undone with forgiveness and love. It starts with me being responsible for my emotions, feeling them, and being a better me no matter what he does." I lay there for a long time staring at him with brand new eyes.

The next day despite my best intentions, I find myself right back in it. His cry of "Mom!" like nails on a chalkboard, a life or death threat to my sanity. Old stories whirl around on repeat, until I catch myself, and in an act of sheer will, I shake my head and say "STOP IT! I won't do this anymore." My inner world comes back into focus. Life is vibrant around me, the birds sing their merry tunes, the sky peppered with clouds, and the wind feels gentle on my face. What if I let go of the old stories and listened to the birds instead? I remember my new intention. *I will find a way to be the mother I want to be.* I will notice the pattern. I will conquer this moment with love.

I can see the monumental realization I had doesn't change the stress and overwhelm of daily life, but at least now I can firmly tell the murderous voice, "Death is *not an option.*"

I face the next day with a new strength, fueled by the power of my conviction to be better. I wake in the morning and write in Sharpie on each of my fingers "Breathe, Create Love, Magnetize, Look Inside, Celebrate." Today, if I feel overwhelmed or at the edge of yelling, I will take a breath and let myself feel the anger, I won't bottle it up any longer. I will surrender to the pain, and let the feeling move through me and out of me. I promise that I will never ever take hurtful action toward him or myself again.

To my surprise, the exercise works, and I am able to calm myself significantly from wild blind rage to a sweet desire for peaceful connection. My mind begins to calm and I'm able to see the world around me through different eyes.

For the first time since 'the ex' left, I begin to dream of what life might be like in the future if things actually went well. I can feel the strength of the process, and decide to call the exercise my Five Fantastic Fingers. I can feel how it's changing me, and I begin to daydream about sharing it with others.

What starts as a daydream, quickly becomes a raging passion inside of me. No one should have to go through what I've been through! I will share my story, I'll teach what I've learned and I'll prevent the suffering of many. The idea of being a Change Maker fuels my soul and powers my recovery over the next few years. I lead workshops teaching the tools that I used every day to keep my overwhelm at bay. Whenever I feel fear or doubt, I return to the vision of myself teaching, sharing, and alive with passion.

Now when we make our favorite breakfast, I am brimming with joy. Pancakes: the gluten-free and vegan variety. My son smiles as he squishes dates, bananas, and chia seeds together. "Okay, next ingredient!" I say, with genuine enthusiasm. We've finally found a recipe my son likes, actually tastes good *and doesn't hurt our bodies*. He goes to pour the pancake mix in and spills it all over the counter. I don't even flinch and instead of being mad I simply ask him, "How can we fix this really easily?" He smiles at me and says, "Easy, I'll push it back into the bowl." He does it by himself as my fingers dance across the recipe. "One last ingredient... " I pause for effect, in a joke that seems to never get old to us. "Did you put the love in?" I look at him and he giggles. "Yup, got it Mom." He grins at me and my heart fills with warmth and pride. I understand with every single part of me, my dedication to 'choosing to live and be a better mom' has made this moment possible. I look at him with tenderness and pride, he's so peaceful now. So am I. Tears pool sweetly in my eyes, I am enchanted with this moment, my son and our family. Most importantly, I am so pleased with myself for making that pivotal decision to do better, be better.

When I look back at that time, I can see now that it was so much more about what I was holding onto inside, than what was happening around me. As I learned to open and feel my feelings again, life became easier, and as I moved through the next years of healing workshops and breathwork retreats, I realized that I was not alone in my pain. I've heard many stories like mine, and much worse. Moments that people just like you and I have lived through, that take my breath away to imagine. Yet, they found the strength to continue on. I invite you right now to commit to really feeling and healing your own stories.

You can, right now, make the decision to no longer blame anyone else for your challenges, or your pains. Imagine what is possible when you take 100% responsibility for feeling your feelings and finding love for them? When you embrace that kind of radical self-love, no matter what the people around you are doing, you become aligned with the force of love. This is the power you hold inside of you.

As a Female Change Maker you MUST walk your talk, and be the source of peace in your life. Your family needs healing, only you can provide. Only you can draw a line through the chaos of your life and know what is acceptable to you, and what is not. Then you can firmly stand with what you believe is best and create yourself as a brand new woman. Now is the time for you to know your power, hold your head higher, and create a new reality for you and your family. Breathe, create love, magnetize, look inside and celebrate! Incredible joy is waiting for you in the next chapter of your life.

Ignite Action Steps

The Five Fantastic Fingers takes five minutes or less from start to finish. It is designed specifically for those moments where you feel so angry you want to scream, freeze, or run away. Use it in any moment of challenge, or as part of your end of day routine to process any emotions you stuffed. You can even write it on your fingers like I did. The ritual creates a repeated brain pathway that goes from "When I start doing this, I am stressed" to "When I finish this, I feel good." Each time you complete it, you hardwire the pattern of moving even quicker from stress to relaxation into your brain and fingers.

If you need to do it more than once, *no problem!* I say, "Doing it twice is better than doing it not at all!" You'll have opportunities to practice any time you get triggered or feel angry. Before we get started, check-in and see how strong the emotion you're feeling is, on a scale of 1-10.

Breathe. Thumb and baby finger together for five breaths to *recognize your awareness of a pattern* of anger or emotion within you. You want to change it and are preparing to shift. Breathe in through your nose and out through your mouth to calm your nervous system. Imagine breathing OUT all your anger, frustration, overwhelm, and stress.

Create Love. Thumb and ring finger together for five breaths to *recognize the love you carry within yourself*, look around for anything you feel grateful for and express gratitude with your inner (or outer) voice. Gratitude: for seeing where you were stuck, your challenge for asking you to love more, for being able to shift it.

Magnetize. Thumb and middle finger together for five breaths, connecting with what you WANT to be happening instead. You want to be patient, loving, kind. VISUALIZE and EXPERIENCE yourself as you want to be feeling. *This is magic, and you shift it.*

Look Inside. Thumb and index finger together for five breaths, then scan your body from head to toe, is there ANYTHING left of that initial challenge? If there is, just go back to Breathe. It will be even easier because of what you've already done. *Make sure you rate your emotions a two or lower before moving on.*

Celebrate. Press your thumbs together five times and breathe. Celebrate! You shifted yourself and are feeling MUCH BETTER! Positive reinforcement is crucial for creating new patterns and celebrating allows us to know without a doubt "This is good, and I am doing something good for myself". If you want to jump up and down with joy, go for it.

Congratulations! You've done it, but before you do anything else, take a moment right now to imagine the power this exercise could have in your life and think of three challenges where you could really use more peace and calm. Now imagine yourself doing it in those situations and how good it feels to choose a new path for yourself.

Elena Harder - Canada
Courage Catalyst and Bulletproof Mom Coach
BulletproofMoms.com
@ @joygasmharder
ℹ joygasm8

Karima Nadine Stein

"Let your heart blossom and it will spread seeds of empowerment."

Intention: By sharing my story, I want to encourage you to start your own journey from your head to your heart. When you reconnect to your heart, miracles happen. Together, we can create a world of people who lead their lives from their hearts and enjoy the changes and marvels that it brings about.

The Contagious Heart

I was educated to be a Change Maker. I had decided to follow this path at the age of 11. Changing the world may seem to be a strange thing for a young girl to decide, but I clearly remember this influential moment. I saw a program on television about the reckless abandon with which humanity treats the planet and its animal inhabitants, and it lit a fire deep inside of me that shaped the person I was to become. I chased that dream with every ounce of my energy, never realizing that the thing I most needed to change was my own heart.

The desire to contribute to a world of love, union, peace, and beauty planted early on in my childhood led me to study Sustainability Sciences. Yet, instead of passionately promoting solutions for a sustainable way of living, I myself was severely ill.

I was 28 years old and I was spinning in blackness. A slight move of my head was enough to make me lose balance. Non-functional digestion and several non-diagnosed causes had left me weighing only 39 kilograms (85 pounds), which was significantly underweight for a woman of my height. Weak and stuck to my bed most of the time, there was nothing I could do but watch my slowly-fading life force. I felt lost and out of control. Nothing to do, only just to be.

I loved control. It gave me a sense of security and, over the years, I had mastered this skill to perfection. A constantly-maintained state of 'doing' became the faithful servant to my hyper-vigilant mind. Being stripped of control made me feel nauseous and insecure. This was not the life I had envisioned of a Change Maker.

I was the 'successful one' of the family. The only one who had finished school and was studying at university. As the oldest child, after our mother and stepfather divorced and she left, I felt responsible to be the mother, to replace what was gone. Being abandoned by a parent for the second time in my life felt as if my arduous patched heart had been ripped into even smaller pieces. Yet, I kept it all together out of love and care for my brothers. As I was the flagship of the family, it also made me the go-to place for my brothers' and stepfather's complaints. Whenever I saw my family, I was either the listener to their sorrows or I was asked to mediate between them. It soon became evident, albeit slowly, that increasing amounts of alcohol were making their way into the house. Disguised as men's quality time or normal teenage behavior, all three of them drank their fair share. My one brother, one of the most bighearted and loving men I know, had been struggling with a deep sorrow following our parents' divorce and I felt absolutely helpless to watch him falling deeper into first alcohol and then drugs. Nothing I tried could get him to change his ways.

Having developed a strong sense for everyone else's pain and emotions rather than mine, it was unbearable for me to step foot into the house which had been *home* to our whole family. In addition, the emotional state of its inhabitants made its ugly self seen in every room. So, whenever I was home, I tried my best to restore some of the cozy and warm atmosphere it once had. It was a bottomless pit. Despite my efforts to help, I became witness to what I perceived as a downward spiral and state of being for all my family members.

My failure to help all of them, especially my brother, haunted me wherever I went. I felt guilty for seeking out a better life for myself and having failed in a responsibility I somehow thought would be mine.

Only once did I break down in tears in all those years, and when it came, it came with force. I fell on the floor sobbing, shaking, and moaning uncontrollably. Nothing anyone said or did could soothe me and I could feel the intensity and depth of my suffering overwhelming them. My friends could not bear to see me in such pain and just wanted it to stop, so they gave me loads of tranquilizing herbs and tea, which worked, yet got me back on numbing my own feelings. Not wanting to be a burden to anyone, I wiped my tears and went right back to trying to hold it all together, stuffing my feelings back in a box and closing the lid with determination.

I focused my energy and passion on contributing to a more sustainable world. Next to my attempts to save the family, I did everything I could to save the planet. On top of my studies, I loaded even more responsibility onto my shoulders by becoming the co-founder and spokeswoman for a student initiative promoting circular economy. I got new roommates and tried putting my life on track.

And then I lost control of my health — the weight loss and spinning blackness being the result of it. When my health issues became significantly threatening and so obvious I had to tell my family, none of them really noticed the urgency of it, being entangled in their own challenges. So used to my not needing anyone, I stayed in the role of helping them, not myself. I was so scared of experiencing another loss of people dear to my heart that I kept up the only interaction which would guarantee attention from my family — playing the role of the strong one, the listener. When my body finally collapsed, leaving me stuck in my bed, none of my family members were there.

With no family support and not having any money for alternative treatments, I was left with my fear of death hovering over me like a ghost. Just before the moment I surrendered to the possibility of my death, my roommate and dear friend, who had been witnessing my decline, offered to pay for me to receive treatment from a holistic doctor. She told me he was working with alternative practices and had helped cure several severe conditions, including her own grandfather's cancer. I knew that if I didn't accept this generous offer, I would be facing death and this scared me more than my fear of depending on someone else's kindness.

After two weeks of daily intense treatments, I was back on my feet, walking again. My vitality and some of the weight came back as the treatment progressed. But now, perceiving the threat of being unable to finish my degree, I relentlessly pushed myself back into working mode. Still in the process of recovery, I did what I was taught would bring a rewarding and fulfilling life — achieving. This is what society tells you to do, after all, and I was convinced that it would make me an influential Change Maker. Although I had just barely reached a functional level, I finished my studies and even won an award for being one of the top students. I then went on to publish a book and fairly quickly got a well-paying job.

From the outside, it looked like I had triumphed over my sickness and worked my way back to what was supposed to be a great life. I continued my mission to contribute to a more sustainable world. Yet the success only became my mask. It was disguising the truth of my broken self and I felt my happiness decreasing even further. I was barely surviving. Inside of me I felt empty. All the strength I had gained from the alternative medicines had diffused into the inner rebellion building up in me. The longing for acknowledgement and fitting in had made me the perfect performer, pretending to be strong when I was weak. Confident when I was insecure. Happy when I was hurting. Just simply functioning.

Secretly, I was wishing for permission to just be myself. Of course, no one gave that to me. So I kept going. In my desperation, I was breeding a dragon inside of me, fueled by my anger and frustration. I hated that I was being pulled toward the hamster wheel that I saw everyone else climbing on and I didn't want to be part of it. Deep down I knew, this was not what my soul was craving. I felt trapped, entering something I didn't want to enter.

In moments of exhaustion that I kept out of the public eye, a soft, warm whisper interrupted the expansive and incessant mind-chatter, "There is a deeper sense to life than this. You have lost yourself." Naturally, I did not listen.

The voice was determined not to be ignored. It made itself heard through my body, putting me back into severe health conditions and this time ripping away the last pillars of security that I had desperately clung to. I was faced with a highly confrontational job situation as a result of stating my truth. At the same time, I lost my love relationship and place to live. I was left with a car full of private belongings and my broken me. And as a side-effect, despite all the fancy achievements, my impact as a Change Maker was minuscule.

A feeling of profound meaninglessness crept into every part of me and finally shattered the meticulously created illusions of myself, leaving me naked and exposed in the process of self-realization. I finally accepted that I had lost myself, that I was broken inside, and — most challenging of all — that I had created this situation myself. This time, I made the decision to face the core of my very own creation. Up until then, I had been pouring all my resources into my family, caring for them, and in many ways trying to save them. At the same time, studying sustainability also made me feel responsible for fixing the world. For the first time in my life, I turned my focus away from saving others and toward my inner world. For the first time in my life, I cared about my own *personal* sustainability.

A long process of self-discovery followed. You would think that living in a body and spending time with yourself 24/7 does qualify you to be an expert about yourself. Well, it turns out that this is not the case. Diving head first into a series of deep meditations, I encountered a proficiently-built dam for emotions that I had installed over the years to keep up my performance. Behind it an overwhelming amount of past emotional experiences were yearning for liberation. Learning to embrace them, feel them and to be vulnerable turned out to be the greatest challenge I had encountered so far. Through meditation and self-development, I finally found tools I could use to access my emotions. Days of tears flowing down my cheeks, screaming, and wild body movements dissolved layer by layer of my collected armor. On the other side of it, moments of pure inner joy and happiness awaited me. I exchanged tears for laughter and screaming for deep-felt peace.

During the process of making changes to my inner world, my outer world also changed. Performance-oriented friendships gave way to true connections. More and more, I found myself surrounded by people who have a positive outlook on life. Taking it in their own hands. The experience of being held in love, while openly showing my agony, my tears and my anger, not only was deeply healing, it created connection. Slowly I could feel my cup being filled and life coming back into my body. Other good things happened also. My mother reached out to me after seven years of no contact. Having dealt with my emotions, I was able to happily embrace her back into my life and establish a more open and compassionate relationship with her.

My uplifted spirits led me to focus on what brings me joy rather than what has to be done and the change in me became noticeable to others. People who had been witness to my change wanted to know how I did it. My own mother reached out to me with questions, wanting to learn and grow herself. I loved spreading my own experience and started to see other lives around me thrive as a result of it. There was no effort in it, no preaching or forcing. Most of all, I enjoyed the process. The ripple effect of my change, by sharing my experiences, was far more evident and reached farther than my efforts of promoting a more sustainable way of living, yet I did not fully understand why.

That understanding was about to come in the most surprising way. One day, in the middle of performing in the choir in the musical "Martin Luther King," it happened. While I was giving my voice, singing to King's message, the gigantic event hall, the people in it, and the voices around me faded away. The words, although I had sung them many times before, opened something up in me. A warm shooting sensation touched my heart. It felt as if my entire being was expanding to at least four times its size and bursting out of my chest. My body became a playground for waves of goosebumps crashing over me one after another. Fireworks of joy, Ignited from deep within me, radiating outward from my center, lighting up love for everything around me.

Suddenly, a holographic picture of a little blond girl appeared in front of my eyes. I had experienced those kinds of visions in my meditations but never before seen them with my eyes open. It was my two-year-old self reaching up to me. Then something occurred which I can only describe as her reconnection with me, with all her gifts and knowledge. Specifically her heart. I could feel the pureness of her being, her knowing of life's beauty and the truth of loving communion. Letting my tears flow, I was unable to continue singing as her message sank into my entire essence. *I understood.* It had been my head, not my heart, that had guided my mission in life for all those years. I realized that the sensation of blackness was a metaphor for much of my illness. Every time I used my head, not my heart, I would often blackout and lose sense of my equilibrium. It became so evident that I needed to *change* and live from my heart. It was as if a veil had been lifted from my eyes.

Faced with challenging life situations and adapting to a performance regime, I had toughened up over time. Closed my heart. Lost the connection to my inner-child and her heart's purity. And in this process, my head had become my master — as well as my own worst enemy and the source of my pain.

My recovery was driven by the very force that was creating my *dis*-ease: my ego, fuelled by emotions, and by the mechanism of survival. The changes that are enriching my life now and the inspiration I have become to others, radiate out of my slowly recovering heart. An open heart filled with life can be seen and felt from afar. It leads to *inspired* actions rather than actions motivated by improvement or lack. Coming from a place of happiness and wholeness automatically spreads seeds of empowerment into my environment. This was just the beginning of my journey from my head to my heart. Yet I now know it's crucial for meaningful Change Making. Whenever I follow the inspired action of my open heart, things flow to me and around me. And it doesn't just change *me*... the light it sheds onto the lives of the people surrounding me is a true gift to give.

There is a saying that "the brain thinks, but the heart knows." Ruling from lack, fear, and an urge to control does not allow you to find your divine gift. It is when we lead from an open and singing heart that true empowerment and miracles happen. So, hold on tight — an open heart is highly contagious!

Many Change Makers devote most of their time and resources to someone else or their mission. I encourage you to honor your personal sustainability first, becoming your very own Change Maker, igniting others from within.

IGNITE ACTION STEPS

Emotional intelligence – Having rebuilt my relationship with my own emotions I now have a deeper understanding of their power. The amount of energy involved and their connection to your thoughts and actions make them a valuable resource to regain sovereignty over your life. There is a difference between feeling them and immersing into them. The latter results in creating a habit of being in a certain emotional state which can turn into a subconscious program running your life. Learning to be aware of your emotions, embracing them but not reacting to them, is both, a challenging yet highly rewarding skill to master.

Be comfortable in just being – Being grown up in a society that promotes doing and achieving as a success mechanism, just being is something most of us have to relearn. Can you make yourself feel comfortable in being present with yourself? Can you enjoy feeling your breathing? How long can you indulge yourself into all your senses in the present moment without any goal, anything to do, think or to achieve?

Have fun – Your heart does not yearn to check off a to-do list. Its desire lies in fully embracing life. It loves indulging in the apparently senseless joy of running barefoot in the grass. It craves feeling and creating true connection and loving communion with the people around us. Tap into what makes you feel alive. Start celebrating life.

Karima Nadine Stein - Germany
Sustainability Scientist and Consultant
KarimaN.stein@gmx.de

Hermian Charles

"Sharing the privileges of justice, freedom,
and equality with others does not lessen your share."

This is an invitation to forgiveness. It is a beckoning to act from a place of love. It's an intention to heal the tears and torn fabrics in our society, to elevate humanity so that all may enjoy the peace and freedom that you personally enjoy. I invoke you to hold the doors to your heart open and to find ways to heal the fractures that leave people unable to be their best selves. May we all be guided by this intent.

Freedom, Justice, and Spirituality

I grew up hearing the phrase, "Where there's smoke, there's fire." This has left the indelible impression on me that there's usually some trace of truth to most gossip or accusation. You see, I am from a tiny island in the Southern Caribbean Sea called Grenada. After 21 years growing up on that island, I only personally knew two people who had been incarcerated. Grenada is a country where justice prevails and those convicted were those whose guilt was beyond a shadow of doubt. I took so much of that for granted, but moving to the United States to pursue my college education showed me a whole other upside-down world.

It was a wake-up call. It was my first immersion into a severely broken, racist culture. Whereas before I experienced colorism or what can be called 'pigmentocracy' in the US, for the first time, I felt treated as a second-class citizen. It manifested itself in blatant ways. The phrase I had always heard in the Pledge of Allegiance, 'Justice and freedom for all,' certainly did not include people of a certain hue. And I quickly learned that the scale of justice was grossly imbalanced in its administration to minority groups (Blacks, Latinos, and Native Americans) as opposed to white Americans.

During my childhood, I attended a Catholic elementary school and then high school in a convent in St. George's, Grenada. Somewhere along that path, I grew distant from the religious doctrines. I knew that we were all interconnected and there was something bigger. But we were not encouraged to question the teachings of the Catholic church. Those who did question did so at their own peril. But what I was taught did not land as my truth.

Once I graduated high school, I stayed away from the church and condemned religion, but as I started asking a better quality question, I started arriving at better answers, more nuanced answers, that uplifted me and swayed the seat of my soul. I started pursuing spirituality that was not based on any religious beliefs.

A few years later, in search of a truth independent of organized religion, I attended my first-ever personal development seminar. That seminar, led by John Bradshaw, had such a profound impact on my life. My entire situational map changed, the way I interpreted power, ownership, and forgiveness. My views were forever altered; a chain of events started where I became a personal development junkie. You name a great thought leader of our day and I bet I have attended their seminar, read their book, or listened to one of their talks. One such seminar led me to examine the guiding principles that were the bedrock of my life. It became clear that there was nothing I treasured more than freedom. I wanted financial freedom, freedom of place, freedom of time, freedom of expression, freedom to choose, and freedom to be.

It became clear to me that I can never be fully free unless others are also free. This freedom, that I hold most dear, is what I wanted to gift the world. It felt like my ministry. My Darma. Freedom for all. I submitted to my soul's calling, whispering to me from all that is. This is my life's mission and I choose to accept it.

So many people around me were not free, and it wasn't situations of their own making; it was because they were preyed upon by what I consider greedy, corrupt, and hate-filled politicians. We have seen the growth of a new industry in the US, the for-profit prison system. Counties pay private industries to house inmates. These private companies quickly figured out that they can grow their profit margin by lobbying, a legal form of bribery where corporations 'donate' to politicians, to get the county to send them more prisoners... to the tune of millions of dollars.

I was a college student during the time that the US Crime Bill was signed into law; I was a young black woman living in New York City, the new ground zero for the war on crime. Quotas were placed on police officers and what once seemed to be casual prejudice became codified into law. A deeper, more insidious type of systemic racism, which was subverted by the Civil Rights Amendment, once again reared its ugly head. More and more, I started seeing harsher policing in neighborhoods of color. Documented, but unknown to most, was the buried text of the crime bill that guaranteed private prisons always be at a minimum of 80 percent capacity. This in turn led to corrupt politicians placing quotas on police officers and turning humans into commodities who feed the prison pipeline. But one cannot guarantee criminality. Some police officers, finding their livelihoods threatened, were known to turn to highly-corrupt tactics of planting illegal drugs and weapons on those they stopped.

Given that the president had already declared the war on drugs, that combined with the crime bill, amplified the situation. The US policies led to criminalizing addictions and issuing harsh sentences for those caught with even the most miniscule amount of illegal substances. The phrase 'zero tolerance' was coined. In some states like California, we saw the introduction of '3 Strikes You're Out', which meant that if you were imprisoned twice, the next time you would automatically receive a life sentence. Today there are people sentenced to life in prison for the ultimate, victimless crime of smoking marijuana.

The introduction of the infamous 'Stop and Frisk' policy which targeted Black and Latino youths in New York City appalled me. Reading about the thousands of police stops that were made broke my heart and made me dread watching the evening news. An awareness bloomed in me of the trauma that these innocent people were being subjected to. I also woke up to the fact that I could easily become part of the statistics and my freedom which I hold so dear could easily be stolen from me. Upwards of 90 percent of the stops made were on people of color, and over 90 percent of the time, they were innocent. Less than 10 percent of the stops were made on white people and, of those stopped, over 90 percent of them were in possession of illegal weapons or substances. Michael Bloomberg, then Mayor of New York City, called for decreasing the number of stops made on white people and increasing the stops on people of color! In the year Bloomberg became Mayor, there were 97,296 stops reported. A decade later, there were 685,724.

Our jails and prisons swelled to beyond capacity and were plagued with

inhumane conditions exacerbated by racist policies and contentious relationships with communities of color. In 2011, a lawsuit was filed to overturn 'Stop
and Frisk' on the grounds of its unconstitutionality. Following the success of
the lawsuit, the statistics plunged to 11,629 in 2017, a number in my opinion
that is still way too high.

Unlike most people I've met on this journey, I cannot claim that my passion
for justice and equality was instigated by a single major trauma in my life. I
have been on this path for several years before a family member was accused
of a crime he didn't commit. The DA was not seeking truth, just a conviction.
Even though I was an eyewitness, I was never called to testify as it would have
invalidated their case. It was purely a numbers game, a question of quotas in
our prosecutorial system where the poor are the ones preyed upon. After we
mounted a rather costly defense, the charges were dropped.

Unfortunately, this is not the case for many victims of over-policing. I sat
in the courtroom on multiple occasions when overburdened public defenders
encouraged clearly innocent young men to 'take a plea.' They would admit
guilt rather than go to trial in exchange for a shorter sentence than they would
have gotten if found guilty. The reality is that many of those kids were often
innocent. They were just too poor to afford a proper defense. And, to my horror,
an astounding number of them 'took the plea.'

Prior to this experience, whenever I heard that someone took a plea, I would
assume that they must be guilty; after all, where there is smoke, there must
be fire. But this was victim blaming and realizing this made my body fill with
rage. I felt utterly helpless.

Throwing money at their defense was not a strategy for change; it was a
band-aid solution. Organizations like The Innocence Project, while tremendously helpful, are not enough. This beast was fueled by greed and hatred, and
it had to be lobotomized at its core. We had to inspire vast systemic changes
to save an entire generation of young people of color.

These events only furthered my drive to be a Change Maker, to help others
ensnared in this trap that is the US criminal justice system. Let me say, I take
objection with the use of the word 'justice' in the way this system is structured.
It serves no true justice, only undeserved leniency to those born of the appreciated color or wealth, or cruel punishment for those unfortunate enough to have
no influence, to be deemed unworthy of compassion. And what this translates
to is that justice is but a distant dream for millions of Americans.

Effecting changes in the US criminal legal system requires reformers in
office. We need to elect judges, district attorneys, and politicians with a vision

and commitment to implement the reforms our country desperately needs. We need them working to transform and decarcerate our criminal legal system if we hope to end unjust policing. By that I mean, people who are willing to decriminalize addiction, homelessness, and mental health impairments. Politicians bent on ending the cash bail system which sees people who have not been tried or convicted of anything imprisoned simply because they are too poor to afford bail. We need people who will create a path out for those who have served time, rather than life sentences for mere mistakes and minor misdemeanors. In effect, people who will spearhead a system rooted in restorative justice and rehabilitation.

The problems are widespread and affect all of us. Though it may seem that white Americans are largely unaffected by the growth of the for-profit prison industrial complex, the reality is that it has cheated us all. It has led to great misunderstanding and mistrust among one another as we all function from our level of perspective. Whites assumed a higher criminal inclination from their black countrymen, and blacks grew to distrust their white counterparts. In telling white friends of incidents I've experienced, I've always felt gaslighted by them. It was like they too believed that where there's smoke, there's fire, and you must have been doing something to be treated that way by law enforcement. It took me years to realize that we were simply living in two very different Americas with our individual experiences curated by very racist policy makers. In short, we have all been shortchanged by these policies. We have been hoodwinked.

Feeling compelled to make a change and be part of the solution, I attended a personal development training addressing the hate we encounter in the world and practiced transmuting it. These exercises were traumatizing. In one exercise, people physically attacked us. In another, we were verbally abused. And there was one where hands were placed around our necks and compressed until some of us lost consciousness. And for us, the only requirement was that we reach deep inside and show our attackers and abusers unconditional love. I clearly remember looking at my teammates and noticing the body postures and eyes while they played the role of the abusers. It wasn't that of strength, instead it was hurt and fear. And at that moment, my brain and heart fused in understanding. Despite the tears streaming down my face, I felt nothing but love, compassion, and empathy. On my knees, I looked into my teammate's eyes and started repeating, "I love you, I love you, I love you." She too fell to her knees and we embraced, sobbing in each other's arms in full awakening, awareness, and understanding. That training marked a turning point in my life. The realization that hurt people — hurt people. To this day, I still walk down the street silently sending love to everyone who crosses my path, seeing their spirit and human-ness instead of their physical form.

In learning to embrace love even under the most challenging of circumstances, I felt strangely powerful. You know the saying, "You don't have to attend every argument you're invited to?" For the first time, I realized that it really does take two people to tango, to get involved in physical conflict, and there is a better way, a higher way. I didn't have to meet hate with hate.

For me, it's about a daily choice to be a Change Maker. Every day I choose to be a beacon of light, hope, and love. Some days it's a struggle and I have to reach out and grab that state as it comes under threat of flying out the window. What came up for me in doubting my state was the realization that transformation is not anchored in any room like a table; it's a state of being. And just as feelings change, so can this and every other state. I have to hold it in my bosom and visualize it in the form of a light engulfing me, the room, my town, city, state, country, and the entire planet.

We need to embrace this broader understanding, especially when dealing with the wrath of righteous anger brought on by those lost on their path. Acknowledge your anger and work through it. Allow it to be transmuted into a force for good. To get to this point, I had to allow myself to feel every aspect of wrath, the constant pain in my neck and throat, and loss of my voice as I was not speaking my truth around this feeling. I had to allow it to consume me until it burned to the ground and then rose like the phoenix into its new form of hope and healing and forgiveness.

Immersing myself into the teachings of the great prophets and Change Makers like Bishop Desmond Tutu, Nelson Mandela, and Martin Luther King Jr., who all volunteered for the sacred task of teaching love and healing to this much-suffering world, Ignites me. Through their actions they taught us that we cannot heal this planet when we are coming from a place of hate and anger. Just as we volunteer to be healers and midwives birthing a new consciousness, those lost souls were assigned to teach us patience and forgiveness as we witness their misdeeds.

Change requires us to look at what's difficult and what needs to be transformed. I invite you to focus on the vision of the world you would like to see. Focus on justice and equality rather than its negative forms. The solution resides in a higher level of consciousness. How can I transmute all this anger into light? How can I assist in transforming this world from greed-fueled and fear-based into a love-based reality? How can I assist in the collective healing of this planet? This in no way calls for a lack of accountability from those who enacted and continue to benefit from these brutal practices. It doesn't require that you seek out the company or support those who cause such pain and suffering. It doesn't mean that we continue relationships or refuse to seek legal or financial redress. It simply means that you have brought clarity, healing, and truth to a situation that was brought into your life. That you *acknowledge* the lesson.

I do not claim to have the answer to fairness and social justice; it's certainly more complex than I can get out in this story and the answer resides in a place of empathy, fairness, compassion, love, understanding, and forgiveness. I encourage you to look at this through the lens of a Change Maker, first changing yourself and then turning that outward, onto the world.

Ignite Action Steps

- Read the works of Ta'Neshi Coates, Michelle Alexander, and Shaun King and learn more about the current state of systematic racism.

- View the films *13th* and the documentary *When They See Us* by Ava Duvernay which speaks more about how slavery is perpetuated to this day.

- Support and donate to the organization RealJusticePAC which focuses on electing reform-minded individuals on a path to restorative justice.

- Donate to The Innocence Project that frees people who are wrongfully incarcerated.

- Participate in local and national elections to elect judges, district attorneys, and politicians focused on change.

- Follow my FaceBook page *Change Makers Living Boldly* that empowers and uplifts individuals and features positive changes on the planet.

Hermian Charles - Grenada & United States
The Unicorn Social Activist & Change Maker
HermianCharles@Yahoo.com

Vivien Hunt

"Change liberates Possibility."

My wish for you is to know that whether you put yourself in the flow of change or choose to wait or resist it, it's already happening. The fact that you are aware of a shift means it's already guiding your story with the potential to connect to all your experiences and to others. Trust that the process of change is working for you and through change you are free to liberate possibility.

Being OK with Uncertainty

How is it that in 2020, people around the world still go to work only to end each day feeling discouraged, disengaged, or disempowered? Compounding over time, too many of these empty feelings can only serve to whittle down the human spirit.

In working with leaders, their teams and organizations, I get to facilitate change and help to create healthier work cultures and happier workplaces. I don't necessarily consider myself a pioneer in this work, yet more often than not when I encounter resistance, a feeling arises in me that I must be ahead of my time.

To be an agent of change, you must be willing to live at the frontline of resistance. Resistance which inevitably shows up in one form or another. So to be resilient to this resistance, you definitely need to develop a superpower.

My superpower is to see the patterns and notice the incongruities, by observing what's working and not working. I have an awareness of what could make a difference and am respectful of the degree of openness in people or readiness to change. I'm also not afraid of the uncertainty change may bring, knowing to trust that things have their own way of working out. Superpowers like mine don't simply appear; they emerge through a long series of life events, which, if those events were to be unravelled, would lead me right back 30 years almost to the day.

Only synchrodestiny can explain how I came to be in Cape Town, South Africa on February 11, 1990. I was standing in the dusty street of the Grayhound terminal, waiting to board my bus to take the long 16-hour journey back to Johannesburg. In the heat of the afternoon, the driver unexpectedly announced there would be an unknown delay. Unknown? What exactly did that mean? No one seemed to have any answers, but it soon became apparent that something was about to disrupt what had been until then a very ordinary day.

A restlessness stirred in the air. My energy shifted and I no longer noticed the hot sun or dusty streets but became increasingly aware of people moving. Moving tranquilly in the same direction, walking past the bus terminal, past me.

At first, it was just a whisper floating above the streets. If you listened carefully enough, you might just catch the word 'Madiba,' murmured softly through the air, lightly hovering. 'Madiba' passed like a childhood secret from one ear to the next. A nervous giggle of delight. Did no one dare to speak out his name, in case the secret was not true?

"What's going on?" I asked a man walking past. He looked at me and his face lit up as he smiled. I saw the joy in his eyes as he said, "Madiba is free," and continued walking. I paused a few seconds to take in the significance of these words. *Madiba* was the name by which Nelson Mandela was called, an endearing name meaning *father*. This was the reverence I witnessed as people walked through the streets, as if awoken from a dream.

Now, if you know your history, you'll know that Mandela had been in prison for 27 years. No one had seen him for much of that time; he was more myth than man. Some stories convinced the public he may even be dead, so to see him at all was something of a disbelief. He truly would be the sign to mark the end of apartheid.

"How long have I got?" I asked the driver. He shrugged his shoulders and that's all I needed. I grabbed my bag and jumped into the street to join the flow of entranced people. As I followed, the pace quickened; clearly word had gotten out.

We were moving toward Cape Town's old town hall, a big town square where, according to rumors, Mandela was due to appear. His release was completely unexpected, unannounced to the world until that very afternoon. No one knew at what time he would appear, but he was expected to speak and I wanted to be there, waiting in the square, waiting to see him.

I had a strange sense of excitement and caution at the same time. South Africa was a turbulent place, a place of uncertainty where you never quite knew what could happen next. I observed the euphoria of people moving, singing, and dancing. My own spirit felt alive and hopeful.

It wasn't long until streams of people started flowing toward the town hall, hoping to get a glimpse of the man no one had seen for almost three decades. Hundreds, then thousands gathered; some newspapers later reported 100,000 people waited in anticipation that afternoon.

The energy of the crowd was building, bubbling energy with nowhere to go. Waiting, waiting. The town square created a container for the excitement which was increasingly rising. Rising, rising.

Yet silence; I only remember silence, observing so many people… excited, hopeful, anxious, nervous. Wondering when he would show. Hopeful and present to the moment. I couldn't get closer than the bottom corner of the square, already packed with people shoulder to shoulder.

Suddenly, on my left, I heard a sharp bang. A man abruptly pushed me aside while people started to scramble. The situation changed almost instantly; glass flying, a number of shop windows were smashed and people started grabbing, looting the small stores underneath the archway which led into the bottom corner of the square. People ran in all directions creating chaos. In a split second, my vision of seeing Mandela vanished and my only thought was safety. I ran past the looters, who took no notice of me, past the police who were rapidly approaching with full force, and ran all the way back down Station Road to the Grayhound bus terminal. As if none of the last hours had happened, I jumped on my bus which was ready to depart and spent the night traveling back to Johannesburg, stunned and disappointed.

"A DAY OF SEISMIC CHANGE," journalists reported.

I learned the following day that Mandela's motorcade had been blocked by people along the streets desperate to see him. For several hours, his car could not advance through to the square. Had I stayed, I would have spent several long hours waiting in the hot sun and chaos as Mandela only appeared on the town hall balcony to address the crowds shortly after 8 PM. What I also learned was that the police had panicked when the looting had started, opened fire to disperse the crowd, killed at least two people and injured at least a hundred.

For me, the awareness that came with that day made visible the joys and struggles that arise to achieve change. That being part of a positive vision, with a wave of people who share a common experience, includes hope, excitement, fear, and uncertainty.

After that day in the square, I was fortunate to see Mandela speak several times at my university. These were seemingly ordinary days, but for anyone who cared to see it, a new vision of what was possible was coming into view. What drew me to his words was his calmness and the reassuring strength in his voice of hope and imminent change. I always came away feeling inspired and grateful, yet largely unaware of the scale and pace of change that rippled behind the scenes of day-to-day life.

Four years later, in April 1994, I stepped forward as an Electoral Monitor for South Africa's first ever democratic election. Together with my sister Sophia, working at a polling station for three days and three nights, we were kept on high alert while the country held its breath, suspended between hope and chaos, on the brink of unrest. For me, the uncertainty served to heighten my awareness. My experience felt surreal where everything moved in slow motion, observing as if watching a movie. What emotions I was feeling, I cannot precisely say, my insignificance magnified by the magnitude of change in which we were all submerged.

Surprisingly, the three days were remarkably peaceful. The resistance and fear, which had been anticipated, were unfounded. Mandela was elected as our new president and a new constitution came into effect on April 27, 1994, now celebrated as Freedom Day.

"A DAY OF MONUMENTAL AND HISTORIC CHANGE," journalists reported.

Being witness to a new South Africa shaped my appreciation of change and transformation, and my view that everything *is* possible. Change is a process, not just one day or one moment in time. It's all the moments that, when strung together, can create something new, powerful, and hopefully even better than what is experienced today.

With that hope, I moved to London and began working on business transformation projects in Europe. It wasn't long however until I felt disconnected from South Africa. Curiously one day, the question I had already begun to ask myself appeared in an ad in the Guardian newspaper.

"HOW CAN WE SUPPORT SOUTH AFRICA FROM AFAR?" This question guided me to co-found the UK charity *The Gumboots Foundation*.

The charity supports projects for children and education in a disadvantaged community on the outskirts of Johannesburg with over 1,000 beneficiaries every year. Creating and building Gumboots reconnected me with South Africa, gave me purposeful work and felt good to intentionally contribute firsthand and make a positive impact.

For many years, the charity energized and fulfilled me, but it wasn't until I trained as a leadership coach over ten years later that my superpowers came alive. I felt inspired to run leadership programs for kids and adults in the community supported by Gumboots. By me choosing to show up for participants, the programs filled with individuals hungry for new learning and opportunities, and from somewhere inside me my creativity flowed, allowing me to see the hopes, dreams, fears and joys of the people I worked with.

During the leadership program, our closing ritual was for each person to share two minutes of feedback with every other participant in the group, expressing what they did well and what they'd like to see more of. This was the gift we gave to each other and learned to give and receive. When it came time to offer this feedback to one particular teenage girl, I looked at her quiet face and shy eyes and sensed no one had ever told her how *amazing* she was. In acknowledging her for her qualities, her smile, her laughter, her voice, I witnessed the tears well up from inside her as *she had been seen*. I noticed how her eyes shone more brightly in response to having someone believe in her. This moment stayed with me, knowing that I can create positive change by helping to Ignite the spark that lights up someone's eyes when they feel hope, joy or self-belief.

"A DAY OF DEEP INTERNAL AND LASTING CHANGE," as reported by me.

What if we all knew that just by passing on hope, joy and belief, we could change our entire experience, environment, or impact? *These are the gifts* by which the reverence of endearment unfolds. Being a Change Maker for me is to create little changes over time that have the potential to liberate big positive impact for you and those around you. Incremental change can lead to exponential change. We are all part of a larger story and that means working with both big and small changes.

My superpowers allow me to support others in building encouragement, engagement, and empowerment. For any of us to show up fully, we need to feel safe, seen, connected, and cared for. Working with leaders, I get to witness firsthand the impact they can make when they show up willing to care, build trust, and believe in their people.

Surely it doesn't take an injustice on the scale of apartheid to advocate for change. Are we waiting for someone to show up for us or are we ready to take the lead?

Whether you choose to show up intentionally or the Universe puts you there, know that you are part of a much bigger story than your own. All our individual moments of change are connected to other people's individual moments of change and, *together*, have the potential to create a wave of positive impact far greater than anything we could ever do on our own.

Ignite Action Steps

My invitation to you is to consciously create ways to show up and experience more positive impact in your day-to-day life. If you feel good, this will ripple out within your organization, family, relationships, and circle right back to your life at home.

One aspect of my work as a leadership coach is to build awareness around healthy and unhealthy behaviors. You may not always recognize the unhealthy ones as, traditionally, some of them have been reinforced or even rewarded. Once you know that behaviors such as judging, excluding, dictating, and limiting (yourself or others) create a toxic environment both externally and internally (on a physiological level), you may choose to simply 'Do less of them.' Likewise, the healthy behaviors that make you feel good on both an emotional and physiological level can make you stronger and even help you to live longer! Notice when these behaviors show up and simply choose to 'Do more of them.'

Your challenge is to make a list of 10 ways to demonstrate and practice daily each of the following behaviors (take into consideration yourself and others):

- Appreciate
- Include
- Expand
- Share
- Discover
- Develop
- Celebrate

Together with your team, colleagues or family, choose the behavior that will make the biggest positive impact for everyone, and consciously and intentionally practice it for a week. After one week, start a conversation to build awareness: What's different? What's working well? What would we like to see or do more of? Then make a commitment as to what you all will do differently, by when and how.

Repeat the process with the next behavior, and so on, to eventually practice each one. What may seem simple can actually create a big impact!

Vivien Hunt - United Kingdom & South Africa
Leadership and Executive Coach
www.leadsourcecoaching.com

BEEJAL COULSON

"Life is a series of lessons and blessings."

My deepest desire is to inspire you to dive into a journey of self discovery, set authentic intentions, and tap into your inner guidance. Take inspired action and trust that you will be guided to live a life on your terms that you love, love, and love.

ALIGNING TO BE ME

My heart fluttered as I looked out at the audience. I felt like I was a singer, with waves of people in front of me, and I was so excited to be there. I was on stage with a translator teaching 350 professors, lecturers, and students about the latest in fashion marketing and advertising trends. I had been invited to be a guest lecturer for a week in a university in Brazil during Sao Paolo fashion week. It was the highlight of my lecturing career. I had loved researching, putting together, and preparing the presentations enhanced with my creativity. It was exciting to share the results with passion to such an amazing audience. There was music, clips from films, lots of photographs and visuals. It was an incredible performance that I had put together. I was no ordinary lecturer! The feeling inside of me as the presentation ended was a pure rush of energy filled with joy as the audience stood up and applauded excitedly in a standing ovation.

My life as a lecturer, 14 years on, was usually far removed from this amazing experience. The closest I got was when I was invited to teach at a university in the south of France for a week every year. I had the ability to create, disseminate, and present information in ways that made it easier, exciting, and interesting to learn. This is what I was great at. Teaching empowered me to support and inspire students. I knew this was aligned with my life purpose, which was to make a positive difference to the lives of others.

Unfortunately, I had fallen out of love with the daily grind of teaching. Feeling depleted from giving with very limited receiving, there was little flow. All the amazing work I did with the students and businesses seemed to go unnoticed. The workload increased, the students got more demanding, their behavior more entitled, and I found myself working way beyond my contracted hours. There had been a couple of attempts on my part to start up new businesses in coaching and fashion, but I did not have the energy to sustain them. There were so many more responsibilities now, but I was not brave enough to walk away and start over like I had in the past. I literally sensed my soul crying every time I drove into work. It felt like I was barely holding things together. Continuing on as I was, it was not possible to envision a long-term future.

Over the years, everything had spun out of control with an ensuing deterioration in my health. The constant stress I experienced as work conditions were increasingly demanding exacerbated the symptoms to the point where it became unbearable for me. I had two autoimmune conditions. One of them, I had lived with for the duration of my entire teaching career; the other, I had just recently been diagnosed with. My body had been whispering signs to me for some time. It started shouting and I lost the ability to digest food. Eventually, it screamed and yelled. This didn't happen in isolation; there were events at work that kept triggering my mind and body's responses, culminating in a total breakdown. I was signed off sick by my doctor, declared unfit to work.

I had hit rock bottom. The medical world had given its diagnosis and prognosis. These autoimmune conditions were chronic and likely to get worse. Additionally, the only solution recommended to me for anxiety was chemical antidepressants.

Four months later, I was relaxing on the lounger by the swimming pool at my health spa, coloring in an elephant in an exquisitely-designed mindfulness book using Japanese water brush pens. Coloring helped me be present. It calmed and quieted my mind so much that I had made it a daily practice. It was in this moment of solitude by the pool that I felt my mind and body starting to speak to me. My inner spirit declared to the Universe that I could no longer continue as I had been.

I decided enough was enough. I had not signed up for this. It was not how I had envisioned my life would turn out. I did not wish to believe the prognosis or take antidepressants. I wanted to heal. Things were going to have to change, and I was going to have to be the one to take charge and get in the driving seat of my life.

A *powerful* feeling blossomed in my solar plexus. I felt the wisdom of a deep inner knowing that I needed to design a life that served me first and foremost. It was a rare and powerful moment of clarity for me. It was as though I was making a silent prayer of my intentions to the Universe about creating a life on my terms.

Above all, I yearned for my health back. What is life without health? I had been feeling an inkling of this for a while, an awareness that grew in bits and pieces. But for the first time in this moment, I felt as if I were in the deep end of the pool, that I *knew* how meaningless life would be without my health. I committed to learning as much as I could about holistic health care and made self-care my highest priority. I was aware that the intentions I desired had been inspired by a Japanese concept that I had taught to my post-graduate Organizational Psychology students called *Ikigai*, which means 'reason for being' or 'what makes life worth living.' *Ikigai* is the point where your passion, mission, calling, and craft intersect. *Ikigai* is the process of allowing the self's possibilities to blossom. And through *Ikigai*, I found myself starting to pull together the various threads of myself.

Looking back on my life, I had found the courage to walk away many times before when

I felt what I was doing was no longer aligning with who I was becoming. I changed to a Business degree part way after studying Chemistry. I left a job in advertising media post MBA, after a short time, the career path too restrictive for my interests. After seven years, anticipating burnout, I resigned from a career in Fashion Marketing Academia to travel the world. I knew I had to listen to the signs from my inner self and body and took action to leave. Each time, I reinvented myself and went on to do greater things. I had to ask myself what prevented me from leaving? In short, I had deceived myself. I was living my purpose, but it was at a cost to my mental health and well-being. It took my mind and body putting me in a crisis for me to actually listen, learn, and change.

It was clear to me I did not want to continue with my lecturing profession. I knew I still wanted to help people and inspire them to make a difference. I had a strong feeling that my next purpose was still unfolding and was connected to my healing journey. Whatever I did, I wanted autonomy. I needed the freedom to work smart, work less, create impact, be valued, feel rewarded, and have a work-life balance so that I was not working to live. These intentions were authentic to me, but I did not know how they were going to manifest.

I knew I needed to honor and nourish my soul through creativity. Music, painting, drumming, dancing... I had deprived myself of these because they did not seem important to someone living with responsibilities. When I was a child, these passions were not cultivated. Culturally, I was brought up being told that pursuing my love for art and music would never result in a favorable career. Today, I know better.

It seemed like the Universe listened to my prayer and conspired with my inner guide to help me realize my intentions with some surprising synchronicities. In the search for prioritizing my health through natural healing, I received an email inviting me to apply to train in a specialized form of Transformational Hypnotherapy. I didn't even need to research it; I just felt it was a deeply powerful method, and not only was it going to help me, I would be able to help others and earn a living from it. I was accepted into the deep immersion course and within a couple of months, I had new letters after my name and was qualified as a Certified Hypnotherapist. I didn't return to lecturing.

Soon after the training course, I committed to my own healing with continued subconscious regression and mind reprogramming, I felt mentally and emotionally liberated from the anxiety and autoimmune conditions. I understood the root causes of them, most of which were formed in utero and in early childhood. My healing journey was further supported with meditation, yoga, breath therapy, and sound healing. I invested in an infrared cocoon and a collection of essential oils. I consulted a nutritional therapist to address the chemical imbalances in my body.

I created a therapy practice at home, and felt elated as my business went global and thrived like wildfire. It helped that I had managed a coaching and fashion business before. I had mastered the tools to uncover root emotional cause and limiting beliefs, and reprogram the mind to healthier ideals. I helped clients overcome fears and phobias, anxiety and depression, be symptom free from chronic medical conditions, lose weight, gain confidence. I supported clients with cancer, heart conditions and those going through fertility treatment. I was a healer! With continuing professional development, I proceeded to qualify as a Clinical Hypnotherapist a year later.

I became a master and a work in progress at the same time.

In this new career, it soon became clear that it was essential that I looked after myself so I could hold space for my clients. I continued to heal, learn, and evolve every day. I restricted the days I worked and the number of clients per week. I swam daily, joined art class and took up African drumming. I regularly attended workshops on health and wellness, and meditation retreats. I took holidays in the sun and went on short city breaks often. This change, not only in career but in my whole life, led to feeling that I was in alignment and I was achieving a work-life balance on my terms. I didn't just want to make a difference to the lives of others, I also wanted to make a difference to *my* life. My mission was evolving!

Clients started asking me to help them discover their purpose, gain clarity on their future and unlock their full potential once they had overcome their challenges. I reflected on my life and the subconscious intentions I had made over the years and realized how they had led me here all along. I became more fascinated with learning about energy and the superconscious mind. I delved into books, research papers and documentaries, attended workshops and events on neuroscience, neuroplasticity, and quantum physics. The quote "If you wish to understand the universe, think of energy, frequency and vibration." by Nikola Tesla had a powerful influence. Curiosity developed especially with my work with vision boards and I experimented with the format when leading workshops in vision boarding for clients.

The deep exploration and experimentation resulted in the creation of a process that led people into their future to discover their highest potentials and embody them in their daily lives. I experimented on myself, my family and any willing clients. It was absolutely amazing and so exciting every time I did a session. To step into the unknown and experience future potentials beyond the mind's imagination was incredible. Each person had the answers from within to their purpose, their passion, their calling and gifts. The inner experience was so profound for them, it was captured and re-experienced daily until it was programmed into their minds. By doing this, the future had no choice but to magically draw itself to them on a fast track. It was like experiencing the life of your wildest dreams, connected to your soul's purpose, and heart's desires all encompassed.

I did a future life session for a colleague living in Australia who had trained with me in Hypnotherapy. She had complex multiple medical issues with recurring symptoms. While she had benefited greatly from the hypnotherapy we had trained in, she was open to having me work on her future with her. I could sense she was exhausted with revisiting her traumatic childhood. My curiosity wondered if she would be free of her symptoms when she was experiencing her future potential. Indeed she was! As we worked together, I could literally feel her positive vibes over the internet! At the end of her session she felt elated and empowered. She asked me if I realized that what I had actually created was super powerful and could potentially positively impact so many lives. I knew deep within this was the case, but hearing it from someone who was also a well-respected therapist and coach made me believe in its validity.

My colleague's results were positive on all levels — physically, mentally and emotionally. She kept repeating she wanted to use the method with her clients and asking if I would be open to training her. She was even willing to travel to the UK to train with me. I was not ready; at least, I thought I was not ready! I was still fine-tuning the process and wanted more case studies. There was also a book I needed to write about it all! Soon after I shared from my heart in a podcast interview about my new creation, and the interviewer, who was a coach based in Sweden, expressed an interest in experiencing it and wanting to train in it! My colleagues in the therapy/coaching industry heard the podcast, many admitting they listened to it twice, as it was so good! I discovered there were more therapists and coaches who wanted to train in my modality, which still didn't even have a name! I knew I was inciting change in both me and something that would Ignite others.

Six months later, in a beautiful hotel in St. Albans, my hometown in the UK, my face radiated with pride as I awarded certificates to the very first group of international practitioners in Quantum Life Technique™(QLT). My heart was bursting with happiness. I could feel energy dancing with joy in and around my body. These few days were purely magical. Time stood still and I had felt so much in flow, doing what I loved and loving what I did. The mission of this magical and powerful modality was given expression — to help raise the collective consciousness of the planet. These practitioners were going to be ambassadors and enable this mission on a global level.

It was important for me to walk my talk and I felt strongly that anyone who would train in QLT would benefit from fully experiencing it themselves. If I and the practitioners could be the example to clients by raising our vibration and consciousness, aligning to our highest potentials, then we would be great role models for leading the way to self discovery and empowered lives.

I regained my mental health and well-being with more energy and vitality than I had experienced for a long time. Activating my intuitive and energy healing gifts enhanced my work as a therapist. I created a pioneering modality that raises the consciousness of individuals and empowers them to lead their best lives. I set up a training academy to teach, mentor, and support others who also wanted to be a part of this mission. I fulfilled the lifelong dream of a second home by the sea in Majorca, Spain. It has been deeply fulfilling to transform the lives of hundreds of people across the world.

As I evolve, my potential expands. Once expanded, I evolve some more, and my potential expands *even* more...

Everything we experience in life is a lesson or a blessing. Challenges are opportunities for us to change, transform, and evolve. Each one of us has the potential for greatness. We hold in ourselves limitless abilities and boundless opportunities. When we choose to step into the power of who we really are (Female Change Makers), we activate our highest potentials and align to them and become the very best versions of ourselves.

Ignite Action Steps

Take daily inspired action to raise your energy and vibration.

Go Within. Connect with your inner self for at least 20-30 minutes daily. Meditate, walk in nature, listen to relaxing music, swim, draw, paint.

Gratitude. Choose experiences/things/people you are grateful for. For each one, identify what it is, visualize it, and then feel the feeling in your body.

Visualization. Create a scene in your mind as if you are living the life you love. Incorporate as much vivid detail and tune in to as many senses as you can, especially into how you feel. Visualize and replay the scene, giving gratitude in advance.

Affirm several times a day, "Everything magically works out for me."

Beejal Coulson - United Kingdom,
Creator / Founder of Quantum Life Technique,
Clinical Hypnotherapist, Author
www.beejalcoulson.com

ANDREA DRAJEWICZ

*"Teach your children to change the world by
changing the world with your children."*

**I believe our children have the power to change the world. Children notice
things around them and they have a deep desire to change the injustices
they see. When adults provide support and encouragement, kids come to
understand themselves as Change Makers. We can all be Change Makers
regardless of age. I hope my story inspires you to solve injustices that
touch you. I want you to know that you have within you everything you
need to change the world. Change requires action, not necessarily big but
intentional actions infused with joy. You *can* make a difference and find
joy in doing it.**

TURNING CHILDREN INTO CHANGE MAKERS

There is a wig lying on my bed just below my pillow. To be fair, it's not
really my bed. It's not my pillow, nor my wig, either. I've taken time off work
to visit my parents and the bed is the one that graces their guest room, my home
away from home for the past two weeks. And someone else's hair is lying on it.

A dozen someones, if you want to get technical about it. The wig is made
of real human hair and it takes up to a dozen hair donations to construct a
single wig. And now those dozen people's hair is puddled on the quilt inches
from where I've been resting my head each night. The sight of it brings up a
complicated rush of emotions that range from sadness to fear to pride.

Most of all, that wig makes me proud.

Not that precise wig; but rather, the thought of it, of everything it represents, and the memory of the moment my soul was awakened to a truth that changed the way I look at the world. At how I look at children. At how I look at myself. It was a wig that taught me the most profound lesson I have ever learned.

A decade ago, as Mama to two young children, I was thinking a lot about how to teach them to be problem solvers. Not necessarily world-changing problem solvers, though that would be marvelous, just little-problem problem solvers. In some areas, our family was really good at this but in others... not so much. Every family is much the same I think. Good at creating independence in some of the little things... and in some of the big things... but somehow never quite getting as good at this as we wished.

I've always been envious of people whose children hand out birthday party invitations that say things like "instead of gifts, please make a donation to *Save the Sharks*" or some other cause... *and mean it.* Their kids genuinely do *not* want material gifts; they're excited to be giving up all personal gain for a cause they're not only just sort of vaguely aware of, *they're actually incredibly passionate about it!* How does one get a child like that? Are some children just born selfless?

One of the people who tops my Most-Inspirational-People-Of-All-Time list is Rachel Coleman of *Signing Time* fame. She is one of those women who you can't help but look at and exclaim, "Wow! How do you do it?" She is Mom to two beautiful girls. Inspired by her oldest daughter who is deaf, she created the *Signing Time* DVD series, teaching sign language to hearing families to eliminate barriers of communication for deaf children. As if that isn't enough, she also started the Signing Time Foundation, inspired by her younger daughter who has cerebral palsy, spearheading projects like inclusive summer camps and the construction of wheelchair-accessible parks. And she does it all with so much joy!

The thing that has always struck me the most about Rachel Coleman is that, no matter the challenge she faces, no matter how emotionally difficult, she not only picks herself up and carries on, she sees in it an opportunity for change and reaches out with both hands to make our world a better place. Somewhere, somehow, she learned that she has the power not only to make her own life the best it can be, but to make as much of the world as she can reach the best it can be, too. I wanted to know how I could learn that; more importantly, how I could teach that to my children.

And then the Universe dropped an opportunity into my lap. I started helping another fantastic mom and her three daughters as they set about changing just one person's life with a small project that grew and grew, showing me that you learn to be a Change Maker by simply trying to make change and that you teach your children how by involving them in making change right along with you. And it all started with a wig.

In 2008, my neighbor and dear friend Sharon and her middle daughter Catherine, then seven years old, decided to donate their hair for wigs for cancer patients. Our kids all attended the same school together and our families were close. That particular year, two of the kids in Catherine's grade had been missing an awful lot of school. They both were fighting cancer.

Cancer is a hard thing for a child to understand. More so when they see kids the same age as themselves lose their energy, lose weight, lose their hair. We all feel powerless when faced with cancer but none more so than a seven-year-old child watching a friend slowly die. No mother likes to see their child hurting, physically or emotionally, and my friend Sharon is no different. One crisp winter afternoon, walking home from school, she suggested to her daughter that perhaps they could donate their hair to make wigs for cancer patients as a way of taking positive action.

Making a wig is not a simple endeavor, especially one made of human hair. And it takes *a lot* of hair! A single wig needs up to a dozen donations, each donation a minimum of 8½ inches long, a length that takes two or more years' time to grow. When Sharon and Catherine discovered this, they figured they had better get a few more people involved. They started a blog and sent emails to the school, hoping to get at least enough donated hair for a single wig. The first blog post was humble in the extreme:

"This will be a terrific mother/daughter thing for us to do and, just maybe, we can help a lot more people if we pass the word along and get other people to donate their hair at the same time."

They asked me for my support making posters and flyers to advertise their initiative. I jumped on board, happy to help a friend. I didn't realize the impact that seemingly simple decision was going to have on my life. I just thought it would be great if they could get enough donations to make a wig; I was not yet invested.

The day of the hair donation event turned into a giant party. The hair salon was absolutely overflowing with people. Kids and families crowded the room and spilled out into the parking lot where a couple of party tents and a barbecue were set up. Everywhere you looked, people were smiling and there was this tremendously contagious *energy* in the air that I could almost feel dancing on my skin. Adults chatted happily while their children raced around with glee, getting their faces painted, eating popcorn and hamburgers, and sharing a celebratory cake. The local newspaper took dozens of photos and the grownups attached to those kids did their share of speechifying and beaming with pride.

Between classmates of Catherine's, friends, neighbors, and word-of-mouth, they ended up with 46 hair donations, $3500 in monetary donations to the Canadian Cancer Society, and a whole gaggle of little girls sporting matching t-shirts, brand-new bobbed haircuts, and enormous smiles.

Those 46 donations resulted in only three wigs. Just three.

After the mad crazy rush of 'donation day' and all the excitement that transpired, I felt hollow inside when I thought of the hours upon hours we had spent together plotting and planning, designing a logo and a t-shirt, reaching out to businesses and community papers for free advertising and donations... Five months of effort and the involvement of over a hundred people for just three wigs. We had done a fantastic thing together. We had connected so many people and kids to a great cause. And it was nowhere near enough to make a difference. My heart was torn between pride and dismay.

Later that year, one of the children with cancer died. The family planted a tree in the schoolyard and installed a plaque my kids and I walked past every morning on our way to class, a sad and lonely reminder of a vibrant life that used to be. My children, saddened by the sight of the plaque, asked many questions and we talked often of the day they had helped Catherine out. Catherine had become a hero in their mind's eye — a Change Maker in their own neighborhood. It planted a seed in all of us.

A year later almost to the day, we went back to the same hair salon to do it all again, this time with Catherine's older sister donating her hair along with many of her friends. We dove into the project with enthusiasm, updating the posters, soliciting donations, and enticing more people to join us.

And it worked — 110 hair donations and over $18,000 donated to the Canadian Cancer Society. That was *110 people*, the vast majority of them little girls, some as young as five years old, donating the very hair on their heads to someone they didn't even know and probably would never see, and they did it joyfully. My daughter was one of the people who happily donated hair that year. So was I.

Nine wigs. I remember standing in the salon that day and running my hands over the neat row of plastic bags that held all the neatly bound ponytails ready for delivery. They filled the counter from one end to the other, 110 of them in a long line. It was easy to pick out the soft brown twist of curls that belonged to my daughter — the hair that I loved to run through my fingers as she cuddled up against me for a story. The hair that I had stuck my nose into so many times, inhaling deeply of the essence that was her. I was so proud of her for doing this, so filled with a buoyant excitement at what we had accomplished, but also still struggling to reconcile the large scale of the event with how small an impact we actually made; more than the year before, but still only nine wigs.

We did it again one more time with Sharon's youngest daughter in the spotlight before they decided to retire the campaign. Over the three years, over two hundred ponytails were collected to be made into wigs and *thousands* of dollars were donated to the cancer society — $27,434 to be precise. By then I had grown used to the idea that each donation was merely a tiny drop in the ocean of need and knowing we had finished filled me with a sort of quiet sadness; a bittersweet knowledge that our changemaking days, as insignificant as they had felt, were done.

But people kept calling. People kept donating their ponytails, even without the campaign, and then emailing us to let us know what they had done. People who wouldn't have thought twice about leaving their locks on the floor of the hair salon to be swept into a pile destined for the landfill now flooded my inbox to ask where they could donate their ponytails instead. Some were friends, but most were the parents of my children's classmates asking how they could honor their child's desire to help out, too. All had been touched by what we had done and wanted to keep it going. For the first time since starting this entire adventure, I understood that this thing I had been a part of had Ignited a spark in all of us. Where I had thought we had done so little, in truth, we had done so very much, and the thought of it kindled a flame of fierce joy in the space behind my ribcage. We had taught the children that they had the power to change the world and now they were asking the adults to help them make it happen again. There was no doubt in my mind anymore about whether we had done enough; we had inspired the next generation to be Change Makers and *that* felt amazing!

The year after *Catherine's Pretty Ponytails* ended, my daughter and I danced our way into the hair salon and, for the second time in my life, I had the distinct joy of watching my baby girl gift a part of herself to someone she doesn't know and will never meet. She did it without prompting — I never asked her to, I merely told her I was going to and let her make up her own mind.

As a Mama, there is nothing quite like watching your child's expression turn to one of wonder and pride as they thrill with the knowledge that they have done something important. That they have made a difference. My daughter changed the world when she was seven and she was so proud of it, and just a little bit in awe of it. As her Mama, I was a little bit in awe, too. But the funny thing is that once a child knows that they have the power to change the world, they keep on trying to change it! Through *Catherine's Pretty Ponytails*, my children learned firsthand that changing the world is well within their capabilities and it inspired them to keep on being Change Makers.

My daughter did it again that year, giving up her birthday gifts in favor of donations to *Charity:Water*. And then her Christmas gifts. And then her birthday gifts again. She has collected money for the *Humane Society* and *Portage Over Poverty*, too. Thousands of dollars and two wells later, she is proud of her world changing. My son is a Change Maker for the *Heart and Stroke Foundation*, for *Unicef*, and has walked mile after mile for hours on end for *Relay for Life*, first at the age of 10 and then again in every single one of his teenage years. Thousands of dollars later, he is proud of his world changing, too. Before *Catherine's Pretty Ponytails*, if you had asked me what it takes to raise world-changing children, I would have ummed and uuhhhed and told you something about meaningful teaching and exposure to opportunities or some such rot. It's all true I suppose, but somehow I just *knew* that the old saw *be the change* mostly meant to be kind. The Rachel Colemans of the world I put in a category that included 'never someone ordinary like me.' Had you asked me, "Can a seven-year-old girl convince *more than 200* of her classmates, neighbors, and even complete strangers to cut off their hair and donate $27,434?" I would have laughed in outright skepticism.

The wig on the guest room bed is a sign. A reminder that children can do the hard work — the *necessary* work — of making a difference; that they can be Change Makers. I pick up the wig and hold it in my hands, turning it over and over as I think about all that it represents. My mom has always had the most beautiful hair. Long and blonde, at times bleached almost white by the sun, other times a darker creamy gold. It has flirted with her shoulders for as long as I can remember. As a child of three or four, I can remember reading the words 'golden spun flax' in a fairy tale and thinking it must mean something like my mom's hair. I was always envious of it, wishing my own mouse-brown locks were nearly as pretty. Now ravaged by chemotherapy, Mom looks both the same as ever and yet so very different. Her beautiful hair is gone but the clear blue eyes and quick laugh are not. The wig in my hand makes her feel more like herself when she wears it, this collection of hair from a dozen other people sewn into something resembling the way her own used to be. It is not new, this wig. Others have worn it before and then, no longer needing it, passed it on. Holding it in my hands, I wonder if some of it might have come from Catherine's baby sister, a blonde.

Sharon and her daughters taught me that even a seven-year-old girl with a small idea can become a Change Maker. I learned that you don't need to be a superhero; you just need to be willing to put yourself out there and work with intention to make change. You can embody the ability to rise to not only meet any challenge but take it further and make a lasting mark on the world in the process. You can teach yourself and your children to change the world by changing the world with your children.

I *am* a Change Maker. So are your children. So are you!

IGNITE ACTION STEPS

Open a conversation with the young people in your life. Ask them what is bothering them in the world, what cause matters to them, what injustice they see that they wish could be fixed. Listen hard. Together, think up ways you could make a difference, even a tiny one, and give them the choice of what to do next. *Then do it.* Paint posters together to raise awareness. Start an online fundraiser. Start an in-person fundraising event. Start whatever crazy notion they have in their heads. Involve them in every step of the process, in every decision, in every action. And have that same conversation with yourself, bringing them along and letting them see you stepping up, using your voice, and taking action.

Andrea Drajewicz - Canada
Writer, Editor, Mama, and Girl Guide Leader
🐦 *@Joyful_Writer*
📷 *@andreacookie8*

DIANA BORGES

"It is in our deepest challenges that we learn the most about life; Forever Learn, Forever Grow."

My intention is that the story of my metamorphosis Ignites changes for you to progress on your own evolutionary path. I want you to know the experiences and false stories from your childhood do not dictate your world. When you are connected to your heart and soul you are more powerful than what you have been told. Embrace the strength and wisdom inside to rejuvenate and rise to the greatest version of you. My hope is for you to be a conscious participant in the evolution of your life and our planet.

ACKNOWLEDGING THE POWER WITHIN

"I don't need love," my inner voices proudly whispered. "I love my lifestyle" was my excuse.

Why wouldn't I love my life? My husband, my daughter, and I lived in a three-bedroom house on a half-acre lot in Sonoma County, California. An area visited by many travelers for our stunning wooded, grass-covered hills, redwood forests, rocky shorelines, mild weather and, of course, wineries. I was the environmental division manager for a consulting firm, overseeing investigations and cleanups of soil and groundwater contamination. Most of the time, I was in the office managing but occasionally I donned my hard hat and supervised the installation of monitoring wells or the excavation of contaminated soil at a job site.

During the first few years in this role, my Fridays off were spent taking care of my daughter, helping her grow from an angelic infant into a beautiful, independent 11-year-old. The extra day had switched into Taekwondo instructor training, errands, and volunteering in Kathryn's classroom. After school, you often could see us at Cafe de Croissant, a warm, apple croissant on her plate and an almond one on mine. Planting flowers or tending the tomatoes, squash, and the rest of the vegetable garden were a release for me. My daughter was often by my side digging in the dirt, throwing the ball for Aura (our Golden Retriever) or in the house playing. Exploring was our family's main pleasure, hiking nearby parks, and traveling. One of my favorite travel memories is our trip to Belgium and Germany. Recalling Kathryn rooted on a pew, in Cologne Cathedral, her brown eyes darting from one enormous carving to another still makes me smile.

My husband Rob and I had met at college, both studying for a bachelor's degree in Geology, a common interest then. I can remember toasting at our wedding with a champagne glass raised in my hand, "Here's to Rob, my best friend, my lover and now my husband. I love you."

Over time, I recognized growing up was not something Rob excelled at. The drinking and smoking pot, while acceptable as college students, were not impressive traits for a 44-year-old man. Being a responsible father, helping paint the family room, and even just supporting me when I needed it would overwhelm him and cause his 'internal circuit board to fry.' I overlooked these characteristics and allowed myself to settle because I loved my lifestyle.

At times, my office responsibilities were as daunting as my marriage. I was the doer, the problem solver, the one other people sought for answers. Grabbing the chainsaw to trim the bushes, resolving issues with my staff while attempting to convince my husband things really weren't that bad at his job were common occurrences. I did it all because I could. I did because it was easy for me. I did because I was trained early in life, like a well-behaved family dog.

As a young girl, I was sexually abused by my father. By the one person who was supposed to protect me, be there for me, and be someone I could trust. The man who had called me 'daddy's little girl' took my innocence away.

School saved me, the connection with my teachers, competing in sports and my friends. I survived the trauma by excelling academically and physically releasing the trapped energies through competition. The acknowledgment and sense of worthiness I lacked were openly delivered in my school sanctuary. My escape at home was a large-canopied maple tree in our front yard. Wedged high between two branches and tucked behind broad leaves, Mom's voice would float from below, "Diana, where are you?" I never answered. I was not going to reveal the one place that made me feel safe.

One courageous day, the warrior within the 10-year old girl unsheathed the sword on her back, stood in front of her father, and said, "No." That act of standing up for *me* ended the abuse and severed my relationship with my father for years. I walled off my heart so that my emotions and memories couldn't ambush me. It took almost 40 years to consciously remember and begin to heal the agony my father had inflicted on me.

A few years later, my sister turned 18, graduated from high school and got married all in the same month. Instantly, I was the oldest sibling in the house when my parents' marriage crumbled to a whole new level. I do not remember how or when I became Mom's protector, but I was. I remember bolting from the bathtub after Mom's familiar plea penetrated the wall. Running into the family room, water dripping off my skin, I stepped between my parents. I screamed at my dad, "Go ahead and hit me, you son-of-a-bitch! It's going to hurt you more than me." The absurdity of his naked teenage daughter cussing back at him jolted him out of his mental state and I stomped back to the bathroom.

During a more turbulent argument, Mom delivered the secret command and the phone was in my hand before I realized. My forefinger dialed the phone number she had given me earlier that month. A few minutes later, my hand opened the door for two policemen to enter. After 'discussions' with the police officers, my father foolishly pushed one of the officers' shoulders. That is when my dad was put in the back of the police car and taken away. Mom, my two brothers and I left that night. That time, we did not go back.

A few years before Mom transitioned from this world, she told me, "There wasn't any love in our house when you kids grew up." That confirmed my feelings; we were a family of six, no love but plenty of yelling, arguing, and cussing. I felt my childhood was stripped from me. The words, the physical abuse and energies I experienced as a child settled in my subconscious. My perception of who I was and my world was molded by experiences and thoughts, creating patterns. Constructing the fortress to conceal the defenseless heart, I learned to not cry and to suppress weak, vulnerable emotions. A powerful and effective human survival technique that stayed with me longer than appropriate. I know now that being repeatedly ordered to, "Stop crying or I'll give you something to cry about." rewired my young child's brain.

Remembrances of my first 17 years are also speckled with pleasantries. Trailer camping in Guerneville and Anchor Bay, California. Screaming on the Wild Mouse ride at Santa Cruz Boardwalk. Running to the next ride at

Disneyland when we visited family in Los Angeles. I felt a sense of freedom while riding horses through the orchards near our home. First trailing my sister on our Shetland pony Coca then inheriting her horse Honey, after she got married. These recollections are dots amongst old memories.

Looking back, it is easy to see how my childhood created my enabling behavior as an adult. Justifying my husband's addictions. Choosing men who were not available. My self-convincing thoughts. It's odd how something inconsequential can Ignite change.

I had just returned from my Taekwondo class on a Friday which my husband also had off. Our daughter was still at school and Rob was lounging on the deck. I opened the sliding glass door to the backyard, my *dobak* still on. "Want to fool around?" he asked, oblivious to the state our marriage had degraded. My foot planted on the step and our eyes locked. "Man, do we need to talk," flashed in my head. It was time for my husband to take off his rose-colored glasses.

We tell ourselves many things. We fabricate stories to help us get through rough times, for survival or, sometimes, reinforce false beliefs. "I don't have the strength." "It really isn't that bad." "He'll change." There are many excuses we use. But when the desire for something different finally outweighs the fear, we find the courage and stand up for our truth. The warrior within me once again unsheathed her sword.

I left my husband and settled into a townhouse less than 10 miles from the home I had known for 16 years. It was my oasis to decorate, to share half time with my daughter, to do what I wanted. Who knew crocheting, eating Butterfinger candy, and drinking chardonnay while watching television could be so recharging?

Determined and reinvigorated by the steps I had taken on this new path, I felt an internal drive for more, an awakening brewing within. An urge to discover *me*. But how do you start when you don't know what you want?

On a bright Sunday afternoon, I unwrapped a Cat Stevens CD case to reveal… nothing. A sealed, brand new CD and no CD inside. I felt this absurd predicament was a sign from the Universe that I was still trying to do too much. This subtle slap upside the head was the final straw that forced me to concede my lone attempts were no match for my defense mechanisms, my ancient fortress. I needed help.

At the advice of the friend who was 'dragging' me down the spiritual path, I began seeing a Diamond Approach teacher — one who uses modern teachings to help transform inner obstacles. Twice a month, I committed to driving 45 minutes one way to work with Janet. To discover my personal truth. To transform my life. And, unbeknownst to me then, to open my heart to *me*.

My motivation grew, and with renewed drive, I found myself on an accelerated path for two years. I attended the week-long Monroe Institute Gateway course to expand my consciousness, learn to navigate beyond the physical world and obtain a better understanding of the real me. I took a Bioenergy program, Qi Gong classes, and many local workshops. I continued my sessions with Janet and had sessions with a Somatic Experiencing Practitioner/Psychologist. I became a dowser and Reiki practitioner, the beginning of my energy healer training. But most importantly, I spent countless hours on personal inquiry and training. Over time, the outer layers of my protective fortress faded, the trapped emotions began to process and... I cried. I had taken responsibility for myself, not everyone else in my life. Responsibility for my actions, my thoughts, my body, my healing, my energy. Declaring myself a priority brought respect and appreciation for who I am.

Over the past 12 years, I have changed physically, mentally, emotionally and spiritually. I started making choices for my highest good and for those involved. I came to recognize that my childhood defense mechanisms that once helped me avoid painful situations were preventing me from truly experiencing life. I learned to trust and believe in myself and in the bigger collective picture that the Universe assists with unfolding. I opened up to possibilities and expanded my reality box. My inner guidance led to the release of my heart's intelligence, intuition, and strength. I quit my job and opened an environmental consulting office. I bought my own house. I finally stopped settling and felt true love in my heart for the first time as an adult.

We are all on our own evolutionary paths, searching for answers, learning, loving, and yes, floundering at times. My path is different from yours because I am in this life to learn different lessons, do different things, and have different experiences. You are not here to 'fix' me and I am not here to 'fix' you. But we can assist and support each other in miraculous ways.

My metamorphosis was far from easy; that is why they call it work. I used to say I would rather spar two people at the same time than go into my heart. The physical confrontation was easier to face than the emotional turmoil confined behind the fortress. Yet, it is only through disintegrating those barrier walls that I connected to my true essence, gained an appreciation of all life, and began to create the world I wanted.

Do I respond to all challenges with curiosity and an open mind? No. I am here to experience life's ups and downs while in this human body. So yes, I allow myself to get angry, frustrated, and hurt. However, I am no longer attached to the emotions, and most of the time... they are not projected onto others. I changed my perceptions and started interpreting situations differently. I now allow emotions to process, shift, and be released in the most appropriate way for me.

By healing the angry, hurt child and forgiving myself, I gained self-love, self-compassion and self-patience. The 20-year-old who went into geology to supervise a drill rig in the boonies far away from the public is now speaking to groups and opening hearts. I facilitate the healing process of others using tuning forks and Heart Access, an energetic modality I created. My work has transitioned from clearing physical contamination to clearing 'energetic contamination.'

I am grateful for my strong constitution and deeply embedded drive that knew there was more to life... for the ability to feel the expansiveness of love and of my soul... for the journey that helped me step into my authentic self and those who played their role in that journey.

My life synchronicities directed me to my current purpose in this life — assisting with the evolution of humanity and our planet. It is because of those teachings and my devoted training I have a heightened understanding of human experiences, the interconnectedness of life and the ability to open energetic portals.

I now have a passion for assisting others with their own awakenings. To help them change limiting beliefs, step into their full potential, experience who they are beyond the physical body and expand their consciousness. I want you to know your energy Ignites ripple effects into the world. When you change, you become a role model for yourself and everyone around you. You can't change your past but you do influence your future. Would I change my past for something easier? Only if the quest deposited me exactly where I am today.

Ignite Action Steps

Life is about love, self discovery, and sharing. About knowing your truth, connecting with your higher self and personal evolution. But all too often, we get stuck in our physical day-to-day activities and perceived obligations. We forget who we are. We forget we have choices. We forget we have the power to change and create our physical world.

Challenges that arise are learning opportunities to assist you in accomplishing the reasons you are here. When they appear, ask, "What is here for me to learn?" Know that changing behavioral patterns and beliefs, so you can step forward, takes *work*. Work that you, not others, have to do because it is YOUR path. Know you have a support system: family, friends, teachers and even "enemies" who mirror things back to you. Expand your tribe.

There is a deep longing inside to love and be loved, for freedom and happiness, to learn and evolve. Gather the strength to defeat the barriers that prevent you from being your true essence. You have the tools and the power within to overcome obstacles. To create the life your heart desires.

Open to Your Truth ~ Reopen communication with yourself. The important answers you seek are already inside you. Take responsibility for your thoughts, words, emotions, actions, health and energy. Give yourself the space and time to transmute the energies from your past. Look in the mirror and say, "I am amazing" because you are. You know more about you than anyone else.

Ask the Universe for Help ~ The Universe assists us but sometimes needs permission. So give it. Ask for guidance. Be open to the divine signs then take the physical steps to confirm your desires. Trust the bigger picture unfolding for you is for your highest good. Know you and all life are part of the collective consciousness.

Reconnect to Your Heart ~ Your heart has much strength and wisdom. It is the key to your soul, intuition, and regaining your power. Fill your heart with self-love, self-compassion, and self-respect. Experience the warmth and support of the love for yourself. Share your heart's energy with your family, friends, world. Allow that love to manifest your physical and spiritual existence. Believe and trust in you.

Love, Laugh, Play, Learn… Grow ~ Take time to enjoy life's magical journey. Schedule at least one day a month to explore, play, or dance. Connect with nature. Know your wants are as important as anyone else's. Be kind to all forms of life, including Earth. We are all energetically connected. Embrace the path you are meant to travel.

Diana Borges - United States
Diana@BorgesExperience.com
Intuitive Teacher, Speaker, Energy Healer, Author, Geologist
BorgesExperience.com

Anne Catherine Færgemann

*"Take compassionate responsibility for your health, and
your future will bring amazing wealth."*

**My deepest wish is for you to find inspiration in my story. I invite you to
feel safe and allow me to guide you with compassion. My hope is that you
are motivated to change your way of thinking, take honest ownership of
your health, and heal your body, now and for the future.**

Honest Body Healing

Let your mind wander back in time to the year 1999. Aerobics classes
were popular, gyms were opening everywhere filled with step classes and low
impact routines. I was the highly-energetic young woman at the front of the
class, instructing aerobics in a local community center. I was attending sports
school, living healthy, and managing my weight. I read and studied books
about health, yoga, fasting, diets, and more.

I started my education as a dietician and had my first child. I walked the
talk. Then, suddenly, I found myself in immense pain with stomach cramps,
needing to lean over the stove when I cooked special diets for patients at the
hospital where I worked. I visited the toilet a handful of times in the mornings,
but it did not really ease the burning pain. I had my own ideas of what was
going on with me, but I had to know that it was not something more serious.

The doctor's tests said that I was fine with gluten (no celiac disease) and milk (no lactose intolerance or milk allergies) and I did not have cancer or inflammatory bowel disease. After both a clear gastroscopy (a camera down the throat) and colonoscopy (a camera up your rear) I was diagnosed with Irritable Bowel Syndrome (IBS), like 25-45 percent of the population, 2/3 of whom are women.

My entire being rejected the diagnosis before I even fully absorbed what he had said. I was not willing to be put in that box, to be given that offhanded instruction to learn to live with it. "Drink lots of water, eat carrots, sprinkle your food with dietary fibers, and goodbye!" is what the doctor had instructed me with.

I was already thinking differently when it came to health, a bit of an extraordinary mindset that was thinking outside the box. I loved life and truly wanted to feel great, but I wasn't feeling great. I knew I had to make changes. I started reading everything I could get hold of at the library and through my studies. There was not much to be gained from this, with little mention of how to diagnose or treat IBS. After some searching, I reached out to the field of Functional Medicine, which Ignited within me a desire to start thinking about health in a completely new way. It was exhilarating! I felt much more empowered. I knew I could change. I realized I could do something about my health… myself. And in finding a philosophy that aligned so well with my own, I felt like I had come home.

Functional Medicine is the medicine of *why*, not the what. Practitioners who incorporate it in their treatments investigate the root cause of the symptoms; if any imbalances are found, these are addressed. Nature's healing remedies are used, such as vitamins, minerals, herbs, healthy fats, amino acids, etc. Questions such as: "Is something triggering the symptoms?" "Can it be removed?" "Is something missing in the body?" and "Can it be replaced?" are asked. It is a whole-body approach and all symptoms are considered, including traumatic life events, spirituality, and emotional balance. A big piece in the puzzle is the body's biochemistry. Laboratory tests are, therefore, used as clinical tools with the purpose to get any imbalance back in shape, for these can be a triggering factor or underlying cause to a problem.

I reached out to two American laboratories who offered testing for Food Intolerance and Gastrointestinal Evaluations, shipping off my samples and eagerly awaiting the results. Not many people in Denmark, where I lived, let alone the world, were testing like this. The Food Intolerance test was, in my case, positive to about 20 different foods. This meant I had to *avoid* those 20 foods! They were a part of my every day diet, but I refused to feel sorry for myself for even one minute as I eliminated them. I was in so much agony by that point that I had to change.

The Gastrointestinal Evaluation read higher markers than normal, but not high enough for it to be indicative of any serious disease. It also showed imbalanced bacteria and yeast flora; that showed I had to take action.

Not willing to accept the idea that I had to live with this, I tailor-made a treatment plan and adapted my diet. I started on supplements such as probiotics, fish oil, and antimicrobial herbs. Within a few weeks, my cramps disappeared and the burning in my intestines stopped. Within six months, I felt great again! I dared myself to try out some of the foods I had avoided. I was able to get most back into my diet, but not gluten. Today, 20 years later, I live a very strict gluten-free life, and there is not a day that goes by where I have any regrets. Going gluten free saved my life. It was a Change Maker!

Life moved on, as it does. Every day, I was grateful for my healing capabilities. I finished my education as a dietician and started working in Denmark's biggest hospital. Functional Medicine was unheard of there. Hospital guidelines had me treating people with a one-size-fits-all concept. Colleagues viewed me as being rather different in some of my viewpoints. It felt rather lonely, yet the fire kept burning inside of me. I knew I wanted to become a Change Maker in my field.

After my second child was born, I quit my hospital job and started working on opening a private Functional Medicine clinic. This dream was becoming reality, side by side with my husband. We worked hard for the clinic to become successful, and through this, make an impact on society. Today, we have clinics in Copenhagen, Stockholm, Helsinki, and Porto. It is amazing to see how my act of thinking differently and pushing for change was accepted by so many people searching for help to heal.

Little did I know how I would have to put my different thinking to use in my own health once again. One random day, I had a routine smear test come back positive for precancerous cells. Follow-up showed invasive cervical cancer. A radical hysterectomy was needed, removing my uterus along with any possibility of having more children. The surgery had been pretty hard on me. I could not stand on my own feet until Day Three as I kept fainting and had very low blood pressure as well as a low-grade infection. The wound kept leaking lymph. And the doctors told me I must undergo adjunct chemotherapy and radiation as well. I was scared and my mind kept ruminating around the thought of dying before I turned 40. I knew I couldn't carry on like that. I had to change my thinking. I decided to turn the '40' into positive energy: I *would* live at least another 40 years!

Once again, a voice Ignited inside of me, pushing me to research more. If I accepted chemo and radiation, how would my stomach react to that? What would be the consequences, at the age of 35, to enter menopause? I read all the official guidelines for cervical cancer; the Danish, British, and American versions. Surgery had removed all of the cancer; the extra treatment was a security measure to ensure the cancer wouldn't return. Accepting that theory went against everything I had learned and stood for. I could not accept that treatment. I met the oncologists anyway as I wanted to hear their arguments as to why I should take this toxic step.

They were shocked that I did not want their 'poisonous radiation' and realized that I was more informed and educated than the average patient… and they couldn't convince me. They called in a senior colleague who proceeded to hammer me with arguments as to why I should accept the treatment. In the end, after hearing my intellectual point of view, he realized that I was not going to follow his orders. He closed my chart and became more relaxed, more human. What he said next surprised me. "After studying your prognosis, I can see why you would be like this," he said. "My job is to recommend you take the treatment, but If you were my daughter, I would support you in your decision. I agree with you, you should not accept." His words sent relief washing through me. "Go home and enjoy life with your friends and family," he said. "You have a long life in front of you." And so I did.

It wasn't easy. I had to work extremely hard to get my health on track. I realized that in disputing the official recommendation, I would have to evaluate other treatment options. Yet again I asked questions such as, "What is the root cause behind this cancer?" and "What nutrients support fast recovery?" I came to the conclusion that I had to make changes to balance levels of antioxidants and oxidants. I received vitamin C injections twice a week for about six months; I juiced and smoothied my way through an entire year, and took all the supplements my research recommended, supporting optimal sleep, healing, metabolism and oxidative balance, muscle strength and hormonal balance. I swallowed them until I was fed up with pills, but most importantly, I swallowed them until I felt healthy, cancer free, and strong.

Recovering from cancer, from this threat to my very life, took time. The mental recovery alone was overwhelming. I felt blue for many months. I changed my lifestyle to spend more time with my children and to have more time for myself. I started expressing my feelings and emotions much more to my children and the people around me, who I deeply cared for. I did a lot of personal work in relation to how I wanted life to play out. Since then, I tell my boys that I love them every single chance that I get. Through this work, I also became much stronger physically, started running, and committed to my yoga practice.

One and a half years after being cancer free and feeling exhilarated, I started experiencing fatigue. Sometimes I could barely stay awake during my consultations with patients. On my days off from work, I started taking naps, yet I did not gain energy from these. My brain was experiencing some form of hyperactivity as well as fog, and I had difficulties reading research articles. As I had to start writing my thesis for my Masters of Nutritional Medicine, this was extremely frustrating. I tried to keep up with my exercise, but if I did too much, I started feeling weaker as if I had a mild flu. And terrifying nightmares invaded my dreams; I would yell out and my husband would have to wake me from them. I went to my doctor, but there was no test that gave a clue as to what was happening, so my doctor suggested depression might be the cause. I disagreed!

I continued living my healthy life, yet nothing I did to fix myself helped. Every day was a struggle. A few months later, on my return from a week in Austria on summer vacation, my husband and I decided to visit a laboratory in Germany to investigate a business prospect. The doctor there was a specialist in infections and we had an animated discussion about Lyme disease, Epstein Barr Virus, Chlamydia pneumoniae and more… and the whole while I was struggling to stay focused and awake. I learned that you could have been infected earlier in life, but could for many years live symptom free, until one day, "Boom!" All dormant infections could become reactivated.

My brain started bubbling over with the excitement of hearing this concept! Once home, I administered tests on myself. They came back positive for several infections, including Lyme disease. I started specific herbal treatment right away. They made me so ill, I felt like I had a full-blown flu for several hours, but then I was okay again. These symptoms are known as Herxheimer reaction, and can occur when microorganisms are killed with an antimicrobial substance, which was what the herbs were. Two weeks later, I started slowly on antibiotics and probiotics to support my gut and I started feeling better. It felt as if the healthy me had started to manifest in my body again. My nightmares stopped. I tried several times to stop the antibiotics, but my symptoms came back within days. I asked myself what the reason for this could be, and realized I had to keep looking for optimal healing solutions. I found a conference specializing in infections. There I trained together with doctors who specialize in herbs and infectious disease. I felt extra blessed, because on this trip I met and shook hands with His Holiness Dalai Lama. His presence empowered me to believe... and felt like a sign that I had found the answer to healing my condition. Back home, I started the comprehensive herbal treatment program. Four months later I managed to get off the horrible antibiotics that by then had caused me severe yeast infections. I continued the herbal treatment and probiotics for another five months, when I finally felt disease free. Now, eight years later, my infections are still suppressed and I feel truly alive.

Would I have wanted to be without disease? Yes, for sure. Disease was not something I had ever wished for. Living a healthy life and doing what you can to stay healthy is not a guarantee for disease immunity. I keep reminding myself of what the outcome might have been, had I never taken responsibility for my own health and done my self-compassionate research to live, heal, and recover optimally. This has taught me a lot about maintaining an optimistic view and I apply it in my professional life. I am the practitioner I am today because of my investigative nature and my own health journey. I have learned to be humble with my patients, not to promise them a quick fix, but to support them with compassion in their healing journey. The entire process helped me become the Change Maker for my patients that I had always wanted to be.

Now that I am healthy again, I am not stopping my research. I am on a mission to become a supercentenarian and turn at least 110 years old. I study longevity and anti-aging theories, and research the mechanisms for prevention of lifestyle diseases (such as cardiovascular disease, dementia, and Parkinson's). I find inspiration for this in my patients and the people around me. My desire is to impact the way individuals perceive their health and awaken the government to be more open to preventative thinking strategies. People need to feel empowered about their health and free to seek alternative options. I want society to know we *own our health*; it is our responsibility, not our doctors', to act and be proactive about it before we become ill.

With my story, I welcome all who wish to do honest body healing. I hope it supports you and gives you clues for your personal detective work in finding the root cause of any symptoms. I hope I have inspired you to shout out loud and go with the powerful force of taking responsibility for your own health, believing in your intuition and letting your heart and love always be there for you. You can be your own Change Maker in YOUR health. Take responsibility, educate yourself and you will find your own healing powers. Making even the smallest change can create a BIG outcome in having the best life you desire.

IGNITE ACTION STEPS

The first step in taking your health seriously is being conscious about your current situation. Start by doing an honest health evaluating body scan. Lie down, or sit in a chair. Perhaps make yourself comfortable with a blanket and a small cushion. You may wish to have a pen and paper handy. Make sure your arms and legs are not crossed, and that your arms are not touching the body. Close your eyes.

Start the body scan by taking a deep breath and exhale slowly. Repeat eight times. Ask yourself, was breathing easy? Was there any tension or resistance? Make a mental note of any discomfort and send love and healing energy toward the spot. Then, focus your attention on your toes and sense if you have any pain or discomfort. Move focus to your ankle, knees and thighs. Continue making mental notes and sending love and healing energy toward those spots. Now, focus on your hips and pelvic area. How does it feel around your sex organs, your stomach, your diaphragm? Is there excess body fat somewhere? Can you feel discomfort in your intestines? Allow all problems to have an honest voice so you can start your journey to heal. Move on to your neck and throat in the same way. Focus your attention on your arms, elbows, and hands. Move up to your head and really allow yourself to evaluate your mood and stress levels.

Continue lying or sitting for a little while, then stretch your arms over your head. Stretch a little to the right and to the left, then slowly open your eyes. Take the time now to note the following:

- Recognize and be aware of conditions in the body. Write them down.
- Accept with honesty, if you have any recurring symptoms.
- Keep track of how long and how often you feel this way.
- Contact your doctor if it persists. Hear their conclusion. Search for more information and question if the treatment is optimal or if there is more you can do.
- Do research, read about the subject on the internet, look for a practitioner that can guide your way to the right people, the right books, the right laboratory tests, the right spirit, the right treatment.
- Follow your intuition and support your body's healing processes. Let love compassionately surround you.

Anne Catherine Færgemann - Denmark
Registered Dietician, MSc Nutritional Medicine,
Yoga and Meditation teacher
www.honestbodyhealing.com

LOUISE GRAHAM

*"True purpose is found within; your truest
purpose is who you are at your core."*

**My hope for you is that you learn that incredible transformation can come,
in your life's work as a Change Maker, when you put yourself first. Putting
my growth, highest excitement, and joy first opened up huge opportunities
for my own transformation and for making a difference in my community.
I want everyone to know that when it comes to making an impact, it doesn't
matter what you do, it's who you are whilst doing it that counts most.**

THE CALLING OF A CHANGE MAKER

There have been many breakthrough moments in my path to following my
life's work as a Change Maker. One of the biggest breakthrough moments
came during Christmas 2018 while sitting home alone, slumped on the couch,
feeling sluggish and burned out, reading the book *Will I Ever Be Good Enough?*

As I read the words, "Daughters of narcissistic mothers absorb the message
'I am valued for what I do rather than who I am'," all the cells in my body
triggered. I was suddenly alert, sitting upright, and drawing multiple lines with
my pen under what I had just read. This message felt true for me. It seemed to
hold the answer to the pattern of depression I had experienced most of my life.
These illuminating words left me feeling more seen than I had ever felt before.

It felt as if my brain had turned into a computer processor as it quickly joined
the dots, reliving scenes from my past and growing the understanding that I

had been seeking my self-worth in what I did for others. I felt an incredible heart-wrenching pain at the confusion of everything in my life before that one brilliant moment of realization and I let the tears come for the years of feeling lost and alone.

We learn that we are valued for what we do rather than who we are. I contemplated these words for days, wondering why they had triggered me so much. What did this mean for my life moving forward? I realized how this one belief and the resulting path of over-responsibility had created so much pain and struggle for me.

Most of my life my mom had been living with deep emotional pain and mental health challenges. Growing up, I watched her break apart while leaving a trail of destruction, terror, and trauma. It was not unusual to witness her lash out in aggression. I remember once coming home from school to find her bedroom turned upside down, glass on the floor, and her car missing from the driveway. She would often attempt to disappear, leaving the rest of us responsible for finding her and bringing her back home.

None of us are just one thing and there was another side to Mom as well. She was incredibly loving and caring, an entrepreneur and self-made woman who had lived through tremendous adversity and loss, yet was always so resilient, ingenious, and intelligent in the way she faced life. I admired my mom a lot and I learned an incredible amount from her. She helped me launch my first business at age 14, writing personalized Santa Claus letters to children all over the world. When I set up my marketing agency at the age of 24, she loaned me the money I needed to buy the computers for it. She was the person who would walk to the ends of the earth for whatever I needed and wanted. The fierce supporter who wrote me the most beautiful letter on my 18th birthday reflecting on her love and wishes for me and my growth.

My relationship with my mom had always been emotionally complex, sometimes sweet and at other times highly traumatic. Most of my life, I had lived with the fear that one day she might act on her threats to take her own life and so I made it my purpose in life to keep her happy, to make her feel loved always. Although I didn't realize it at the time, I received almost all of my self-worth from what I did for her and I carried that unhealthy codependent pattern into my work, believing that my value was in what I did for others.

I recall the day my life changed beyond all comprehension: September 11, 2013. I was expecting friends to come by my apartment and so, when the intercom sounded, I let them in and left my door ajar while I went to brush my teeth. Coming out of the bathroom, I saw not my friends but two police officers standing in the doorway. Having reported mom missing just a few days earlier, I thought at first that they were there to interview me further about her disappearance, but as soon as I saw the expression on their faces, I knew everything was wrong. "You're not coming in," I told them, not wanting the news to be made real. "You're not coming in!" But of course they did and they told me the news that Mom had been found dead. In the instant that they voiced it, that they said it out loud, it only confirmed what my soul already knew was true. At some point in the shock-filled moments that followed, my friends arrived and tried to convince me that the police weren't sure, that it might not be true. But I knew. I knew that it was real. That night, after eventually falling asleep, I woke up screaming, I felt like I had died with her. For years afterwards I often wished I had.

When my Mom died I hadn't been in contact with her. After some highly traumatic and abusive episodes — one of which where our lives were in danger — I made the brave decision to seek therapy, putting some distance between her and I. I had been so tied to protecting my Mom and looking after her well-being that I was neglecting who I was. That felt like an extremely brave decision. I knew that it was my Mom's greatest fear that one day I would leave. She had shared this with me many times and I was aware of my own fear that if I should leave, she might do something to hurt herself. Still, I decided that healing our relationship was more important, and I reminded myself that fear was a false illusion.

A few days before I was due to complete my three-month course of therapy and space from Mom, I received a phone call from her boss. He was asking if I had heard from her. He was concerned that she hadn't appeared for important meetings and suggested that I check in to make sure she was okay.

As she was working overseas in Spain, I asked a family member to go to her house to check up on her. After finding out she hadn't been home, I called the police and reported my Mom as a missing person... September 11th, they found her body in her hotel in Spain with her suitcases packed and her passport laid out on the day she was due to return home. She had died of a heart attack. I can't begin to describe the shock; I still think there are parts of me still in shock when I think about my Mom no longer existing in this world.

I threw myself into the busy work of the repatriation of her body, tussling with the insurance company, paperwork, house clearing, funeral plans, and all other distractions before I finally came into my body to feel the crippling effects of grief. My grief led to the darkest years of my life as I battled clinical depression and feelings of worthlessness resulting in my own self-harm and self-abuse. I felt completely lost. I was no longer a daughter. I struggled to hold things together, including my business. The external things I had tied my self-worth had disappeared and I was feeling like there was no place for me in the world. I spiralled in a black hole of days spent in bed, isolated, alone, and thinking of a way out. I had completely lost myself in clouds in confusion and indecision. I wasn't sleeping, wasn't socialising, was hardly eating, and barely surviving. I wanted more for my life but didn't know how to get it.

One evening, I found myself distressed and alone sitting on the concrete steps of my apartment building with no energy or will to climb the stairs. In that painful moment, I found myself hitting my head on the concrete steps… I didn't know why I was doing that but I had seen my Mom do it in times of distress. I had lost control and I didn't know what else to do. A new awareness woke me up and I knew if I continued I could do some serious harm and I knew I wanted more for myself.

I had been running a successful boutique marketing agency in Scotland for several years and I was feeling divided. Part of me wanted to stay committed to my work and my business, which meant staying in Scotland, and another part of me was screaming for a change of scene, for adventure and travel.

Scrolling Instagram in the wee hours of the morning, I came across the hashtag #digitalnomad. Following my curiosity, I found a place in Bali called Ubud and something just clicked. I craved being nurtured and supported with every cell of my being, and I felt as if this were a place I could go where I could let go of responsibility, indulge in opportunities for self-care, and release the pressure and heaviness of what I had been feeling for so many months.

I sent my friend a message, "I am moving to Bali." to which she replied, "Louise, it's 4 AM in the morning. Let's chat tomorrow." By the time we spoke later that day I had already booked my ticket.

In December, fifteen months after my mom died, I flew out to Bali for a holiday and to scope it out as a place to live and returned to Glasgow in January with a decision to make. Bali had blown my mind! I had felt the happiest I had ever felt and yet I was scared of all the 'What if's' — What if I can't cope and I am there alone? What if I lose everything? What if I don't feel safe? I made a pact giving myself two months back home in Scotland to see how I felt. Maybe my little holiday had been enough and packing up my life wasn't the right thing.

In February, my depression returned. I had been for lunch with a friend who had always told me to keep working on my business, to not make any rash moves whilst grieving. He turned to me and he said, "Louise, I think maybe you should take some time for yourself and follow your heart." His permission made me feel seen, feel heard, and was all I needed to hear. A week later, I was meeting with my clients to ask them how they felt about me living in Bali and servicing their projects remotely, working out how I could let go of my home, my office, my team, and all other responsibilities as I figured out what I needed to do to compress my life into one suitcase.

In April, I moved to Bali and started my journey of getting to know myself. Who was I? What was my purpose and who could I become? I immersed myself in self-help and self-growth, attending every workshop on offer. I loved the thrill of discovering who I was whilst nurturing my body with healthy food and an incredible community. I made connections beyond what I had ever experienced. I felt alive again. I walked the streets of Ubud, soaking up the energy as tears streamed down my face, doing Kundalini yoga under the stars, and being amongst so much nature and so much love. I could feel my heart getting fuller and fuller. Within months, there was no sign of what I had come to call depression and I was starting to feel renewed again.

A year and a half later, I returned to the UK for my Dad's wedding and ended up settling in London. After a year of working building brands for others, I had once again reached burnout. My relationship with myself and others was suffering; I was sensing some red flags for my mental health and I reached for that book…

I am valued for what I do rather than who I am. That sentence in that book opened up a new question of the nature of my work. I asked myself how my childhood narrative of being valued for what I do for others could be leading to the deep periods of burnout I was experiencing. Something about my work and the way I did it felt emotionally unhealthy, like I was supporting an old pattern. It didn't feel like growth. I thought about how I had spent my time over the past few years and where my highest excitement was. I realized that every book I had ever read, all the spare time I had, was spent learning about self-growth, spirituality, personal development, and human transformation. I hadn't picked up a marketing book in a very long time.

I love asking myself important, deeper questions. I always find so much strength in doing this, and so I asked myself another question, "What does emotionally-healthy work look like?" I realized that if I had a personal mission, my mission would be to use my zone of genius to create *more* human transformation, to raise the consciousness of humanity. I knew I didn't want to become a life coach or a marketing coach. I wanted to use my years of knowledge and experience as an award-winning marketeer, use my personal strategies of resilience and creative problem-solving to help others make more impact, change, and transformation in the world.

I loved the idea of being someone who could help Change Makers find opportunity in their greatest challenge. Even more so, I loved the idea of a world of work where I could help and support others to support themselves. I set a goal to work with 20 Change Makers and their biggest challenges, which led to launching an even bigger goal to do 60 breakthroughs in 60 days by donation. This then led to the creation of a growing Change Maker community, facilitating over 75 breakthrough sessions in eight months, and at Christmas I launched my own not-for-profit project, *Glasgow Basket Brigade*. I had just moved back to Glasgow with a desire to ground myself more in the community. I was feeling a strong heart-calling to launch a Glasgow Chapter for the Tony Robbins *Basket Brigade*. I wanted to do great work in the world but I didn't want to lose myself in the process.

I had always had a big heart and a strong heart calling to help others, but my inner narrative said, "Don't do it! You'll end up burned out. You just moved house and don't have the time or resources for this. You'll give too much of yourself. You won't have healthy boundaries around it and your mental health will suffer." This belief was rocked to its core. I had no experience of running a social enterprise, no money, and no contacts but I had evidenced enough new perspective on this through my recent breakthrough work that I decided to share my idea, be open with my fears, and watch for what wanted to unfold.

I put an advert on a local Facebook group asking for support, sharing my big vision, insecurities, and laying out exactly what I needed to launch the *Glasgow Basket Brigade*. In 48 hours my post received 420 comments and I had over 200 emails. In 10 days I had put a leadership team together. Within 48 hours from launch, our *Glasgow Basket Brigade* campaign had gone viral, being picked up by the local and national media and the city was so excited by what we were doing that we reached 400 volunteer sign-ups in a matter of days opening up to a waiting list.

We partnered with local businesses and schools, kids from all over the city collected packets of custard, gravy, and stuffing whilst companies sent us truckloads of mince pies, Christmas puddings, Christmas crackers, and everything else. The kids even handmade over 500 Christmas cards to go inside the baskets.

On the 21st of December 2019, 400 volunteers gathered for a family fun day to make and deliver 500 Christmas food baskets for Glasgow families in need. In little under eight weeks, we had raised £10.5k and bought enough food for just under 2,000 people to enjoy a Christmas meal at home. I had never experienced energy or flow like this. I felt so much support in our mission. Everything we needed was offered to us and I was more energized and on-purpose than I had ever been. Now, I am dedicating my time as an Impact coach & mentor to support conscious Change Makers to thrive in their life's work, to find more clarity and flow to create real change in the world. I am watching myself and my life's work grow at a whole new level as I step into my highest alignment and growth as a Change Maker who puts herself first.

It took me years of looking outside of myself to understand that true purpose is found within. I learned that it is not what I do for others but who I am whilst doing it that matters most. I realized after years of seeking, that all seeking, is life simply seeking itself. That we need to slow down to speed up. Go after your life's work, that's where flow is. Your life's work is your greatest evolution and natural gift coming together as one. You *are* what you believe a Change Maker to be. Nothing is outside of you.

Ignite Action Steps

Bring awareness to your highest calling. Get curious and use deep listening for synchronicities and other ways that you are being guided. Connect to your inner knowing and heart intelligence. Ask more questions; answers will be found in moments of presence and stillness.

Louise Graham - Scotland
Impact Coach for Conscious Change Makers,
Social Entrepreneur & Community Philanthropist
www.louisegraham.me

Rosalyn Palmer

"The greatest change you will make in the World will come from within."

I share my story to share the secret that your inner self holds the true key to change. Only once you move beyond a need to change your external circumstances and instead stop and feel the feelings you've been avoiding can you truly be at one with your best and most authentic self. I hope my story inspires you to change yourself from the inside out and then go out and change the world for the better.

Change Yourself Then Change The World

Back in the early 80s I hitchhiked around Ireland with my then university boyfriend. We were studying Irish literature at the time. He had a penny whistle and would sit by the roadside in whichever middle-of-nowhere place we were stranded in and screech out a terrible tune. We had only a backpack each and very little money. It didn't matter, as we managed to hitch lifts at each stage of the journey. It was a very different world then. Hitching was commonplace in rural communities as few people had cars. Most drivers obligingly stopped for us, often not going to where we had planned, but we went with them anyway, letting chance direct our travels. There were no Airbnbs™ then, nor mobile phones, yet we always found lodging and I never had to spend a night in a field full of cows, despite bringing a rudimentary tent along with us just in case.

My favorite lift came when we were deep in the lush emerald green of County Claire. It was the end of a long day of adventuring and we had been standing there for a while with our thumbs out, getting a tad concerned about the rapidly approaching dusk. A battered old blue van rattled into view. I flagged the driver down. He was charming. I told him where we were headed and asked if we could hitch a ride. His eyebrows rose almost to his hairline and the words that came out of his mouth next were priceless, "Jeesus! If you want to go *there* then you don't want to be starting from *here!*"

Those words have stayed with me ever since. This is how life — or the thought of changing it — feels as you say to yourself, "If only I didn't have to start from here!" But you have to! *Here* is the only place you *can* start from. Even if the thought of where you are at this very moment is so painful and disappointing that you would rather not even think about it, it is still the only place from which you can begin. In fact, the more painful your current location in life is... the more it is causing you to suffer... the more it is compromising your health, wealth, and welfare... the more urgent is the need for you to think about it just long enough to work out what is causing the pain so you can create new and immediate strategies for lasting change. And sometimes the smallest shifts can have the most dramatic results. It's like a tanker that changes course by only a few degrees in the middle of the vast open sea. To the naked eye, that minuscule change is unnoticeable, but the resulting course often takes that ship not just to a different country but a different continent. So too can a miniscule shift in your life's path via a journey of self-discovery lead to a new version of your life, a new continent of you.

My whole life I have had to shift directions repeatedly and, luckily, I often instinctively got it right. Drawing on my faith and a good grounding in my upbringing, education, and sheer internal grit, I navigated many forks in the road and derailments in my life beginning with my early career. In the mid 80s, I graduated with a degree in English Literature and fell into the fledgling industry of public relations (PR) in London, UK.

At first I worked for a Theatrical Management company that produced London West End and touring theatrical productions. I loved every second of it. What could be better? Shows, costumes, theaters, and temperamental stars swearing at me. Long hours. Terrible pay. Champagne at my desk and bagels on the way to work on the underground after five hours of sleep. Soaking in the amazing plays and even just being in the theater every night. I loved the theater life. Sadly, the company went bankrupt and, finding myself out of a job, off I went to work for the UK's leading theater program publisher.

I was based in my beloved London to start. Some months later, following a management buy-out, I found myself moving from my shared flat to a regional print works in a depressed part of the north of England. I felt so alone and iso-lated. I'd moved with a promise of promotion, a better salary, an expensive new car, and paid-for accommodation. Those promised outward shows of success had turned my young head. I thought that changing my external circumstances and getting the shiny rewards and money was a good idea.

Six months after my move, I knew that this wasn't the truth. Alone, away from my friends, and utterly disconnected from the world and things I loved, I was feeling nearly suicidal. I struggled to get through each day, convinced if I could just stay the course, things might get better. After all, I had every reason to be happy! Except... I wasn't. And three months after that, the management buy-out failed and I was made redundant. I returned to my shared accom-modation in London only to find that several of my former housemates had moved on. Everything familiar was gone. I was left with a room, no job, and sharing a home with strangers. It was brutal and depressing, completely unlike those carefree days when I carried all I needed on my back and depended on the kindness of strangers to get me from place to place. Yet somehow I came through. Every day I got up, got 'suited and booted,' and applied for every PR job I could find. Soon I secured a job at the leading PR company in the UK — the famous Lynne Franks PR upon which the TV series and movie *Absolutely Fabulous* are based.

I felt like a Change Maker. As I sashayed into the trendy office every day clutching my coffee, wearing my designer suit, I thought I had arrived. All the hard work and risk taking and tenacity I'd put into my career felt like it was finally paying off. I'd certainly changed my misfortune and I changed from a regional company to the glamour of THE best and brightest PR agency of its time. Celebrities, fashion designers, and models adorned the office. My second day on the job was spent on the *Orient Express*. A breakfast soon afterwards was shared with the Oscar winning actor, Daniel Day Lewis. I met my future husband in the VIP area at a top nightclub. I walked as tall as my 5 foot 2 height allowed with my head held high. I felt I had made the necessary changes and I'd arrived. Not quite a 'wolf of Wall Street,' but definitely a cub. How wrong was I?

Needing to learn more about marketing and advertising, I changed jobs several times. Little by little I adjusted my course, always keeping my sights trained on the distant shore labeled 'Success' and yet with the recession of 1991 I was made redundant again, cast aside totally unfairly as my hard work and loyalty were neither seen nor rewarded. It felt like not just a glass ceiling but a glass box was all around me. This time, determined not to tie my fortunes to yet another sinking ship whose direction I could not control, I set up my own PR company in my spare bedroom with the small severance package I received. My dog, Rosie, was my first member of staff. The furniture was second hand. It wasn't much, but it was mine, and I focused every single ounce of my energy into making it thrive. While success came quickly, it was a demanding mistress. I had to project just the right image and wear a mask that made it look a lot better than the financial reality and near exhaustion of 20-hour days depicted.

The thrill of achievement drove me on. External signs of success started to arrive. I had the beautiful house, lovely car, private members' club, personal trainer, and housekeeper. I dined out in the best restaurants in London. Skiing and holidays… designer clothes… first-class travel around the globe… my external world had changed beyond recognition, yet inside I felt broken. It should have been a life of ease but it was a life of dis-ease, overwhelm, and utter disconnection from anything that really mattered. I was an empty void when I wasn't pumped on the adrenalin of business or external events and, deep in my heart, I knew it.

The long hours and adrenaline-fueled days affected my health. I knew I didn't like the new patterns of behavior, but I didn't know how to get off the merry-go-round. My Ayurvedic doctor told me that mental or physical breakdown was about to happen. The thought scared me so much I put my PR company on the market, desperate to fix myself. I thought I had pulled it off when we were able to sell and move overseas. Yet that is where the world as I knew it imploded.

Over an 18-month period, everything I knew and identified with changed. After the sale of my company, stripped of my home, status, identity, and daily routines, I channeled my energy into the kids and exercise. Into book clubs, voluntary work, and walks on the beach. For the first time in my life, I was starting to build connections instead of business plans and it felt good. But the dis-ease caught up with me. A diagnosis of breast cancer hit me with all the force of a freight training coming in the wrong direction. I had to sort out treatment in the US. Have my children looked after. Fight to stay alive.

We moved to a remote organic farm on an out-island in the Bahamas. When I was recovering from cancer away from family and friends there, I learned to finally let go for a while and I was never more filled with joy. I learned to live in the present moment and engage with myself. To be still. To observe. To appreciate all around me. To connect deeply. I discovered I could paint. I wrote poetry and prose. I watched uplifting movies. My favorite was *Groundhog Day*, a story of hope and redemption. It spoke to me.

It is over 25 years since the movie *Groundhog Day* was released. It is one of the few movies that (ironically) I can and will watch repeatedly. For me it has everything. Humor, pathos, a central dilemma and ultimately, hope. If you are unfamiliar with it, the movie centres on Groundhog Day, a popular tradition celebrated in Canada and the US on February 2nd each year. The phrase 'Groundhog Day' for me means wanting to change but repeating your behavior over and over again and trying to change the external factors until you learn from it and finally break free of the cycle of behavior.

This is what Phil Connors (played brilliantly by actor Bill Murray) does in the movie. At the outset, Phil is a sophisticated TV weatherman with an ego to match. He finds himself stuck in having to live out the same day repeatedly and he goes through a progression of emotions rather like the stages of grief. This all plays out against the backdrop of a small American town that he is contemptuous of at first, surrounded by people who are living the day for the first time, unaware of his dilemma.

Phil moves from disbelief to selfishness to despair and even suicide before he accepts his lot. The day does not change, the location does not change, and the townspeople do not change. It is Phil who changes in his mind and heart. He turns his worst day into the best day of his life by transforming from within. He finds values of connection, kindness, selflessness, and living in the moment. He finds hope and joy.

When everything around you changes, when everything you cherish has been taken away, you can only go within. Past the 'conditioned self' to the 'authentic self.' To the essence of your being. To the place you fear — when you are so caught up on the merry-go-round of a busy life — that you can't even find or identify with. It is the most amazing transcendence when you move into the present and engage with life directly and authentically.

Even as I had found presence and joy in my time of isolation and gaining back my health, I was still overwhelmed with external changes. My parents fell into ill health, my father having a stroke and my mother developing terminal pancreatic cancer. My financial bedrock vanished, lost through a series of poor investments. My marriage crumbled under the financial stresses. My home, my health, my marriage, and nearly my sanity changed in an instant. All structure was removed and all the norms destroyed.

Walking along arguably one of the most beautiful beaches in the world where I was living, pink sands lapped by crystal clear azure waters, I could barely see the end of the beach for the tears. There, then, in what is arguably paradise, I realized that everything I had known, everything I had identified with, everything that defined me as *me* had been taken away or was about to be taken away. The only resource I had was to leave all of that new life behind, fly back to England with my children with no security, no job, no home… to be with my family and take it from there, seeing what I could rebuild.

Recently I discovered a book about my life-saving movie *Groundhog Day* that analyzes its messages. *The Wisdom of Groundhog Day* resonated so much with me that I am now in touch with its author, Paul Hannam, who says about it, "A happy and fulfilling life is built on love, not fear; on helping others, not ourselves; on gratitude, not craving; on being present and following our hearts."

This conversation made me realize just how life changing my own Groundhog Day truly was. After the glittering career and familiar life came to an end, I had had to change from within. I had to adjust my course and fix my gaze on the life I wanted to be living. I had to choose my thoughts and change their meaning if I were to have any hope of moving from feeling trapped to feeling fulfilled. I had to change every aspect of how I approached life and it led to the most amazingly transcendent and authentic transformation. I was able to engage with others and put others first. I became Head of Marketing and Communications for an international charity supporting some of the most stigmatized and vulnerable people in the world: people with leprosy. I then trained as a therapist and coach and now heal others from the traumas and hurts of the past. I work with individuals, groups, and companies to exorcise the chains that hold them back from lasting and joyful change.

The world has changed incredibly recently. Freedoms many of us took for granted have been removed and uncertainty has crept in. Globally we have fought an invisible but deadly enemy and all the systems and daily routines many of us clung to and hid behind have been stripped away.

Allow this change to change you. Change Makers have to go through a sort of hero's journey to dig deep into themselves and be stripped bare of the masks they hide behind. I certainly was and it was the making of me. I was able to find myself. Be still with myself. Get to know myself and then go beyond myself to pay the kindness and compassion I felt for myself forward to heal and support others.

These aren't just words. This is the blueprint for how I've lived and how I've survived. It's hard to make that journey within and oftentimes scary, but what's worse is to feel disconnected from your true self, asking yourself, "Is this as good as it gets?" So be inspired. Be Ignited. Be courageous. As Lady Macbeth says to Macbeth, "Screw your courage to the sticking post and we'll not fail." You have the grit, the tenacity, the courage to see it through and trust me, it's absolutely worth it on the other side.

Ignite action steps

If you're not living the life you would like to be living, if you want to change your life and stop the *Groundhog Day* of being trapped, then start inside. Ask yourself every day:

What inspires me? Can I do some or all of that today? Perhaps it is only a question of what you can do. What you can change. So, the MOST important question every day is to ask yourself first is: What is achievable TODAY? If you have external restrictions placed on you, you can still achieve the following (that spells CHANGE):

- Choose your thoughts and change the meaning. Reframe how you think about your circumstances. Get enough sleep to reset your brain pattern.

- Hydrate your body well. Keep drinking water or similar.

- Always exercise and move your body. I love yoga and this can be done almost anywhere. There are wonderful free online courses such as Yoga with Adrienne. Just dance around your kitchen or go for a walk. Whatever you do, just MOVE.

- Never do anything that is not good for you or those around you or the World. Ask yourself if it is a good thing before you do it. In your heart you will know and make the right choice.

- Go inside: meditate or be still. If you can't sit and meditate, download one of the hundreds of meditation or hypnosis recordings available. I have a great selection!

- Eat well. Eliminate sugary junk foods. Treat your body like it is your best friend.

Rosalyn Palmer - United Kingdom
Advanced Rapid Transformational Hypnotherapist & Coach
www.rosalynpalmer.com

Diana Lockett

*"Our experiences do not define us; they inform us and
can catapult us toward our deepest purpose."*

**My longing is that you, the reader, will remember that in spite of, or per-
haps because of, your history, you have the power to heal, to connect to
your soul's purpose and to become your own unique Change Maker in the
world. You are a miracle and your voice matters. May my story help you
unlock the potential of your life, encourage you to turn your pain into your
purpose, and use the gift of your voice to Ignite a difference in the world.**

The Space Between the Words

As a little girl, I loved talking, singing, and making up stories. I spoke so
much that my twin sister didn't need to speak until she was almost four years
old, as I not only spoke for myself, I also spoke for her. That's how vocal I was
as a young child. I don't recall the specifics of it, but I grew up hearing that
narrative… a lot. And talking and singing were some of my favorite things to
do during exciting events, holidays, and family gatherings, and especially at
Christmas time.

I loved Christmas. I adored everything about it: the way the lights danced
on the tree, the excited feelings of the little girl in me, waking up Christmas
morning, and opening the carefully wrapped presents. I enjoyed the feeling of
my family coming together in celebration and singing carols, both in our community, at church, and at home. My father would put on his favorite Christmas

songs and we would sing as we decorated the Christmas tree while my mother prepared a feast for our family. I would sing along at the top of my lungs, even if I didn't know the words or was out of tune. These are some of my earliest joyful memories and they included me using my voice as a self-expression instrument, until one Christmas day when my voice was silenced.

My family used to call me 'Chatterbox.' I'm sure it was meant to be funny, but I received the message that my voice was too much with each passing joke about "Diana is the chatterbox of the family," and "We can never get a word in when Diana is around." This didn't feel like a badge of honor to me. As a little girl, I received the message that I was too much, my voice was too eager and was not welcomed. I felt ridiculed and shamed. I would come home excited to tell my mom about my school day to find her asleep, medicated, on the couch... again. In time, I learned that, as a good little girl, it was best to be seen and not heard. I would retreat quietly to my room with my excitement crushed and my words swallowed.

I remember one particular morning when this conditioned belief was reinforced. I was seven years old. I woke up with the excitement that always engulfed me on Christmas morning. The tree was decorated, the carols playing on the record player, the smell of Christmas dinner filled the house. I was excited to open my stocking and see what Santa had left for me. Chocolate, socks, candy and... a wind-up chatter teeth toy. The red and white plastic ones that you wind-up and they chomp up and down.

My family laughed as they affirmed that this reflected 'Diana the Chatterbox.' I remember the feeling of my shoulders drooping, the deep contraction in my heart, the sense of my throat closing. I remember the beliefs that arose at that moment when that mocking gift confirmed what I had been told and what I began to believe about myself. My voice was too much. My voice was not welcomed.

That was the day I began to silence my words. In that moment, I told myself my voice didn't matter. And over time, I allowed that belief to create my identity, my thoughts, my feelings, behaviors, and habits. I learned that it was best to be quiet. That was my initiation into the journey of the powerlessness of silence.

I kept quiet during childhood physical abuse with silent tears as my Dad expressed his fury. I kept silent during teenage sexual assault where I didn't dare make a sound, not even a tear. I kept to myself during infidelity and betrayal. I kept quiet when I was forced to have an abortion. I kept silent through an acrimonious divorce, even when I was locked out of my house. I kept to myself when my 'friends' started a public slaughter on Facebook, questioning my worthiness to open a new business after previous failures. I lost all words when everything I owned was taken away and I had to declare bankruptcy. Each of these experiences in my life led me to swallow my voice, dismiss my pride, and relinquish my power a little more. I put a lid on all my feelings and instead of expressing myself, I held it in as shame.

The shame grew until it became a dark monster that threatened to swallow me whole. In time, I felt incapable of holding the humiliation anymore and my feelings and thoughts turned to hopelessness, depression, and suicide. Some days it took everything I had to negotiate with the demons in my mind. The need to feed my children and take them to school was the only thing that could lift me up and give me purpose, but still, all this in silence. I was unable to share my fears, my anguish, my darkest secrets. What I had to say, after all, didn't matter.

Even though my relationship with my own voice was not a powerful one, I went into a profession to help others find theirs. I became a Speech Language Pathologist in my early 20s and, for 30 years, helped children who were minimally verbal or nonverbal. My mission was to match their voiceless needs with a communication system to give them a voice. I didn't realize that in doing so, little by little, I was finding my own.

Throughout this time, I started practicing yoga for self-care. I fell in love with the healing properties of yoga and the *hope* it brought to my life. I became a Yoga Instructor and eventually opened up a Yoga Teacher Training Academy. Every day, I felt like an imposter. When I taught, I was simply regurgitating what my teachers had taught me, which I realize now we all do at the beginning until we find our own voice. In the quest to go deep and find my authenticity, I started sharing my story. In the quiet moments between my words, I began to notice that people *listened*. They listened and they used my teachings to inspire their own lives, to find their genuine voice. The more I shared my story, the more it impacted my community, my students, my friends. And myself.

Teaching yoga brought me back to my purpose and allowed me to access gratitude for the blessings in my life. In spite of having hit rock bottom, even with a leaky roof over my head, I recognized that I had my health, my kids were thriving, and I had an impactful message to share. I knew with certainty the Universe had my back and I was ready to trust that and welcome change.

It was a profound revelation.

The transformation that followed allowed me to make a conscious decision to turn my pain into my purpose. I became resolute in my steps to create a personal evolution and my daily mantra became "Life is happening *for* me." I began to find my own words. To appreciate my own unique voice. In love and gratitude,

I patiently allowed my words to come forward and be expressed through me. I realized that I had been standing in my own way for so long and holding myself back. I hadn't trusted myself. I had allowed myself to be defined by… everything and everyone! My parents, my schooling, my religion, my society, my friends (the not so good 'friends') and my experiences. I began to evoke questions such as "Who was I?" and "What legacy did I want to leave behind?" along with "What was my purpose in my life?" These became my North Star questions and the inquiry brought me to explore my beliefs, thoughts, feelings, actions, and the results that I was longing for in my life. I saw the misalignment in who I was and who I wanted to be. I made a commitment to myself that if I wanted to change my life, it was up to me. And it would begin right now.

There were many changes made that year and one of the biggest was to have a compassionate relationship with my feelings as part of my plan to reclaim my power. I decided that if I longed to find my voice, to express myself, I had to have the courage to feel my feelings as the thermometer that would allow me to recognize how I was showing up each day. I knew that I longed to release the tension of shame that I held inside. The shame that had engulfed me for most of my life. I learned how to express my grief and release a lifetime of sorrow. I discovered how to use my breath as a tool, to connect with my body and its sensations and to trust it as my inner guidance. I did the deep practice of forgiveness, for myself and others. I noticed tension began to leave my body and create space for clear intentions. That work guided me to a new and present path and I began to feel my own inner goodness.

Well almost… I was now confronted with the one emotion that I avoided for so long. It called to me. I heard my inner voice: "Do it.", "The idea of it is scarier than the experience.", "You deserve it." I knew from the research that touching my anger would release my shame and allow me to connect to my passion. My default response to anger was to shut it down, to put on meditation music and calm myself. I am a Yogini, after all, and I did not have a healthy childhood imprint of anger.

On a gray day in Amsterdam during a Heart IQ™ circle, I let go. I surrendered to my anger and my shame. I witnessed these expressions leave my body as messy, loud, primal sounds of uncontained rage that had been confined for decades. I moved my body… I found my voice… and I fell in love with it.

The most beautiful gift was how the strangers in my circle received my anger and shame with love, encouragement, and celebration. I felt an immediate relaxation in my entire nervous system and a spaciousness in my throat. I felt my wholeness and completeness.

I learned that day that my self-expression was a gesture of self-love. I discovered that forgiveness is a practice and I have all the tools I need inside me. I decided that I am worthy to feel and express myself and embraced that power comes from my heart.

I knew from the teachings of many wise leaders that when we numb one feeling, we can numb all feelings and begin to live a life of mediocrity. I knew that the unwillingness to touch any part of my pain and my emotional ranges leads to them being suppressed and showing up at the most inappropriate times and in harmful ways like judgment or rage (we call these 'shadows'). I had been living that life and was very good at numbing out (with 'good' habits like yoga and exercise) but had not allowed myself to fully feel the spectrum of my embodied emotional range. I now realize that was a 'spiritual bypass.' When I welcomed the time to stop and feel all my emotions AND express them in a healthy manner as they came up, what came out wasn't scary anymore. It was clear, it was on purpose, and it was veiled with passion. And from that passion grew the increasing clarity that I was on the path toward exploring my life purpose. Touching the emotional ranges of anger allowed me to find my voice to express my excitement, joy, love, and gratitude.

When I went home at the end of that powerful experience, I brought along an old, reclaimed friend. I found my voice and welcomed her home. From that day on, my purpose became *uncrushable*: to help people to find their voices so they realize that they matter, what they do matters, what they feel matters, what they say matters. My mission was ignited with passion and clarity.

Within a year, I was invited to speak on a stage with The Global Change-makers™ with a commitment to help entrepreneurs to become healthier in their emotional and energetic systems. I went on to co-create powerful communities through my Yoga Teacher Training program, helping people find and express their unique gifts and voices. I began to offer my powerful teachings with humility and love, merging the ancient teachings of yoga philosophy with current neuropsychology, Shadow work, positive psychology, and coaching. I now find so much joy in my work coaching others to help them become clear in their lives, to access their joy and purpose and to express their own words with clarity and love. I find myself so energized when I help businesses create cultures that are transparent, mindful, joyful, and cooperative to increase productivity and become conscious Change Makers in the world. And I have stopped filtering my thoughts and now allow the Universe to use me as a vessel and let Grace speak through me.

Today, when I share, I share with the conviction of someone who has turned her deepest pain into a fiery mission in her life. I feel my resilience, power, and strength. I feel my joy, purpose, and immense gratitude for all that I have gone through. This is my new thermometer as I move through life.

We all have gifts. We all have powerful voices and messages. What I say matters. Just like YOU. With that assurance, I can sense the vastness of the ocean in me, as it is in you. I can ride the waves of Grace when life takes its unexpected turns and I know that I am not defined by my experiences. I made the choice to change so that, as Alan Cohen says, "My history is not my destiny."

What genuine expression is needing a voice in your life? I believe that when you touch your truth and meet your pain with compassion, there is a vulnerability that allows your authenticity to shine through. As the Sufi poet Rumi said, "The wound is the place where the Light enters you." When you learn to hold space for your pain, you can remember that, in that space, you can realign with your truest vision for your life and go from a path of barely getting by to a path of unfathomable joy. I've learned that if I don't like the answers in my life, I have to change the questions and I have to challenge my beliefs. When I change the lens of my perspective, I am met with clarity, ease, and purpose. Today, my deepest question is no longer "How will I quiet my voice," but "How can my words change the heart of the world?"

Ignite Action Steps

Here are some steps that I have developed and practice that I call "Be REAL and RE-ALign to Thrive™." They are designed to awaken you to take responsibility in your life and find your own unique gifts, power, and voice.

R= Remember that you are a miracle and be willing to see the miracle in others. When tension, stress, and life get in the way of remembering the gift of your life, ask yourself: "If I was to take 5% more responsibility to show up with love in my life today, what would I do?"

E= Explore what emotions and energetic experiences are present in you. Practice daily meditation to quiet your mind and be able to tune into the sensations of your body. Sensations are the language of the body and can inform you about how you are doing. Rather than attach to the emotions, label the sensations and sit with them for a few moments (e.g. instead of "I'm sad.", tell yourself "I notice my heart feels heavy and my shoulders are drooping.").

A= Allow whatever surfaces to be part of your experience. Soften and hold space for all of your sensations and experiences. Trust that it is all part of your embodied journey. Release what needs to be released through movement, sound, in circles, etc.

L= Love yourself no matter what comes up; your life experiences do not define you. Use a mantra: "Life is happening FOR me." or "I am the loving creator of my life.", or "I can realign to thrive in my life." Recite these daily.

When you practice being the REAL you, it will take you on a journey to be:

I= Inspired: to stay with the moments that are painful and trust that they will show you the path to your deepest purpose.

G= Grateful: for all the experiences, as they are the catalyst for change in your life.

N= Nonjudgmental: with yourself and with others as you cultivate loving compassion.

Diana Lockett, M.Sc., E-RYT - Canada
Realignment Coach, Founder of Realign To Thrive™
Dianalockett.com

CRISTINA PUJOL JENSEN

"Find your voice, find your way"

When do you make a change? Usually we have a catalyst to make a change when something goes wrong. What about when things on the outside look right, but on the inside are not quite right? What is going to drive *you* to make a change? I want to inspire you to find the essence of your own voice and get out of your own way. Your inner voice is a compass and your mindset is the engine. Find your own compass and fuel your mindset. That will shape your destiny.

MAKING CHANGES FROM THE INSIDE

I can remember being barely 16 years old, sitting across from my mother at the kitchen table and trying to figure out what career path I was going to follow for the rest of my life. My mother was my biggest supporter and cheerleader as I went through this first big life dilemma. I loved studying and wanted to pursue a degree at the university but didn't know which degree to choose. I was a nerd, one who freaks out with an 8 instead of a 10. I loved math, but I also liked sports, biking, and hiking. I wanted to experience the whole world: there was so much to try and I had to choose only ONE thing. Oh boy! What if I didn't like it? What if I didn't make it? I knew I was very privileged to have *that* kind of choice, no one in my entire family had had that opportunity before, and it felt intimidating. Pencil and notebook in hand, I crossed out all the options that I didn't want, leaving me with two. Two choices between futures that I'd never tried out before. Telecommunications or computer science engineering... It was unsettling.

I wanted something that would challenge me to grow and stretch my capabilities. I applied to three universities and I was accepted into all three; the first to answer was one offering computer engineering. I liked their study program and the location, Barcelona, in the region my father came from. My choice was made. I dived fully into it, pushing mentally and physically through the hard program for six years until I got my Masters degree. I finished on a Friday, and on Monday I was already working at the same university.

My job was really exciting and I loved what I did those first few years, but I was also in love with a guy. Two years into our relationship he left to study in Colorado. Eventually, I made the difficult decision to quit my job and follow him to the USA. From the moment I arrived, everything was new. The language, the customs, the people. I felt the desire to leave the bubble of university life where I had been working and experience the corporate world. I landed a job very quickly with an incredible company and started adjusting to my new way of life.

At the same time, I became proactive in my reawakened love of dance and joined a Latino Dance Group. The leader of this group, Carmen, was a charismatic woman who managed to 'convince' me to teach a specific form of dance from my region in Spain: Sevillanas. In my mind though, I was an engineer not a dancer. After nine years of this engineering thing, somehow my identity was tied to my title, and it was a nice and prestigious title. I had danced earlier in life, but 'Dancer' as a career was not on my radar. But there I was day after day, standing at the front of a mirrored room, teaching adults and kids to move, organizing choreographies, and performing in other dance forms like Salsa, Merengue, and Bolero. And all the while still working a very demanding job in engineering.

Dancing was calling me more and more. I was falling in love with it, discovering the feeling it gave me, the connections I made, the community that was created, the traumas I helped heal in children and adults, and the confidence I saw growing in my students... and in myself.

I also loved the part of me tied to my identity as an engineer. I loved computer science, my work, my colleagues and bosses, and the intellectual challenge of it all... but something was missing. I didn't have a strong desire to climb the 'ladder' of corporate success. My job was truly demanding and yet my mind would often wander off into the dancing world, drifting through the sensations and feelings teaching dance brought out in me. I felt conflicted. I enjoyed engineering, but I didn't see myself still doing it in 10 years. It was hard work, but it was also a good salary. Not wanting to shy away from doing hard things, I started questioning my motives. I didn't want to quit just because it was hard. I thought that I should only quit if I really didn't like my work. Little did I know all that was coming ahead.

My partner got a job in another state, so I took this as an opportunity to taste something new. I traveled for six months to Costa Rica and Cuba to study dancing and experience it directly, without computers or a job. Wow! What an amazing experience! I learned so much about myself, about other cultures, about following passions and dreams, about taking risks, about the meaning of connection and dance, and of giving and receiving. And I started rekindling with an old friend: my inner voice.

On returning to the States, I knew I wanted to start a brand new career with dance included, but I didn't know what that would look like. Then, a big and unexpected change blew up in my face: my partner ended our relationship. Here I was in my most vulnerable time: no job, no home, and no secure legal status in the US. I was lost. I didn't want to look for a computer science job; that felt like going backwards. So I focused on helping a dear friend start some dance classes. I began teaching with him and our close work relationship soon transformed into a close romantic relationship as well. Our classes exploded and soon we had a big following. It was tremendously exciting, but part of me was unsettled. Something was just not right. My identity was still tied to being an engineer, not a dancer. And I realized that being an engineer was so much more socially acceptable. It amused me to notice people's reactions when I introduced myself as an engineer rather than a dancer, even in the USA where dance as a profession is much more valued than in the Latino cultures.

Sadly, full-time dancing didn't provide the income I wanted and somehow I missed engineering. I decided to give my CV to one of my dance students, a shy fellow who happened to be one of the higher-ups at a software company. It was funny to be interviewed for a job by this dance student who I knew as overly quiet and shy, but who was very confident and strong in his job. He became my influential and inspiring boss during the day, but in the evenings on the dance floor, I was his.

Things were good. My life felt like it had balance. I was able to explore my passions and was feeding both the left and right sides of my brain. I was able to express both my masculine and feminine sides, being logical and rational while also emotional and passionate. But all this and I still felt unfulfilled. What was my problem?

I knew deep down inside that the choice to go back to engineering was driven more by my need for money and security than anything else. Again I found myself in an amazing workplace, but I was not proud of my work. I was not motivated by it. I knew I was not giving my best and *I didn't want to*. I felt the transformation I had started should not be leading me down this road. There was another path for me to follow, but which one? I had always liked and done hard-core software design and programming. Maybe it was time to lift my head out of this arena. I started exploring different roles in the engineering world. How about not designing programs but teaching them? I liked teaching, maybe if I switched to the training team…? To the marketing team…? To the support team…? Still, I wanted to leave work quickly every day at 5 PM to teach dancing. The transformation that had begun years earlier just wouldn't leave me alone. And so one day, after trying many other things, I decided to quit.

I set up a meeting with my boss to let him know my final decision about quitting my job. I went into his office with this intention in my mind and with great determination, or so I thought. By the end of the discussion, he had persuaded me to stay at the company for just a little while longer. I went home feeling confused. I started exercising in our home kitchen gym (Yes, in the kitchen!). Suddenly, I felt very dizzy and got a splitting headache, then started feeling nauseous. Thinking I had overdone the effort on the chest workout, I took some ibuprofen. The feeling worsened and, along with it, the world around me started sounding strange, muffled and unreal. Despite how I felt, later that afternoon, I headed to the Swiss Consulate where I was scheduled to perform.

At the Swiss Consulate, as we started to dance in the main hall, I told my partner to grab me strong and tight, as I could not hear the music well and felt dizzy. The noise of all the people was unbearable. "It is only one performance. I can do it. This feeling will pass," I told myself.

I made it through the first event and we changed costumes and went on to the next. I reminded myself, "One hour to teach, and then dance, and then done!" We did the one-hour class, my head pounding with noise, my body hurting with some indefinable pain. As I walked off the stage, I just couldn't take it anymore. I felt terrible so I asked my partner to take me to the emergency room. After six painful long waiting hours in one of the best hospitals in Boston, I was diagnosed with a bad ear infection. My dizziness and hearing problems made sense. I could handle the pain and discomfort knowing it would have an end, or so I thought.

I was advised to see a specialist, so I got an appointment a week later, and that is one that I will never forget. I sat on the chair at the doctor's office, and after inspecting my ears with his various tools, the doctor told me matter-of-factly, "You don't have an ear infection." I felt a brief moment of relief before it dawned on me to ask, "What DO I have?" The doctor coldly dropped the bomb on my head, "You've lost your hearing completely."

"Excuse me, WHAT?" I thought. In the most calm manner I could muster, I said to him, "You know, English is not my first language. Let me see if I understood right. Are you saying that I will never hear again in my left ear?" His direct answer was, "Yes. IF you had been correctly diagnosed with a virus last week in the emergency room, maybe the treatment that I prescribe today would have given you more chances of recovering some of your hearing. But now, the chances are slim or none." I sank in the chair, wanting to cry, to shout, to scream. WHY???

Rapid-fire questions pounded in my head. Can I also get the virus in the other ear? How did this happen? Will I become totally deaf? What is my world going to be like if I can't hear? What happens with my engineering? How can I *dance* if I can't hear the music? How can I *teach* if I can't hear my students?

I asked the doctor, "What about the OTHER ear?" "It's a virus," he said. "It won't affect your other ear." I felt myself screaming inside. "REALLY? You don't know what caused this in the first place, but somehow you can ASSURE me that it won't happen to my other ear?" I felt helpless and hopeless.

I was brought to another room to do a hearing test. I tried my best to be a 'good student,' to hear every beep and sound, every tone and buzz, and to press the button that indicated what I could hear. It felt like a life or death test and I failed miserably. Hearing the news, I could feel my entire self shrinking into my core and becoming numb and lifeless. My hearing was lost completely in one ear, and my brain had decided to fill in the void with a constant and very loud plane engine droning in my head 24/7, resulting in tinnitus. My world had changed in a very unexpected way. I hadn't listened to myself, and my body was giving me a wake-up call the hard way. If you don't change when you know you need to change, the message will become louder and louder until you listen. And boy, was the tinnitus loud!!!

I entered a very hard time in my life, hoping that my brain would learn to quiet the noise at night and struggling to learn to live with this sudden hearing loss (SHL) and tinnitus. I wanted to be able to sleep and hoped that the prescribed medication would bring some of my hearing back. I explored alternative medicines, acupuncture, herbs, you name it. I was putting all my effort into bringing back sounds on my left side. I had to learn how to communicate differently. My brain was filling in words that I missed in sentences with other random words.

My life changed overnight, literally. I missed hearing the music in full stereo, but I could still hear it. I missed silent moments but sometimes my brain would give me a break. I started training my brain to understand the world around me in a new way. Which sounds are far and which are close. Which direction are the sounds coming from. How to handle multiple conversations happening in the background. How to position myself around people when they talk. How to increase the volume of what I hear. Most importantly, I was determined not to attach deafness to my identity or let it hinder any part of my life.

I gave myself tools to adapt to this new change so that it would not define me. I kept dancing, teaching, and working as an engineer. I know I pissed some people off because I didn't hear them. I know sometimes I sounded dumb as my answer didn't go with the question. But I did not let it define who I was or what I could be. I created a supportive environment around me. And I learned to tell others what I needed to have a good conversation and a strong connection. I didn't choose this change but courageously found ways to adapt. It wasn't a choice I made, but it was *my* choice in how I dealt with it that made me stronger. It empowered me to become the Change Maker of my own life.

Sometimes, once we start thriving, we realize that we're thriving at the wrong thing. That even though everything seems to be great, it might be time to make another change. After all the changes I had been through, after all the challenges I have overcome, I have learned that in good times, starting from zero can be a truly conscious and powerful decision. It is not an easy one, but the drive to change can lead to something better. Something powerful. Something that brings abundance to your life. I have never regretted any of the choices I have made, as they have brought the learnings that make me the person I am today: Leadership Coach, Speaker, Author, Trainer, and Dancer. My inner voice has become my compass. I see now that choosing only ONE thing was never my path. The steps to my happiness have been me experiencing and doing *all* the things that I love, and learning to listen to myself

There is always a way to thrive no matter what the circumstances. You always have a choice. Don't let things outside of you define you, instead, *listen* to your inner voice and *hear* what really matters to you. Find out who you are independent of any titles by exploring and connecting to your values. Look back, see your trajectory, and realize that you can do many things, make conscious changes, and live by your own beliefs.

"As you start to walk out on the way, the way appears" - Rumi.

IGNITE ACTION STEPS

- **Don't believe everything that you think and feel.**

- **Decide who you want to be.** Remove the noise in your life so you can hear your own thinking and feeling. The beautiful thing about reinventing yourself is that it can be done at any age, needs few to no resources, and can be done as many times as you want. Some useful questions: What is my identity tied to? Is it my job, titles, income, or is it my values ? What do I stand for? What pillars support my BEING and then my DOING? What are my main values in life?

- **Build a growth mindset:** you can always learn new things and better how you currently do what you do. **Experiment boldly,** keeping your mind open. Ask WHAT questions and not WHY.
    What are you going to focus on?
    What meaning are you giving to…?
    What are you going to do now?

- **Begin to act.** Make conscious decisions *every day* and act on them as you transform into the real you. If you don't start acting, nothing will change.

- **Find people who support your journey.** Connect with people who bring out the best in you and also those who challenge your status quo or comfort zone.

Cristina Pujol Jensen - Spain
Leadership Coach, Speaker, Author, Trainer, and Dancer
CondicionateParaTriunfar.com

CHARLOTTE SØEBERG

"True power is being you."

My loving intention is to be courageous and see myself as who I truly am, with both my vulnerabilities on one side and my powerfulness on the other. I invite you to see your true self fully and nudge you to change your painful patterns into healthy and harmonious ones. My sincere hope is, by reading my story, you will be one step closer to living a life where your beautiful YUMMY self is able to flourish and thrive.

TAKING MY OWN MEDICINE

I have been looking everywhere for that note I wrote when I was 17 years old. I know I wrote it on a piece of paper and have kept it for more than 30 years. I even remember putting it in the neat, brown leather cover of my old address book. But it is not there anymore. However, it is still imprinted in my mind, as a blueprint for my whole life. I understand now, as I didn't then, that what I wrote on that piece of paper would subconsciously have a very great impact on me throughout my life.

What I wrote was something along the lines of, *"My intention throughout my life is to embrace every person that I will ever meet exactly as they are, and always make them feel safe and loved in my company."*

It was a beautiful teenage vision *per se*, I thought. I remember how good and special it made me feel to write it, and the love and power that I felt behind it. I felt a warm flush of pride at the thought that I had taken a shortcut into wisdom that was unusual for someone of my age. Yet, what I did not know at that time was that I had a pretty (f*cked up) = unhealthy understanding of what love was. It took me many years of challenging experiences and many broken relationships before I realized what was going on.

I grew up with very loving and well-intentioned parents. Both with big hearts. From an early age, I figured out that the only way I could get attention and feel love from my father was when he would help me with my homework. So, as I remember, I did *a lot* of homework with him. I sometimes wonder if this is one of the reasons why I became a medical doctor? Most of the time, though, he would be in his own little world, smoking cigarettes constantly and writing down formulas on a piece of paper calmly and persistently. He was a very intelligent chemical engineer and very passionate about his work, yet he was not very present with the family in general. My mother, whom I felt very connected to emotionally, was clearly suffering as much as I was from his lack of presence and engagement.

My mother is a very beautiful, happy, and positive soul and has always been. Yet sometimes when my father would do something that would upset her, she would come to me and complain. From a young age, I absorbed her feelings and tried to say or do something that would take her pain away. I could not bear to see her upset. It was as much because I loved her dearly as a survival mechanism that I learned to talk to her and tried to soothe her. Quite often, I would be upset with her, and filled with guilt at the same time. More often though, I would be furious with my father. I tried to the best of my ability to deal with the emotional pain. My mother would praise and thank me, telling me how amazed she was with my skills in making her feel better. She even told friends and family how brilliant I was at this. But this ability was not without consequences.

Throughout my childhood, I constantly had bad stomach pains. Part of it was due to food intolerances. There was another pain though. It was deep and sharp and hurt like a burning knife twisting around in my navel. I felt like this especially when I saw my mother was upset. Even though supporting my mother emotionally had a cost, I am extremely grateful that my mother 'nudged' me to practice and develop a profound empathy and ability to be present. For the last four decades, I have used these skills every day in my relations with my loved ones, with my beloved friends and in my professional life with my patients. I have been told both professionally and privately that I am an empathetic, trustworthy listener, and communicator.

As a physician, my ability to be present is the foundation of my success.

However, the beliefs I documented in that note when I was 17, and the service-minded behaviors that were a result of them, helps me connect with my patients. These beliefs also help me develop deep lasting friendships with beautiful and amazing people. Yet, in my love relationships, my subconscious beliefs turned out to be more destructive and would show up after a while and eat me (us) up… alive.

Right after my 50th birthday, a very loving and intense relationship that I was in, suddenly ended — again. I had not seen it coming and sure enough I was in deep grief and sorrow for months — again. I was so fed up with yet another broken relationship. I felt like a failure. This time, though, I decided to deal with the pain and sorrow in another way. I would wake up in the middle of the night, my mind spinning like a roulette wheel, bringing me wide awake within a split second. My whole body hurt, mostly in my chest. But instead of suppressing my feelings and building yet another armored fortress around my heart, I would just surrender into my feelings of grief, sorrow, pain, and despair. To the absolute best of my abilities, I let all the difficult feelings rush through my body, through each and every cell, with my defenses down. Sometimes the process would feel like a penetrating corrosive acid bath, but I *was* determined to deal with it differently. I promised myself to open up my heart fully and let the love that I so badly wanted to give to instead flow toward myself and heal my unbearable pain. I would even say out loud, "Just come to me pain. Let me feel you. I can take it. Here I am with my broken yet loving heart." Healing of my own wounded emotions felt so much healthier and authentic. Despite the pain, it felt loving and right, and I recovered faster.

During all those sleepless nights, I promised myself that I would get professional help with clearing and changing my subconscious beliefs and whatever else was needed to step into my true power. I was more ready than ever to change my destructive relationship patterns. No more walking on eggshells ever again. I realize that the repeated, unbearable, and hideous pain in yet another broken love relationship was what made me ready to finally become a true change maker. A change maker in my entire life, including in my career as both a family physician and a mindfulness instructor. I have learned how to be of greater contribution to everyone around me, without depleting myself of love and energy, preventing a future burnout or illness.

One and a half years after the break up, feeling better and living my truth, I was walking to my car when I had an unexpected Ignite moment. It was a powerful moment where everything seemed to fall into place and where all the loose ends came together in a beautiful pattern. A kind of connect-the-dots pattern that showed me on a larger scale what had been going on. I knew bits and pieces, here and there. I knew deep inside that I was doing the right things, even though I didn't really understand it all. Finally, the whole picture started to make sense to me. I sat in my car, and leaned my head against the steering wheel as I absorbed what it all meant. At last, I felt I was harvesting the fruits of all of my self-development work throughout more than 30 years. A satisfied and relieved smile appeared on my face as I felt my earned internal power.

It came to me very clearly; I had to use the message on that note I wrote as a teenager, on myself. Interestingly enough, I had intuitively been doing that after the painful relationship break up around 18 months earlier. In that difficult period, I finally started taking my own 'medicine' by giving myself the space to embrace ME exactly as I was and how I felt. Precisely as it was written in the note all those years ago, I was able to make *myself* feel safe and loved instead of focusing on *others* feeling safe and loved by me. Which meant that I was ready to truly and compassionately do so toward others.

I was aware all along from my learnings in self-development, on a conscious intellectual level, that I was supposed to love myself to be able to truly love others, though I had not been aware how strong my sabotaging subconscious beliefs had been tossing me around in my internal emotional tumble dryer. Until recently, I did not have the supporting blueprint nor the tools that I have now to practice loving myself for being me.

Looking back on those nights of surrendering to exactly what *is*, I was *finally* able to *fully* be myself, with both vulnerabilities and powerfulness present at the same time. And because I kept doing it, this became my turning point toward true change. A profound change in my understanding of what love is, seen from a more healthy adult perspective. A change that is of great contribution to both myself and others.

One of the most useful and practical processes I learned in manifesting change is how I learned to fill myself up with love and energy and take care of my inner child. Before I learned this, I would be pulling the love directly from my heart, giving it to my loved ones, which would feel both painful, draining, and depleting of my energy. Step by step I learned by intensely practicing to fill myself up with love in excess. I did this by opening up from the top of my head and feeling a loving, warm, golden light endlessly pouring from The Great Mother through me. In my imagination and using all my senses, I would fill up my heart and all my cells with beautiful warm and loving energy. I continued this process until feeling saturated with love and at peace. After this amazing, wonderful and satisfying infusion, I would let the love overflow and consciously direct any excess energy toward my loved ones, patients, and everyone I have an interaction with.

It turned out that in the written note, when I was just stepping into adulthood, there was a hidden subconscious belief behind that intention. A belief that I had shaped from my understanding as a little girl, that I had to take care of my parents, please them, and sometimes set aside my own needs, for them to love me. The key problem then became that I loved myself more *for my abilities* than *for who I truly am*. I valued myself for my dedication to be there for others which would sometimes require me to twist myself into pieces, often to the detriment of being my true self. This was exhausting and rarely ever beneficial. I did this because I did not want to be discarded.

I now know that my unhealthy belief behind the beautiful intention I had on the note, was, *"I am not worthy of being loved if I do not take care of and please my loved ones."*

I worked intensely and repeatedly with an experienced and empathetic professional to clear and change the subconscious beliefs that blocked me from having a healthy love relationship, and I am extremely grateful that I did. If I were to write my famous note again now, I would write, *"I am enough exactly as I am and I am worthy of being loved for being me."*

After doing all this work, I started dating a wonderful man. I realize now that my perception toward men and love relationships has also changed. I now focus on other important values in our relationship, compared to what I did before.

I am aware that sometimes my new partner is triggering or mirroring some of my fears and shadows. However, I understand that it is at these exact moments, I can choose to let a deeper healing and transformational process take place. Only if I dare to be 100 percent honest with myself and acknowledge which destructive subconscious beliefs are driving me toward the challenges that I am experiencing, can I take action to change them. This way the challenges can be turned around to become a blessing in disguise instead of a path toward attracting more of the same kind of challenges into my life. A blessing that has the potential of healing my wounds.

Today, I am working on staying forever true to myself in my new healthy relationship, knowing that my true power, beneficial for both, lies in being me. My loving actions toward my partner come from another level of perception due to my healthy, transformed core beliefs. I now have been imprinting subconsciously, that I AM worthy of being loved for who I am and not only for what I do.

Now it is easier for me to know what feelings belong to whom. I take responsibility for my emotions and let my partner take care of his. Yet offering my support to an extent that is accepted and wanted from both sides. This way I can act from a conscious place of love, instead of from an underlying subconscious place of fear of rejection.

I have a strong belief and hope that you are in the process of creating a conscious, healthy, honest, compassionate, uplifting and very loving relationship with yourself. I believe that the foundation and power of being a true change maker in the world starts with your enhanced and harmonious love relationship with your true self. May your next step in creating a conscious healthy life be one where you are the maker of change. Love yourself for who you are and that CHANGES everything.

IGNITE ACTION STEPS

Be with exactly what is

We often tend to want to control our life, our circumstances, our emotional reactions and even other people's lives and reactions, instead of accepting exactly what is. We can learn to lean more into, accept, or even surrender to the things that we know we have no power to control anyway. Use three to five minutes every day for two weeks to sit down in a quiet place where you are undisturbed and close your eyes. Pick an incident that happened to you during the day, that was out of your control somehow. Now replay the incident for your inner eye and realize how it feels in your body. Try to describe it to yourself. Talk to yourself in your mind. For example, I can feel it in my stomach. It is a tingling sensation. I also feel a restlessness in my legs and I feel like running away. Be with all the sensations and allow yourself to feel whatever comes up. Keep focusing on the bodily sensations. Stay with it for three to five minutes. Do not try to change anything. Do not analyze. Just be with it exactly as it is. Now imagine that you open your heart and send warmth to the body parts that are involved. It will usually feel less intense after a while, especially if you do not resist the process.

Changing your beliefs

The first step to changing a subconscious belief is becoming aware of it. Think of a category in life where blockages or destructive patterns seem to come up for you repeatedly, for example in emotional life, love life, financial life, or in any other category.

Step 1: Sit down with a blank piece of paper and on the top write down your goal or vision in present tense like it already happened. If you choose to work on emotional life, a specific goal could be: I honor, respect and love every feeling I have. It is easy for me to understand the message behind my feelings and this makes my emotional intelligence expand every single day.

Step 2: Write down limiting beliefs. 1) Take two to three deep breaths. 2) Set an intention to be open to whatever is going to come to you. 3) Start each sentence with, *"I have a belief about emotions that…."* and then finish the sentence. It could, for example, be, "I have a belief about emotions that if I show too many feelings then I am weak." or "When I get angry I will push people away." Keep writing until you are empty of beliefs.

Step 3: Look at the list and ask yourself about each belief: How does my life feel like with this belief? And is it really true?

Step 4: Read your goal again and ask yourself, "How does it feel when I have reached my goal?" Keep this elevated emotion inside while doing step five.

Step 5: Write down beliefs that will support you toward your goal. Repeat part one to three of Step 2. For example, write, "I have a belief about emotions that my emotions are the compass of my soul or that when I learn to embrace my own feelings, it is easier to embrace others or my emotions are not me, rather they are passing thoughts that create a physical sensation in my body to teach me something."

Inner child work

Right before you go to sleep, close your eyes and place your right hand just underneath your navel and your left hand on your heart. Take two to three deep breaths to get in contact with yourself. Now make an intention to get in contact with your inner child. See your younger self playing somewhere, maybe out in nature. Get in contact with how he/she is doing right now. Just let any picture or emotion show up. Embrace however he/she is feeling and do not try to change or fix anything. Imagine that you effortlessly send him/her love directly from your heart to his/hers. While doing this, make sure to open up the top of your head (Crown Chakra) to let endless love from The Great Mother fill you up constantly. Imagine asking him/her what he/she needs from you. It can be with or without words in your imagination. Accept also if he/she does not answer you. Just be with him/her and let whatever unfolds happen without judgment. Do this exercise for three to five minutes every night for a minimum of two weeks.

Charlotte Søeberg - Denmark
Medical Doctor, BA psychology, Mindfulness Instructor
and Personal Development Inspirator
www.charlottesoeberg.com

MARÍA EUGENIA ANÉS DRAEGERT

"Embrace vulnerability and be known for who you really are."

It is necessary to live with an understanding of how fragile we are, to recognize that, from our vulnerability, we can connect with others more deeply from a place of love. From there, we can find the strength that leads us to take charge of our lives, to make resolute decisions that solve our problems. My hope is that you have the courage to experience vulnerability and know that you are capable of overcoming and solving whatever may be happening to you.

GETTING TO KNOW VULNERABILITY

My story contains three different experiences I have had with vulnerability. They have helped me become a better version of me.

I was raised in the '80s in South America by two amazing parents. My mother, Milagros, is intelligent and empowered. People describe her as a Jill-of-all-trades. She is one of those women who does not stop for anyone or anything, always hard-working and a relentless learner. My father, Nino, has amazing qualities of humility, tolerance, and love for others. He is a feminist; he is one of those men who takes you out shopping for party outfits when you start going out at 15. The combination of these two amazing beings resulted in four daughters, who I can rightfully describe as intelligent and having hearts full of love.

My sisters are three spectacular human beings. Gaby, my twin, is the one who did not follow any rules when she was younger, but now is my anchor, my northern point when my compass diverts its course, the one who is always there when you need her and even when you do not. Mary is the angel who landed in the family; she is like an angel on earth. She has that special something that makes her truly unique. She is the best possible friend you could have. Mary would give everything up for her family. The youngest is Fernanda, the millennial of the family who arrived 25 years later. She is so innocent. She seems as if she were Mary's daughter, so similar in souls are they, the very personification of innocence. Unlike all my other sisters, I am the structured one in the family, like my mom, but also frequently spontaneous and playful.

One of the most relevant moments of my life happened when I was 15 years old. We received the news that my older sister Mary had lupus. I remember that moment with the sharpest clarity: we were sitting on the porch where we grew up. My mother bravely shared, "I have something to tell you. Your sister has *systemic lupus erythematosus.* She will be fine, but she must take care of herself because she has a health condition." I did not understand what that meant, but judging by the looks of uncertainty and seriousness on my parents' faces, I knew hard times were ahead and that our family would face this with a good attitude. However, I was still so young and not sure if it was because my mom was so confident, and therefore gave us plenty of calmness, or if my family was just believing my mom's hopeful convictions.

When my sister found out, she took it as if she had been told something totally ordinary, with zero drama and a lot of maturity. That impressed me. They told her she had an immune disease which did not have a cure. That it was life-long. That she had to take care of herself, could not be exposed to the sun ever, and had to wear long sleeves and use an umbrella at all times. That would have sent any 20-year-old into the worst confusion and uneasiness, but not her. Mary said, "OK. Let's see how it all unfolds."

And so we did exactly that. Into our lives came years of trips to the capital for medical exams. Cyclically, the lupus always attacked some organ: skin, lung, or kidney and critical episodes would hit my sister yearly. But she was always there, defending herself from those attacks. And we were always there with her, with a lot of family love, giving her the confidence and tranquility she needed to keep going. Families have a choice in these situations and we chose to band together in strength and love.

I was sad and confused, because we had never experienced such a critical and complicated situation. It was further exacerbated by the convoluted situation in

Venezuela that made medication hard to find. That, plus the difficulty in traveling, represented a daily struggle. We had to search for medication throughout the entire city, even in other countries. I noticed that my family did not dare to express their feelings most of the time.

During my sister's most critical episode, we limited our interaction to dealing with our daily needs like eating and buying medicine. We became like robots. However, none of us ever lost the drive to go on, and I was always the one leading everyone else. In retrospect, I realize how this situation started to make me more thick-skinned, and to reinforce the leader in me. Likewise, I noticed it is crucial to maintain hope. With open hearts and minds, I was able to recognize angels when they appeared in the shape of friends, strangers, and doctors, and they helped us in getting what Mary needed. It was extremely gratifying for me to realize that we are never really alone in our struggles.

My sister started her process of recovery and, with a lot of personal care, plenty of medication, and development of self-awareness on her part and in everybody surrounding her, she is now fully recovered and living happily. And she even overeats! God gave us the chance to remain by her side and we are forever grateful and forever changed.

The doctors today confirm that my sister is a miracle of life, that the love from her family and her urge to live was what made her survive. From this journey, I extracted many lessons. This year and a half meant huge change for everyone involved. Life played us very hard, but we hit back with love, faith, resilience, self-confidence, and self-knowledge. All of these traits, so well defined for each member of the family, helped me develop the abilities that made me a better person today.

Contrary to all expectations, her vulnerability with regard to her health did not inhibit her from being the great wife, mother, daughter, sister, and working woman she is today. Witnessing my sister's health struggles and seeing up close how life-changing it was, not just for her but for the entire family, *changed* me profoundly. Her story made me look at other situations in a different light. Through her vulnerability, I found my strength, self-knowledge, and resilience to get ahead despite so much adversity.

I see many people dealing with similar, critical situations, who rise above while others have their health, have so much going for them, yet are miserable in their lives. We sometimes think we live in a box, assuming that nothing bad will happen, and when it does, we need to step out of our limitations and find our strength, hope, and our angels. We need to fight for that! Now look at yourself, value who you are, and recognize your ability to move forward in your personal and working life. Be the change you want to be!

Undergoing Vulnerability From Another Perspective

I was 21 years old, working for a transnational company, starting from the bottom and trying to climb the corporate ladder. Despite being a strong and intelligent woman, I was the victim of a number of situations of harassment and microaggressions. Those situations did not escalate because, every time one would present itself, I defended myself in a rational, self-confident manner. I did not let those moments go overboard and result in sexual harassment.

I remember the first one very clearly. My boss invited me to a work meeting in the restaurant of a hotel, later to invite me to his room. My body started to shake. I felt humiliated. Why was he doing this? With a trembling voice, I gave him what I felt was the obvious response, that he had me all wrong and that I didn't have to accept something like that, even if it meant my dismissal.

The second instance happened three years later with another executive. We traveled together in his car to an event where we were to give a presentation. When we were headed back to the office, he took a detour toward a motel. When the car turned off the road, I felt the same humiliation, the same shakiness as the first time. Once again, I used my voice and my power. I asked him what he was doing and threatened to report him to Human Resources unless he returned us to the office or let me get out of the car and take a taxi.

The third was ten years later, with yet another superior, the CEO of the company. In an after-office meeting, he tried to put his hand inside my shirt. After ten years of this sort of behavior, I no longer felt humiliated. I no longer shook from fear. Instead, I stopped him in his tracks, as I had many times before. In a very controlled tone, I told him that he was mistaken. The next day, I presented my resignation letter, which was not accepted. Instead I was sent to another country because I did not share the same 'spirit of leadership' as this CEO. Since that moment, my other bosses have not tried to make such advances. I am sure it's because I have a new attitude. I don't show my vulnerability to *them*, I reserve it for those who love me. My position now is that of a strong and intelligent woman *who holds myself in equal standing to them*.

In those situations, I lived my vulnerability. Like so many other women living, suffering, and wishing to be entrepreneurial leaders, I knew I needed to stand in both my vulnerability *and* my strength. Women have such a hard time climbing that corporate ladder. It may be because people do not trust their ability to direct a company, or because they assume the roles and stereotypes that are so clearly defined in many societies: that women take care of the children and do the housework, not be leaders.

I tell you this because I realized that I was scared before and I felt vulnerable. Maybe it was because I was very young and going through these experiences for the first time. Now I know that you need to find the courage and rationality to face them with zero drama. You need to get through them and become stronger for the next time it happens, because... be sure that it will happen again... and you must be an advocate of change!

Embracing Vulnerability, I Found My Purpose

With all of this on my mind, and going through experiences from which I only salvage the lessons learned, I started to work on myself. I tried not to have inner voices that distracted me from being the person I wanted to be. I did my best to figure out how to get through the days, how to face complicated situations and come out better. I learned how to diminish my ego and *welcome* vulnerability, accept myself as I am, and be aware that I have the strength to get ahead in any situation.

I went to therapy and had heart-to-heart conversations with family and friends. That's how I learned where my inner voice was coming from and I started acknowledging it. I talked a lot with my friends, Susana and Diana, who are feminists and intelligent women, about how we could contribute toward a society with equal opportunities for men and women. We wondered how we could make a better world for people who think differently and break the traditional rules of conservative societies in Latin America. We both agreed that, sadly, inclusion and diversity are far from being a reality, but we wanted to be inspiring role models for other women.

I felt powerless because I couldn't understand how to collaborate and resolve this situation. Being in the corporate world for so many years, it was part of my daily life to become a robot and accept that I didn't have the same equal opportunities as men. It was an uphill battle to achieve a promotion or even have the same salary, or the same capabilities. Many times, it was frustrating that showing my vulnerability resulted in men taking advantage of me in many situations.

With this aggravating concern, I found my purpose: to support women, giving them tools for their empowerment and making them more aware of their capabilities, so that they could continue advancing toward executive positions within their organizations.

I believe it is necessary to lower the volume of our self-criticism and evade the perfectionism that characterizes us as women. Many times, this will not let us move forward and it stops us from applying for higher positions which require additional studies and more experience. Women, especially entrepreneurs or corporate workers, need to recognize the social vulnerability that might exist in their surroundings, and the vulnerability which comes from being a woman in roles that break the stereotypes in many conservative societies.

With all this awareness, with my co-founders, we launched an undertaking called **Corewoman**: an innovation laboratory in New York and Latin America dedicated to closing the gender gap. We launched our brand without having everything ready! We had an idea of what we wanted, but it wasn't as structured as we would have liked. But we did not let perfectionism beat us to it! We decided to launch as we were so we could start making a difference immediately! Today, everything is much clearer. We have a presence in six countries and have worked with more than 3000 women of different social stratas and from vulnerable areas. The learning has been amazing! We help them strive for their economic independence and confidence in themselves. In the entrepreneurial area, we provide tools for those who start from scratch (as I did) to help them reach their own individual goals.

While working with those women, I became so much more aware that we could improve our capacity as confident individuals in order to achieve our major goals. How we speak, how we answer, how to listen more and react less, and how our body language speaks on our behalf is the message we give out to the world.

Now, I have conviction that women can and should be vulnerable and show ourselves as we really are. Society is changing. It is necessary to stop, evaluate ourselves, and see how we can collaborate from a place of vulnerability to be able to adapt to and embrace inclusion and diversity.

Writing this story has been a magnificent lesson to get to know myself even more and to recognize what legacy I want to leave behind as a Female Change Maker (something that is very difficult for many women to identify). Today, I know that I no longer want to be a robot. I want to feel and connect more with people. The way to do that is by showing myself exactly as I am: a transparent, vulnerable, intelligent person with a great desire to live in a better world. I feel closer than ever to discovering who I am and I wish that for you. I want you to live in the present, yet see your future possibilities. To embrace your womanness and love your vulnerabilities. We all need to be aware of our capabilities for change. Have the courage to change. In changing you become a better version of yourself and that inspires the next woman, to become her own powerful Change Maker.

IGNITE ACTION STEPS

Every time negative feelings or insecurity invade your thoughts, be aware of it. Stop for a moment, separate them, isolate them and tell them, "Today, you're not going to sabotage me!" Believe in yourself! Increase your levels of self-confidence and self-esteem to be able to go out into the world and play big. Turn down the volume of that little voice of internal criticism and turn up the volume of the mentor that comes from within!

Set your expectations of the world. Don't expect to receive from people the same thing that you would give them. Each person is unique and everyone is different. Learn to raise your voice as a woman. I'm not talking about yelling, but rather placing your point of view on the table. Do not doubt your capabilities and how far you can get if you believe in yourself!!! Believe that you are enough! From that place where self-love lies, you can open many paths that you never would have thought were available before.

Let's be women who support women. It is so powerful when we get together for the common good, inviting men to the table to have enriching conversations. Additionally, if we want to be included in conversations, let's treat men with the same compassionate respect.

María Eugenia Anés Draegert - Venezuela
Co-Founder and Develop Markets Director – COREWOMAN
www.corewoman.org

NICOLE STOKER EVANS, PT, DPT, CSCS

"The Other Side of Fear is Where You Find Your Greatness."

My hope for you is that you will come to the realization that fear does not have to be a lasting paralysis. Experiencing and acknowledging fear is not a weakness. It is a vital aspect of our growth. Feel confident in knowing that you too are capable of walking through that fear, pushing forward, and coming out on the other side as the very best version of you.

KEEP MOVING FORWARD

It was an ordinary Tuesday morning like any other when I woke up, reached for my phone on the bedside table, looked at the date and thought "Oh, my gosh…" Exactly six months ago to the day, I had taken sole ownership of my company. I realized in that moment, lying in the tiny patch of sun that warmed my side of the bed, that I had made it. I hadn't failed. My company was still running. Not only was it running, it was *thriving*.

I had been told that I wouldn't last this long on my own. There was a part of me that insisted on believing the persistent voice telling me I wouldn't make it, so this realization — that my business was doing everything I had hoped — was intensely powerful. I had spent the last six months, since my divorce and taking ownership of my company, putting one foot in front of the other and simply moving forward. Not moving forward was *not* an option for me, or at least, it didn't feel like one. I had too many people depending on me to keep going. Those people, my kids and my employees, saved me during those six months by keeping me focused. That morning, pushing back the covers and getting ready to start my day, I knew I was capable!

For years, in my mind, I felt I wasn't enough on my own. I felt that the successes that I had must have been because of someone else. I wasn't even sure how I had gotten to where I was. I just knew that I hadn't let fear take hold of me and stop me. There were times when fear crept in loudly and felt deafening. In those times, the fear making it physically difficult to breathe, I would sit in my favorite corner of the couch, paralyzed by the choices I needed to make, by the impact those choices would have on others, and would question it all over and over again. I didn't trust myself yet, to make choices on my own, but it was different now. I was making the decisions, and it felt good. My actions were all true to who I was and what I believed in.

I felt so much better about my company now than I did when I was married, had a business partner, and was making significantly more money. It was refreshing to be making my own business decisions without the judgment and influence of others. I was able to sleep at night knowing that I believed wholeheartedly in what I was doing and was proud of the exceptional service my company, Synergy Physical Therapy, was providing. I genuinely wanted a company that stood for Synergy... where the patient and physical therapist work together to accomplish an even greater goal to achieve a functional and empowered life. I now have that, and it is a great sense of relief to know I did it without compromising my values.

This exciting shift in momentum was the start of a very different company vision and a very different version of myself. I no longer anxiously wondered if my business would fail. My mindset shifted on that day from "How do I survive?" to "How can I help my company, employees, and patients thrive?" I started thinking more about the culture of my team, how I wanted that to look and feel, and how we could provide not only great support but also the best and the most forward thinking care. My passion for the profession and my own learning grew in leaps and bounds.

As a child, I was always striving to be the 'best' or what I thought was the best. At age six, my belief of being the best meant being the best in class or striving to be the best on the court or on the field. I would hear my parents, teachers, and coaches say that we should all be striving to be **our** best, but I could never get a solid grasp on what that looked like for me.

Each time I found myself at the top of my class, it surprised me how unsatisfied and unfulfilled I felt. It was the same dissatisfied feeling as when I didn't find myself at or near the top. I kept thinking that once I'd reach success, I would feel differently, but the feelings of excitement, accomplishment, and being the best never showed up. I'm not sure that I ever found out what I was fully capable of at school or in sports, which is a regret I sorely hold with me to this day.

When I reflected on why that may have been, why I was never willing to go all in, it alway ended up pointing to a fear of failure. I thought, "If I don't try my hardest and fail, it won't hurt as much, because I didn't try my best." The problem with that is the everlasting question of "What if?" that we sometimes don't get another chance to answer. I don't know what would have happened or where I would have ended up in my academics, athletics, career, and relationships if I would have genuinely pushed my limits, been vulnerable, and given it my all.

People have always seen me as a confident individual, and I always wondered how they didn't see my fear. That fear felt so visible and tangible to me. I was confident only within that box I lived in, within the walls I created for myself, as I knew I could succeed there.

I took that same mindset with me through my high school, undergraduate, and graduate college experiences. I graduated near the top of my class throughout my schooling but was still afraid to really push myself outside of my comfort zone or beyond where I already knew or thought my limits were.

I had always wanted to be a physician, more specifically a surgeon. I wanted to make what I felt was a definitive and positive change in patients' lives. When I met my husband, I wanted to pursue my dream of becoming a physician, but I would need to move to another state for schooling. I had just been married and was reluctant to move, so I looked at what I considered to be my backup plan, physical therapy. At the time, it felt like settling, and I really struggled internally with letting go of that dream. This disappointment I held on to for quite a few years. There was, however, a part of me that felt relieved because I didn't know if I would even make it through medical school, if I was intelligent enough, or if I would fail and people would finally see the failure that I consistently felt.

When I first graduated and became a Physical Therapist, I felt I was right where I was supposed to be. I had the opportunity to spend ample time with my patients, to see them through their entire recovery process, and to witness the benefits in their lives. Despite the changes that happened, I am excited to go to work each day, working with patients and employees that are driven and motivated to improve their lives. I'm grateful each day to be part of that progress and success.

My husband and I decided to open our own physical therapy practice during my last year of schooling. It was an exciting and daunting adventure which dominated our lives for several years. We opened three physical therapy clinics and a store, had two children, and I managed to, slowly, over time, lose bits of myself. My kids and my love for them kept me going. I spent every free moment making wonderful memories with them. They brought me happiness and let me forget about how unfulfilled I was in other aspects of my life. We've all heard or read stories about women or men losing themselves, forgetting who they are, letting go of their interests, and for all kinds of reasons. It's interesting, though, how it happens without you realizing it. We fill our time with things that we feel will bring us that happiness and those things are somewhat successful in filling that void. However, if we haven't dealt with the real issues, we soon find ourselves right back where we were... unfulfilled.

In those 13 years of marriage, I lost my authentic voice. I'm not sure that I ever took the time to really find it prior to being married though, and maybe that's why I lost it so easily. On paper, I had a great life. People referred to us as the power couple. We had a successful business, a beautiful home, and two adorable children. However, there were times when I would reflect on where I was, what I was doing, and why I didn't feel fulfilled. I could never come up with any great answers. It got to the point where I couldn't even remember what the 'old Nicole' was like. I had stopped talking to any of my childhood and college friends. I hadn't played volleyball, a sport I loved, in nearly 10 years. I was spending less and less time doing things that I previously found enjoyable, and I was doing my best to be the wife and mother I thought I should be. The problem was, I didn't feel like I was the person I wanted my kids to see and know. I was going through the motions but was a shell of myself.

I realized that, at work, my and my partner's approaches to the business and patient care were very different. Our views on life and what we each placed importance in also didn't align. I had a harder time with these differences the longer time went on. I was consistently making hollow excuses for why things were the way they were, why I wasn't as engaged in family functions, or the reasons I wasn't going out with friends. I rationalized so many things to myself and even started to believe my own stories.

It took a very unexpected friendship to help me start to see myself again. It was not someone I would have expected would change my life. Yet there they were, standing strong beside me and giving me the courage to take small steps toward unlocking the person, mother, and business owner that I desperately wanted to be. I thought for a while that my new found strength was because of them and wondered how they saw me as this strong and capable person. This unexpected blessing in my life reminded me to simply reflect on who I was. They took the time to ask the questions no one else was asking. Was I happy? Was this the life I wanted for myself? For my kids? Was I willing to make a change?

Up to that point, I had wondered if it was all in my head since no one in my life ever said anything or asked questions about my happiness. I guess I had done a decent job of painting a picture to others of a happy life. I think it goes back to that 'perfect life on paper' issue. Even though I was so far from the person I had once been, from the person they knew me to be, they said nothing. I will be forever grateful to this friend and the courage they had to ask those questions and to help me start to see my life and myself with more clarity.

As I started to open my eyes again and see things clearly, I felt rejuvenated. I felt excited about life despite the fears that I had about doing it on my own. I soon realized that 'Doing it on your own' isn't even a thing! It takes countless people woven through our journey to guide us to success.

This tiny glimpse into the other side of fear helped me become less and less paralyzed by it. I learned to move through it, not to walk around it or give it space in my life. I learned that, when we move forward, we aren't leaving things in the past unless that's where they need to be left. We are forging those experiences and lessons into a place where we are now capable of taking control of our own life.

I can now say that I am deeply proud of Synergy Physical Therapy, what it stands for and the people who have helped me create it. We now have four clinics and employ 48 outstanding individuals with an enormous collective passion and energy for the field. We are known for giving exceptional care and training top-notch future physical therapists. I feel so blessed to be where I am today and to have the opportunity to share my passion, inspire, and lead such a wonderful group of individuals. I am grateful to be on the other side of those fears I had five years ago.

It is not a weakness to be afraid. It's the choices we make *after* the fear that really count. I believe that the biggest hurdle we all face is not understanding what our true limits are. Unless you are willing to go there, to push yourself to the edge of what you thought possible, you have no idea how far you are destined to go.

I can now confidently say I love my life. I am a better person. A better mother. My sons now get to see my authentic self, and I love that. I enjoy the freedom to be myself and want my boys to embrace their uniqueness as well. We talk openly about the successes and struggles of schooling, athletics, work, and life in general and they happily give me advice and suggestions on how to improve my tennis and volleyball game. Their unconditional love and support through this journey has helped and encouraged me to get to where I am today. They are excellent examples in their willingness to walk through fear, and they always encourage me to do the same. I have found the strength in my life that I so craved.

My childhood belief of my limits was just that... a childhood belief. It was not my reality. It was not until I stepped outside of my limiting beliefs that I discovered what I could be. I *changed* my perception of myself and *made* a conscious choice to push outside my box. As a woman and female business owner, I instill change in others by encouraging people to find what they are passionate about. I have a firm belief that we all have unique gifts and talents. We are all meant to be great at something. Step outside your comfort zone and really take a chance. It will be fulfilling, and in doing so you can thrive in every aspect of your life.

Ignite Action Steps

Over the years, I have learned that there are a few simple things we can do to work through fear and hold true to ourselves. I have listed my favorites below.

Set a timer. Make a choice now, when things are going well, that when you find yourself in that paralysis from fear, you will set a timer. When that timer goes off, you make a conscious choice to get up and move. It doesn't mean that you have to deal with the issue at hand right then, but you do have to move. Get up from the couch. Get out of bed. Get outside. Get moving.

Find those people in your life who allow you to be *you*. Don't take them for granted. Oftentimes, these people are our family, but sometimes, you're lucky enough to find that one unexpected friend who really truly accepts you for *you*... that person (or those people) who gives you the freedom to be you is invaluable. Cherish them.

Regularly take time to think about who you are and who you want to be. Talk with someone you trust about this. Share what you desire for yourself so they can help hold you accountable. Otherwise, it is too easy to lose ourselves in our day-to-day work tasks, chauffeuring our adorable kids around, trying to get dinner on the table, making time to exercise, and all of the other tasks that we put value in throughout our day.

Commit to making time for at least one thing that you really love to do, and don't feel guilty about it. That's the toughest part! However, when you see the positive effect it has on you and how that flows not only into everything you do but also into those around you, that guilt will dissipate.

The other side of fear is where you find your greatness so push your limits and see what you discover.

Nicole Stoker Evans, PT, DPT, CSCS - United States
Doctor of Physical Therapy, Business Owner,
Certified Strength and Conditioning Specialist
www.synergyptnv.com

DIANA PELÁEZ

"Weave the threads of your present to build the tapestry of your future."

I want to share with you that you have the power to transform lives. When you believe you can make a difference in other people's lives and you dream of all possibilities, a universe of creative opportunities will emerge for everyone. By uncovering other people's passions and strengths, you can show them how to dream about the *impossible* and make it *possible*!

SOWING IN THE SOUL

A Tapestry of Families For Powerful Communities

My family has always been passionate about baseball. My grandfather and later my father owned the Willard baseball team in Barranquilla, Colombia. Baseball was what our family did. Growing up, I spent countless hours traveling from stadium to stadium, watching the games, and watching my parents use the games to change the world. My parents loved to use baseball as a tool to instill values and provide education. The sport was the vehicle to help children and youth create their own life project and get away from the dangers of the streets, drugs, and crime. Growing up and going with my parents to the games allowed me to see how they helped everybody: the man selling corn-on-a-cob to the crowd, the ones taking care of the cars, the bat boys, and of course, the baseball players.

My family's passion for social change has been part of my day-to-day life. My mother would go street by street in neighborhoods, towns, and cities in

Colombia looking for children and teaching them to play baseball. People loved her. The kids were always crowding around her when our car arrived before a practice. I remember the children running over and hugging her. They showered her with beautiful words, compliments, and gratitude. She was always around, always had time for everyone, and always had time for me. She made me feel so special. She was my hero. I didn't like baseball much or maybe I just didn't understand many things about it, but I remember coming home from school and she was always available for me. I know how she did it. I always saw her struggle in a world of men, but she never gave up. Going along with her to games and practices, I got to see a part of the world where opportunities and possibilities were not easy to come by. That experience shaped who I became, without me even knowing it. What is most amazing is that her passion is still intact to this day. And, after all those years, I have come to understand that her passion is now mine. I realized that we are one, that we vibrate with the same energy, and helping others is part of our essence.

Watching her showed me how changing and impacting other people's lives was transformational. It showed me what would become *my* life's path. Since I was a child, I saw both my parents bring new possibilities to vulnerable populations, showing them other ways of living, assuring them that they are not doomed to poverty and that being born poor does not force them to remain poor forever.

Through baseball, helping others became a part of my DNA. Many of those kids are now adults: Renteria, Quintana, Theran, and Ushella are now in the United States Major League Baseball. And they still adore my mother, calling her and sharing their joy with her regularly. At my mother's knee, I came to believe that education is the best tool to transform lives and provide opportunities for those who have not yet had the chance to start their dreams and become Change Makers.

As a young woman, I decided to study law at a university in Colombia not too far from home. For four years I spent my days immersed in law books and classes, but I soon realized it was not my calling. Something was missing. I took a year off to live in London, England.

In London, I was free to follow any whim that caught my fancy, at least for a little while. I spent the first few days waking up and wandering the streets, having a coffee at a little cafe, visiting museums, soaking in the art, marveling in the architecture, and adoring the vibrant colors I saw there. I immersed myself in reading, exploring literature I had not read before that was far more interesting than my law books. I traveled — exploring everything around me on my own. I had never done those things by myself before and the joy I felt in my newfound freedom was almost unimaginable. I lived in a shared flat with three other students, no longer enjoying all the comforts of living in my family home with my parents in Colombia. I became self-reliant and capable of so much more than I had ever dreamed.

One rainy afternoon, I was walking down the street and I passed by a Montessori school. That night, talking to my flatmates, one of them mentioned my sister had attended Montessori schools. Intrigued, I stopped by the school the next day to get more information about it. The school was situated in a beautiful house and it radiated such an *energy*. Within seconds of stepping inside the building, I just *knew* this was it. This was what I wanted to do. It was an Ignite moment for me.

I started studying early childhood education. I loved education so much that I became determined to be a Change Maker in my hometown. I didn't want to bring more traditional education to Colombia; instead, I wanted to help children be autonomous, creative, and *happy*, and to know that they are fully capable of reaching for the stars.

With that crystal clear vision, 23 years ago my family and I founded a kindergarten in Barranquilla, Colombia, with the idea of using innovative, out-of-the-box ideas to deliver the best experiences for children to feel whole, supported, and happy. We called it *Happy Time*. There, we allowed children and families the ability to invest in quality education for their children.

Thanks to the success of *Happy Time* and its sustainability for over two decades, with close to 3500 graduated children, a door I never imagined opened. The opportunity arose to transform communities and generate the equity I had always dreamed of by bringing my experience with *Happy Time* to the public sector. This is how the *Tiempo Feliz Foundation* was born (which means Happy Time Foundation in Spanish).

I had no idea that *Tiempo Feliz Foundation* would not only change the communities I was working in, it would come to change my entire life. The idea of doing it was both exciting and intimidating at the same time. With fear, desire, many ideas, and a great team, I threw myself into the unknown. All we had was a compass that allowed us to have a clear horizon of where we wanted to go. I learned that facing this world is not easy, but when dreams are strong, any obstacle that presents itself can be overcome.

With time, I understood that the only certainty in the world is change. *Tiempo Feliz* and *Happy Time* are my daily inspiration. They have given me the opportunity to accompany many children and families through the process of shaping their dreams — strengthening the emotional health of their communities, helping families and individuals as they develop their own life story. My work is based on three main pillars of action: education, family training, and promotion of creative use of free time. Based on these pillars, we have been able to touch many hearts. Working with each of those who are part of the foundation, and understanding their needs, interests, and knowledge, has allowed us to create an inspiring, transforming, unique, and collective process. Every story is like a thread, that when spun together, creates a beautiful piece of art.

The panorama of the reality for children in my country is bleak, and abuse in all its forms prevails in Colombian families. Acknowledgement of these facts has driven me to direct all my efforts toward changing this reality. I strongly believe that by sowing in the soul the desire to change and the idea that there are other ways of living and sharing, parents will feel empowered and conscious. Helping these communities became my passion and obsession.

My life story has always led me to think about others, about education and how to generate opportunities for building equality. I now dream about the impossible and make it possible. My commitment is to positively impact the lives of all the people in Colombia, all children and their families and show them their potential. That has led me to embark on an adventure full of challenges, stumbles, and yet, much happiness. It has allowed me to grow day by day and be able to reach many communities, providing them with the power to transform their own stories. It has given me the chance to look them in the eye and say, "Yes, it is possible and we will do it together!"

My big challenge as a Change Maker is to transform the stories of unsafe and unprotected communities and neighborhoods into safe and protective environments filled with happy, committed, and empathetic children, youth, and families — one story at a time. With that in mind, the many programs and strategies we have created at *Tiempo Feliz Foundation* are aimed at preventing child violence, insecurity, and hopelessness by generating spaces for learning, co-developing community response, and creating collaborative support networks.

I have always wanted to inspire others to believe they can make a change. I want to invite them to touch their hearts and awaken their senses, to show them that where there is a Wheel, there is a way. That they know opportunities are there, and challenges must be taken to grow, evolve, and create each person's own story.

The first pillar of my mission is education. I have always opted to deliver high-quality education for children, education that manages to transform processes and generate equitable and solidary communities. For me, quality education is about maintaining high standards in pedagogy, proper nutrition, training, and support to families. We provide exceptional educational spaces with high-quality learning materials according to the age of the children and their needs in harmony with their community roots, customs, and traditions. Likewise, quality education demands qualified, well-trained, and highly skilled human talent, and transparent and efficient money management.

When I think of education, I dream of breaking down barriers, of fully developing the potential of each child, of giving them a powerful opportunity to overcome their own history. Education impacts all areas of life giving you knowledge and makes you more confident to go out and achieve things. Imagine you are weaving a tapestry — you know how to do it and you have developed the skills; the yarn will be spun together and without gaps.

The second pillar of my work is family training. Family is the first circle of safety and support for children. If the family is aggressive, the child is unprotected and faces negative situations in their life, which affects their integral development. We accompany families in their parenting processes, training and educating them in knowing what children are like, what they can expect at each age and stage of development, and we give them practical tools for handling common childhood situations. We train families to prevent child violence, strengthen emotional ties between parents and children, recognize their own family history in order to heal difficult moments of their childhood, and deliver tools of friendly, loving, and respectful parenting patterns. I am convinced that training and accompanying families through their parenting journey is the magic key for reducing childhood violence.

The third pillar of my work is the promotion of creative spaces for a more positive use of free time. Not knowing what to do when you do not have an occupation or a hobby is the single biggest risk factor for falling into the consumption of psychoactive substances, crime, and school dropout — deadly traps for ignorance and poverty.

When I think about what we do, I make an analogy in my mind. I imagine a train representing the first and most important pillar of education, full of wagons loaded with raw materials to construct dreams, such as literature, art, and music. I imagine our team traveling on this train, visiting parks and empty lots, providing the tools to many children, youth, and families for them to fill those spaces with inspiring stories, life dances, and songs full of meaning. I have found that this complements formal education, generating recreational spaces that children can use in their free time, preventing kids from doing drugs, hanging with the wrong crowd, and dropping out of school.

My journey through the lives and stories touched by the Foundation reminds me every day that where there is a desire to make change, there is a way! Every day, I am encouraged to continue delivering threads to weave new stories together and help change lives.

So many amazing moments have resulted in this endeavour. I remember the day one little boy came up to me and whispered, "Miss, please, can you take care of the toys?" I asked him why he was telling me that and he said, "My father is a robber. He is going to come here and take these things and sell them."

I was shocked. I couldn't believe what he was telling me but immediately I started thinking this was an opportunity! I had to make this boy see this situation as a strength instead of a liability. I had to show how everyone deserves to have all the beautiful toys and school supplies to create with. We started working with all of the families, making them a part of the school and our different programs. Today, those families are the ones who take care of us. *They* protect us. They know that we are there to help them build a better world, in their families, in their community. That what we do is worth fighting for and is what they deserve. They deserve to be treated equally, to have those circles of poverty broken. This is when you see the real change.

That is why I wake up every day to work in the morning and keep innovating. I want to make a contribution to my country by showing the most vulnerable how the impossible can become possible, how dreams can come true, and how education can become a right and not a luxury. I am convinced that with my work I do not carry services for people, but I deliver a suitcase full of threads and needles for weaving stories. Stories of triumphs, overcoming challenges, fulfilled dreams, and transformed lives. Along the path I have witnessed that education is a living entity that breathes and with adequate nutrition, it can evolve into unimaginable lengths.

Dreaming is part of my inspiration. Dream with me and we will build a better world, transforming, impacting, and changing lives. We can break the barriers and limitations of today allowing tomorrow's possibilities to emerge. You could choose to be a Change Maker, to lead change in your community, in your work, or in your life starting immediately. You don't need much: only the desire to do it. Dream big, believe in yourself, use your curiosity and creativity, and always remember that what may seem like a failure, an obstacle, or a problem may be an opportunity to grow.

Ignite Action Steps

- Ask yourself, "What is limiting me?"
- Ask a community leader, "How can I help?", "How can I support you in what you're doing?" This might open a door to a big opportunity for someone you haven't met yet.
- Find a passion that you can share with others in your community.
- Dream BIG.
- Have gratitude.
- Give back.
- Be willing to be a Change Maker in your community.

Diana Isabelle Peláez - Colombia
Licensed in Children's Education
www.fundaciontiempofeliz.org
www.happytime.edu.co

Asifa Akbar

"The Universe is counting on you to be your best
self; allow what you love to guide you there."

My intention is for you to realize you are already a valuable Change Maker. You have innate worth, gifts, and purpose. No system, person, circumstance, or experience decides your worth; only *you* get to define YOU. The biggest impact you can have on others is through your own conscious self-transformation. Strive to be the best version of you and encourage others to do the same; this will be your greatest offering to humanity and the best way to honor your Creator.

"No Less Than the Trees and the Stars"

Change is the essence of life: change that we witness, that we bear, and that we initiate. The most powerful change is our own conscious self-transformation and intentional aspiration to be the best version of ourselves.

My story is one of navigating life's changes. I spent the first decade of my life in South Africa before emigrating to Canada with my family at age 11. I remember once, when I was 5 years old and still living in South Africa, my maternal grandfather, my Nana, drove us to a nearby town to visit his daughter, my youngest aunt. En route, I spotted a windmill churning steadily in a field. "When the wind blooows, the windmill goooes," I chanted in a playful sing-song voice, my nose pressed against the back-passenger window. "Ah, you're a poet!" Nana exclaimed, his words leaving an indelible mark in my heart. Nana loved poetry. He was always penning witty, loving verses for family on special occasions. Perhaps that's where I got it from, my love of words and language.

Nana's stained-glass bookshelf was filled with delicious vintage items: classics by Dickens and Shakespeare, poetry by Tennyson, and scriptures of the world's major religions. I often leafed through them as a child, marveling about mysterious lands and ancient cultures, relishing in beautiful words. My grandmother, Nanima, was a woman of words in her own right. She enjoyed telling us stories, folk tales, and family history as she sat in her favorite chair enjoying her savory snacks.

My grandparents lived in a cozy Victorian-style house with a pillared veranda and large yard lined with many shade-giving fruit trees we climbed as children. Their home was a safe haven and sanctuary welcoming family, friends, neighbors and wayfarers from far and wide, yet it was also corralled in a segregated neighborhood marked only for people of Indian origin in small-town Pietermaritzburg, South Africa. Their home was an oasis of security despite growing social unrest that would eventually dismantle the unjust racially segregated system we lived under. Though they are gone now, people still talk of their generous spirits to this day. This was their powerful legacy: simple, consistent acts of kindness and compassion.

Changes we witness

In my childhood years, before my family's move to snowy Canada, I witnessed much personal change that provided invaluable lessons about embracing a 'new normal' and choosing to live to the fullest, despite circumstances beyond one's control. The most profound lesson came from one of my greatest muses, my beautiful Nanima. At mid-life, she was diagnosed with cancer in her cheek. She underwent delicate surgery removing a jawbone and numerous skin grafts. It was a tense time, and I missed her terribly when she was hospitalized.

I recall, vividly, the day she came home. She lay in bed in our house and as I entered the room quietly, I could not recognize her face — it was scarred and hollowed on one side. I felt nervous. Then suddenly she smiled with her eyes and greeted me. On hearing her familiar, warm voice, I instantly knew it was my beloved Nanima, who often sang joyfully while cooking aromatic dishes for us at her stove. It didn't matter that her face was different now; all that mattered was our Nanima was home! She began to heal physically and, before we knew it, was back to her energetic self, opening curtains and windows to bright sunlight and fresh air, waking us up early against our will, urging us to "Rise and shine!" She was a survivor, yes, and her face was scarred, but this did not stop her from gracefully embracing profound personal change, living to the fullest, and being her authentic best.

Post-surgery, in her early fifties, she learned to read and write for the first time, fulfilling a cherished life goal. I was in primary school and loved going to the library with friends on Saturdays. Each time, I would make sure to check out (through the segregated checkout system) not only *my* favorite novels and stories to read to my little brother at bedtime, but ones I believed my Nanima might enjoy and find easy to read (like the Beatrix Potter tales). At home, we read together and I would help her pronounce words. She was determined to succeed and practiced reading and writing diligently. In no time, she was strutting gracefully across the stage to accept her graduation certificate. She was not only a survivor, but had made a conscious, intentional effort to thrive! She proved that though life may throw unexpected curveballs at us, how we choose to respond, determines our quality of life. We can still strive for our personal best and highest potential. Like the sun, full of zest for life, she chose to rise and shine through adversity. She chose to flip the script and write a new story.

Before leaving for Canada, we stayed with my grandparents. While social unrest brewed and my older siblings bravely participated in student boycotts against *Apartheid,* my grandparents' house remained filled with an anchoring sense of love, belonging and security. Around that time, I recall often craning my neck, on tiptoes, to read a famous poem on a scroll hanging in my grandparents' living room, *Desiderata.* It was a good-bye gift to my oldest sister from her best friend. One line in the poem always stood out: "You are a child of the universe no less than the trees and the stars; you have a right to be here." It struck a chord in my innocent, childhood heart because I often heard that people were fighting for 'equal rights.' Indeed we had a *right* to be there, I believed. But, soon we were to be plucked from our roots and transplanted to a foreign land; we had to flee.

Changes we bear

We arrived in the frozen Canadian prairies in early December. Struggling into winter parkas and thermal boots, we waded through knee-deep snow we were seeing for the first time. Amidst a sea of different accents and faces, we often committed *faux pas* like standing on the wrong side of the road for the bus. It was the early 1980s, and our mammoth adjustment was fully underway. For me, this period combined not only the awkwardness of culture shock, but the growing pains of adolescence. It was 'the ugly years.' Scrawny, awkward, still growing, I didn't feel pretty then, and longed for the beloved country we left.

In South Africa, I had been popular at school. Classmates would literally yank my hands in different directions to pick me for their teams. In Canada, I was one of about five students of color at my Junior High and unfamiliar with the popular culture. There were many mortifying moments. Being made fun of for the distinct South-African English I spoke. Being teased for my choice of Halloween costume, Halloween being a tradition unfamiliar to us. The boy with his locker next to mine who would often let his books fall from the top shelf onto my head. And in gym class, being the last girl standing when it was time to pick teams. I felt like I did not belong. I felt like an outcast.

I often had to stand up for myself. One boy and his pals would often tease me and others and throw spitballs onto the back of my head. One particular day, I reacted to his antics by calling him a 'pig.' He responded with, "You're worse because you're brown!"

On confiding with my mother, my father rushed to advocate on my behalf, urging the principal to address these incidents. I recalled my grandmother's wise advice, "If anyone says anything about the color of your skin, tell them if we were cut open, we'll all bleed the same color." By Grade 8, however, despite my grandmother's lessons about the importance of character over outer appearance, I became highly self-conscious and my self-confidence plummeted. In high school, my poor self-image continued. I had not yet found ways to independently script my self-worth; instead I internalized others' negative messages, allowing their biases to define me. This left me increasingly unhappy and what I felt inside was what I projected on the outside.

Changes we initiate

My parents always inspired my siblings and I to be independent, critical thinkers, and high achievers. Dad was a talented orator, often holding friends and family captive with his charismatic lectures and storytelling. An old-school lawyer, he taught us the value of using words and language to advocate for social justice, and avidly wrote letters to local Canadian newspapers whenever he felt strongly about a social issue. He understood the power of using words to effect change. Mom was ever ready with encouragement, motivational quotes, and inspiring stories of triumph over obstacles, not unlike her own. Like her mother, she firmly believed in second acts, that it's never too late to do anything you set your mind to. Together, they instilled in us that we are each captain of our own ships; at any time we can initiate changes for the better in our own lives.

When I started university, like most young people, I had yet to fully learn how I could script my own life path and thrive with inner self-confidence.

Though I had a strong sense of social justice and was always ready to stand up for the underdog, I was only beginning to gain confidence in how I could advocate on *my own* behalf and direct *my own* journey. Real life lessons awaited after undergrad.

With a B.A. and my first credit card in hand, 16 years later and three years after Apartheid officially ended, I returned to South Africa for a visit. Sadly, Nanima had succumbed to cancer a couple of years prior, but Nana was still there to uplift me with his soulful jokes, stories, and wise advice. One afternoon during my trip, as we bonded in the warm sun-drenched garden, he pointed to a colorfully blooming African Violet, wistfully indicating that it was Nanima who had first nourished it to life. Like Nanima's evergreen, life-affirming spirit, it was still thriving!

As we chatted leisurely, sensing something deeper, he gently advised, "You should be more confident." I nodded self-consciously in agreement. "As long as you keep reading the Quran, don't worry about what anyone else thinks," he continued. The trip affirmed familiar bonds and roots, and with my Canadian cultural outlook, I suddenly felt a lucky sense of belonging not just in one, but two places: South Africa and Canada. Feeling empowered, and having completed my first solo trip overseas, I returned home with renewed self-confidence, challenging myself to one of my most profound experiences with self-initiated change. Deferring grad and law school, I embarked on a once-in-a-lifetime opportunity to participate in the *Japan Exchange and Teaching Program.*

Japan was a magical adventure. I was stationed in the picturesque mountain town of Shizukuishi, where I would have a pleasant experience of local fame. Foreigners were still a rare sight there then. Students would clamor to take pictures with me and townspeople would shower me with kindness and hospitality. I appeared on a TV game show, in local newspapers, and was asked to give speeches at opening ceremonies of an annual ski festival. As I grew more accustomed to Japanese culture, however, these novelties soon faded and I began to invest more in the teaching experience. Into my second year there, I began thinking about a longer-term impact on my students. One in particular caught my attention, a diligent, smart, but quiet student: Tsuyoshi San.

Perhaps compelled by memories of my own awkwardness growing up, I often called on him to participate, praising his efforts in the least assuming way possible. In time, I noticed small transformations. The more positive feedback I provided, the more his confidence seemed to grow. Soon he began eagerly seeking extra help for written work during lunchtime. Then an idea came to me. I volunteer-coordinated a Global Issues Group that was collecting school supplies for underprivileged students in Vietnam. I decided to ask Tsuyoshi to write a letter to the students in Vietnam, which we would publish in our next newsletter; as part of developing his English-language skills. Thrilled to be asked, he was overjoyed to see his own thoughtfully-written letter in *print*, and in *English*. What seemed like a small gesture turned out to be a very important one. Before I left Japan, Tsuyoshi's mother thanked me personally for helping her son learn English, sending flowers and a gift. Perhaps I made an impact after all? On returning to Canada, I would continue to hear about his accomplishments. With his bright mind and newfound confidence, this student from a rural Japanese high school went on to earn a university degree and is himself now teaching English, Japanese, and Social Studies.

Through this I learned something powerful: small intentional initiatives can have an enduring, meaningful ripple effect. As my grandparents' example showed, change-making does not have to be on a grandiose scale; a little kindness goes a long way. Life is not a seesaw. Lifting others up, does not bring oneself down. On the contrary, all are uplifted in the process. With conscious intention, anyone can author powerful stories of change, through the things they enjoy doing.

Self-transformation

In recent years, facing systemic and other obstacles and consistently not feeling valued and respected for who I really am, I realized this is not how I wanted my story to go and I started to seriously contemplate my purpose in life. Wasted skills, talents, and gifts are a travesty for anyone. I often take a stand when others are being treated unfairly, yet perhaps have advocated less on my own behalf. Was it the skeletal remains of a sense of unworthiness or of not belonging, whatever the root causes? Discomfort propels growth.

After my father's passing five years ago, I was jolted with a sense that my 'someday' is now. With only so many things under our control, I began to think about the things I *could* change. I gradually began taking a conscious *KonMari* approach to my outlook. I wanted to declutter not just in the material sense, but my life in general. I started asking myself, honestly, what activities spark joy for me? What am I passionate about? In quiet moments, with my intuition guiding, clarity gradually came.

I am always motivated by a sense of social justice, by a desire to help others realize their inherent worth and right to be their best selves, and I love writing. I love using words, language and storytelling to inspire, paint hope and encourage, to advocate, to resolve and to heal. With this newfound awareness, I now consciously look for opportunities to use words in my own authentic way, as a vehicle to motivate, empower, and support others. I am embarking on the most important kind of change-making journey: conscious self-transformation, a labor of love toward my best self.

Each of us is as unique as our fingerprints. We all have inherent worth, innate gifts and talents, and a purpose to fulfill while alive. Each person's spot in this Universe has already been reserved. Messages of not being good enough contradict our essential purpose. Ultimately, only *we* get to define ourselves. It is our birthright to thrive and to pen our best life stories. Each one of us can adopt Nanima's wise and powerful words, "Rise and shine!" as our personal mantra. Dare to do what you are passionate about, and use your life lessons as an offering to help elevate yourself and others. In this way, you can have the most meaningful and enduring impact on yourself and humanity.

Always remember: "You are no less than the trees and the stars; you have a right to be here." Allow what you love to guide you, and make the impact only *you* were created for, Change Maker. The Universe is counting on you to be your best self.

Ignite Action Steps

To uncover your purpose, first discover your passions. What sparks joy in you? Pursue those things, and relinquish any feelings of doubt, fear, guilt, shame, and any badges of unworthiness or negative conditioning you may be unconsciously holding onto, *regardless of the source*. What Ignites your *best* self? Do those things. Consciously look for opportunities to express and use your passions and you will fulfill your purpose. If you are harming no one in doing so, others' opinions of you are irrelevant. Gather all your experiences, including resilience and tenacity and use them to propel you. Yes, there will be obstacles, often unjustifiable ones, but keep going. Flip the script, adjust your sails, try something new, if necessary, but always strive to be the best YOU. Dare to follow *your* joys and passions.

Asifa Akbar - Canada
M.A., LL.B., Author, Coach, Researcher, Analyst, Lawyer-Candidate
shineyourbestlight@gmail.com

Arshiya Bhan

"To rise, to love, to succeed; self love must fall over me."

I share my story to help you realize how influential your energy is. My wish is that when you read my story, you open your arms to spirituality and, through self discovery, you face your fears, crush your anxiety, and jump into change.

The Power of Your Inner Energy

Imagine waking up in the morning and realizing you have nothing to worry about. You look at yourself in the mirror and say, "I am fearless."

I felt that way when I was a child. In my younger years, my most authentic self was always apparent, even at play. I was carefree, vulnerable, and celebrating my existence every single day. I often wonder what happens when we become adults. I questioned why we limit our happiness? Why do we run away from self-love despite knowing deep down it's the best kind of love? As adults, I'm curious if we subconsciously know how backwards our lives have been conditioned to become. I certainly didn't. And, it took a major life change to help me see it.

In my early twenties, I was walking across the York University stage at my graduation for Early Childhood Education. I was anxious, unhappy, and feeling defeated. Although this was supposed to be a celebration, it wasn't. I knew this vocation wasn't my purpose. I had chosen to 'settle' for a conventional lifestyle, believing teaching was a safe career that would support me financially. Yet, there I was; my fingers feeling like ice as they closed around the diploma. Later that night, after all the effort, instead of being buoyed with energy from my success, I went home and I cried for hours. I was suppressing the creative part of me.

I was missing my inner child.

Ever since I was young, I have always been passionate about the arts. I enjoyed dancing, acting out scenarios, and spilling my thoughts through writing. But more than any other art form, it was dance that kept me alive. Dance was my ultimate passion, my escape from reality. It empowered me to create stories through different movements of my body. It allowed me to lose myself in different characters. Sometimes I wouldn't even dance to music, but would use my poetry as inspiration for my soul's stories.

It was my definition of unconditional Love.

Prior to receiving my degree in Early Childhood Education, my passion for the arts led me to pursue a degree in Fine Arts and Journalism. I was surrounded by the amazing creative energies and the diverse life experiences of my fellow students at York University, in Toronto, Canada. At the time, I thought this was the greatest decision of my life. I had it all figured out. I was auditioning for acting roles, dance gigs and writing opportunities, hoping for a breakthrough. I spent hours scouring ads in newspapers, going to auditions, taking spontaneous trips with friends to explore new avenues and find new ways to pursue my passion for the arts. I had some success doing this, but mostly failures. The muscles in my neck would get tighter and tighter with each disappointment, feeling the pain as I failed again and again. I started to question my self-belief. I began to lose hope.

Dance was the light to my darkness; it gave me the courage to keep fighting.

Reality hit when a countless number of auditions didn't result in a callback. It destroyed my inner peace and also my bank account. I felt as though I didn't belong in the arts. The feeling of being lost is an excruciating pain that affected me from scalp to toes.

I *knew* I had to make changes.

One gloomy night, walking home after another failed audition, I felt that excruciating pain encompass my entire body once more. I asked myself, "Who am I?" There was a power in this question, an energy. It called to me and roared through me, encouraging me to dig deep and get real with my own beliefs.

At first, my response was silence. I couldn't describe who I was. I felt all over the place. One minute I wanted to dance, and the other minute I wanted to write. Most days, my anxiety over finances overwhelmed and discouraged me. This question had Ignited something in me. It *Ignited* my spiritual journey.

That's when I decided to enroll in Early Childhood Education. I felt so defeated by lack of success in following my passion that I let my fears take over. I thought taking a different path would give me financial stability. I didn't have to totally give up on my dream; I could use my skills of dance and theater in lesson plans for the children. I assured myself that this would keep my passion alive. I saw it as a win-win situation; I could achieve what I wanted in both art forms.

Or at least I thought I could.

And yet there I was, on that stage, shaking hands with the Dean and my professor, my heart sitting leadenly somewhere around my knees. My inner being knew it was a mistake.

My soul knew I had a different purpose.

Shortly after graduation, I landed a job working with young children. I started juggling my passion for the arts with a weekly 40-hour work routine. It felt like I was living in the middle of a non-stop tornado. My calendar was piled with dance performances, content creation, my job, and trying to fit in a fun and interesting social life. I was starting to burn out. Realizing that I needed to keep my body strong, if I was to keep up the pace, I added fitness into my dance life. This fusion made me realize our body, mind, and soul are connected. The combination of the two was a perfect way to connect with my inner self. It led me to my intuition and gave me an idea.

It was raining heavily one night as I dashed into the dance studio after work. I had arrived an hour early for my class, one I was taking for fun. I was craving solitude, needing to be away from my own frantic energy, wanting to figure out what I was doing with my life. I decided to turn off the lights, lie on my yoga mat, and close my eyes. I asked myself the same question I had back on that graduation stage, "Who am I?"

This time, I had an answer. I went back down memory lane to when I was a child. As a young girl, I was always being told by others that I had so much energy. I would dance and dance for hours, having no cares and loving my freedom. Feeling the echo of that child in my muscles, I realized I had the power to face my fears. I began to connect the dots of my life while lying still, in meditative silence. That was a major Ignite moment for me. I understood; my inner child had always been part of me. I realized my energy was influential. That it shaped me, and through me, shapes others.

That experience taught me that stillness gives us clarity. I realized the decisions that I made in the past had led me to this confusion of figuring out "Who am I?" This was supposed to happen because it's part of my spiritual journey.

On the heels of this awakening, I started analyzing my career as an Early Childhood Educator. I loved teaching, but not necessarily in the field I was in. I was choosing to be vulnerable and real with my feelings in this moment, choosing to listen to my heart instead of my fear. I made the decision to start my own class and was rewarded almost instantly with a feeling of liberation. This was another Ignite moment for me and sparked the beginning of *my* change.

The year of my 25th birthday started my re-birth. I had begun my journey to connect with my passion, inner wounds, vulnerability, and fears. Despite not knowing where I would be heading, I felt strong. I knew this would be helping people. I believed I was being guided to make my purpose become a reality.

The vision of Belly AB Fitness started with workshops across Toronto. I started with only friends and family, eventually building up the courage to create workshops for the public. Whenever I taught these workshops, I felt connected with myself and the people who were participating. I would see everyone putting so much energy in my workouts and dance routines while having huge smiles on their faces. And in those moments, for the first time in my life, I didn't feel lost. I felt connected with my soul purpose. I realized in that moment that before our bodies exist, we are all energy. It was a reminder for me that "your energy is influential."

And this time, I believed it.

I was starting to feel motivated again. I felt happier knowing that I am making a difference with my soul purpose. I continued in this way for about eight months and then I decided to take another leap of faith.

This was a scary moment for me. But it wasn't a feeling of failing. It was a moment of growth. Of reaching further. Of *change*. And that part scared me. Many of us are afraid to trust our gut instincts; perhaps that's why many of us are avoiding change. I chose to trust my intuition. I allowed my inner voice to help my passion turn into my soul purpose.

The element that made me realize how powerful our inner voice is was practicing spirituality.

I started to feel more powerful as I was healing myself and helping other people at the same time. I started to realize that the structure of my class was also changing. I was incorporating what I was learning in my personal life. Dance and fitness were the two elements that focused on our physical and emotional self. But I wanted to incorporate the most powerful element of all: *Spirituality*. This gave me the clarity that my class is not just about fitness; it's wellness.

It's a combination of mind, body, and inner soul.

I have changed so much since I connected with this element. It has taught me the power of stillness, to appreciate life and to live in the moment. It helped me understand the power of forgiveness, and unconditional love. It has taught me to connect with my core values and my higher self. But one of the biggest take-aways from practicing spirituality is my acceptance for my vulnerability, and all the parts of me.

As I received more clarity, I had to make two very important decisions. One was to question my life. Was I going to stand on both sides of a teeter-totter at once, living a comfortable life with a full-time job and pursue my passion on the side? Or was I going to take another leap of faith and commit to my passion for the arts wholeheartedly with everything I had?

My second decision was about the class name. The name I had for what I was doing was restricting my vision. I decided to take a few weeks to meditate and connect with my inner voice.

As an entrepreneur, making decisions and being accepting of change is important. The beginning of any new venture, of any new phase in a business is the most difficult, but I understood that recognizing any red flags in the early stages is all a learning curve and is so important to the process.

Apparently, I had a lot to learn.

I took this change as a lesson, and as a blessing. For weeks, I brainstormed. I collected over 200 words that felt right to me in this quest to encompass the vision of my brand. I tried connecting words and phrases that already existed, but nothing fit.

One night, I wrote down all the elements that are part of my vision. I asked myself, "What word connects with dance, fitness, and spirituality?" I wanted something powerful, but soulful. And then it struck me. I thought of practicing the breathing that I usually do during meditation. I started to sound out 'u-m-f' while taking deep breaths. It felt strong for me. And another I tried another sound 's-r-a' because it was calming. I put the sounds together, and the word "Umsra" was born.

I cried after that. The combination of those words made me feel complete.

It was a feeling of coming back to *home*. I needed to dive deep into my creativity and brainstorm, to think outside the box. To let myself be free. It represented a clarity that allowed me to execute a plan and bring my idea to life. I put on my Change Maker hat and started working. I trademarked the name, knowing that it meant commitment and devotion. It didn't feel like work; it felt like waking up to my passion. I was happy, and making other people feel the same. I knew that was something that I could make a lifelong purpose.

Looking back now, I realized all the answers existed within me. But had I not experienced the feeling of being lost, I wouldn't have been able to find my purest form and my soul purpose today. Being vulnerable and finding self-acceptance helped me make the decision to quit my job, give up my financial stability, take the risk, and dive into Umsra with both eyes wide open.

It was a change I was excited to make.

Spirituality can be a powerful part of our lives. It can help us to grow, to heal, and to figure out what we really want from ourselves. We all have the capability to be passionate about our vision and help others feel connected with their inner selves along the way.

Our life experiences can teach us that challenges are a blessing in disguise. It may be frustrating being lost and uncertain at first, yet knowing subconsciously we all have a purpose.

We just have to create it.

It may have taken 27 years of my existence to realize that. But I wouldn't have it any other way. We all can be Change Makers and help the world become a better place. Change is beautiful. Find the beauty in yours.

IGNITE ACTION STEPS

My first step to becoming a Change Maker was believing in my inner energy. Let me help you connect with yours.

- The first step is to notice your feelings.

- The second step is to express these feelings through journaling, or meditation.

- Thirdly, engage in enjoyable solo activities. For me, dance was my stress reliever. Notice how your body language changes, and focus on your breathing. Is it heavy? Is it calming? Focus on every detail.

Arshiya Bhan - Canada
Entrepreneur, Artist
www.umsrauniverse.com

JENNIFER NEWTON

"Real freedom comes from alignment to the truth within us."

I wish to share with you ideas that can reconstruct our earth. A new earth co-created through alignment to inner truth and reverence to Mother Gaia. I wish for you to experience true freedom by allowing the mindsets of fear, delusion and greed to fall away so that the destructive, old paradigms can dissolve and give rise to peace and a new way of living, in integrity, with the earth and all beings.

CO-CREATING THE NEW EARTH

I had always felt displaced. I was born in South Africa and grew up in Zaire, now the Democratic Republic of Congo. When I was ten years old, my family moved to the United Kingdom and I was sent to boarding school. I recall putting on my school uniform for the first time; the starchy white shirt was hard and constricting, the tie like a noose around my neck, and the thick and scratchy woolly tights failed to warm my now numbingly-chilled skin. I felt like an alien. The wildness and freedom that I had experienced in Africa was such a contrast to the strict and rigid authoritarianism of school in England. I decided there and then that I was never going to become institutionalized. The interior world of my mind, which was full of imagination and feminine spirit, didn't mold to the artificial and man-made indoor landscape and lifestyle I was forced to survive in during my school years.

However, my sense of displacement proved to be a blessing in disguise and one of the most necessary aspects of becoming a Change Maker. The constant relocation I experienced throughout my childhood prevented any serious ingraining of cultural and social conditioning, and it was impossible for me to get too attached to any one particular set of belief systems about the world.

Travel was in my blood and I left for university in Ireland, followed by a brief stint in the Caribbean before settling in fast-paced, neon-filled and rather chaotic Hong Kong. There I was surrounded by masses of people who could be seen going about their lives through the windows of the skyscrapers where they both lived and worked, scrambling to the top, the most expensive real estate, like laboratory rats in a tunnel. Strangely, however, it was there that I was fated to set up my interior design company. I was passionate about what I did for a living to such a degree that I never considered it work. It was my calling in life and it deeply fulfilled my artistic nature. It also fitted perfectly with my fundamental desire to escape into a fairytale, to be somewhere more beautiful and otherworldly, to be in a plane of existence that was more suited to my sensitivity and heightened sensibilities. I was always dreaming of being somewhere other than where I was; the world seemed cruel and cutthroat, and working as a designer enabled me to create my fantasy places. There was so much adrenaline in Hong Kong. My body was not at home in that environment and I constantly felt on edge. My shoulders tense, adrenals shot, unable to sleep in a city that was enslaved day and night to a power grid of synthetic light and distorted noise. I felt disconnected from everything and I was always aspiring to design a place that would somehow accurately reflect my inner world.

In Hong Kong, like the UK, I never felt like I belonged. The city seemed an ill-fitting, coercive grid overlay to the natural world. My consciousness felt boxed in by all the squareness around me. It was far away from the freedom I felt in my early years in the tropics and there was a deep-seated pining to return to nature. It was a quality that I brought into my work, and every project I did was infused with a natural aesthetic. There was never any makeup or perfume in my bag. Instead, it was always filled with samples of rock, stone, wood and pebbles to use in my designs.

I perceived a certain mindset behind the construction of the developed world. It seemed to me that the design of the city was informed by a need to dominate and control, be bigger and better, rather than harmoniously coexist: colonize rather than collaborate. The phallic skyscrapers seemed to suffocate the natural energy lines and songlines of the earth and overbear the skyline with no respect for any of the other species we share our home with. The architecture and urban planning organized the way people lived and moved in a robotic, linear way. It seemed dehumanizing, and cut people off from the intrinsic nature of their being. Apartment blocks were like cells in a vertical prison and I felt like I was designing in gilded cages.

It was not long before I needed to escape and find my freedom again. I craved a more artistic community, somewhere where I could ease the sense of displacement I felt within a world that had somehow been hijacked by corporate greed, and I was not finding it within the man-made construction of reality around me. During this time, I also noted the 'greenwashing' in the construction industry. As much as I was trying to design in a way that was ecologically beneficial, the options mostly consisted of what was 'less destructive' for the environment, rather than a solution that worked in synergy. I knew that if we were going to save ourselves from extinction, a total revolution of the mind and how we perceive the earth was required, not just a few minor adjustments.

I no longer wanted to participate in the cycle of consumerism that seemed to engulf me and consume my every waking minute. I could not imagine saving up and paying my whole life to live in a home owned by the bank, when I knew that I could build one from the earth straight beneath my feet for a few thousand dollars. I didn't want my life, my home, my time, my soul to be owned by the financial empire. I wasn't willing to pay a corporation for electricity when I could provide my own. I couldn't conceive that I had to pay the government for water when they had no more right to take it freely than I did, and certainly no right to charge for it. I didn't want useless products cluttering up my life and mind, holding me back and tying me down to a world of global slavery that I refused to be a part of.

Living in Asia, I had seen first-hand in Burma, India, and China the workers who were slaving in factories to feed the consumer greed of the West. The freedom we have in the West is borne from the exploitation that occurs behind closed doors in these countries, and it became clear to me that it was false freedom and collective delusion.

I could not unsee what I had seen. I could not close my mind after it had expanded into new dimensions. I was committed to creating the change I wanted to see in the world. I wanted to live a life I had chosen, not one dictated to me by the corporate agenda, and I chose to have my days to flow with synchronicity and spontaneity.

My strong desire to be a Change Maker and trailblaze another way of living was Ignited. I attended a month-long mud building course in Thailand and learned all about natural building, holistic living and how to grow my own organic food. I was on a different trajectory and my soul embraced the wave of peace and *rightness* that washed over me, knowing that there was an alternative way… and I had found it. I embraced permaculture as a business design model, placing equal weight on the community and the environment and dislodging profit from the sole leading role. I attended another month-long course on deep ecology and started to gravitate more and more toward an attitude and consciousness that was deeply communing with the animal and plant realms of the natural world.

This conscious disconnecting from the world of Wi-Fi and constant online connectivity, this immersion into the realm of the organic, in the living earth, in building a connection with life in all its forms around me, so hidden to those trapped on devices … it Ignited my heart. I made a commitment to myself to follow the path of freedom, not just for myself but for all beings, to embrace my truth and sense of integrity however that meant, whatever the consequences and wherever it led me. I refused to be part of the man-made matrix.

It led me to the Indonesian beaches of Lombok. After traveling in Asia for a few years, I got on my motorbike and moved to a very undeveloped area to fulfill my inner commitment. I bought a beautiful piece of land in the mountains a few minutes away from pristine, world-class beaches and began to build a little wooden cabin on stilts and three mud huts. Surrounded by the natural beauty of the jungle on the little piece of the mountain I inhabited, my dream expanded into a retreat and learning center for holistic living. To me, the concept of owning a piece of the earth was ridiculous and egotistical; humanity had no right to enslave the earth to their own agenda, but it seemed that in today's world that was the only way I could proceed. I wanted to be an honorable steward, guardian of the land — to leave it better off than I had found it, to replant, to reforest, to regenerate. The holistic center was my own little fairy tale, living in beautiful symbiosis with the spirit realm of Mother Gaia, sovereign beings on a sovereign earth, and with no real need to leave.

In that expanse of land, I saw infinite abundance: banana trees, coconut trees, grasses that could be dried and woven into roofs, clay and sand from soil mixed with water that could be molded into bricks, baked in the sun and used to build houses, jungle vine could be used instead of nails. The different clays and limestones that lay usually ignored beneath our feet, I turned into waterproof polished plasters that delighted even my most difficult clients. There was groundwater beneath me; it just required digging a well. With simply the earth and falling rain drops, utopia was possible. I set about sculpting it into being, with my savings as well as the endless support and contributions from friends who believed in this dream, and my mother, always my biggest supporter. I spent our money not on buying materials but paying the locals in the village for their labor in helping me build. With 90 percent of materials straight from the site or the village, we constructed a center for people to learn basic technologies such as how to filter water with earth and gravel, how to build a solar water heater, how to create bio composting toilets and how to live from the land and grow organic vegetables. It was the way to experience a life in direct connection with the earth, to live from the heart, to learn the art of living simply.

There must have been something deep in my psyche, a recollection of mud huts in Africa, but I loved the simplicity of building with mud and the inherent integrity of it. Mud was a way of building that was not only directly connected to the earth; it was *of* the earth; there was no division, no separation, no domination or exploitation. There was a pure harmony to it, an intrinsic beauty.

Building with mud or rammed earth has no absolute rules and regulations. It's intuitive, sculptural, gentle on the hands, and artistic. You could design with curves and free-flowing shapes that could blend fluidly into the contours of the land. It was a radical contrast to building with concrete. There were no toxic chemicals required. It had always seemed deluded to me that we would build homes that destroyed our real home — the earth. Building with mud reflected a mindset of ease and flow, harmony, joy, fun, and reverence for the earth. There was no one precise way to build, many different variations and techniques could be used, and instead of measuring out exact quantities, you had to arrive at an inner knowing, a 'feeling' of when the mix was workable. It was a radically feminine approach to building and the opposite to how we build in the 'civilized' world. There was no corporate empire behind it. No greed. No predation. You could feel the heartbeat of the earth.

However, my dream soon became my nightmare. I came to realize that I was living in a patriarchal Muslim community ruled by men and their jungle law. People's minds were wired for theft and violence in a karmic wheel of samsara where there was no escape from the suffering. It was incredibly challenging to build or co-create in that community. I was amidst a mindset of selfish greed, where each man was out for himself in a culture that annihilated the qualities of the feminine in favor of brute force. Kindness was seen as weakness, and women had absolutely no voice or role other than being alive to breed. Creative spirit was radically suppressed in favor of power through domination. It was a cycle of destruction.

Leaving London and then Hong Kong, I had run as far away as I possibly could from the mainstream to the jungle of Indonesia where I planned to create my dream. And the paradise I thought I had found was toxic. There was no foresight, understanding of the consequences of actions. There was no connection — no sense of shared purpose, of teamwork, of satisfaction. My paradise was never going to be possible if the community lacked the beauty and creative spirit of feminine energies. What I started to realize was that if I wanted to get out of the matrix, there was no external place I could go.

In Hong Kong, people had more money than they could ever possibly need and yet they were still striving for more, unsatiated, unfulfilled. In this village in the jungle, people had all the natural resources they needed to build true paradise on earth and yet their focus was on fighting and stealing from each other, which just led to contraction and destruction rather than co-creation and abundance. On the outside, both were radically different and yet the mind states were the same. Both were plagued by fear, greed and delusion, and these traits were at the foundation of society. They have colonized our minds and the earth for too long, leading to the ecocide we now face. We are destroying ourselves and if we want to survive we simply have to choose a different way. Change is no longer a choice; it's survival. It became clear to me that our prison is the conditioning, the unquestioned programming that we succumb to. The matrix is just the world we unconsciously create through our collective negative thoughts and beliefs.

The mindset drove me away again, the fact that the gifts I had to bring to the community were undermined, exploited and taken advantage of rather than honored. I decided to sell my retreat and approached the local real estate agent to put my place on the market. I moved instead to the nearby island of Bali where there was a small but growing community of like-minded souls who held the same intention of co-creating a more simple and holistic way of living in integrity with the earth. The Balinese hold a deep understanding that they are part of the earth, that their bones and the soil are one.

Today, I put all my newfound design and hands-on experience to work on projects with others who are envisioning the same shared dream, with female leaders who are driven by the greater good and their own inner knowing and connection to the divine, source of all creation. These are the changes I dreamed of making in my childhood. As pioneers of a new earth, we need to commune with what is directly reliable, with that which nourishes the soul, rather than merely following old established dogmas, doctrines and collective concepts of the mind that we have been conditioned into. We need to step out of the coma and courageously choose instead to follow the voice of our own inner truth.

I have learned that freedom and creativity go hand in hand. Our freedom, our salvation as a species, reigns in reclaiming our feminine wisdom and embracing its inherent ability to create in alignment with higher states of consciousness. Within my community of truth seekers, artists, writers, healers, teachers and dharma buddies seeking freedom, in my mixed Balinese and international community of like-minded spirits, I have found hope. I have discovered a place where the feminine creative energies flourish and thrive, where generosity and kindness are abundant, and connections to all living things are honored and respected.

Freedom comes in reclaiming our minds and cultivating new states of consciousness. Beautiful states of mind will be the building blocks of the new earth: generosity, loving kindness, and intuitive wisdom. These qualities of the feminine are blanketing the earth. The old world of domination, greed and consumption that we have unknowingly fallen into, are falling away. We can all look forward to a world seeded from love, and a deep, intuitive knowing. That is now birthing. It will be Female Change Makers who lead us into the new co-creativeness, collaborating for peace, and freedom for all.

Ignite Action Steps

- Tune in and listen to your inner voice. It is the softest sounding, the quietest voice to hear. Learn to follow your inner voice. Learn to act on your inner truth. In times of crisis and the unknown, it is this voice that will lead humanity out of the darkness.
- Audit every item you bring into your home or consume. Choose items that honor the earth and are created locally, from beautiful states of mind.
- Plant seeds in your garden and observe nature's intelligence blossoming into infinite diversity with just water, earth, light and love. Trust in the power of the earth to provide.
- Water the seeds of beautiful states of consciousness by cultivating intuitive wisdom, loving kindness, and generosity.

Jennifer Newton - Indonesia
Director/Designer
www.wildsensoriadevelopment.com
◎ @wildsensoria_development

STEPHANIE BARROS

"Set your life alight and seek out those who fan your flame!"

My wish for you, dear reader, is that my story reminds you of the knowing and power that lies within you, and always has — the knowing that you were meant for more and the power to take complete responsibility for Igniting Your SPARK to change your life, exploding your unique potential to live fully.

IGNITING YOUR SPARK

I will never forget the day I received my wake-up call from the Universe. All my life, I had lived by the plan laid down by my family, society, and culture. I was a relatively 'good' girl, did well at school, got a decent job, got married, bought a house, and had a child, but… at the age of 29, I was ready to take my own life.

I was sitting in the chair where I fed my daughter, sleeping pills in one hand, water in the other, completely sleep deprived, and feeling utterly defeated. I didn't know why I felt so desperate when by all accounts I was relatively 'successful.' But deep down I was miserable; the person I thought I could be was lost. At the core of my being, I felt cheated and believed there was no way out other than to end my life. It was my newborn daughter who 'saved' me. Looking at her beautiful face, seeing her hazel eyes gazing up at me with complete and utter trust, I realized she needed me, and I was the person who was ultimately responsible for her.

A year later I was separated and on my way to being divorced. I had moved out on my own and saw my daughter only every other week. I was utterly lost. I knew I had made the right decision to leave my husband, but I still didn't know how to be 'happy.'

For the next 10 years, I muddled around. In fact, I re-lived the same life. I continued my corporate career, bought another house, had two more children, and remarried. Of course, I thought this was the answer because it was with the 'right' man this time. But again, one year after being remarried, I once more found myself unhappy.

It was at this time my brother introduced my husband and I to his mentor. At first, I wasn't interested, but my husband had recently started his own entrepreneurial endeavor and, in the attempt to be a supportive wife, I agreed to accompany him to a workshop. That one decision changed my life! I can viscerally recall the moment at which I felt the 'Universal Slap' that woke me up and Ignited my SPARK. I could almost hear the admonishment from the Universe asking me, "What had I been doing all this time; had I been sleep-walking?" And the hard honest truth was... I had been. It was time for a change. I needed to wake up, be personally responsible and take control of MY life. And since that moment, I have never looked back.

I changed entirely based on the SPARK that was Ignited in me. It was terrifying to overhaul my life in so many ways, but I knew I had to do it. I had to change. And for me, this change, this journey, was made up of five steps.

Unleash Your Spirit

Regardless of your beliefs, albeit religious or otherwise, I do believe most people understand that we all have an inner spirit. An inner essence that isn't our mind or our body. It is the true life force that makes us who we are. One of my favorite sayings was coined by Pierre Teilhard de Chardin, a French philosopher and Jesuit priest. He said, *"We are not human beings having a spiritual experience; we are spiritual beings having a human experience."*

I had forgotten what my spirit was truly like. In the unconscious dash to play out my life according to the plans of others, I had somehow muted my spirit. Occasionally it would bubble to the surface in a laugh, in a moment where I was in 'flow,' or in an experience when I was truly present. But most of the time it was like being in a soundproof room with only a vague dull feeling that I could be something more.

When I set out to change my life knowing I was meant for more, I focused on unleashing my spirit. I realized that my self-concept was flawed. Primarily because it was a result of others' expectations and not my own. I was always comparing myself to someone or something else. My self-concept equaled a strong, capable independent woman with a successful career, wonderful marriage, great children, financially well off, and happy.

Sounds great, right? "Strong, capable, independent woman" — nothing harmful in that... it was something I'd heard my whole life from my dad who wanted nothing more than to ensure his daughters could stand on their own two feet. I adopted it as part of my self-concept. But the issue arose in what I made it mean. Being this woman meant that I couldn't trust someone else (like my husband) to support me financially, which meant I wouldn't allow myself to be in a position where I didn't earn my own money. 'Successful career' — again nothing bad about that, except... successful by whose standards?

I realized I had not made conscious choices about who I wanted to be, or the person I wanted to become. Rather, I had adopted others' views of me and then had mangled them into a self-concept that was causing me stress. As I started to work on myself, I realized I couldn't easily manipulate my self-concept into something I was comfortable with. I tried to attribute different meanings to it, but no matter how hard I tried, they wouldn't stick. It was so frustrating, I just wanted it to *happen*! Eventually, I came to understand it was because my underlying self-esteem wasn't rock solid.

At the time, I wouldn't have described it as low self-esteem because I didn't really have the language or know how to label it. What I did know was that I was continually worried about being 'found out' and exhausted from being the person I was assuming others expected me to be. I did some research and discovered some of the common self-defeating behaviors and negative habits that are symptoms of low self-esteem. Going down the checklist, I ticked at least 9/10! It took a little investigation before I discovered some literature that helped me. I worked through the recommended exercises to aid in boosting self-esteem. I did them daily for at least a year. I realized the messages I had been relaying to myself for over 40 years were destructive. When I took ownership by improving my self-talk, the cracks in my self-esteem dissipated.

Today, I am much more comfortable with my self-concept and my self-esteem is sturdier. I am okay for people to see me for who I truly am. Unleashing my spirit is a constant journey of growth and self-development that I am happy to have finally started. In everything I do, my inner essence now shines.

Power Your Performance

Although I had been relatively successful as judged by others, when I committed to being personally accountable, I was dismayed to realize I wasn't performing at my full potential. I knew I had more in me, but I didn't know how to access it.

As I delved deeper, I realized what was holding me back… FEAR. And it was suffocating me. I was constantly putting myself under pressure to perform, and physically and mentally stressing myself out. I was afraid that when I had that next health check, went for that next promotion, or had that difficult conversation, I would not be 'good enough.'

What I had to do wasn't to find a way to perform better; I had to acknowledge and release my fears about not being *enough*. I had to accept that my fears were *my* emotions, and I would only experience consistent debilitating worry if I continued to believe in the false illusion that someone else's perspective could hurt me. I needed to remember that I am the only person who determines how I feel. In letting go of the fear, I opened myself up to realize my true performance potential.

I took action to translate that potential into actual performance. Luckily, that took me less time than figuring out that I had to own my emotions, given the multitude of opportunities I had to learn about performance through my corporate experience. Every day at work, I took every opportunity I could to try new strategies and push myself further without fear. After much experimentation, the model I found that resonates best for me in all areas of life is the 'High Performance' framework from the High Performance Institute (HPI).

I used the framework in a variety of ways. I worked on seeking *Clarity* to get clear on my purpose and life goal(s). I focused on generating my *Energy* to ensure I had both the physical and mental energy to sustain continual high performance. I increased my *Productivity* by using the tools that assisted me to focus on the right things. I developed my *Influence* by increasing my capability to establish and maintain great people skills. And through it all, I demonstrated my *Courage* by stepping out of my comfort zone and doing what needed to be done. This framework has worked so well for me that I became a Certified High Performance Coach. I know firsthand how good it feels to get past your limitations and go after your potential and I am so passionate about helping others do the same.

Working on each of these levers changed my life. It gave me a consistent level of performance far greater than I could have imagined and brought me much closer to my full potential. It effected change in other ways as well. Me, who had never put on a pair of hiking boots or gone camping, climbed Mount

Kilimanjaro — something I would never have believed possible! That climb led to other changes. I left my corporate executive career. I started traveling the world with my family… an adventure we're still on today.

Act with Authenticity

I've observed that over the course of my life I have 'acted' in many roles — daughter, sister, friend, colleague, wife, and mother to name a few. In each role, I was a slightly different version of 'me,' usually the version I thought was needed by the other person. I barely gave any thought to who *I* was and who *I* wanted to be in each interaction.

It was not long after I received the 'Universal Slap' that I was fortunate enough to attend a really unique course in Lausanne, right on Lake Léman in Switzerland. There I learned what it meant to 'Act with Authenticity.' As part of the course, a group of actors came in to 'teach' us how to be ourselves more. The premise was that to increase my 'executive presence,' I needed to find my authentic voice and learn how to use it and show up — with more skill. I was petrified at the thought of standing in front of a group of corporate executives and speaking to them about who I was. However, when I finally did it, I was amazed at what came out of my mouth and humbled by their standing ovation. That was just the start of the journey for me to find my 'authentic voice.'

Next, I had to define my values — the me I was going to be no matter what. I explored a few different ways to define those values, but the one that resonated the most with me was when I learned about the 'Code of Honor.' It is a set of rules that defines how you operate. You start by establishing your mission or purpose, then define those values that reflect you and determine the rules that enable you to achieve them.

When defining this for yourself, it is the values by which you want to live your life and interact with others, irrespective of the 'role' you are in. The rules you attach to these values then provide you with the guide for how to be the best authentic version of yourself. Your values reflect who you want to be, the unique you. Having a code that you create and choose to guide your decisions and interactions makes life easier!

"Authenticity is more than speaking. Authenticity is also about doing. Every decision we make says something about who we are."
Simon Sinek

Rebound with Resilience

Over the years, my understanding and perspective on resilience has changed. Once upon a time I believed resilience meant 'keep your chin up, a smile on your dial, and persevere no matter what,' irrespective of the situation or circumstance. I have come to understand that resilience isn't just showing a brave face, but rather being brave enough to truly allow yourself to feel the depth of emotion that a situation may generate. Instead of bottling emotions up, or tamping them down, giving yourself the space to really experience them. But that's not where resilience ends (or else it wouldn't be resilience would it?... it would just be wallowing in whatever emotion you were experiencing). Resilience starts with allowing yourself to experience the emotion AND then working through the emotion to come out the other side.

My perspective of resilience is now that there's nothing wrong with a fit of despair, so long as you pull yourself out of the pit of despair! The mere act of getting yourself out of the pit and moving beyond the situation is what real resilience is. So, the next time something happens that has you feeling low — make it okay to feel what you feel. Exercise some self-care and self-compassion. And when you feel ready, take the next step and breathe. Remember... your experiences shape you, they don't deflate you.

Hone Your Knowledge

For as long as I can remember I was a 'good student' as deemed by traditional education: school, university, corporate seminars, although it was ALWAYS related to recognized qualifications that would improve my credentials. I was not even aware that there was a type of learning that was focused on improving *you*, not just your skills. And I certainly had no idea how much of an impact such learning could have on my life. The accelerated learning workshop I attended where I received my 'Universal Slap' is referred to as 'Shock Learning.' As I discovered, it is the kind of learning which enabled insights I might not otherwise have had the opportunity to develop, like my realization I had been sleepwalking through life!

Growth learning adds knowledge and skills to your repertoire that you did not have before and enables you to do things that you could not do previously. While some of this happens through the traditional methods of learning, I realized that I could also learn from thought leaders, speakers, trainers, facilitators, and gurus all over the world... and I didn't need to sit in a classroom to do it. In my experience, this type of growth learning, in addition to shock learning in the form of seminars, workshops, and coaching programs, is what really creates transformational change in your life quickly.

From everything I've learned during my journey, I know we can all grow and change. I believe you were meant to live the life you desire. You have the power to take complete responsibility for Igniting Your SPARK to completely change the trajectory of your life, just like I did, exploding your unique potential to live fully.

IGNITE ACTION STEPS

- **Unleash Your Spirit**: by consciously choosing your self-concept and fortifying your self-esteem.

- **Power Your Performance**: by focusing on those levers which will make the most difference while keeping your health and relationships strong.

- **Act with Authenticity:** by communicating consistently with your unique voice.

- **Rebound with Resilience:** by acknowledging and experiencing difficult emotions and moving through positively to the other side.

- **Hone Your Knowledge:** by learning, growing and getting support for transformational change… continuously!

Stephanie Barros - Australia
Certified High Performance Coach, Facilitator & Speaker
www.stephanie-barros.com

Christy Parker

*"Relationships are everything in life; the one you have with
yourself is the most powerful you will ever have."*

**It is my sincere hope, desire, and intention to inspire you to radically shift
your current paradigm. By sharing my story, I hope you will see how I built
a relationship with myself, discovered beauty in the mess, created order
from chaos, and found the silver lining in situations. Every relationship in
life is a lesson or a blessing, if you allow it to be a catalyst for empowering
your transformation. Embrace your inner hopeless romantic and fall in
love with YOURSELF.**

Escape Your Cage and Learn to Soar

Several years ago, my life looked very different. I was spending hours and
hours at the office, constantly traveling on business, and seemingly dedicating
every ounce of energy I had to climbing the corporate ladder.

But behind all that busyness was a secret. I was in what I considered a
tremendously toxic marriage. Not knowing what to do, how to address it, nor
having the courage to leave… I simply shut down and sank into the survival
mode I knew: avoidance. I spent countless hours at work, far beyond what
was required and expected. When requested to travel, I jumped at it. Anything
and everything to numb the pain I was enduring. The only good thing that
came from this was that I quickly climbed the 'corporate ladder.' Little did my
supervisors or colleagues know what was truly happening on the inside or why

I seemed so dedicated to my work. It was an escape. Pure and simple. But, in truth, I was a hot mess and spiraling fast. Sadly, the costs were incredibly high.

This was my third failed marriage. My relationship with my children, my family, and my friends suffered. And, more significantly, my relationship with myself evaporated; it felt like it vanished into thin air. During this period of time, my spirit was being deprived of oxygen, smothered under the leaden weight of guilt. I felt like I was dying, constantly feeling guilty from avoiding my loved ones and not having the courage to face the truth. I saw myself as such a failure. Again! And self-forgiveness seemed elusive.

I was desperate to find solace, understanding, or anything resembling a lifeline. A friend of mine, a woman who felt like the sister of my soul rather than just a regular friend, suggested I look into the world of personal growth. There, for the first time, I came across some of the most amazing thought leaders. The more I read, the more I learned, the more I started to feel alive again. One of the first authors who truly resonated with me was Caroline Myss. Relaxing in my bubble bath, listening to her audiobook, I could *feel* her words echoing through every chamber of my soul. Through her work, I began to understand the significance low self-esteem had played in my life and how I had unknowingly been sabotaging myself over and over again.

For the majority of my adult life, I had been obese, tipping the scales right at 300 pounds. My weight was keeping me from achieving my full potential. But, as with most significant choices in life, there comes a pivotal moment when you are just tired of the struggle and the potential benefits all of a sudden far outweigh the known risks.

For me, this particular moment came one unseasonably warm autumn day when I went to the local fair. The fair was one of my absolute favorite things to do with my family in the fall. I had always been an adrenaline junkie, but by this point, it was difficult for me to even push myself off of the couch because of my size at the time. Yet, blinded by complete self-denial, I went to the fair with full intentions to enjoy most, if not all, of the wild, crazy, intense rides. I craved the wind in my hair and the sensation of my stomach first floating then dropping. I couldn't wait to throw my arms in the air and scream with joy while going down the roller coaster. Most of all, I wanted to ride *the gravity-defying Twister*. After waiting in the ridiculously long line full of anticipation for my adrenaline fix, *finally* it was my turn. It took several tries just to hoist myself up into the suspended seat and required a huge amount of effort; it was mortifying! But that was not the most embarrassing part. Having a throng of people witness my struggle was horrific enough, however, when the ride attendant came to secure my safety harness over my abdomen, it would not latch despite multiple attempts. The attendant, embarrassed for me, had to ask me to leave the ride. In front of everyone. I was completely humiliated, and I vowed right then and there that I needed to change.

One of my first acts of courage was to finally move forward with gastric bypass surgery. Despite my decade-long fear of surgery, I realized that it could be my salvation. Being in the healthcare industry, I knew the risks were great and, quite frankly, I was terrified. I had researched it for a decade and had always been unable to imagine doing it. Now, determined to change, I found the courage and a 'why' that inspired me to take the first step of researching the best surgeons in my area and scheduling a consultation. A year later, I found myself sporting a chic hospital gown and my life has never been the same.

Within twelve months, I had lost about half of my total body weight. As the pounds shed, the real me started to emerge and my self-esteem started to grow. Ironically, the more I could see who I was meant to be, the more my depression accelerated. I was looking and feeling better, yet I still felt like I was in a cage. I didn't feel free to step into who I was. Despite my new size, I still saw my old size and it took me time to embrace who I was becoming. More and more professional opportunities were unfolding. I had increased energy to enjoy playing with my kids. Yet, I felt like something remained just out of reach. I did a deep dive into my soul to figure out what was missing. Through all the determination and effort it took, I needed to find my purpose.

From the outside, I had it all: a seemingly happy marriage, two fabulous kids, a beautiful home, and a successful career. But, what was my purpose in life? I was having a very difficult time understanding who I was now. I would think about who I could be. I would visualize what I wanted and my heart would just pound out of my chest. Fear would cover me from head to toe, stealing my breath, and paralyzing me. All I wanted to do was breathe... and I began a quest to do just that.

I mustered the strength to leave my marriage and begin a life on my own. It was the most dramatic change I had made yet. I struggled with only having my kids part of the week. When it was my turn without the children, living in deafening silence was incredibly difficult, and despite trying to hold them in, sobs would escape from time to time. Exhausted by emotion, I realized I simply needed to surrender. Surrender to the quiet, surrender to my feelings, surrender to the drastic changes that had occurred and find the silver lining in what was one of the hardest times of my life. I instigated this change because I knew it was right. But it was not easy. And in embracing it — no TV, no phone, no distractions — is where I started to find myself again.

In the quiet, I continued to learn as much as I could. One of the most impactful books I read was *The Code of the Extraordinary Mind* by Vishen Lakhiani. For the first time, I granted myself permission to challenge many of my long-held beliefs and to shift my paradigm to one which supports my role in creating my own reality. Wrapped up in my low self-esteem was the belief that I was shy and not able to make friends easily. One way to challenge that, as I began my transformation journey, was to willingly step out of my comfort zone and meet more people.

I really did believe I was shy. I had traveled fairly extensively for work, but you would never see me in a social situation outside the conference room. I would always retreat to my hotel room to work and find every excuse to seclude myself. So, I decided to treat myself to a trip just for me with the sole intent to meet other people interested in personal growth. Enter *Mindvalley Live.* This conference in Los Angeles was a life changer. I used the many, many Skymiles I had accumulated over the years, flying first class and allowing myself to be open to meeting as many people as I could. The experience, at first, was much harder than I thought! Despite my excitement, anxiety quickly set in. I saw everyone happy and hugging and it was the opposite of what I had lived with for most of my life. Again. My heart began to race and my breaths became faster and more shallow. Helpless, my eyes welled with tears and began to search for any exit. Frustrated and confused, I reverted to my coping mechanisms of seclusion and retreat. But, slowly, I realized how kind and receptive each participant was. The facilitators of the event recognized this was a common experience for many of us and created multiple opportunities for me to connect with others and network. By the end of the weekend, I had made some amazing friends and even felt brave enough to approach others who seemed to be struggling too. The fulfillment I felt was new to me. For the first time, I felt accepted. I felt like part of the group. These were my people, my tribe, and I felt comfortable being among them. I felt like I belonged.

Another long-held belief was that I would never have the courage to travel abroad. As my network of international friends began to grow, possibilities began to present themselves. I soon had the opportunity to travel to Italy with some of them. Having experienced the liberation of abandoning so many of my limiting beliefs, I literally jumped at the chance!

By opening myself up to expanding relationships and ideas, I also found serendipity showing up at just the right times. I was having breakfast with new friends and one of them asked me if I earned Skymiles. With all of my travel, of course, I had at that point accumulated quite a few! After affirming that I did, he shared that I could use my Skymiles for international first-class tickets. What?? So, not only in one conversation did I learn that I could go to Italy, but that I could go first class for my first trip abroad!! Yah!

Once again, I stepped into the unknown and embraced it fully. I was still a little terrified by the idea and, before leaving, I asked everyone I knew who had traveled abroad multiple questions about packing, customs, and navigating different airports… but then I just did it!

I traveled domestically all the time. I had been in airports constantly for work. But somehow, sitting there at the gate with my passport in my hand… it felt different. Looking out through the airport window, I saw the plane through the glass windows at the gate, and it was *massive.* I had never been on such a large plane before in my life and I was more than a little intimidated, but the first thought that popped into my mind was, "I'm getting on *that* plane!"

Stepping across the threshold into the plane was surreal. My first-class suite was intimately lit, the lighting low against the darkness outside. There was a bed with a pillow and earphones and my own TV. There was a menu where I could select my meal, the flight attendants hovering nearby, ready to take my dinner order or provide anything I might need throughout the trip. The freedom of it all was exhilarating!

And it was all because I changed my self-perception and told myself, "Yes I can, I'm worth it, I deserve this." I had always compared myself to others, finding myself lacking, and this was the first time I had stepped over the threshold of what was possible. I embraced my true self-worth and saw my amazing potential.

My two weeks in Italy were indescribable. Spending time exploring a few cities, enjoying morning cappuccinos, and sampling some of the most delicious pasta I could have imagined were undoubtedly some of the most significant memories of the trip. But, they all paled in comparison to the conversations and laughter with my girlfriends. Spending two weeks with a few of the most amazing women that I have ever met left me forever changed. My relationships with these women transcend friendship… we truly consider ourselves soul sisters.

A few months later when the opportunity to travel to Estonia arose, there was no hesitation. The fears of traveling abroad alone and spending time with strangers felt like a distant memory. By this point, I was transformed and there was no going back to the person I had been. What was so exciting for me was that I knew the journey was just beginning. I now understand how significant relationships are in my life and how they are the catalyst for some of the most amazing shifts and evolutions. This is true for *all* my relationships whether it be with friends, colleagues, children, romantic partners, and family.

The beginning of this profound understanding came not through my relationships with others, but through my relationship with *myself*. Taking the necessary time to fall in love with who I was and who I could become was the first critical step in my transformation journey. Granted, I'm still learning who I am and what my potential might be… but, it's been fabulous! And, it's only enhanced the beauty of all of my relationships as I evolve and grow. A hard lesson at times, however, is how relationships also change over time. Some grow with me… and some I outgrow. I have had to learn that outgrowing is perfectly ok and part of the transformation process. The key, I have found, is to identify the beauty, gift, or lesson in any relationship and honor that… even if the relationship eventually ends. Each relationship is a gift.

It's not uncommon for me now to be asked why or how I am so positive… in work and in life. The answer, at least for me, lies in all of the amazing relationships I now have. Literally relationships which span the globe. I'm still learning and evolving, of course (aren't we all??), but I no longer have fear of the same things I once did. Abandoning self-limiting beliefs and stepping into the unknown, I feel, is now part of my purpose. I gain so much joy and fulfillment in my life as I help others see the lessons, the gifts, and the beauty to be found when they embrace a healthy and loving relationship with themselves.

In life, we all encounter challenges, struggles and self-limiting beliefs. We go through intense times and they can either define us or refine us. Learning from each of these moments gives us the gift to make a *change*, change for the *better* and create *massive* change in who we are. The choice is yours on how you view every situation and then define it. Ask yourself how will you step forward? What ways can you improve? And, what *change* do you need to undergo… so you can emerge knowing …YOU are worth it... YES you can... and you DESERVE it all.

IGNITE ACTION STEPS

Everyone is on their own journey. By taking a few simple actions you can create massive change of your own.

Listen to your body. It's your soul's way of communicating with you. If you are feeling anxious, take a deep breath and find the source of this feeling. Acknowledge it. Embrace it. Thank it. Then, resolve it.

Spend time in silence. Eliminate whatever you identify as a distraction and allow your quiet little voice, which has likely been suppressed for years, to finally be heard. What is she saying? What does she want? What is she afraid of? What is her deepest desire? Listen to her. She is your best friend. Always has been. Always will be. Get to know her again.

Identify one thing that scares you. Then do it. Whatever it is. Is it traveling? Is it having a difficult conversation with someone? Is it owning your truth? Whatever it is… do it. The confidence you will gain from doing just one thing you thought you never could will absolutely give you the inspiration to do more. You will become *unstoppable*!

Make a new friend. Go for coffee, out for wine, ditch digital and go analog. Reaching out and connecting at an authentic level connects you soul to soul and allows you to discover their true story and who they really are.

Be bold! Be brave! Ride that roller coaster! For me, it was a literal roller coaster that changed my life. What's yours? Why aren't you chasing it? Life is full of ups and downs. It ebbs and flows. Enjoy the ride!

Dr. Christy Parker - United States
Transformational Leader and Coach,
Inspirational Speaker, Passionate Intrapreneur
in *@christy-parker*

Elena Rodríguez Blanco

"Today is the day you had been waiting for."

Your life on earth matters, and the world is a better place because you are in it. This story is an invitation for you to create and design a business and a lifestyle that adds value to you, your family, society, the environment, and the planet. The world is lucky because you are in it. Ask yourself *generative* **questions, questions that produce multiple possibilities. Then take action and inspire change so as to make the world a better place for everyone.**

An Urgent Conversation: People, Planet & Profit

"What if? What if?" It was all I could hear from inside my mind as I sat there on one of many identical cold plastic chairs surrounding the enormous table in the meeting room. I felt like a living vessel of ideas. They wouldn't stop pouring into my brain. Or were they coming from my heart, I wondered? From somewhere beyond? My colleagues and I were all facing the projector, listening to our next steps to maximize earnings for the quarterly profit review. They were tapping at their laptops and seemed oblivious to my thoughts. The presenter was talking his way through a PowerPoint and exponential graphs in his habitual monotone delivery style.

I wasn't daydreaming, I was paying attention. I was listening to the words because my internal questions were related to the content being discussed.

Every time he mentioned something as a matter of fact, all I could think was, "What if? What if we added *a shared value strategy,* one where we could bring real value to society?" Or, "What if we try *another idea* to involve more communities while following a strategy?" The most recurring question, the most pressing one in my mind, was, "What if the way we think about business and live our lives are based on the wrong assumptions?"

Rob Hopkins, an innovative author and environmentalist inspired new thinking in me. He shared how newly discovered sea creatures in trenches eleven kilometres deep are found to have plastic in their stomachs. That bees and other insect populations are on the verge of collapse. How society is dangerously polarized, and there is a resurgence of toxic ideas. His most powerful quote is, "When we lurch from financial crisis to financial crisis without changing the fundamental imbalances, that makes their occurrence almost inevitable."

We have entered 'those times,' and the conversation in the meeting room made me feel detached from it all, as if it was extrapolated from the current world itself. The company was making plans that didn't take into account the reality that was around us and it was becoming hard to ignore. No one was considering the bigger picture: the systemic effect we are having on the earth, the interdependent ecology in which every choice we make has consequences for all life forms on the planet. How can we care about the world and ourselves at the same time? I wanted to put up my hand and ask… but I didn't.

After the meeting, I continued to ask myself, "What if there is indeed another way to look at this exact same thing? What if the premises on which we have built these theories are questioned? What if the conflict, the problem, the situation at hand is here to invite us to change, to move, to see with different eyes?" I realized that we are all completely intertwined and we need to take action toward a new way of doing things.

All of us in that room had come from many different countries and backgrounds, and had worked hard to find ways to be educated to follow the clear and best career path that was presented to us as business people and future managers. We all had been hired because we had an MBA (Masters in Business Administration), possibly the most expensive Masters in existence that comes with promises of career security attached. I had worked incredibly hard for mine, determined to get a leg up and gain insight into our economic and financial systems and the ways we could make the economy grow.

Coming from El Salvador, it was not easy. I had to prioritize if I wanted to make that happen. Unlike many, I had the opportunity to study at university and I worked hard to achieve the grades that would allow me to have a paid scholarship. But my scholarship only covered part of my tuition, so I used my savings from my first five years of working to pay the remainder of my expenses while studying. I felt I was one of the lucky ones who had made it, proud to be holding the same textbooks that everyone quoted when talking about financial futures.

The same unstoppable growth I learned about in textbooks was being discussed in that room. It was always the same questions: How can we increase our quarterly earnings? How can we make our company grow? It was a cancerous question, one of unprincipled and unthinking selfish growth at the expense of the host it was growing in.

I was working at General Electric (GE), a company with an annual revenue of $213 billion, larger than the combined earnings of entire countries! And GE is not alone. In fact, *every* company's goal is to maximize shareholder profit. The conversation about growth should always be on the table, but if the people discussing how to get there, come through the exact same training path, using the exact same reading materials, I wondered how we could initiate any change? And, how could we Ignite new thoughts over time?

More questions kept arising, this time with clear direction: "What if growth is meant to maximize *all* value and create *shared* value? What if maximized meant *beyond* the shareholder to *include* stakeholders as well — that is, society and the environment? What if instead of just growth for growth, we plan growth cycles like nature does, enriching our ecosystems so that they can better hold during those cycles? 'What if' kept coming to my mind.

I knew the answers to those questions were not written in any business book I had read during my MBA. These were questions that the books had no answers for; rather, they required a leap of faith and trying out something different. My questions were full of hope and also fear. Is there a way to do business that benefits people, planet, then profits?

There were already symptoms appearing as to how 'business as usual' was creating more harm than good. For example, in Central America, a high proportion of the illiterate population was being convinced to sign loans with ridiculous interest rates to 'make money fast' without any explanation of the consequences. At the same time, environmental disasters started emerging: the oil spills, the rapid progression of species extinction, and forests disappearing. These stories were becoming more and more recurrent, part of our everyday dialogue. We ignored the connections and didn't start a global conversation.

My body ached with a deep-rooted pain every time I watched the news. I could feel the blood in my veins heat with rage when I saw pictures and clips of businesses making careless decisions toward the environment, toward our shared home.

The consequences of these stories were still to be revealed and understood by the masses, yet one could already sense the ending was far from what 'economic theory' had promised.

Before I started working in corporate and had to continually worry about sales earnings reviews, I spent time volunteering on different projects, mainly in El Salvador where I had lived since age six, and giving back was just the environment back home. Even though I had left El Salvador, my soul country, years ago, I remained in touch with many non-profit organizations that were doing fantastic work solving some of the social and environmental challenges that were happening in the country. While this work always filled my heart and soul with joy, there was something missing.

I calmed my conscience by saying at least I was doing something. On many occasions, the truth is those actions are not really creating any *real* change; they are serving as a Band-Aid™ for a much deeper symptom that many times we ignored, or could not even identify in the first place. I sometimes felt like those actions were more about us volunteers 'feeling good' than actually affecting any long-term change on a large scale.

I knew I could do more and my heart beat faster when I compared my small ten years of on-the-ground contributions with the billions that I was now helping GE to generate for themselves every year. And while both coexist, the reality is that **business is the most effective way to make money and catalyze change in a capitalist society**. What if that money I was helping GE earn could be earned while also helping solve some of the many problems our world is facing? Can it be both? Can the purpose of business go beyond its textbook and legal definition of maximizing shareholder profit? What would that look like? How would that work?

I left GE a year later with a mission to further my understanding of these challenges the world was facing. I had experienced firsthand the atrocities of civil war and violence, as well as the upheaval of a natural disaster during my 15 years in El Salvador. Still, I wanted to name the lived experience with some actual academic and scientific research and theory. It is easy to be biased with your own perception of reality and I was seeking a broader framework, and perhaps an even more comprehensive understanding from the people who had been studying what was actually happening for years. Was there a way to rewrite the story? What action steps could we take? Was it too late? So many questions.

I applied for another improbable scholarship. Despite now being 'older' than my peers and in a different stage of life, my curiosity coupled with unseen forces working to make this happen landed me a full scholarship to live and study in London for a year on this precise theme. I spent one year focused on understanding the theory of social development and the challenges we have in the world from the perspective of professors, journalists, world leaders, and other peers with the same exact questions I had. That, to me, became the real power of learning; you join with others who are looking for answers to a question in the same realm. And it was that year that a pilot class came out called: 'Business Models for Social Change.'

Back then, very few people had started naming the possibility of joining Business and Social Change as part of a strategy, and not under a side label. I knew that was the reason I had gone back to study, to understand how I could use the tool of business as a catalyst for good.

No textbooks, no guidelines, just a couple of recent case studies of what some companies and organizations were doing. Well-funded ideas that were emerging from the companies that had the same purpose. It was exciting! It felt like we were doing something that hadn't been done before, bringing an urgent conversation to the world. Finally, I could use a new business language to talk about the causes that I cared about! And, it wasn't framed in victim language; it was honest and empowering. This was an arena we just had to start doing things in and test. No one had the answer; we just had to walk the path and be the Change Makers.

It was then that it became clear to me; my body filled with excitement, an adrenaline rush at the idea that re-defining the purpose of business could be one powerful idea that could change our future at the pace that we need.

So where do we start? *With generative questions.* With thought provoking questions that invite us to rethink our paradigm and our perception of what is possible. The task at hand required us to be beyond creativity and innovation. It would require a reconnection with imagination in order to connect to an outcome that didn't exist yet and hadn't been done before. It required trust, that possibility CAN happen, within you. It was about designing a blueprint for your path, a *belief* in business that would be unique in its DNA.

Generative Questions are not about following advice or following answers that one may know in advance. Instead, they allow concepts to emerge from the individual's mindset through creating a common collective. Using Generative Questions, people are able to listen to the problems created by societal, community and environmental myths. They question typical worldviews, uncovering real processes and actual needs. In this way generative questions are a combination of ideas, hopes, doubts, values and challenges in an amicable paradox uncovering both what is and what will become.One example of a generative question is: How can we make sure we can increase our ability to adapt to change and transform in life?

Filled with this new thinking, it was time to take action. The only way to learn would be to learn by doing; that is, building a social business. There was one person I deeply admired, Professor Muhammad Yunus, a Bangladeshi social entrepreneur, banker, economist, and civil society leader who was pioneering the concept of microcredit and microfinance and who in 2016 was awarded a Nobel Peace Prize for his work. As I was not yet a social business, I self-defined as a social entrepreneur, an electrifying business title. My objective was to develop, fund and implement solutions to social, cultural and environmental issues through a business that makes money. I wanted to combine, in core strategy, profit and revenues with social outputs. I needed to bridge what up to now had been two separate worlds — that of making money and scaling, and that of helping others and doing good — into one unique business model to grow.

I still remember the cold tone in my father's voice when I told him I wasn't going to look for a job that spring. As an economist, he has a mental spreadsheet of all investments made in time, money AND opportunity cost into my education. Of all the opportunities available to me, in ways that he and my mom hadn't had. I knew I was choosing this unknown path. Holding a vision that seemed... well, unreasonable. I knew I had been shown my life mission: **making business a catalyst for social change in the world: people, planet, and profit.**

It's been 15 years since I first made this choice and I am still building businesses that challenge the way we think, the way we work, the way we travel, and the way we spend. I strive to ask better questions each and every day. To go to bed knowing that today, I did the best I could with the resources I have to make living in this world worth it.

Until now, we as a society have left it in the hands of non-governmental organizations (NGOs) and foreign aid to take care of the most pressing societal problems in the world. Businesses, on the other hand, have the potential to do both at the same time and operate at a faster rate. In 2013, I founded my first B Corp certified company to become part of a movement of businesses that 'meet the highest standards of verified social and environmental performance' and 'aspire to use the power of markets to solve social and environmental problems.'

Business is the vehicle that can really drive change at the scale and efficiency we need. With the most talented of people working together to solve what is to come, we can *change* how and why we do business, leaping forward and designing new models and more sustainable lifestyles.

This is the day you had been waiting for. What is your generative question on how you can create change?

IGNITE ACTION STEPS

We all need to ask better questions, look for better answers, and take action now! If we all apply our gifts and talents, no matter how imperfectly, looking beyond ourselves to better the world, we can change the world for the better.

Wherever you are, no matter what you're doing, leave the place you're in better than you found it. Whatever you do, think seven generations ahead: What impact will your actions have on future generations? Make that impact a good one.

Look at your talents and your gifts. Look at the challenges the world is having. Find ways to apply your talents, your gifts, to the problems at hand and change the world's story. You can make money, live your passion, and support the world at the same time. **Think people, planet, profit.**

There are people already doing this; you are not alone. Tap into the resources around you; together, we can have a powerful impact on our future.

Ask yourself generative questions? What assumptions and beliefs are you basing your life on? Are they true? Think beyond yes or no questions and invite others into the process of "How might we create change?"

Elena Rodríguez Blanco - Spain
Serial social entrepreneur and Impact Investor
www.elenarodriguezblanco.com

REV. PRIESTESS ANANDHA RAY, MA, MA, DTR

"Adversity can be a gift that can Ignite the spirit to soar to new heights; adversity can be the seeds of change."

The shadow times of life can be moments that we wish we hadn't experienced. The story of your past is unchangeable. What has happened to you actually isn't the story of your life. Rather, what you do in response is what determines who you are and defines your legacy. It is in overcoming struggles that we gain strength, courage, compassion and empowerment. This is where you will find your silver lining. It will always be there; I hope my story inspires you to discover yours.

BEAUTY FROM DARKNESS

I stood in the classroom with 50 attentive Belarusian dancers awaiting my instruction. In an instant, I felt a warmth rush over me. I opened my mouth to speak and nothing came out. Silence filled the room; an expectation hung in the air as the beautiful dancers looked to me and I remained voiceless. "I don't want to do this," I thought.

I was serving as a cultural ambassador on an international tour representing the United States in the very first tour of Belarus by a contemporary dance company from the US. We were three cities into a jam-packed 5-city tour. We taught workshops, did concerts, gave print and television interviews… it was non-stop. It was right in the middle of teaching an intensive pre-concert workshop that I froze. Me, who never lacks confidence in teaching dance. Me, who has two Masters degrees. Me, who had been chairperson of a university dance department and wrote the coursework for the university to offer a dance major. Me, the artistic director of this professional dance company representing the United States. And Me… was frozen.

Despite my experience and level of competence, I stood motionless, my feet welded to the floor, my arms held stiffly in the air as they prepared to guide the class. I embodied the silence of a statue, forever reckoning this moment in time. I realized I had spent most of my career buying into a paradigm in which *I no longer believed*. This idea of teaching steps to dancers, of showing them how to move… no longer appealed to me.

Years before, I had almost died of anorexia. My body had become rail thin and every movement required enormous effort. It took eleven weeks of hospitalization and years of therapy to begin to unwind the deep rejection of my core self. It was a darkness that seeped into the framework of my soul. I lived in my mind, a place where I was at war with myself, a place I called the great abyss.

Dance gave me a means of expressing those things that I could not talk about: the terrors of the mind, the desolate loneliness, the paralyzing fears. Dance offered me a means to heal. I understood unequivocally the value of dance to give voice to those things that could not be talked about.

In the course of my life, I was unable to talk about these aspects. I had to maintain professionalism and 'healing' and 'spirit' or 'soul' were words that do not attract financial funding. Dance healed me, but as a professional choreographer who depended on grants, this healing work had to happen in secret. The dance methods that called me, that used me as a vessel toward creating them, bringing them into the world, dove deeply into understanding movement as a language of our humanity.

Yet, I was frozen. On this prestigious international tour, teaching enthusiastic young dancers, sharing my choreographed dance phrases… in that moment I could not continue the traditional format of offering dance; I knew that was not my way. With the hungry eyes of these students trained on me, I wanted to offer them *more*. I wanted to show them the deepening connection through dance that I knew was possible. I wanted to guide their spirit to dance, and allow their body to express the language of the soul. I wanted them to understand the resources of their heart, the *language* that had become so intimately my own. In that instant I fully understood an inner directive to create a bridge between what I knew in my heart was the true value of dance, and the old ways of teaching dance steps. In my rehearsals with my professional dancers, I had changed the idea of teaching dance and created an innovative way to wield it as a powerful healing force. It was a radical departure from the norm. It was unheard of. And it was my secret; I was not offering this to the public — I had an image to uphold.

In that suspended moment in Belarus, my past and all of my future unfolded right before my eyes. I began to comprehend a new awareness. In that instant of realization, as if it were my life flashing before my eyes, I remembered my younger self, teaching myself ways in which dance was healing the soul-wounds of living in the abyss of anorexia. I realized the medicine that movement had been, the *wholeness* dance brought me. For me, dance has always been a means of expressing the unspeakable beauty of the human soul. I had learned of dance therapy and dove headfirst into the vast sea of understanding it as a healing vessel. I divided my focus and became a dance therapist, specializing in the treatment of patients with eating disorders. Dance therapy is like a movement meditation with your eyes closed. The therapist is the only one who can actually see the movements of the dancers. As a choreographer, I was inspired by the beauty of the movement of the patients. And, they had no training! I was struck with the knowledge that I wasn't meant to be a therapist and there was more that I could offer.

Dance was a bridge and I was its architect. I was meant to learn about dance therapy only so I could understand how dance heals. My life journey would be to connect the healing power of dance therapy with stage performances as artistic expression, to alchemize the beauty of the publicly unseen moments of this expressive form into an evocative form of dance that was not meant to be watched, but rather *witnessed*. The first dance I created in this way expressed the feeling of a cry. I didn't tell the dance what to be about, but rather I allowed it to speak a truth of pure, raw humanness. The choreography gave voice to extreme movements, an exaggerated backward arch of the spine, reliving the desperate feeling of having a scream locked inside that created a pressure in your core without any place for it to escape. It was a silent and secret cry, held deeply hidden from the world. I was surprised when audiences told me that what they interpreted was that the dance was about the effects that one who has been abused as a child endures for the rest of their life. It wasn't my intention at all. Although I had been abused, I had never talked about it… but the dance told the story.

Performing it took a lot of courage. One performance in particular was terrifying. I had been asked to perform this dance for a conference for Survivors of Child Abuse. In this conference, hundreds of survivors would be there... as well as perpetrators of child abuse that were required by law to attend. They would line up against the back wall, unwilling, not wanting to be there, standing while the rest of the audience sat in chairs. As I positioned myself to perform for this audience, my body reacted in terror, unwilling to respond to my commands. After we performed, there were few dry eyes in the audience. Surprisingly — and satisfyingly — even the perpetrators in the back of the theater had shed tears. They FELT the experience, through the expression of the dance. After the performance, a survivor approached me, saying, "I never knew that something so ugly could be made into something so beautiful." Beauty from darkness.

Those memories of how dance had healed me flooded into my mind, solidifying into a burning awareness as I gazed back into the eyes of those attentive students in Belarus. Feeling a surge of courage flood into my upraised arms, I lifted my chin. What I had created... my new way of teaching dance... was *completely different* than any other method that existed, yet it held the potential to unlock healing through the expression of our shared human authenticity. I was compelled to take this risk. My soul was determined to give these students the powerful experience in dance that I knew was possible... that had become my lifeline... that was my new way of understanding the humanity we all hold inside of us. At the moment, when I could not form words with the Belarusian students, in the stillness that seemed to last forever, a quiver of fierceness grew, bringing the courage that it takes to make change. It was time to 'lean in' to my conditioned fear of teaching something so unexpected, so non-traditional. It was frightening to present these changes to the public. In following my truth, it meant changing the very foundation not only of how I created dances, but also of the way that I taught dance to everyone.

I would open their bodies to manifest their truths, to discover *their* voice in dance and in that moment, completely depart from the way that dance had been taught. It was time for *Change*. The roaring silence of that moment was deafening. The dancers were excitedly waiting to see what I would do next. I stopped class. I changed course midstream. "We're going to do something different," I said. And I led them on a journey.

As my words began to form again, I gathered the students into a circle. I shared with them that there was so much more to dance than the steps alone. I expressed my desire to see dance that touched the soul, that resonated in deep emotional spaces. I led them to unlock the components of how dance is a language of its own. Arms akimbo, legs slicing the air, athletic lunges, and creative expressions spoke through movements that sprang from their *hearts*. They danced with tears in their eyes and brought tears to mine. They touched my soul deeply. It ended in a thunderous applause and hugs. THIS! This was what I knew dance could be, a deep connection of souls even when we speak different languages.

I carried this newfound courage home to California. In my dance studio, I began offering this work to the public in the form now called Quimera Ritual Dance. I never looked back. No longer teaching dance steps, I shared processes that inspired creativity and opened channels of dancing heartfelt, deeply personal and profoundly creative expressions. It was a new way of thinking about dance and I felt incredibly vulnerable sharing it. It combined the expertise of my three distinct Masters' degree topics: choreography, kinesiology, and dance therapy. The fusion of these three disparate forms created an innovative way of understanding dance. And as I taught it, I witnessed the rapid explosion of students' athletic abilities. Right alongside their transcendent physical improvement, I witnessed old wounds healing. They stepped more confidently and with courage into their full expressiveness in dance and in life. Their souls were healing.

This innovative form was doing a really unusual thing; it was bridging the dichotomy of two opposite worlds: 'dance as therapy' and 'dance as an exquisite athletic art form.' The fear of the inner darkness was retreating, not just for my dancers but for *myself*. While the art that resulted was profound, reviews were mixed. Wildly popular in European countries, in the United States, people walked out stating, "This is NOT entertainment." And I couldn't disagree. It wasn't my intention to entertain.

And then I received a letter from an audience member. They described how they had come to the concert feeling suicidal but had left feeling *changed*, feeling understood, and no longer alone. Every cell in my body felt connected to the letter writer. I was simply overwhelmed. Someone in the world had decided to live because they saw themselves in my dance. Of the many letters I received over the years, five were from people who had been suicidal and left the concert *changed*. It drove me to continue what I was doing despite the naysayers or the people who said my dances were too raw and needed a happy ending.

I *had* my happy ending. The people behind those letters also had *their* happy endings.

And as for me, I wanted to know more about how and why dance could heal such deep wounds. I wondered if this type of healing dance might have been present in the world before, or if indigenous and ancient movement ceremonies might have had this healing quality. I was curious about how movement is used in sacred ceremonies. I wanted to know more about shamanism and dance. But I still had a company to run, tours to manage, and classes to teach.

That idea, the need to know, to understand, never let me go. When I retired, the time opened up for me to explore the shamanic, transformative connections of dance. For two years, I cocooned myself into the world of ritual and ceremony, exploring every avenue I could find. I began to understand how it was that creating human connections through the language of dance communicated spirit-to-spirit, soul-to-soul. In surprising ways, ancient rituals and ceremonies danced into my life. Through these experiences, the compelling mystery that ritual and ceremony evoked… the shamanism of dance… was seeping into my consciousness.

I attended private indigenous international ceremonies by invitation only, and danced in Grandmother's Moon Dance Ceremonies in the moon-cast shadow of the Teotihuacan pyramids in the desert of Mexico. For four consecutive days, we danced until the sun came up. We sang in sweat lodges, and gathered in circles to absorb new learnings. We fasted and didn't sleep. The third night, I began having visions. From the land of shadows, Owl entered my life and gave me eyes to see through the darkness. Soon, the ceremonies and rituals I had participated in solidified into one message whispered over and over in my ear. "Offer your dance as a ceremony." I was understanding how dance allows a person to enter shamanic states, to communicate with energies and spirits, and even to visit with loved ones who have passed on. The ways in which I could speak about it and teach it to others were clear to me now.

And so this journey deepened. I began to explore this calling from a goddess of dance. In Egypt, in ancient times, the priestesses of Isis would dance outside the temples to heal the passersby. My calling continued to expand and I began a year of initiation to become an ordained Reverend Priestess of the Goddess Isis. As part of my ministry, I began the service of offering dance as a monthly ceremony. People gathered and stepped into healing ceremonies with me. Every new person was so inspired that they would invite another for the next month. In this small way, the gathering grew rapidly.

Once I was ordained, my first assignment as a Reverend Priestess was to train others. I was invited to lead six dancers in a year-long training to be ordained themselves. All six accepted, throwing me into a state both nervous and excited. They were only the first, and it is in this way that Quimera Ritual Dance was formalized. My work expanded profoundly, reaching out to those who were ready to transform through the beauty of movement in ceremony and ritual, in workshops, retreats and in year-long trainings. Carrying forth a deep connection to the humanness of being human… the emotional expression of challenges, as well as the celebrations of life, called forth a community of spiritual connections through dance. A healing tribe was formed to use dance as a means to speak the language of the soul. People's lives change profoundly. Issues that plagued them for a lifetime, unwound and were resolved. Their arms filled with grace, limbs moved more fluidly, spines more supple, and souls embodied freedom and risk. People shared with me over and over again that, in just one session, they felt like they had experienced ten years of therapy.

Stepping far outside of the norm in the dance community, creating radical change, a new dance form emerged, bringing healing to myself and others. Dance that is not always 'pretty' but *beautiful* in ways that are eternal. If my early life had not been laced with adversity, I might never have developed the vision to see the world differently. Adversity can be a force that changes our future. Yet it is NOT our life story; it is only the beginning. As counterintuitive as it might sound, the very things that we call adversity just might be some of the greatest gifts you will ever embody. In the telling of your life stories, it's easy to define trauma as only a negative. Even if you were dealt the most severe of experiences, *the way that you redefine your story is creating the next steps of your future*. Every story has a component of empowerment in the telling of it… when you understand the GIFT within it. May the shadow and light of your future be illuminated through the *empowered* understanding of the totality of what made you the Change Maker you are *becoming*.

IGNITE ACTION STEPS

Find your silver lining.

The way we tell our stories creates in us a path to become better or bitter. Think through a story of trauma in your life. Follow the thread of that story. What did you do because of it? In the end, how did it affect you to change in a positive way? Imagine that *your* life has aligned to give you the perfect experiences to bring you to a place where you have already become, or are becoming a transformative Change Maker.

Rev. Priestess Anandha Ray, MA, MA, DTR - United States
Master Teacher, Choreographer, Visionary
www.quimeraritual.dance
www.anandharay.com

Holly Olp

*"The only constant in life is choice; change is just
the direction those choices take you in."*

**My hope is that by reading my story you realize that at this very moment,
you ARE changing. When you decide what to eat, how to speak, what you
show up for... you are changing. Appreciate that every action you take is
your CHOICE, and use this power to change in profound ways and toward
the direction of your dreamiest, healthiest, happiest life.**

Running Up the Down Escalator

I remember the moment clearly. I was in my usual spot, sitting on my couch
with a late dinner of cheese and crackers and a glass of wine, scrolling social
media posts from the online fitness challenge I was participating in. I had seen
the same woman post daily through the entire challenge, but for some reason,
this day her post struck me. She was a single mom and she had just finished her
workout. She proudly shared her sweaty selfie as proof of her commitment. I
admired how she had not finished her workout until after midnight in her East
Coast basement. All the while I was sitting on my pillowy couch, in my kid-free
bachelorette pad around 9 PM Pacific Time, already in my jammies. I hadn't
worked out and didn't plan to, despite being part of the same challenge. "I can't
work out that late!" I thought. "That's crazy! Besides, *Coming to America* is
on TV and I can't miss it."

A wave of shame came over me. I realized that actually I could do all of it.

And the reality that poured over me felt about as nice as a bucket of ice-cold water.

I could work out at 9 PM. I wasn't too busy. I was sitting smack dab in the middle of the time I thought I didn't have, caught scrolling Facebook and watching TV instead of doing something I could, should, and *wanted* to do for myself.

That was my Ignite Moment. Sitting on the couch that night, I had no idea that it was where my life would change, but I now know that defining moments are real and that that was mine. Since then, I've learned that the moment alone is not enough; the time leading up to it and the time following it is where the magic happens. That is where I realized that all the juicy lessons and challenges influenced my transformation. That Ignite Moment was the tipping point where the me I was before, and the me I would become, were suspended, waiting to see which way I would go.

We've all heard the phrase "Change is hard" and it seems spot on, doesn't it? The reality is, that couldn't be further from the truth. Change is effortless. It happens whether you like it or not. Change is just the end result of all of the big and little choices you make each and every day.

A year prior to my Ignite Moment, I had already dropped change bombs all over my life. I had been unhappy for many months, but with a master's degree in 'suck it up' and a minor in 'let's not feel this,' I had held it all in for far too long. The thing about feelings though, is that those darn things can Houdini out of the tightest situations, no matter how locked away you think they are. Mine certainly did.

The facts were all there. I was in a relationship that wasn't going how I'd imagined. I was feeling undervalued and unloved and no matter how hard I tried to be impressive, lose weight, and look pretty… I wasn't getting the love and attention I was seeking. I was in denial about how I truly felt about the relationship, and in my futile efforts to fix things, I had become someone I didn't enjoy. I wasn't fun anymore; feeling needy and desperate. Each day that I let my feelings go unspoken was another day spent in something I knew wasn't right. Staying, changed me for the worse. Ultimately, recognizing this about myself was what tipped the scale and prompted me to move on. So, *abracadabra*! I had reached a point where I couldn't deny my feelings anymore and I needed a change.

Making that choice was hard. Admitting defeat is never easy. Splitting the friends, leaving my lifestyle, upending my routine, and finding myself alone felt uncomfortable. And even though I knew I needed those changes and I wanted to open space for something better, that discomfort caused me to doubt my every move.

Professionally, it was the same story, and at the same time. Remember that magic trick my emotions performed? As it turns out, emotions aren't limited to your personal life. Unfortunately, when you bottle them all up to the point of overflowing, they don't spill out into tidy, organized piles so you can handle one thing at a time. I had been working my butt off and was really proud of what I'd accomplished in my first 15 months at my Barbie dream job. I was preparing to ask for a raise when I received an invite from our department's VP. I thought it must be some sort of recognition lunch for me and all the hard work I had done, and I was so flattered. But when we sat down to lunch, I realized I had it all wrong. She started explaining how our department worked and what her expectations were for our team. My mouth went dry. I had heard this all before. She had lumped me in with all the new team members and this was their welcome lunch — I. Was. Mortified.

There I was, so excited that the woman who signs my checks wanted to take me out to lunch for all my hard work — the one who ultimately would be the gatekeeper to the promotion I was about to ask for — and she was oblivious to when I started and how hard I'd been working. She had no recollection of having taken me for that same welcome lunch ten months earlier. I'm sure my face said it all because she instantly asked how long I'd been there. I mumbled my start date, but I didn't have the nerve to tell her we'd already done this whole thing. Needless to say, I left feeling completely defeated and undervalued.

I knew I needed to leave that job. The wind had been taken right out of my sails on a professional level and it certainly wasn't making me an enjoyable person to be around, at work or at home. That general 'unfunness' I felt was spilling over into my personal life and my relationship as well.

This brings me back to 'Change is hard.' That period of my life was definitely difficult. Realizing I was in the wrong places, with the wrong people, doing the wrong job… tossing out all the time and effort I put into obtaining those things… deciding to change… it was hard. The deliberation, the doubt, the decisions… were hard. But once the decision was made, the changes that ensued felt effortless.

At a time when I was evaluating everything in my life, the thought of changing jobs felt incredibly overwhelming. Ultimately, I made the decision to move. Professionally, I found a much more supportive workplace, but it also meant a pay cut, losing touch with my former coworkers, and deviating from my 'master plan.' All those factors were huge sources of discomfort and doubt for me.

I wish I could tell you that this is where my story turned around, but I've never been one for straight lines except when they come in flannel. With a newly-vacant social calendar, paid vacation, and sane work hours, life was measurably better and I was emotionally free as a bird. I started filling my time with brunches, dinners and drinks, mini-vacations, girls nights, TV watch parties, and a dozen other versions of wine plus friends.

The weight I'd lost in my fight to feel loved in my failing relationship showed back up and brought some friends. I hated getting ready to go out. My fragile confidence cracked with every marathon outfit picking session as I rejected option after option in my closet. I had little energy and, despite the job change, had very little drive.

Looking back now, I see that the thing that was missing in all aspects of my life was challenge and growth. I was floating, choosing comfort, and living life like it was happening to me, not by me. Sure, it was fun, this 'aftermath' of all the changes I'd just experienced. I thought I WAS living. But while I thought the changes were done, the reality was the changes HADN'T stopped. My choices, small daily things like whether I should go for a hike or eat a stack of pancakes, whether I should stop by the grocery store or order Thai takeout, whether I should work out or continue watching '80s movie marathons... they all continued to move me and change me. The change was so effortless and gradual that I didn't feel it until my pants wouldn't button and I found myself on the floor of my closet bouncing between anger directed at my denim collection and tears of general self-pity at the mess my life had become.

Here I was having made two massive positive decisions for myself, followed by a bunch of tiny, insignificant choices: pancakes and mimosas. Takeout? Extra peanut sauce? And obviously *Coming to America* because it might be seven months before it was on TV again. When it comes to moving forward, I was as effective as running up the *down* escalator.

And yet there I was, on my couch, about to be hit over the head with my Ignite Moment. The one where I knew I should workout, I could workout, and I saw right through myself and the epic lameness of my excuses. Once I saw the reality of that one moment it was just the tip of the iceberg. In evaluating all my other choices, the results were finally too big to ignore.

I decided to step up my game. I spent the money I thought I didn't have and invested in a full workout plan. I showed up in the fitness challenges more and, most importantly, was honest about when I didn't do the work. I still went out with friends, but chose to eat at home more in between outings. I took my vitamins. I drank more water. It wasn't a massive overhaul, just a general cleaning up of all the tiny choices I made daily. By flipping a few more to the healthy side, by choosing differently, change flowed effortlessly to almost all parts of my life.

The first change was the energy. By introducing vitamins, more water, more home-cookin' and fewer mimosas, my energy skyrocketed. I distinctly remember one day stopping in my tracks and thinking about just how good I felt. My new normal felt like Dorothy from the *Wizard of Oz*, when she steps out into the full-color version of her life after living in black and white — I just didn't know what I had been missing!

From there, people at work started asking me what I was doing differently. My family noticed more happiness in my voice and that I had started a new healthy routine... and they wanted in. And my online fit friends casually mentioned that maybe I should help lead others.

It was all new and exciting. I was enjoying how I looked and getting ready was fun again. I was challenging myself for the first time in years. I was feeling amazing, and that fueled me to make even more positive choices. But let me be clear — fear and doubt still followed with every new scary choice, including when I said yes to becoming a fitness coach. I didn't consider myself a leader just yet. I knew I had taken the right steps and I felt good, but I had no idea how to convince anyone else to follow my lead. Fortunately, by that time, I had done so many things I thought I couldn't do, that I knew I should keep challenging myself and go after this.

By choosing to become a coach, I put myself way outside my comfort zone. I had to share and promote myself and my business. I had to lead from the front and share more publicly. I had to ask people if I could help them and invite them to join me. I had to give tough love, talk about sensitive things, share my failures, and generally flip off my introverted tendencies. That choice was hard. Through the past six years, I have never felt like it was easy. Even when I don't feel like it and that comfy spot on my couch is calling my name, I choose every day to show up. Add value. Share. Inspire.

But dang, the changes that followed those choices have been some of the greatest things that could ever happen in a life. My own personal changes and my work leading others has added so much vibrancy to my life. My fitness routine gave me confidence in my strength and helped me question my limiting beliefs. Remember that space I opened up for greater love and opportunity? I made the tough choices to create that space but I also learned (through trial and error) that even the small choices matter if I want to move forward. Since getting my choices aligned, it's been a whirlwind of love and opportunity, and my life has evolved in tremendous ways: more self-love and confidence, a happier relationship, more opportunity for growth, and a continuous flow of positive energy and change.

Today, I am in the most love-filled and supportive relationship, one that far exceeds what I used to dream of. Professionally, my work now takes me into locations where I present and facilitate workshops for companies all over the world, and my fitness coaching business wakes me up each day with excitement. Both have opened up new channels for me to help others change how they live, move, think, and act. Not a week goes by that I don't have someone sharing an Ignite Moment of their own!

When I look back at all of those scary moments of self-doubt and tough choices, I see that these choices have so completely changed me. I can't help but thank the Universe for that Ignite Moment on my couch and the opportunity I have here to help you recognize yours. I've gone from the wrong job, the wrong relationship, living on a whim, inside my comfort zone, introverted, and lacking self-confidence... to someone who is proud of her lifestyle, lives with great energy, steps outside her comfort zone, and loves the direction she's going. I'm now someone who leads workshops, writes books, and helps people around the world change in new ways. It all came from a few hard choices, a lot of little easy choices, and the changes that followed after.

I hope you see some of *you* in my story and use this as a guide to shape the parts of your life that don't feel quite right. You have more control than you think and you are capable of more than you give yourself credit for. It's time to align your choices and start walking yourself up the *up* escalator!

IGNITE ACTION STEPS

- Identify any big areas of your life that you know don't feel right. What is it about them that doesn't feel good? What does your gut tell you is the next right step?

- Prepare for it to be hard. I know now that when fear and doubt follow me, I'm usually on the right track. Fear, doubt, and discomfort are what draw you back into old habits and your comfort zone. Recognize that even in your comfort zone you are changing — but rarely in a positive direction.

- Identify the small choices that you are making each day. They are count-less so let's start with the ones that pertain to your energy, health, and happiness in some way. Are these smaller choices in alignment with how you want to live and feel? Or are you running up the down escalator and getting nowhere?

- Recognize that you don't have to be perfect. Pick a few to choose dif-ferently today. How did it make you feel to choose better?

- Repeat tomorrow and again the next day. You'll be surprised how much a few small choices can quickly change how you feel. Hold on to the good feeling and let it fuel you when the choices feel hard.

- Love yourself enough to embrace the hard stuff. Positive change is always on the other side.

- Lastly, teach what you've learned to others while you are learning it. You only have to be one step ahead of someone else to be a leader.

Holly Olp - United States
Wellness Coach; Behavior Change Specialist
www.hollyolp.com
🔘 *@hollyolp*

MELISSA ELEVEY

"Love is always the answer."

My intention is that you realize how powerful you are. Through your seeming ordinariness, you can create extraordinary change in the world. You don't have to search for years to find your purpose... you were born *as* the purpose. When you fully step into the beauty and magnificence of who you are, you will transform and come alive. And when you do, your love and joy have the capacity to light up everyone around you. My wish is that you see how beautiful you truly are and how powerful you can become when you embrace your uniqueness and follow your soul's song.

ACCESSING YOUR GREATEST POWER

My entire life, I thought I had it all — little did I know the Universe was about to show me otherwise. I was running around in a world where I could make anything happen. This. Was. My. Life. A great life. Anything I wanted, I got. I had set goals for the next 10 years and my life was on target. I had a million things I wanted to achieve and — just like that — I did them. And unbelievably, they usually turned out way better than I had imagined. This gave me an amazing rush of energy every time. I felt that spark alive in my heart, the passion was there, and everything flowed. I had it all, and I knew it all. Or so I believed.

Then, one day... BOOM! Darkness descended.

Life had other plans for me.

My body had had enough. Foreign sensations started plaguing me — pains were shooting through my body, my muscles felt as weak as jelly, and crippling fatigue overcame me. I had no idea what was going on. I thought I was dying.

I felt blindsided. I didn't see it coming. There were days where I could barely muster up enough energy to drag myself out of bed. And there were also those days when I couldn't even get out of bed. In my high-achieving world, this was unfathomable. Sure, there was stress to my lifestyle and it would sometimes slow me down, but nothing like this. And, quite frankly, I didn't have time to pay attention to it. I ignored it until I no longer had a choice. But now, my fit and healthy self was a distant memory.

Having been an independent woman my entire life, I now had to let go of the need to do everything on my own and finally ask others for help. I really craved care and support from others — I needed it in order to get through my days. However, I appeared normal and physically healthy to them. They had no clue about the health challenges and struggles that each moment presented to me. I often wondered if I would ever feel 'normal' again.

I was devastated.

Especially because what was most important to me was taken away. From the time I can remember, I was active every moment possible. Either walking around with a skip in my step or outside riding my bike, jogging, or playing sports. I loved it more than anything. It brought so much joy to my world. And now, here I was, not even able to manage a short walk outside amongst nature. I was intensely missing the feeling of the cool breeze brushing past my cheek as I frolicked in the great outdoors. I was desperate to return to my usual self and determined I would get there. And although I couldn't see the light at that point, I always believed that I would get better — I just had this inner determination and an inner knowing.

This energetic, exuberant, and creative soul had become part of the living 'lifeless.' The types that are walking around doing things, but when you look into their eyes, you can instantly tell the fire in their soul was put out years ago. Unbelievably, this happened to me. I was now one of them.

How did I let this happen? When did this happen?

Looking back, it was easy to see. I made a choice when I returned home from a year of soul-expanding travel overseas. I decided that it was time to '*be like everyone else.*' I had my fun and I should settle into a 'normal' life. The kind of life that everyone else seemed to have. I just wanted to fit in and feel more connected to others by being more like them. So I did. I changed myself to 'fit in.' I changed how outspoken I was by adopting neutral opinions. I started dressing differently, choosing mainly black instead of the colorful tones that I usually gravitated toward. And I chose to stay in a relationship with someone who was a 'nice' person, yet not supportive of me, and who didn't spark excitement in my soul. Looking back, it was obvious that when I tried to fit in with other people, I completely lost my sense of self. I lost my sparkle. I lost my brilliance. I faded away.

My life went from being passion-fuelled to being anxiety-ridden — in search of approval for being someone who I was not. Looking back, those soul depriving years were the darkest years of my life.

Deep inside a black hole, it was time for me to face the devastating truth — that a woman who was on top of her game had completely lost who she was. I became numb to the experiences of life. I'd forgotten what made me feel joy. And with the crippling fatigue, I was too exhausted to try and figure it out. It was in these moments that I started to ask myself the question, "What the hell was I here for?"

This question exposed a fear I didn't even realize I had. A fear of my existence being useless. Of not being needed by anyone or anything on this planet. In those dark moments, everything just blurred into one heavy, overwhelming mass of helplessness.

This was the beginning of the journey. The journey where I *finally* had to start listening. Listening to myself. Listening closely to what my heart really wanted. Who am I? What is my purpose in life? What am I here to do?

Those questions hit hard. Tremendously hard. I felt I couldn't start living my life until I knew the answers.

I was bobbing around like a cork on the ocean, waiting... waiting for the answers to become clear. I needed to find my purpose! Searching for it was like searching for a magical key that would unlock the reason for my existence on this earth. It would reveal the gifts that I am meant to share with the world. Once I found this elusive magical key of purpose, I believed that everything would be fine again. My life would all of a sudden have direction and become meaningful.

I read books, attended courses, experienced new places, and pushed myself out of my comfort zone in every way. Despite my growth and expansion as a person, I was still directionless and continued to bob around on what felt like a vast and lonely ocean.

During my 'search' for purpose, I discovered amazing places and met many incredible people. Of these people, there were those special few who had something magnetic about them. They naturally became my teachers... my mentors… my guides — whether they knew it or not. I wanted to be around them all the time because it felt so good to be in their presence. They seemed to spring out of nowhere, usually at times when I needed them most. They had a profound influence on my life and ultimately on who I became. One of them was George.

George was a down-to-earth guy, the kind of person who didn't care what you looked like or did for a living. He lived for the moment, had joy in his soul and always saw the countless possibilities available at any given time. I met George when I was still going through a phase of incredibly heavy fatigue. Although I was weak, I agreed to catch up for a mid-morning stroll along one of my favorite beach coastline trails. I didn't know how far I would manage to walk that day, but was simply happy to be outdoors with good company. With the sun shining down, we shared many laughs and also our dreams — the ones that make you feel alive when you talk about them. I was enjoying the sun on my back and breathing in the salty coastal air. I felt light and flowy — I'd completely forgotten about any worries I had. And then, a fair distance into the walk, BOOM! It was clear. I looked up at George and declared, "You know what? When I hang out with you, I never feel tired."

How could being around a person create such a supernatural effect? That a perpetually exhausted person no longer felt the least bit tired? That a lifeless soul could feel energized and excited about life?

What was it about George and the other incredible people I had met like him that they could have this mystical effect on me? And also on all those around them?

They had the fire alive in their soul. And with that fire, they seemed to be able to light up the spark in all those they met. In that moment of realization, I understood that, just like them, *I was the purpose*. All I had to do was step into it. I realized that if I became fully alive as myself, I might be able to help others see the beauty and magnificence within themselves. As the sage Rumi said, "A candle loses none of its light by lighting another."

What inspired me most about George and the others like him was that they lived a life full of play, fun, and laughter. They seemed free and happy. Joy beamed out of them. Their spark was alive, and this spark always seemed to flow to everyone in their presence. I noticed other people transforming when they spent time with my teachers, the light in their souls re-igniting, even if only for a moment. George and all the other teachers like him in my life were living examples of the practice of unconditional love. I discovered unconditional love from a fellow human is one of the most beautiful gifts to receive and one of the most beautiful gifts to give. In that presence, I felt that anything was possible.

George also had this knack about him. Generosity flowed from his being. Especially generosity of time and generosity of spirit. He also created this beautiful safe space where people felt comfortable to share their truth. I never felt silly when I shared my crazy thoughts and ideas. It was because he listened without judgment. I always felt encouraged and supported. And the more I was encouraged to be me, the more I *became* me.

The more I relaxed into the beauty of my uniqueness and lived as my soul's true essence, the more I began to notice the sparks Ignite into flames. I could feel the fire flaming in my soul. I felt alive again!

I continued to fill my life with more thoughts and activities that fueled my soul's desires. At the same time, I noticed my fatigue disappearing a little more with each passing day. When I began to embrace the fun inside every moment, all the seriousness in my life disappeared. Instead of darkness and heaviness, my days became filled with more joy and giggles — which I could now share with the people who entered my sphere, be it strangers, acquaintances, or loved ones.

I learned that when I honored and admired the unique beauty of my own soul's signature, living fully in every moment, I shone more vibrantly to the world. It is our vibrance and love of life that inspires others. We instantly become an example to the world that being our unique selves is the path to pure freedom and joy. And it is our kindness, encouragement, and unconditional love that gently guides and supports us toward that path of expressing our soul's truth.

We don't have to do something big to change the world. Know that through our seeming ordinariness, we can and *do* have a powerful impact each and every day. We don't have to do anything special to inspire or enliven people. Simply be who you are, share your aliveness with others, and love. Love unconditionally. Your love has the power to transform the world!

Realize how important and amazing you are. Know your brilliance. Each and every person has an important role to play in this tapestry of life on earth — whether we know it or not. We are all Change Makers — and we need each other to realize our full beauty. We are each a colorful and vibrant strand in this tapestry that becomes even more stunning when woven together. When one single strand is missing, the tapestry all of a sudden becomes a little less beautiful, a little less complete. You are important. You are special. You are amazing. And, know that there is no magical key of purpose. We are here *on* purpose and we *are* the purpose. The answer is that simple. We *are* the key.

My dear Change Maker, you are enough. You are more than enough. You are way more beautiful and way more powerful than you could ever imagine. And yes, you can transform the world, one person at a time, by being the most joyous, passionate, and alive version of yourself. We need people who can remind us of our beauty, who inspire us to believe in life, and to follow our dreams once again. You can help others tap into their aliveness and create a ripple effect. Let's light up the world by sharing our joy, laughter, encouragement, and most importantly, our unconditional love.

IGNITE ACTION STEPS

We are all going through our own unique journey in this lifetime, yet, we all need each other. By being ourselves and expressing our uniqueness we inspire others to step into themselves fully and shine as their own unique expression. What we see is what we have — we are all a reflection of each other. So focus on the beauty within yourself, within nature, within others and that will light up the world.

- **Fill your day with fun.** Having more fun not only brightens up your day, but it also brightens up the day of those around you. Drop the seriousness by starting to look at the world again with child-like eyes. Let everything amaze you. Have curiosity. Aim to find the fun in everything — the things that make you laugh and smile. See the beauty and joy in every moment. And when you find that joy, remember to share it with those around you.

- **Share with others what you admire about them.** Sprinkle more kindness into the world each day. It's important to never assume what is happening in anyone's world — especially if everything looks fine from the outside. Consider the people you interact with during your day, they may be strangers or people you know, and share with them what you genuinely like or admire about them. Positive comments always lift a person's spirits and their confidence. Although you may never know the power of those words, the comment that you express may be the inspiration for them to make a decision that positively changes the course of their life.

- **Practise unconditional love daily.** Appreciate people for who they are, what they say, and what they contribute. Your unconditional love provides the container for them to feel safe to express who they are without any judgment. What you see in others exists in you — so be compassionate and seek the beauty in everyone. Your unconditional love is what gives people the strength and confidence they need to take the risks to follow their heart. Remember, nobody is perfect and mastering unconditional love is a daily practice. Start with yourself. The more you love yourself for who you are, the easier it is to be compassionate toward others and love them without judgment.

- **Encourage others and support their dreams – even if it's not what you would do or how you would do it.** We all have different dreams and different paths to follow in this life. We also have our own lessons to learn along the way. If someone is following their passion, then support them in that. Their desires are what lights up their soul and is the fire that makes them get out of bed every day. Think about how wonderful it feels when someone supports you. When you show interest in other people's dreams, just watch their eyes light up! It is a magical moment. Provide suggestions or guidance only if they ask. We might know of a better way or a shortcut, but we all learn most through making our own mistakes. Allow people the freedom to learn from their mistakes as they follow *their* path.

Believe in your unique magnificence. Let your joy light up the world!

Melissa Elevey - Australia
Dreamer. Creator. Adventurer. Lover of life.

Rosa Maria Kallas

"Grounded in your values but lenient in your beliefs,
know that every moment is a new possibility."

My wish is for you to let go of all the dreams holding you back, of all the logical equations that don't seem to make sense, and of all the expectations preventing you from experiencing yourself, in this lifetime, to the fullest. My hope is for you to set the intention of freedom and expansion, freedom from all beliefs that are limiting you and an expansion even bigger than your own dreams.

1 + 1 = Possibilities

The world is unfair. In every country, there are circumstances; in every marriage, there are disappointments; in every family, there are wounds; and inside each person there are imperfections. Knowing that so many things might seem unfair and out of your control, what are you hoping for and what are you still waiting for?

I got tired from wishing things would change. Lying awake at night, scared, wanting, praying, hoping, for things to be different. I wished for my mother's mood swings to stop, for my biased country to wake up to equality, for people around me to be more appreciative, for life's circumstances to be fair. I had wished so hard for so long, until one moment *changed* everything. That moment made *me* change. That moment made my *dreams* come true.

My story begins, where most stories do, in early childhood. I grew up with a dad who was all heart, all emotions and kindness. He raised me to believe everything was possible, the only thing you need is love, and if you find love, nothing can ever stop you. A bit unrealistic, wouldn't you agree? Lucky for me, but not really, on the opposite end of the spectrum was my mom who thought my dad was, well… delusional! She believed life was unfair. She thought we needed to stay on guard and alert all the time, that life was filled with disappointments.

I grew up not understanding right from wrong. I felt torn between optimism and realism and struggled to make sense of both. I couldn't uphold a relationship or a job, because I was constantly chasing after true love, neverending passion and a wholesome inner feeling. I chased what Dad described as the 'Holy Grail' and what Mom never believed existed.

I have felt this feeling in moments. It is the warmest, coolest, truest and safest feeling ever. It actually feels as if you are immersed in clouds that are holding you tightly and hugging you softly and you catch yourself whispering from the inside out, "I'm home; everything is gonna be alright." It is a moment so light yet so safe, so warm yet so pleasantly cool, and you are in the midst of it, going with the flow of the wind, not caring where because each step feels like home.

My 20s were my quest for the truth, the truth about God, about us, about our existence. Curious, I traveled. Living in various monasteries, spending so much time running after love, running after God, only to realize there was no need for me to look any further than myself.

I struggled with broken relationships, thousands of dollars spent in efforts and hopes unmet. Details at this stage don't matter much and you have probably already lived parts of these stories yourself — the failed connections, the broken dreams, life disappointing you, you disappointing yourself. We all experience the unexpected and the extraordinary. By now, we just want the solution for it all.

At 24 years old, in my room, I scream in frustration. My parents rush in, "What's happening, what's going on?" they asked. I scream again, "What is the purpose of it all? When will things make sense? And then what!" That year, I landed at the top of my class with an internship at one of the biggest advertising firms in Lebanon. A few months into it, my passion started fading away as I couldn't uphold my values anymore. Such a competitive environment, where creativity gets crushed every day and you need to step on or step over someone in order to become something. It just wasn't me.

I started missing work, unable to wake up early anymore. I began losing motivation. I felt empty, purposeless. This wasn't my first heartbreak, but it was the one that tipped the scales. In my head, 1 + 1 equals 2. There is no other possibility. Falling in love meant happily ever after; finding a job I felt passionate about meant success; being a good person meant good things happened to me. You see, 1 + 1 always equals 2, so how come things in my life weren't adding up?

Is it not enough to love, to work hard, to be a good person, to have good intentions and do your best? Disappointment after disappointment, I started shrinking, like I was no longer my body. I was just living in it. Like wearing an oversized coat, losing touch with my extremities. Have you ever felt that way? Quarantined inside of yourself, you try to smile but you cannot reach your lips, you want to wake up but you cannot move your legs, you need to make sense but you cannot find your thoughts, you are far away from yourself, trapped, inside of yourself.

"What's going on?" my mother shouted. I couldn't answer her. "Enough!" That is all I could say. On that day, I was angry. My feet and hands, boiling. My body shivering, my eyes crying, my mouth shouting. I didn't have anything to ask myself anymore, nothing to wonder about anymore, nothing made sense anymore.

Suddenly, I catch a glimpse of something on my right side and turn to see one of the most *beautiful* sights I had ever seen. I still remember it to this day. I see the window of my bedroom, so big, so bright, so beautiful, sunlight shining through it. I could smell the flowers from the garden down below and taste the life inside of the trees. Intuitively, I see myself running toward the window. I open it, grab the sides firmly with my two hands, so cold and rough underneath my fingers. At that moment, everything made sense, that moment had possibilities, "Jump!" I scream from the inside out, "Jump!"

There was one string pulling me outwards and another pulling me backwards. I stopped. It wasn't my mother's scream nor my father's shock, it was something else. I took a few steps back, dropped to my knees, and as soon as I hit the floor, everything dropped within me. My logic. My equations. My expectations. My anger. Everything changed and I was never the same.

On that day, in that moment, I realized that life doesn't owe me anything. It does not follow any logic because it cannot be apprehended; and it is not fair because it is outside of all judgments. I realized that 1 + 1 DOES

NOT = 2. That opened the door for amazing new possibilities.

A week later, my aunt calls from Miami asking me to spend some time with her. Without hesitation, I put my job on hold and accepted her invitation. I was open without expectation, free to explore my new understanding; *when nothing makes sense anymore, everything becomes possible.* I had no clue why I chose to go, but I went anyway, only to find myself a few days later walking into a crowded reception room at a hotel on Hallandale Beach, Florida. A sign was posted on the door stating 'GLOBAL NLP TRAINING.' Five minutes into the coach's introduction, I simultaneously felt both light-headed and grounded. Aware, awake and with eyes open, I didn't know what was happening to me.

"Are you feeling anything weird?" I started asking people around me, and they had no clue. Everything and everyone looked ok. I wasn't. The coach continued her presentation about the benefits of NLP (neuro-linguistic programming) and the feeling of a heavy head and hazy vision stayed with me. I was amazed. I was in awe of everything the coach was saying. Right then and there I understood that feeling of oddness. It was just me. It was my soul recognizing its purpose. At that moment I heard my inner whisper. *Everything was ok, everything was alright, I'm home.*

NLP and coaching were neither in my plans nor in my equations, but I became aware of them both on that same day. There in Miami, tens of thousands of kilometres away from home, oceans apart from my own plans, and a Universe away from my own expectations and possibilities.

I came back home to my country, Lebanon, in the midst of all the difficulties imaginable. Lebanon, as a country in the Middle East, is a patriarchal society filled with sexist views about life, capabilities, success, and business. I decided to open my own training and coaching company to start the change I wished to see. Every day, I laughed at the sexist jokes and endured biased opinions; by then, they did not matter anymore. What mattered the most was simply doing my best. I had learned, life doesn't owe me anything, regardless of the circumstances. *I* was the one evolving.

By now, in my mind, 1 + 1 didn't equal 2 anymore. 1 + 1 equaled endless possibilities. And, with endless possibilities, I grew. I did what no one has dared to do before; workshops in the wilderness, dance-off competitions between company executives… *everything* that challenged their belief system, I did it.

Grounded in my values, each step felt like home. Lenient in my beliefs, I went with the flow of life. Growing and expanding, the possibilities became endless. An understanding formed between me and Life. Neither owed the other anything.

Remaining grounded in my values but lenient in my beliefs *changed my life.* It unleashed a fire in me waiting to be Ignited. From one company, I branched out to creating retreats and wellness events, and eventually opening my own well-being center.

All these projects came naturally. Even finding my soulmate and life partner manifested itself organically. I am planning our wedding and, to say the least, he wasn't what I had expected, yet, he is everything I need.

The truth as I understood it. The biggest mistake one can do is to plan for what's *'right.'* There is no right time or right circumstance for anything. No amount of meditation hours can quiet your mind, no number of books can fix your life, tricks can't make your marriage work and people will never be able to fill the gaps inside of you.

Dollars, positions and positive quotes written on stickers will never be able to make you feel your worth. Success will always remain relative. For me, success isn't measured by achievements but instead by developing the ability to understand Life.

Shifting my mindset from a TRADER's mindset to a COLLABORATOR's mindset, manifested my dreams. Everything became possible. Traders are those who negotiate with Life; *I want to receive THIS in exchange for THAT.* They have expectations, plans and schemes; they have the *'Because,'* the blaming, and the shaming.

Contrarily, Collaborators and Change Makers are those who *cooperate* with life. They focus on growing their own potential, on manifesting their own values, on doing their best despite everything. They are, at the same time, lenient and resilient. A new paradigm. A more organic dynamic.

We have one life. Spiritual, religious, or atheist, regardless of what you believe in about the afterlife, you will never be you again. You will never have the same body, mind, family, position or circumstances. It is a shame to waste your potential waiting for a good trade. You cannot negotiate with life. You can only express it through you, allowing it to pass through you, Igniting your spark! That spark that is the very best version of you.

No one owes anyone anything. Now, knowing that, will you still do your best? A question to think about. An answer that will CHANGE your life.

Ignite Action Steps

Ignite your steps for it will make you sparkle! Each person is unique; it is not about attracting the life you want and more about opening up to the life you were meant for. For me, my Ignite moment was a single instant in time. Everything came together to pose a divine question, *"Knowing that no one owes me anything, will I still do my best?"* The answer changed my life. You can ask yourself the same questions that guided me inwards and then set the stage for shifting your mindset from a TRADER to a COLLABORATOR and experience life surprising you.

Let's go! Bring your journal and start writing. Answer the same questions more than once; our first impulse might not be our truest.

First Step: Identify Your Mindset.

- Write down the names of the people who are not meeting your expectations in one column and, in parallel, answer the following question: *Knowing that [this person] might never treat me the way I treat them, would I still operate out of my best self?*

- Write down the goals you are struggling to reach in one column and, in parallel, ask yourself: *If the odds of me realizing this dream are low, would I still pursue it?*

If you have answered negatively, then dear reader, you are a Trader... trading with life, wasting your qualities and running further away from your soul's purpose. If you answered positively, then Collaborator, the Universe is lucky to have you.

Second Step: Shift Your Mindset

Try to notice your thought patterns and the emotions that rise each time your expectations are not being met. When we understand the link between thought and emotion, when we remove our reactivity, Life will unfold itself to us in a whole new way.

	TRADER'S MINDSET TRADEOFF		**COLLABORATOR'S MINDSET** TWISTS
OPTION 1 Low energy levels	Surrender *[Thought]* Regret *[Emotion]*	*Switch to* 	Be Collaborative *[Ask for New Ideas]* Perseverance *[Emotion]*
OPTION 2 High energy levels	Revenge *[Thought]* Anger *[Emotion]*	→	Be Creative *[Create New Ideas]* Motivation *[Emotion]*

Question everything you have wished for and everything you have regretted. Question whether you are smarter than Life or whether life is more knowing. Actively shift your thoughts and your emotions to positively impact your life. Humility and a collaborative spirit change everything. Our openness and intention to collaborate *with* life is the driving force; let yours drive you toward new possibilities.

Rosa Maria Kallas - Lebanon.
Inner Guidance Coach, NLP Master Practitioner, Social & Emotional
Intelligence Coach, Hypnotherapist, Motivational Speaker & Life Coach
www.rosamariakallas.com

KATARINA AMADORA

*"To be a Change Maker is to go bravely into the fight, take
a stand, and use your voice to advocate for change."*

**We are powerful when we band together. The tipping point required to
create a powerful movement is just 3.5% of any population. It is my intention to instill passion within you so that you will be inspired to take action.
I desire everyone to care about where their food comes from and how it
is produced. I dream of a world of activists who are willing to vote with
their pocketbooks. Together we can take radical action in small and big
ways to spread this message and instigate change. I believe that a small
group of committed individuals can change the world.**

CULTIVATING CHANGE

The key to vibrant health lies in the small choices that we make every day.
Each bite that we eat impacts our health on a cellular level. Our cells are constructed from nutrients in the foods that we eat, and we are constantly replacing
cells that die out. When you eat junk, your body lacks quality building blocks.
I believe that in order to stem the tide of exponentially increasing health problems and to decrease the cost of caring for people with these conditions, it is
essential that we make a seismic shift in how we produce food and how we
make decisions regarding the way we fuel our bodies.

Over the course of my life, the world has changed dramatically. When I
was a kid, we only had 13 channels on the TV and there was no such thing as

a computer. I even remember having a milkman who delivered milk in glass bottles right to our front door. I grew up in a small rural town in Kansas. There were 13,000 people in my town which may seem small now, however when I was growing up, that was big compared to the tiny towns around us. Many of my childhood memories consisted of visiting my grandparents' farm each weekend. My cousins all lived within a 30-mile radius from the farm and we would frequently converge there on Sunday afternoons. I remember getting into all sorts of mischief on the farm. My cousin Danny was often the instigator. I vividly recall one Sunday afternoon when he had the bright idea to steal eggs from the henhouse and use them to make mud pies. We got into so much trouble!

My grandfather's farm was the standard quarter square mile lot that he had inherited from his parents, Swedish immigrants who had met and married in rural Kansas before the turn of the last century. Grandfather had grown up farming that land. He followed the traditional practices of rotating crops to keep the land healthy. He would plant winter wheat in the fall to harvest in June, and plant sorghum, which would be harvested in the fall before planting more wheat. These cycles could, of course, be thrown off by bad weather, droughts, or rains coming at the wrong time, which could cause him to miss a planting season completely. Farming has always operated at the mercy of the elements, causing farmers untold amounts of stress over factors that they are helpless to control.

Much of our time at the farm revolved around food… we would gather eggs, help dig potatoes, and pick cherries or watermelon when they were in season. We would always have a big family dinner. Certain things tasted much better back then. My grandfather's watermelons were so sweet... much sweeter than the ones I find in the supermarkets today. I really miss his tart pie cherries and the sandhill plums. There's nothing quite like a pie made from fresh pie cherries. My mom would make plum jam which was delicious on fluffy omelets… one of my favorite breakfasts.

Back then, most farms were similar — typically small and most had been in the same family for generations. Many of my classmates were in youth organizations such as 4-H or Future Farmers of America because it was almost expected that they would take over their family farm. I grew up in 4-H, though I was more interested in sewing, cooking, and knitting, and all the other creative projects. I loved the way that 4-H helped me develop leadership skills and I loved exhibiting my projects in the fair every summer.

In 1975, my grandfather worked on Jimmy Carter's campaign for President. Grandpa was so excited that a farmer was actually campaigning to be President and he took on a leadership role in the campaign headquarters in my home town. Jimmy Carter was a peanut farmer and I remember stopping by campaign headquarters almost every day after school to say hi to my Grandpa and help myself to some of the peanut-brittle that they always had in ready supply. I was so excited when Carter got elected… I think that this was the last time Kansas ever voted for a Democrat for President.

Maybe this has something to do with a big shift that occurred in 1985, shortly after I graduated High School. Jimmy Carter declared a grain embargo against the Soviet Union in response to their invasion of Afghanistan. This precipitated a huge farming crisis, further aggravated by skyrocketing interest rates above 21 percent, accompanied by a steep drop in land valuation. (Many farms lost two-thirds of their value in a very short time period!) This followed after a time of expansion in the late '70s because prices had been strong and demand was high. Many farmers had expanded, optimistic that this would continue, taking out large loans to purchase land or update their equipment. When Carter enacted the grain embargo and thus cut demand, it coincided with record grain production and caused a massive drop in prices. As commodities bottomed out, the price for grains dropped far below what it cost the farmers to produce the crops.

Already, many farms had been barely getting by. It was common practice to take out a loan in the spring to pay for seed and supplies, which would be repaid in the fall when the harvest came in. As the land continued to drop in value and interest rates remained high, many farmers couldn't repay their loans. A combination of bad weather and manipulation in the markets caused further instability. This collapse in the farming industry resulted in many of these small family farms being lost to bankruptcy or sold off to the highest bidder. Farmer and banker suicides went through the roof, and this phenomenon has remained a significant problem to this day. It has been documented that farmers continue to commit suicide at a rate *double* that of veterans, and *three to five times greater* than the general population.

As more and more farms were lost to foreclosure, land value continued to drop. Our family had to adapt. My uncle, who had taken over the farm, managed to keep it by shifting to raising cattle rather than grain. Farm by farm, more land was gradually taken over by huge industrial farming operations. Big industrial agriculture giants profited handsomely from this as they bought up these farms for pennies on the dollar. Industrial farming has been touted as important for increasing efficiency. Instead, it crushed the hopes and dreams of generations of farmers.

During this time period, GMO seeds also came into common usage. They were promoted as being the scientific answer to feeding the world. With the use of GMO seeds, the use of glyphosate increased exponentially. In many cases, crop rotation was abandoned in favor of monoculture farming. This required ever-increasing amounts of fertilizer and pesticides to increase yields at the expense of depleting the soil and resulted in large amounts of toxic runoff entering our streams and waterways.

GMO seeds are engineered to allow the plant to express proteins that were not present in the native seed. Some, called 'Roundup Ready,' have been engineered to be resistant to glyphosate. Others contain genes that cause the plant to manufacture endogenous pesticides which make the grain toxic to bugs. Because this pesticide is part of the plant, it cannot be washed off. This means that anything that consumes these foods takes on a large toxic load which bioaccumulates up the food chain. For the most part, these GMOs have not been tested to see if they are safe for human consumption... they simply entered our food supply without us even knowing what we were eating.

As GMO seeds became more prevalent, crossover contamination has been observed that allows weeds to take on this gene for Roundup resistance. In addition, Monsanto, the company which produces these seeds, has sued farmers for planting seed which tested positive for the Roundup-ready trait because of accidental cross-pollination from a neighboring field. It has become increasingly difficult to even find seed which is untainted with foreign DNA. In addition, now most GMO seed is genetically programmed to produce sterile seed, forcing the farmer to constantly buy their seed from Monsanto. When the programmed cell death gene cross-pollinates with surrounding non-GMO fields, it can cause *these* fields to produce sterile seed. If it gets out of control, this may endanger our entire food supply. Having grown up visiting my grandfather's farm, it hurt my heart to see the impact that it was having on farmers.

Even non-GMO crops like wheat have seen a huge increase in the amount of Roundup used. For the last 15 years, it has been common practice for farmers to apply glyphosate to their wheat fields a week or so before harvest as a desiccant. This kills the wheat and causes it to release the grain, making it cheaper and easier to harvest. The net result is that the amount of glyphosate consumed by every man, woman, and child in the United States has increased exponentially. I have become a passionate advocate of raising awareness and calling for changes in our farming practices because I see this as one of the greatest threats that we face today.

It's interesting... if you plot a graph of the use of glyphosate year by year since 1960, and you superimpose that graph with a graph of the rates of diabetes, cancer, heart disease, autism, ADHD, or autoimmune disease, you will find those graphs have an uncanny similarity. Of course, these types of epidemiologic studies cannot prove causation, but the correlation between the two is damning. What is hard to unravel is how much is due to glyphosate, how much is due to GMOs in general, and how much is due to the increased use of fertilizers and pesticides over the same time period.

I remember growing up with a kid named Dennis. He was a skinny, blond boy who we called 'Dennis the Menace' after the popular comic strip character. He had diabetes. When I went to his house one day, I discovered he had to have an injection every single day. I was horrified. I hated having shots, let alone every day. His Mom said that he had 'juvenile-onset diabetes.' At that young age, I already knew that I wanted to be a doctor, and I was eager to learn more about why his body stopped producing insulin.

By the time I got to medical school, this terminology had changed. 'Juvenile-onset diabetes' had been replaced by 'Type 1 Diabetes Mellitus' because so many kids were now getting the adult-onset type, which was now called 'Type 2 Diabetes Mellitus.' Type 1 is caused by pancreatic failure. Type 2 is caused by insulin resistance.

In medical school, I learned about the pathophysiology of disease and how to treat symptoms with pharmaceuticals; however, the role of food and nutrition is seldom addressed beyond understanding the pharmacology of vitamins, minerals, and specific nutritional deficiencies related to their lack, such as scurvy and rickets. At the time, I was just trying to keep up with everything that I was learning and I did not recognize this gap in my medical education.

It wasn't until I read the book *Grain Brain* by Dr. David Perlmutter that I started to see it. I had been curious about gluten for a few years because I had a daughter with high-functioning autism. There was much debate about whether gluten might contribute to autism; however, there was also a lot of misinformation out there. I didn't know who to believe. Perlmutter laid out his argument so clearly. My background as a protein chemist came online and my medical understanding started connecting the dots. I decided to eliminate gluten from my diet and I cut out all wheat products. Over the following two years, I dropped nearly 30 pounds and I felt healthier than ever. My moods also became more regulated and I was able to discontinue antidepressants that I had been on for nearly 20 years.

In my early 50s, I finally put all the pieces together when I participated in a revolutionary new program called WildFit which was inspired by evolutionary biology principles combined with a functional medicine approach. By returning to the way that our ancestors ate, people experience profound shifts in their health and well-being. The program utilizes behavioral psychology methods to instill permanent change. I came to understand how we as a society have been brainwashed into eating *so many* toxic, dysfunctional foods, and the massive impact that this has had on our health. I became angry as I realized how inadequate my education had been in the realm of nutrition. I also learned about the field of functional medicine, which had been in its infancy when I was in medical school. I am so grateful for this new understanding, so much so that I decided to become a WildFit Coach. I sincerely regret that I did not know about the Functional Medicine approach when I was deciding on a specialty. I now feel that *this is the way that medicine should be practiced.* Sometimes, I wonder if it would be too late for me to go back and complete a Functional Medicine residency program… a choice that was not yet available when I left medical school in 1997.

Everything I've learned along my path has led me to be an outspoken advocate for changing the way we eat, the way we farm, and the way that we understand nutrition. As a WildFit Coach, I love being able to help my clients transform their health, but I want to take this to the next level.

My goal is to influence people worldwide to make different nutritional choices. I want them to become advocates for their own health and to make their voices heard to advocate for change in the way we farm and produce food. I believe this starts with changing the individual decisions that we make each day, but that this alone is insufficient. We must expand our focus to take on the food industry as a whole. We must be vocal proponents of change, asking for what we want and refusing to spend our money on toxic crap. We must lobby those who represent us and let them know that we are watching how they spend our money through the Farm Bill. The focus must be shifted away from subsidizing big 'factory farms' using unsustainable farming techniques and shift toward regenerative practices.

We must all be Change Makers, for this has far-reaching implications. The way we farm impacts our greenhouse gas emissions, our access to clean water, and so many other factors. Learn more, get involved. Call your congressperson. Join the regenerative movement. Find out what you can do both locally and globally. Together, I believe that we can make a difference. We only need 3.5% to start a massive movement. Be one of those who instigate the change.

IGNITE ACTION STEPS

- We must vote with our pocketbooks. When we refuse to spend money on toxic non-foods, it becomes less profitable to produce them. Ask for what you want in your local market and refuse to spend your money on anything but good food. As the demand for healthy food increases, companies will step in to fill that need. Together we can make a difference.

- When we eat better, we will enjoy better health and more productivity in our lives, as well as lower medical costs. Educate yourself and spread the word to your friends. Take charge of your own health and nutrition… speaking as a doctor, remember that doctors don't know everything. Your body knows best, if you learn to listen to it, it will make all the difference.

- Support small organic family farms, which will also reduce your carbon footprint. By eating locally, we help these farmers to earn a living so that they can provide for their families and produce more healthy foods.

- Put pressure on your legislators and refuse to drink the Kool-Aid that Monsanto is promoting. What you do matters. Contact your Legislator. Call your Senator. Let them know that we are watching. Tell them we want funds in the Farm Bill to go to family farmers who are producing organic crops and promoting regenerative practices. Let them know how vital it is that the Farm Bill also include funds for Mental Health Services. Tell them that funding big industrial farms that use extractive practices is unacceptable. The more they hear from us, the more they will understand that we are watching what they do, watching where they spend our tax dollars, and that we WILL hold them accountable on election day.

- Donate to organizations that are promoting regenerative practices around the world. Educate yourself regarding how you can get involved in making a difference in your community. Be a Change Maker.

Katarina Amadora - United States
MD, Certified Hypnotist, Certified WildFit Coach, Rev. Priestess
www.AmadoraTransformations.com

JOANNE FEASTER

*"Out of adversity, change, and challenge comes
hope, inspiration, and creativity."*

I would like to provide you with hope. To guide you if you're lost, stuck, or overwhelmed and give you practical pointers for making change. I want to prevent suicides, by raising awareness for and reducing the stigma around suicidal thoughts and mental health issues. May my story give you reassurance within yourself and if you are supporting others with their mental health concerns.

HELP! I NEED SOMEBODY...

I am sitting at my desk, in the quiet stillness of the late night hours, my children finally asleep after a full day of high-spirited chattering and needing my attention. It's Mar. 17, 2020, around two and a half weeks after my Ignite Moment and two and half years since I first admitted to having suicidal thoughts.

I intended to start writing several days ago, but events have overtaken me. With the COVID-19 pandemic currently sweeping the globe I, and those around me, are going to need to be healthy, physically and mentally, in the days and weeks to come, so the timing of my story seems very appropriate.

This date holds special significance for me. It is my wedding anniversary — a very happy occasion! Today is the fifth anniversary of my cousin delivering her daughter, Alice, stillborn at 36 weeks of pregnancy, a tragedy that had a profound effect on me. And on Mar. 17, 11 years ago, the announcement of a major organizational restructuring where I worked triggered a downward spiral that led me to receive a medical diagnosis of ill mental health for the first time.

Looking back on my life before this, I can identify numerous episodes of ill mental health that were never 'diagnosed' but were managed with the support of my family. This time it was different. I felt *isolated* and *underachieving*. Close colleagues were losing their jobs and they were far more deserving than me. Despite the support of those around me, I couldn't pull myself out of the hole I was gradually sinking into. I dreaded work and would sit in the car unable to go in until I rang my husband for support. It affected my mood and behavior outside of work. Enjoyment of *anything* seemed impossible.

My doctor signed me off work for two weeks citing *stress* and referred me to the local Primary Care Mental Health service where I received fantastic support. My colleagues were very helpful too and, four months later, I believed I had good strategies in place to prevent a relapse. However, in November, another situation at work triggered a decline and I sought medical help again. To my surprise, I was diagnosed with *depression*. I felt guilty, ashamed, a bit of a fraud like I wasn't 'really ill'; I was just not good enough to do my job. I kept thinking of people dealing with far worse than me.

This was the first time I was prescribed antidepressant medication. I was reluctant to take it as I was trying to conceive and I feared for the health of my unborn child. Fortunately, Toby, my brilliant advisor from the Mental Health service, identified a specific medication that would present the least risk whilst giving me vital relief.

Two years later, I went through a redundancy process at work. Relief washed over me. The payout would give me breathing space and time to heal before I considered my next move. Later that month, I was thrilled when I found out I was pregnant with our first child. *The very things that had kept my mental health fluctuating seemingly vanished!* At that stage, life seemed good. One significant outcome of fertility testing was that I was diagnosed with an underactive thyroid, a known factor for depression. I was confident that by having my longed-for baby and the correct thyroid medication, I would stay mentally well.

Parenthood was a big shock to the system for both my husband and me. Nothing could have prepared us for the sleepless nights, the feeling of powerlessness when you can't comfort your crying baby, or the isolation and loss of identity. In the same way, nothing could prepare us for the love we felt for our beautiful daughter and the rewards we got every day: the cuddles and smiles, the wonder that comes from observing a little human you created develop and grow. We conceived our second baby much more quickly, a relief that quickly turned to pain with a very early miscarriage while we were on holiday. Our son was born a year later. The prolonged bouts of depression and anxiety that had plagued me didn't return and I was happy and managed well.

Jun. 16, 2016 marked the start of my most recent period of mental ill health. In the throes of the Brexit referendum campaign, I was experiencing a sense of loss and emptiness — a good friend was about to leave for a new life in Australia. After struggling to make close friends since university, I had finally found someone I could confide in… and now they were leaving! We arranged a final play date at an indoor play center on the outskirts of Birstall. While there, the local MP, Jo Cox, was attacked by an unknown assailant and was left bleeding to death in the street. The attacker was reportedly heading our way. The kids were happily playing just a few feet away and I was flushed with adrenaline trying to find out what was going on. The attacker was apprehended a short distance away. I felt a mixture of fear coupled with the biggest sense of relief. My friend left for Australia that weekend, leaving me to deal with all my feelings about it without her. I felt very *alone and isolated* once again.

The following year, just before my son started nursery school, I began to feel *lost in the changes* that had come and those still on the horizon. My husband encouraged me to return to the doctor and seek help. The doctor, one I had not seen before, was a lovely empathetic woman. As we went through the appointment, she started questioning me about my feelings and mental health. Under her gentle yet direct questioning, I opened up and my tears started flowing freely as I whispered then sobbed that, *"Yes, I have considered harming myself."* It was the first time I had ever said it out loud to anyone.

That afternoon I lay on the bed filling in the lengthy online referral forms for the Improving Access to Psychological Therapies (IAPT) services. I struggled to see through my tears. I was terrified that there would be a knock at the door and my fitness as a mother would be questioned. My parents were with me that day and my mum came up so I told her what I had told the doctor. She wrapped me in a big, warm hug and told me gently that everything would be okay: I was now getting the help I needed and I would get better again. Later that night I told my husband, slightly fearful of his reaction because of the wider reaching implications; he cuddled me and we lay on the sofa watching mindless T.V.

I had been prescribed antidepressant medication and taken my first pill that morning. Lying on the cold bathroom floor in the middle of the night, feeling faint and sick, I questioned whether I had done the right thing. I wondered, had the side effects of the medication been this bad the first time round? The doctor had advised that the pills can make you feel worse for the first one to two weeks of taking them, but that by four-six weeks I should notice a marked improvement in mood. The severe side effects only lasted for the first night. The medication took the edge off my darkest thoughts and, toward the end of the year, I felt much brighter. An idea had formed to start my own business and I began working toward that.

The next two years were very up and down and I remained on the medication. The roller-coaster nature of my mental health was becoming increasingly unbearable. Living with two disparate states of mind was particularly frustrating and difficult for both myself and those close to me. When I'm depressed and anxious, I feel quite detached from the world going on around me, like an observer in my own life. I can engage in work and social activities with competence and a modicum of enthusiasm, but I don't enjoy life. I lack motivation, energy, and sparkle, feeling constantly tired and isolating myself wherever possible. At the other extreme I feel super confident, full of creativity and ideas, loving connection, and bringing people together. Sometimes, I get so busy and full of life and ideas that I struggle to rest properly, or to let others keep up with my now fast paced and super-charged mind.

In the summer of last year, after taking the painful decision to close my own business and lacking any direction as to what I would do next, I returned to the doctor. She increased the dosage of my antidepressant medication and this helped take the edge off my fleeting, yet increasingly frequent, suicidal thoughts. As I trudged wearily through the process of dismantling my business, it felt like each item I closed down was a nail in the coffin of my confidence and self-belief, dismantling the hope that I was capable of doing something remarkable with my life. The spark that had briefly returned was quickly extinguished.

In early December, whilst in the midst of my daughter's birthday celebrations and chaos of pre-Christmas planning, I got an unexpected call. Would I do some freelance event delegate management work? Deep down I knew I had to give it a go and I was right. The anxiety that had plagued my mornings for months was absent on my first morning at work, replaced by eager anticipation. Being in a hard-working, friendly, and supportive office environment five days a week during school hours did wonders for my confidence. By Christmas there had been a remarkable turnaround. The fog in my head had lifted and I could see the world clearly again, see my family and friends for the supportive and loving people they are, see that I was mistaken when I believed that no one really understood or liked me. Aside from me having a job, nothing intrinsically had changed.

Riding the crest of the wave, I returned to becoming active on social media.

When I'm happy and energized I want to share almost every thought! I had been strongly influenced over the last year by those aiming to help others by sharing their own vulnerabilities and now I felt compelled to *come clean* myself. I did a Facebook post revealing my decade of mental health struggles, first in *The Career Mum* group (somehow it seemed easier to share with 4000 strangers first!) and then on my own timeline. The reaction was 100% positive and supportive and I had a handful of people contact me individually to say that my story had resonated with them, made them feel less alone and, in one case, was the catalyst for them seeking professional help. I glowed inside and felt like a huge weight had been lifted from my shoulders.

In January I decided to join *Inspiring Women Changemakers,* Anj Handa's online community. I had met Anj the year before at a mentoring circle organized by *The Career Mum* group. The social consciousness and campaigning spirit I left behind was reawakened. I love helping people; kindness and compassion are two of my core values. I now knew I wanted to be a Change Maker; I just didn't quite know how.

Suicide is a traumatic and sensitive topic for many. It remains, to a large extent, undiscussed and therefore unaddressed. It was the death of my Nan in 2006 that unexpectedly presented me with my first personal experience of suicide. Whilst at my parents house, we received a call to get to the hospital urgently. My mum and I rushed over and as the rest of our large family gradually gathered, we could not contact one of my uncles. My cousin cycled round to his house and made a shocking discovery. He had taken his own life. The rest of the evening was a strange affair. I took comfort from the whole extended family being together again. We spent hours catching up, taking turns to sit at my Nan's bedside and having an impromptu picnic. My Nan died in the early hours of the following morning. I felt loss but also relief that her pain was over. I drove the couple of hours home that Sunday night on auto-pilot, tired and emotionally drained from two deaths in the family within 48 hours. Every time I drive that route now it takes me back. I went to work the following day and didn't tell a soul. I kept the tears I shed hidden in the bathroom. I now consider that a big mistake. I never dealt with the trauma, the double funeral, or the grief; instead I dismissed my emotional anguish and just carried on. In retrospect, that weekend was a trigger, marking a lengthy period of low moods, inner sadness, and stress. For years I deliberately omitted any reference to suicidal thoughts around friends and family. Sharing felt like a step too far, that others might take offence at, or feel hurt by. It was something to be ashamed of and keep hidden.

It was the death of British television and radio presenter Caroline Flack on Feb. 15, 2020 that was the catalyst for determining my new mission. She was 40, like me, and I had enjoyed watching her on *Strictly Come Dancing*. She seemed confident and full of life so it was a shock when she took her life. What made the most impact was that I knew how it felt to think that it would be better if life ended, feeling like a burden on my family and friends. To just want the pain to stop. For it all to be over.

Various discussions in *The Career Mum* group and then two key factors led me to a conclusion. I read an incredibly powerful poem called "The Morning After I Killed Myself" by Meggie Royer; the ending gave me goosebumps: *I tried to unkill myself, but couldn't finish what I started.* Then, around a week later, I sat alone on the sofa and watched an emotional instagram post by Caroline's former boyfriend, Danny Cipriani, a heart-moving monologue about his realization of the importance of being more open about his dark days. I questioned myself; what had stopped my thoughts from turning to action?

The answer occurred to me while I was in the shower — it was voicing those thoughts that had saved me! I reached out for help in the form of doctor visits and medication. I'm aware of the controversy around the impact of antidepressant medication. For me, it helps to take the edge off, it numbs me, stops the crying, and it removes almost completely the suicidal ideation. Getting relief from those most painful of thoughts is so important and necessary to enable my recovery. In the long term, recovery can only come from within, from changes to the way I think and therefore feel. Alongside the self discovery and healing process, I also needed the love and support of those around me.

A week later and by chance I had finally finished the last pill of my antidepressant medication, having been weaning myself off it over a long period, and I felt like celebrating! With a little trepidation, I published a second Facebook post where I openly admitted to having suicidal thoughts and noted what had helped me to get through the difficult times. The reaction was again 100% positive and supportive. Many people commented that I was brave and strong for sharing my deepest secret. I finally felt free! It takes great strength to pull oneself back from the abyss. That was the Ignite moment that changed me and helped me know what change I can facilitate for others.

Now I'm in a sweet spot of self-awareness and ongoing discovery and learning. I'm connecting with others and undertaking relevant training with a view to make my twin passions of mental health and female empowerment align with the work I do. I'm using the Japanese *Ikigai* model of clarifying my passion, defining my life purpose, and in turn helping others. I now believe I can be an *Inspiring Female Changemaker*. My life is not without its challenges or disagreements, but it has purpose, drive, and most importantly hope of a better future for all.

Personal note: *If you are in the depths of despair and possibly experiencing suicidal thoughts, I hope my story gives you inspiration, a reason to keep going, and a belief that you can get better too. If you are supporting someone with a mental health issue, particularly depression and anxiety, I hope my story gives you insight into the thought processes the person you are supporting may be going through, and reassurance that, just by being there and listening, you can make a difference, doing more good than you can possibly imagine.*

IGNITE ACTION STEPS

If you are experiencing suicidal thoughts or ideation, find one person to tell and tell them as soon as possible. Who that person is will be different for everyone. The act of telling them doesn't even have to form a sentence, it can simply be asking for "help." Believe that it can and will get better, even though it doesn't feel like it.

If you are dealing with mental health issues yourself: be honest, kind, and practice gratitude. Get exercise, get out in nature, appreciate the little things in life and look for the positives. Find your tribe and spend time with them — people who appreciate you for what and who you are, who make you feel respected and safe, valued and loved.

If you are supporting friends, family, or co-workers with mental health issues, remember that the most important thing is to be there. You don't need to fix them. Listen if they want to talk. Accept that they may not know how to express their feelings and thoughts right now. Give hugs, encourage them to take part in activities they used to enjoy, suggest that they contact other friends and family. Signpost them to appropriate professional advice — doctors, counselors, support groups.

It is ok to need help! When you're feeling vulnerable it can be hard to voice that request. However, the rewards for doing so cannot be underestimated for you and your family.

Joanne Feaster, England - United Kingdom
Freelance Administrator and Mental Health Campaigner
www.joannefeaster.com
🔗 *@joanne-feaster*

María Paulina Mejía

"See how magic begins to unfold before your eyes... believe."

I believe, without a shadow of a doubt, that within human beings dwells such a powerful force, that despite how terrifying and hurtful the experiences we endured, we can always rise above them empowered and confident. Hang on to your True self and believe in the impossible while taking the necessary steps toward self-discovery, acceptance, forgiveness, trust, awareness, and above all loving yourself enough in order to make a change. If you decide to join me in this belief, your world will feel like heaven on earth.

I Found The Real Me. So Can You.

It all began under the sheets of my abuser. I do not know how many times I was forced under there. I cannot remember her face. I blocked it, I am sure. I needed to survive I suppose. What I can definitely recall is my tiny body lying next to hers, struggling to understand why. This is my second memory of my existence. My first memory is a dream — a bad, bad dream. I was in bed when, all of a sudden, I felt something or someone hitting the mattress from beneath. I was too terrified to look, so I waited. There it was again. The banging became so hard that I bounced up and down on my bed like a stuffed toy. I tried to scream but my voice would not come out. A mirror hung from the wall, filled with the reflection of a wicked witch who stared and laughed at me. Soon after, I heard giggles coming from under the bed. This time, I leaned forward, sliding my upper body down the side until my head was hanging, and

I took a peek. I could not believe my eyes. A multitude of green dwarves were partying under my own bed. As soon as they saw me, they ran out and began to crawl up my blanket. I leaped off the bed and rushed out of the bedroom into the living room. The little monsters chased me around the coffee table until I was exhausted. I figured my only escape was to climb up the wall to the window and jump. But I was too tiny to reach. So, in the middle of my fruitless intent, I woke up. I was only three-years-old.

After years of digging in my subconscious mind, I finally came to understand the real meaning of that dream: the witch was my perpetrator; the green dwarves, the fears her abuse had imprinted on me. But it did not stop there. It never does. You see, when you have been sexually abused as a kid, not only do you feel scared, but for some strange reason, many grow up making sure that the abuse repeats itself, again and again. And that was exactly what I did. I became shy and erratic to the limit, and the perfect prey for middle school bullies. I picked the wrong boyfriends. I had to; otherwise, I would be betraying my own secret promise. At twelve, I hid a bottle of *aguardiente* liquor in my closet and took a few sips after arriving home from school, so I could withdraw myself from reality. I began smoking cigarettes. I tried to take my own life a couple of times, and I married a man with whom I ended up experiencing ice-cold solitude. I became an expert in self-doubt, self-pity, and self-destruction. Needless to say, the world was an unsafe and, therefore, frightful place to me. I tried to hide from it in every way that I could; but for some obnoxious reason, it was always able to find me, just when I was about to succeed.

As years went by, I started to feel the pain of other people almost as if it was my own. It was unbearable to me. I spent many nights crying in silence, trying to make sense of a world that seemed evil. That is when, at 19, I thought I would become a psychologist. In my head, this would be the perfect match between my urge to help and humanity's hurt. I could even turn into a Change Maker.

I started at the university in a cold brick building in the often overcast city of Bogotá. Shortly into the program, I realized I had to deal with my own demons. I had already been to therapy and, as much as it helped, I felt like I needed something more… expressive. I dropped out of psychology and signed up for drama classes. I had been hiding behind countless masks in order to get by and, somewhere deep inside, I knew theater could force me out of my self-incarceration. Eighteen months later, I was feeling like a normal human being for the first time. I searched my talent toolbox and remembered writing was something which not only did I enjoy while growing up, it was one of the very few things I was good at. I enrolled in journalism. The night before my first day of class, I lay on my bed staring at the ceiling, wondering if this time I would make it. My head was blurry and my stomach crunched. I twisted and turned, battling to fall asleep. Dawn hit and I had to get up and face reality. Outside, the world seemed like a hazy movie watched from afar.

My whole life, I had failed at school both socially and academically — one more thing my abuser left me with. I dreaded sitting in a classroom and feeling like an idiot again, but a part of me insisted that I give it a try. To my surprise, not only did I make friends quite easily but, almost magically, I became one of the most outstanding students in my class. My grades were so high even the teachers were impressed. *Something in me had shifted.* For the first time, I was glimpsing a chunk of the real me. A version of me whose emotional rough edges were starting to heal, allowing my long-time hidden strengths to surface.

I got married a year later. Two years after that, I gave birth to the most adorable little girl. My husband and I believed we had an unbreakable love, but our financial situation was so deficient, the pressures began to erode what we had and, at the end, there was only silence between us. We separated. I was devastated. He was the only man I had ever wanted to spend my life with and now he was gone. He married six months later and had a baby girl nine months after that. The pain was unbearable, stealing my breath away so much so that I passed out in the middle of the street a couple of times, having to be rescued by strangers.

I left university before graduating; I had to work, I had no choice. I was 29, a young divorcée brought up like a princess in captivity with no money, no degree, and a daughter to feed and raise. "I have to catch up with myself," I thought. I needed a degree I could complete while working full-time and through which I could be of service to my community. Elementary education fit my needs. How ironic! I would be standing on the other side of what used to be my worst nightmare: being a school student. A class day lasted eight hours and as my daughter's father had vanished, I brought her to class with me. She never complained. "We will graduate soon," I said to her. Too young to know what I meant, she just smiled. What to me felt like a roller coaster was a fun adventure for her. She trusted me, though I did not.

Classes were on Saturdays, but I had to read lectures, prepare for tests, and write essays every night. I slept less than four hours, waking up at 4:30 AM every day for work. By fifth semester, I had won every Mention of Honor, an award the faculty gave to the best student in the class. By sixth semester, I was consumed and about to throw in the towel. Every bit of my body ached. My brain was about to explode and my heart was so weak. I fantasized about disappearing... and then I saw my daughter. That sweet little person deserved the best of me. I had to unbury my strength from wherever it was concealed. I slowed down a bit, spending more time focussed on her, but to my surprise, I only moved down to second place. I graduated right after my thirty-third birthday. I could not believe it! I would have jumped up and down in front of the entire auditorium had I allowed myself a little spontaneity.

Over the next 11 years, a lot changed. I wrote my first three novels and dove deeply into my soul. It was not for a pretty reason though. Completely frustrated with departmental restructuring, I quit my job. I packed my tiny car, a Skoda, with our things, made space for our Labrador in the back seat, and moved us to Bogotá! I was offered a job teaching kindergarten English, something I was a complete amateur at. International private schools normally offer teachers' children a full scholarship. That place was supposed to be a kids' hidden learning paradise and we were bubbling with excitement... but it turned out to be the opposite. Six months into fifth grade, my daughter was emotionally executed by her female classmates. Their bigotry toward her authenticity and self-respect ended up completely isolating her. I never thought I would see the happiest child in the entire world throw herself on the floor in pain and twirl like an injured animal.

The situation became insufferable. She sobbed day in and day out. I did not know what to do. Many times I sat on my shower floor for hours, letting the water slide down my head mixing with my tears. I cried out for help, but her predators viciously denied their attacks, so nobody did anything. I pulled her out of school 15 days before the end of the school year, fearing that it was either that or see her fade away. Driving away from the school that morning I wondered what I had done so wrong. Life had been against me since the beginning. I had been trying so hard for so long. And now my daughter... I was worn out in every way.

We moved back to our hometown. Things were apparently going well until torture struck again. One more time, my daughter was being bullied. Considering she was just recovering from the previous experience, her psyche broke. Slowly but surely, she entered a state of self-denial and self-harm that quickly transformed into an eating disorder. "Really?" I thought. "I will be heard this time. Oh, yes, I will!" My chance to act as a Change Maker was right before my eyes and I was taking it. I met with the principal almost daily. I wrote an entire pedagogical dissertation in hopes it would help my daughter and other kids enjoy a safe learning environment in future. With the school's approval, my daughter took her classes from home. But her inner light dimmed day after day, and her body weakened. I felt like I was falling into a deep black hole. If I let myself drop, I would never come back up again. A mental health institution and one suicide attempt later, she managed to finish ninth grade.

In the middle of all of this, the Universe smacked me on the head. My daughter, clear-headed despite her emotional pain, saw a profound truth. Sitting on the balcony, surrounded by orchids of all different colors, she begged me to stop living *for* her, and start doing what I really loved. "You'll get sick if you don't," she said to me. I had spent every waking moment since she was born trying to prove that I could do it, and realized I needed to take care of me. I promised her I would do exactly that. The healing process began. I had already gone through so much and I was still standing. There had to be a good reason for it, I presumed. Out of the blue, a colleague mentioned an angel therapist. I had never heard of something like that before, but I sensed that information had reached me for a reason. I booked a session and was sent home with some spiritual tasks to complete as homework. Among them, I had to use the Ho'oponopono on me, a Hawaiian ancient spiritual practice of reconciliation and forgiveness. I was curious so I did a little research. "If this worked with severe psychiatric cases, I'll try it with my daughter," I planned. Little by little, she felt the desire to heal.

Though I thought I was doing this for my daughter and myself, the truth is it was impacting the people around me. In a way, I had already become a Change Maker. I felt like something magnificent had taken over me. My inner demons appeared to be at rest. For the first time, I was experiencing real peace. I was profoundly connected to everyone and everything. I even felt unconditional love. At last, what I had gone through as an individual and as a mother was disclosing its purpose. As if I had been writing that story in my mind forever, I wrote my first novel in only 60 days. I was elated! I barely slept and hardly ate. Six months later, I had written three whole books.

During my daughter's hospitalization, people I had never heard of before showed up on my laptop screen speaking the language of love and compassion in a way that made perfect sense to me. I was shifting again. I was healing and while doing so, my real self was revealing itself to me. I felt comfortable in my own skin. I loved myself, everyone, and everything. Embedded in this energy, my urge to serve others became stronger. Instead of teaching academics, I used my own transmutation process to help others put back together the pieces of whatever aspect of their lives they thought was shattered. One more time, my Change Maker persona was seizing control. I couldn't wait!

I created *Pedagogía para la Vida* (Pedagogy for Life). PPV covers my books and *Un Café con María Paulina* (A Coffee with María Paulina). My books, novels included, depict how attainable self-transformation is, and open a door to self-observation, self-forgiveness, and consequently, self-reconciliation. Through *Un Café con María Paulina,* I accompany internal healing and transformational processes for individuals, couples, and groups. PPV embraces a good part of who I was born to be: someone who survived her own tyrant beginnings, overcame watching her own daughter crumble, and still continued on despite her dreams crushed since early on.

That real me was so full of love to give, so many amazing things to achieve and witness, that she would by no means allow herself to give up. So I pushed. I did not have anyone to lead me through this journey. Therefore, I hung on to the teachings coming my way and trusted my intuition with my life. It was an astounding trip back to me and so worth my while. My daughter graduated from a school near home where she excelled academically and was appreciated. She now lives a full, healthy life. She shares love and happiness, and raises spiritual awareness in her own, even comic, way. As for me, I am writing my sixth book and *Un Café con María Paulina* keeps expanding.

In my farmhouse where I live with 26 animals, surrounded by centuries-old trees and vast pasturelands, I look back at my life and take delight in how powerful we humans can be. My tears are now of happiness because I know that, no matter how obscure our days may seem, there is always a bright light awaiting only a step away. A childhood which, on more occasions than I can remember, felt unlivable, ended up showing me the way to self-forgiveness, self-compassion, and self-love. It taught me to accept life as it is… I can now see the beauty and the blessings in every circumstance.

From my *estudio en el aire* (office in the air), I created a sanctuary with a wide open view of the world before me. It allows me to be part of nature and enjoy the beauty around me. It represents how we can have what we envision in our lives. I am confident that we are equipped to be, do, and have whatever we wish for. The faster you open to who you truly are, the faster you will be able to enjoy the loveliness of self-discovery and the bliss within your True Self. Getting in touch with your True Self is your ticket to self-LOVE. And self-LOVE is the direct path to plenitude. It is now your turn to worship yourself. Tap into your heart and take steps toward *you* becoming one spectacular Change Maker. Believe me when I say if I could find the real me, *so can you.*

Ignite Action Steps

Whenever you are sailing through rough waters I, lovingly, invite you to try this: Sit in silence and close your eyes. Open your heart. Throw a question out into the Universe about anything that concerns you. Listen. The energy of your experiences will give you simple yet powerful answers for you to take action *fast*. Breathe…

Keep a journal. Accept what comes up with no judgment; write it down and go with it. Trust yourself. Let us see…

If you are struggling to appreciate yourself, take a moment every morning, as soon as you wake up, and in the quiet of your bedroom, repeat these words in your mind, while allowing your heart to vibrate in pure love, "I fully love and accept myself. Thank you." Do this for as long as you believe necessary, be grateful for *every* single thing you already are and have, even if you do not feel it, and see how magic begins to unfold before your eyes. Now… believe.

María Paulina Mejía - Colombia
Life Pedagogue and Writer
PedagogiaParaLaVida.com

CYNTHIA VITRANO

"With determination, dedication and discipline anything is possible."

I feel it is important for people to understand that you are not alone. I want you to know that whatever you are going through, I can relate. I want others to know that we all need to be who we are. That determination, dedication, and discipline makes anything possible. Let go of control and fear, freeing yourself to all the possibilities before you. My role as a parent has taught me how rewarding this is.

KEEPING THE 'DANCING' SOUL ALIVE

When I first became a mother, I never imagined that parenting children who have deep passions would end up transforming my own life so completely. My journey as a protector and confidence builder started when I arrived in the United States at the age of thirty and found out I was pregnant with my first daughter, my first love, Isabella. I had been living and working as an English teacher in Japan for nearly ten years; my experience with children was not insignificant, but it never prepared me for what was to come.

Becoming a mother was an amazing and frightening experience all at the same time. To finally experience unconditional love, to have a piece of your heart walking around in the world was terrifying. All you want to do is protect this little being. I still remember that first week with Isabella, not sleeping, watching her every breath to make sure she would survive, not wanting to leave that beautiful little soul for one second. I went through the same experience with my other two daughters, Sofia and Natalia. They are all precious in their own unique way. To this day, I can still watch them sleep and I will always remember those first feelings. They are such beautiful gifts and I am truly blessed and forever grateful they chose me to be their mother.

Sofia, my second child, was born two and half years after Isabella who fell in love at first sight and wouldn't leave her side for a moment. They were inseparable. As a mother, this was a beautiful bond to witness; I could not ask for anything more special between these beautiful little girls. Natalia came along quite a few years later, turning the duo into a trio, and so our journey together began.

Growing up, each one of the girls took dance classes, each gravitating toward their own style. Isabella became more interested in gymnastics, showing determination, drive, and perseverance. These amazing qualities enabled her to become a state and regional champion in gymnastics. I had practiced gymnastics during my childhood, but the intense competitive nature that Isabella endured was on a whole new level. In awe, I watched my firstborn transform herself through enormous effort into the true definition of what you call an amazing, hardworking athlete. The hours of training involved, the dedication, the struggle, and most of all the passion and love she had was something quite remarkable. Watching her compete, watching her lithe body fling itself into the movements and contortions of her performances was an exercise in motherly restraint — my heart in my throat, my breath stuck behind my ribs, every muscle tensed in anticipation. I hoped beyond hope she would make it through the performances without injury; that she would survive the physical risks of the sport.

Sofia started dancing at around three years old and was the cutest little performer. She had drive, passion, and a fire for dance that was so strong I had no choice but to nurture it as much as I could. Sofia's father has been a professional dancer his whole life, so when Sofia expressed that she wanted to follow in his footsteps, it made him feel truly special. Knowing that your child wants to experience your passion makes your entire being radiate with joy.

Sofia continued to excel as a dancer and was always put in the 'good dancers' routines. This came with a lot of pressure, not only on the child but also the parent. Dance is completely different from gymnastics. While injury is still a risk, the bigger risk is getting so deeply consumed by your child's performance that the lines blur between who is doing the dancing and who is the supportive adult. Being the parent of the child who makes a mistake in a routine is not a fun place to be either. In the dance world, competitive dance parents seemed to be unconsciously caught up in wanting perfection and thus missing the joy of a dancer's expressive soul, whether they intended it to be like this or not.

When Sofia was around ten years old, we moved her to a different dance studio. The training was more intense at this studio; the hours increased significantly as we went from fifteen hours a week to twenty-five hours a week for a child of her age. Sofia went from one ballet class a week to three or sometimes four as we allowed her to join the YAGP program which competes in NYC, the top competition in the US. I was stressed, often worried and concerned for her well-being. I had knots in my stomach and bouts of anxiety due to the pressure to be perfect. I hoped beyond hope she would not let her internal dialogue diminish her abilities; that she wouldn't be too hard on herself.

After a year of intense training and becoming more aware of the top competitions in the dance world, Sofia ended up in a group of 'advanced' dancers that showcased the studio's technique, training, and professionalism. This required her to train even more, which in turn brought on injuries due to overuse of particular muscles. The studio used teaching methods that were different from what we were used to and Sofia was working harder than she ever had before. Looking back, I realize the teaching methods used in this program were not entirely in alignment with our family values; they did not honor the child's inner drive or build up self-esteem; they were not supportive or encouraging.

The intense energy at the studio had started to take its toll. Sofia had started to express to me that she felt like she was not a good dancer. I became aware that one of her teachers had been belittling her, picked on her, crushed her spirit, and was destroying her passion for dance. That broke my heart. It made me sick to my stomach to know that a trusted adult would do this to a child; something needed to change. There had to be a better way.

Even with these emotional troubles, Sofia wanted to continue training at the studio. My entire body rebelled at this notion, needing to protect her. After much discussion with her, we came to see that all she needed from us was to support her in her decision; that we needed to honor her voice, her desire, and her dream. Knowing that it was going to be a tough year, we enrolled her for the following season. We reassured her that we supported her unconditionally in her commitment to learn and grow through overcoming the challenges, and if she ever felt uncomfortable we would look for a different studio.

We felt a little ease with our decision when the studio had the opportunity to audition for 'NBC's World of Dance.' We felt like Sofia's dedication had paid off. The teacher put together a group of thirteen dancers for the audition

— twelve dancers who would be in the routine and one alternate in case someone got injured. Our celebration was short-lived when we learned that the children were not told who the alternate was (well at least, some of the children were not told, though others knew). On the day of the audition, Sofia's gentle, loving heart was crying for that thirteenth child who only at that moment found out she was the backup. My heart sank as Sofia told me, imagining how crushed that child must have felt, thinking they were in the routine only to find out at the last minute they weren't. My heart bled for the spirit of that child and I hoped beyond hope that her mental well-being would not be affected.

After weeks of waiting, the group finally received news that they were going to be on national TV for the whole world to see! The children were ecstatic. To some, the announcement was the pivotal moment they had been waiting for. All their hard work and training had been recognized. For many, it was their entire life's dream come true and the start of their potential commercial career in the industry.

The show was being filmed in sunny California but the kids all lived in Las Vegas, an hour's flight away. Each time they needed to be on set for filming, they flew the team, along with several adult chaperones to the studio in Los Angeles. There they would spend long days working on their choreography, rehearsing for hours and then performing for the cameras, all the while keeping on top of their school work as this was a requirement in the state of California. It was exhausting for everyone involved.

The group made it all the way to the divisional final before being eliminated by the team that would later win the whole show. The winners were incredible. The amount of dedication, unity, and hard work all of the dancers on the show exhibited was next level. But back on Sofia's team, the pressures, challenges, unsupportive tactics, and emotional turmoil left our dancers divided. In addition to the defeat, they were mentally exhausted and utterly shattered. Some of the children within our group turned their backs on their passion and quit dancing altogether after this. Sofia was almost one of them.

Sofia expressed to me that she no longer wanted to dance and didn't step foot in a studio for nearly three months. It broke my heart to see my little dancer lose her way because as a parent you only want what is best for them. We work hard to nurture and support their passions and talents, to give them the best possible chance to live their life's purpose. I felt like we had failed Sofia.

Sofia was asked to do one last competition with the studio during spring break. I was reluctant and it went against my strong gut feeling of unease to let her participate as it meant that she would be on the other side of the country. However, Sofia was still a dancer, it is sewn into her fiber, her courage and determination are attributes that I admire even to this day. As it would happen, my worst fear came to life and due to all the pressures and anxieties she had endured throughout the season, Sofia suffered her first panic attack and got disoriented and lost. Once again, I felt like I had failed, but this time my little dancer was on the other side of the country and I was rendered helpless. After what seemed like forever, Sofia was found and with the help of some very loving parents and teachers, they reassured me that she was going to be okay. My mind went into overdrive, thinking about solutions to the pressure and expectations that were so evident in this industry. It was at that moment I became *Ignited* with the desire to create a safe, nurturing, and soul-uplifting environment for all children who want to flourish and become the best version of themselves — not only as dancers but as a person in this game of life. I knew the time to do it was right now.

I set to work creating a training program that I felt would be the next generational way to train young dancers, which enabled me to partner with an amazing technique teacher from LA and then purchase an existing dance studio that needed a full renovation. I was now in it for the long haul. One night, shortly after the purchase, I went into the studio, turned on the small light in the corner and looked around. I wasn't looking in as much as just absorbing the energy of the space. I could smell the sweat of the kids who had been in there from the last class of the day and envisioned nurturing and supporting every single dancer who walked through the doors. I was caught up in a feeling of so much joy and relief that I was going to be able to do exactly what I wanted, how I wanted. I knew that my vision was going to make a change in the philosophy of dance by honoring the soul of every child and guiding their spirit toward accomplishing their dreams.

I realized in that moment that we are all masters of our own destiny. You can BE, you can DO, you can EMBODY whatever your soul desires. For me, that was creating a space that I knew would be 100% dedicated to nurturing all children who entered the doors. As a studio owner, my goal is to bring about change for the better so that children can thrive, grow, and not only learn how to dance but get to experience some important fundamentals of life: how to be loving, kind, and considerate to our fellow dancers, teachers, and parents.

My intention for the studio is that we be there for each other, to support, encourage, and enjoy the beauty of dance and all that it holds. Our children only get to be children once, and to overshadow it with competitiveness or negativity ruins it for everyone and doesn't build self-esteem. Mindfulness and self-love should be just as important as precision and technique. If we had a little more self-awareness and compassion then the world would be a better place.

It has been quite the eye opener becoming a studio owner. I have acquired the best teachers in Las Vegas who align with the same philosophies, which is the emotional care of a child's well-being in an environment that is safe and nurturing as well as disciplined and focused. The expertise that the faculty embody in the industry is incredible and I feel truly blessed and honored that they chose to embark on this journey with me to make the dance environment a better place.

Nurturing and honoring our children's spirits doesn't contradict the joy of competition and the sheer amount of dedication and willpower that they put into it. Our studio provides opportunities that enable children to further themselves in the pursuit of their dreams to become professional dancers. They learn teamwork, dedication, perfecting their craft as well as being part of a group. They also learn the power of community by loving and supporting one another in the competitive tract, in our recreational and special needs classes. Because we spend so much time at the studio, I am a huge believer in that which you surround yourself with, you become.

Where once I felt fear, I now see dancers who are enjoying their craft and participating in opportunities to perform at benefits, assisted living facilities and charity events. My own girls have all benefited in different ways; they enjoy their renewed passion for dance by feeling more confident, supported and are completely immersing themselves in the environment we have created. I have peace within myself knowing that my child and other children can express themselves without judgment. Becoming a Change Maker has instilled a level of confidence that I didn't realize I had and has reinforced my determination, dedication, and discipline.

If I can leave you with just one thing, my dear Change Maker, it is that we are all on this journey together: growing, learning, crying, and enjoying what life has to offer. We are all one. Through *determination* you gain the strength to be who you really are. With *dedication* you can reach your goals and anything is possible. *Devotion* allows you to express your passion and *discipline* gives you the tools to succeed.

IGNITE ACTION STEPS

Let go of any fear you have. Fear borders on control so a bit of freedom goes a long way in allowing what is meant to unfold, easily unfold.

Evolve into who you want to be. It is important to be comfortable in your skin to discover the true essence of who you are. Then you can show up and be who you want to be versus what others impose.

Change is good! Don't fear it, be different. It enables you to step out of your comfort zones and discover new attributes. It strengthens the qualities you like and dissolves the ones that don't align with your true purpose. When you choose to change, you reclaim your ability to receive all the gifts the Universe has in store for you.

"Seeing is believing, but sometimes the most real things in the world are the things we can't see" — you just have to BELIEVE.

Cynthia Vitrano - New Zealand
Principal - Summerlin Dance Academy, CEO - Gifted Management Group
www.Summerlindance.com

Sibylle Mani

*"Balance your strengths and vulnerability to achieve
the changes you wish to see in the world."*

**I set out in life to use my strength and privilege to change the world for
the vulnerable. But, it wasn't until I embraced my own self that I found a
balanced strength. My wish is that by reading my story you begin your own
inner journey of self-discovery and inner strength. That you walk through
the storm of indecision and vulnerability, and embrace your true essence.
That essence will support you along the way to the life you are destined to live.**

Discovering the Female Change Maker Within

As a teenager, I discovered my life's purpose. I was thinking about the
meaning of life at that time. I was reading books and deciding what I wanted
to do, fascinated by people like Martin Luther King and Mikhail Gorbachev
and other activists and revolutionaries. I wanted to be like them. I wanted to do
more than just be helpful to others, I wanted to start a revolution and change
the world. It came to me so clearly and I could see all the pieces of it at once.
I would be unencumbered by a husband or children, I would be engaged in
local political groups and NGOs doing positive work around the world, and I
would start a revolution.

The purpose I built for myself was this: *Be strong, independent, adventurous,
ecological, and stand for social justice by using your privilege to give the less
privileged people in the world a voice.*

This strong belief drove me to focus on human rights and humanitarian assistance, work in Uganda and Afghanistan, and develop a participative sustainable process in Switzerland. My life was going smoothly, just as I had dreamt it would. Until it all changed.

I grew up in a very social family where magazines about development work were all around and my parents were strongly engaged in different social and political projects. Creativity, honesty, social engagement, modesty, and social justice were core values. It was a caring homelife, one that encouraged me to trust in the world and to follow my own dreams. I had been socially engaged at church and political groups since I was young and I committed to live my life in the moment and not be materialistic.

I started out as a Kindergarten teacher, and although I loved the creativity of this work, that world was too small for me. I spent some time working as a volunteer in a children's home in Romania and that led me to study social work with a focus on community development.

After graduation, I worked as a youth worker in my hometown Spiez, Switzerland and also volunteered at a local participatory sustainable Local Agenda 21 process. Through that process, many different people came together to develop an action plan for a sustainable, balanced Spiez for the next 20 years. I was the driving person behind the plan and got the support of others in the town. This was a unique process where I could feel the spirit and power of my vision creating a global impact for our residents. I saw when an idea falls into the right hands, with the right people, at the right time... it was magic, where global thoughts came into local actions — an approach I always believed in.

Even though I loved my work, I realized that I was tired of staying in the same place and I felt that another phase in life was waiting for me. I decided to organize a 'Peace Bike Trip' from Switzerland to Israel and Palestine, to raise money for the YMCA/YWCA in the Gaza Strip. I wanted to support this important worldwide youth organization focusing on youth development through delivering a wide variety of youth activities, including providing sport facilities, holding life skills classes, and promoting humanitarian values and engagement. I cycled for 67 days, riding 4800 kilometers, and raising $10,000. During the ride, I met youth groups and we discussed their understanding of peace, democracy, and social justice.

The growth I experienced throughout that trip was unbelievable. At the beginning, the trip was more of a personal challenge with a good purpose, but when I reached Syria, I met human rights activists who told me their stories of having been tortured in prison just because they stood up for their citizens' rights. While talking with students at the University in Damaskus about their understanding of peace and democracy, I was interrupted by one of them who told me, "You have to go now! The national security has found out about you and they think you are going to mobilize the students for a protest." I was shocked, but I had no time to think about it. "We have no time, let's go!"

I hid myself in the home of a Kurdish lawyer living in an illegal settlement in Damascus for three days. About every three years, these settlements are destroyed by the government, but the people always rebuild because they do not see another future for themselves. Seeing and hearing all those stories, an inner voice just clearly said, "What am I doing on this bicycle? What is the meaning of traveling like this when people are facing these kinds of injustices?" With no doubt, as a privileged Swiss, I *do* want to focus my life on supporting less privileged people and amplify their voices regarding injustice and human rights violations.

From that day onwards, every kilometer I rode, I grew, *I changed*, feeling the power of this clear focus in my life. I hardly recognized the person I was when I crossed the finish line in Bethlehem.

Returning to Switzerland, I talked about my bicycle trip and my work in Palestine on many different occasions, in various places, and with people of all ages and communities including political groups. With all of them, I shared the tremendous impact the trip had on me. I spoke from that vulnerable place deep inside of me, expressing my change of attitude during this trip, and how vulnerability can change society's beliefs. My openness made them reflect about their own prejudice and stereotypes about the conflicts in Palestine and Israel.

That change of focus trickled over into my personal life as well. I wondered how I could talk about social justice, peace, and reconciliation on a global scale but not be able to implement it in my own interfaith-intercultural relationship?

Sharing with the locals, talking about my bicycle trip, the audience members, while admiring my strength, said they could never do this. But having seen how my emotional vulnerability had resonated with them earlier, I decided to go even deeper. I wanted to get really real, raw, and honest. So I asked the audience, largely made up of rural women, if they were married. Ninety nine percent said that they were.

"You took this commitment to get married and raise children," I told them, "but you think you couldn't do this kind of a bicycle trip. For me, those kinds of trips are the adventures I love to take and do not fear. But getting married, to me, looks like a huge adventure that I am fearful to jump into. So, everybody has their own strengths and fears to deal with in life." Silence. Confused eyes looked up at me and then, shy smiles growing into shining eyes, the rural women started sitting up more straightly in their chairs.

My intuition brought me to work for the Civil Peace Service of Germany and they offered me a position in Uganda, Africa. I felt a lot of inner turmoil as I was not ready to leave behind my commitments in the Middle East.

This decision to let go and move to Uganda was hard but one of the best I've ever made. The three years in Uganda were full of different personal and professional experiences. I got to know myself differently and the way I looked at the world changed completely. My understanding of values — the meaning of reconciliation and justice systems, the way of talking and behaving — were all questioned. Even the way I *listened* to the people changed. In the first months, I felt like a small child ever so slowly discovering a new world.

In my new role as a civil peace advisor, I led Justice and Peace committees, worked with a psycho-social support program for prisoners, conducted community awareness programs through drama, worked with street children, and established a platform for performing artists — all with a very small budget. It was not easy, but I did it. My energy was flowing once again; I felt in the right place.

Three years into the project, my contract was not renewed, with an extract from the letter stating: "Dear Sibylle, personally I fully support you, but it is difficult for the traditional setting here. You are 20 years ahead of us." I read the letter from the acting Italian Bishop at the time and felt sad and hurt.

With a very heavy heart, I left Uganda and arrived in Afghanistan. There, I worked for the German International Cooperation (GIZ) in Kabul, supporting a national human rights organization. I found local people with a similar spirit to mine. After more than 12 years focusing on this path, I walked with a group of people in Geneva through the big corridors of the UN to talk about human rights violations in Afghanistan. I, as an ordinary social worker, was being able to coordinate the submission of the first shadow report on torture to the UN CAT commission in Geneva from the civil society side. My Afghan colleagues received threats, but they didn't give up. Excitingly, for this most sensitive of cases, a prosecutor process was initiated in Afghanistan. I felt so honored, so full of gratitude when I saw that the UN CAT commissioners listened to us with full attention, and when I saw the impact I was able to achieve for vulnerable people on an international level. Supporting others in raising their voice — my dream had come true. I felt, I *am* a Change Maker for humanity on an international level! I drifted off to sleep that night with this realization filling my dreams with light.

I was influencing changes not just at the international level, but also on a smaller scale. I worked on developing a program for juvenile offenders in northern Afghanistan. At the beginning, we faced significant criticism, however, our success was applauded by the top management of GIZ. One inmate of the juvenile rehabilitation center, who was affiliated with the Taliban, refused to join, yet six months later, he had become the captain of the sports team. Watching others change their lives reinforced for me how important it is to work on issues not just at the international level but also on a personal scale.

Although I began to feel tired of the restrictive, security-driven lifestyle in Afghanistan, I accepted an offer to become Country Representative of Caritas Germany in Afghanistan, a Catholic-based NGO in Kabul. I felt very honored to get this role. I started with a lot of enthusiasm, thinking, "Now I can make strategic decisions." It was my dream to lead with a modern leadership style, to empower and inspire people. However, my role had a lot of responsibilities but little authority; established strategies and procedures had to be followed. The social assistance projects were long-term and innovation was not welcomed. I was dismayed at my naiveté.

I was used to being independent, following more the needs and interests of beneficiaries than strategic interests; I was confronted by the predefined procedures and standards that I was expected to follow. My ideas of modern leadership were only partly supported. I kept trying to make changes but could not be as effective as I wanted to be.

In my new role, I was part of international meetings, discussing how millions of dollars were to be distributed for emergency crises. Surprisingly, I was in charge of enormous budgets. Realizing how international politics and strategies are implemented on the ground in humanitarian aid was interesting, but at the same time worrying. I questioned, "Is this the way International Aid is working? I thought that was history, but it seems not."

The majority of my time was taken up with work, leaving little availability for my personal interests and ideas. Living in Afghanistan, where security measures are strict, my daily movements were drastically restricted. My dream of giving service to the most vulnerable people in a political 'hot spot' had created a one-sided life taking place in a small space. Online personal growth and sport programs were the few things I was doing regularly in my free time. Internally, I was restless. I lost my focus. And when the relationship with my boyfriend came to an end, it was the last straw for me amidst the very difficult, high pressure circumstances. The feeling of hopelessness overwhelmed me.

My purpose and focus that had been so clear and steadfast until then suddenly crumbled. I felt lost and did not know anymore if I was still on the right path. I began asking myself, "Why is it that I can support thousands of people I don't know, but I cannot remain close to and support the one I love? Is that the price I have to pay for this work? Is it worth it? Where is my own emotional resilience when dealing with challenging personal situations?" I longed for answers to these questions.

The time had come instead to step back, regroup, and gather my energy so I could stand for the bigger changes again in the future. I needed to look into my inner, to look into my own change to reflect, and analyze where the new phase of life was going to take me. It had to happen, to bring me a step further to making me the person I was meant to be, integrating my female side more concisely. More importantly, I saw that I needed to rebalance, regain my self confidence. I needed time to recover, reconcile with the situation, and rethink my purpose. I had been afraid to lose my freedom by being in a relationship; instead, I got lost in life.

At work, I couldn't hide my situation well and so I carefully shared it with the team members. Unexpectedly, the reaction was a positive one. "Yes, Sibylle, we can understand this situation. We are here to take care of you. We will do as much as we can to support you." Some of the staff opened up and shared their own experiences with having a heartbreak. I stood there, the privileged Swiss lady, emotionally vulnerable and exposed, in a place where the people struggle daily for survival, and I felt *held* by my Afghan colleagues and friends. Their compassion and strength showed me that through sharing our vulnerabilities, we create a bond. We are not alone on this earth, and we need to remember that. We need to connect with others. We need to be courageous enough to be vulnerable.

Being surrounded by love and support from the most unexpected source was a powerful moment for me. My vulnerability turned out not to be a weakness but a blessing. A strength. Suddenly I realized that standing in this vulnerability made me a more understanding, sensible — and interestingly — even more respected female Change Maker. In that moment of unconditional support, it felt as though I was leaving one skin behind me and rediscovering my own vulnerability and purpose. The only thing I am sure of is if we all take small steps, be patient with ourselves, and stand in our insurgency, trusting that something new is waiting for us after the storm — strength is found. A female Change Maker arises, steps forth and keeps unfolding.

IGNITE ACTION STEPS

- Trust your ability to be a pioneer in creating and developing unconventional love relationships that can integrate your purpose and bring joy to your life.

- Stand to your innovative and creative personality, and admit that you need space and freedom to make it flourish and have an impact on the purpose of your life.

- Be patient with your ideas and vision for change, so that you are able to achieve some, instead of getting lost in trying too many things at once.

- Balance well. Know when it is worth struggling and when it is better to let go.

- Stand bold and proactively practice leadership in vulnerability, as it establishes trust and belonging inside the team. These new approaches are inspired by a more conscious leader where people are empowered to perform their best in a creative, low hierarchy way.

- Stand and struggle with the people you want to support and do not compromise for any organizational structure.

- Give your soul time and space to digest all your experiences and emotions to be able to explore how you have changed in a joyful, growing way.

Sibylle Mani - Switzerland
Social Worker specialized in community development, social justice and human rights, Master of Advanced in Managing Diversity
sibylle.mani@bluewin.ch

SONIA CHOPRA, DDS

*"The storm you are experiencing today is
building the woman you will be tomorrow."*

**My intention is to remind you to keep going, do not give up. Embrace
your struggles and see them as gifts; they have the power to teach you and
help you grow. One day, when you look back at your life, you will say, "I
wouldn't change a thing." So DON'T GIVE UP. The best is yet to come!**

FINDING THE BEAUTY IN BURNOUT

Burnout was one of the hardest experiences of my life, hands down. If you'd
have told me at the time I would have found beauty in that moment, I would
never have believed you. But that experience is what shaped who I am and
what my life is like today. And, believe it or not, it all started with my teeth.

I was born with an anomaly; eight congenitally missing teeth. This left
me with dental problems from the time I was born. More than that, it meant
I rarely smiled, at least not big enough to show my teeth. My parents didn't
realize the impact it would have on me until I started to lose my baby teeth
and several adult teeth never grew in. As I progressed into my teens and my
teeth never erupted, we knew I was going to have a problem. Not only was
I self-conscious about my smile, every time I went to the dentist, I routinely
had numerous cavities; eight always seems to be the number. Eventually, my
baby teeth fell out — or rotted out, I should say — and it was time to manage
all the missing spaces.

In the summer of 1995, after I graduated high school, my mom decided to close the gaps. She wanted me to actually eat when I went off to college. That was always the only thing that my mom was worried about, what I ate!

I spent my summer weeks not at the pool, but at the dentist's office. I had a dentist appointment once a week for what seemed like an eternity. As my teeth were restored into form and function, I developed a new problem… a toothache.

My pain started out vague and I couldn't tell you which tooth it was coming from. The dentist just told me that everything looked fine and they didn't see a problem. I was sent home to deal with it, a pain that the doctors started to tell me was all in my head. As I headed to the door getting ready to leave, I overheard the dentist telling my parents that I was just trying to seek their attention. Fear filled me. I covered my jaw with my hand, feeling that pulsating throb. The pain was changing me, making me a different person, and I wondered how much longer I was going to have to live with this.

Eventually, my dentist got so frustrated with me that he sent me to the oral surgeon to get the painful tooth removed. He still couldn't find anything wrong and never made a definitive diagnosis. My mom, a physician herself, was so frustrated that even she didn't know how to help her own daughter. All she wanted was for me to feel comfortable again, so she went along with the plan.

We showed up at the oral surgeon's office with me crying in anguish as I sat in the dental chair. My mom was emotional and stressed as she talked to the surgeon, a colleague of hers. I don't recall much of that day due to the haze of pain I was in, but I do vividly remember the look on his face as he stared at the referral sheet, questioning. I mean, I was only 17 years old and I was already missing eight teeth. I could tell that he didn't want to make it a ninth. But, I was hurting so much and my mom just didn't know what else to do. She wanted her baby to stop suffering!! What's a tooth, right? You can always live without a tooth.

I could see the battle in his mind, and although reluctant, he made the pull. My jaw was numb, so there was relief, at least for the moment. As the anesthesia started to wear off, the pain came back… and with a vengeance! It was at that very moment that I knew what just happened: they had extracted the wrong tooth!

I was devastated, filled with fear and didn't know how to end the pain. I saw seven different doctors throughout that year and no one could diagnose the problem. Over time, my body gave up, exhausted by a serious infection.

The left side of my face swelled up to the point that you couldn't even tell that I had a neck. I looked like my chubby-cheeked Cabbage Patch Doll, but I wasn't cute. I was bedridden and febrile.

Since I couldn't take any more teeth out, I was referred to an endodontist, a root canal specialist, what I call a tooth saver. And he really saved *me*. He was the first person that was able to tell me what was going on with my body. He treated me like an empowered voice in my own health. He taught me that my experience of myself and of my pain... *mattered*. He did the root canal on the infected tooth that I had so badly needed. Free of pain, I was just so happy to *sleep* again! Finally, my body was going back to normal. And not only did he relieve my pain, he saved my tooth. "Why wasn't I introduced to him in the first place?" was the main question running through my head.

This man changed my life in so many ways with his simple compassion, understanding, and explanation. He shared with me those qualities and I knew that I wanted to carry them with me for the rest of my life. I have emulated him ever since.

All of this happened when I was in college, thinking about my future and my career. I remember vividly sitting on my dorm room bed, flipping through the little booklet detailing the different college majors, wondering what my future could look like. Going with the flow of being an Indian woman and the daughter of a physician, I knew my choices were limited to those of a doctor, lawyer, or dentist. After so many visits to the dentist's office, it wasn't scary to me anymore. It's what I wanted to do. But I knew this wouldn't be an easy path and I kept thinking, "I can't do this. I'll never get into dental school." I also didn't want to disappoint my parents or the Indian norm. Looking back now, I realize part of this stemmed from a belief I'd had since I was a child.

Growing up I was always shy. Lacking confidence, I never let myself be *big*. Small, close-mouthed smiles, hesitant answers in class, never volunteering to be team captain for anything. I just *knew* I was not good enough. It came from not being placed in with the 'smart kids.' Barely ten years old, I was put in the lower reading level group in school, and in my mind, this had immediately labeled me 'not good enough.' I was crushed! From that day onward, I would never raise my hand to answer questions in class. Most of the time, I actually DID have the right answer and then I would get mad at myself for not speaking out loud. What a vicious cycle, right? My gosh, it affected my self-confidence for *years* and created roadblocks for me my entire life. This feeling of being 'less than special' stayed with me throughout

384 / S<small>ONIA</small> C<small>HOPRA</small>, DDS

the years. Even today, I feel this 'story' or this 'belief' can creep up on me unexpectedly.

Dental school was a challenge. I had to learn new skills: hand-eye coordination, working backwards in a mirror, wrestling a tongue and lip, and dealing with the scared person attached to it all. Then one day, one of my male teachers pulled me aside and told me that I should perhaps find a new career path. I felt completely smashed into the ground, as if someone took their shoe and stomped on a bug and was trying to get the guts off. It was a rock bottom moment for me.

After crying for weeks and wallowing in my teacher's harsh words, I knew I had to pick myself up. To do anything less was not in my DNA. This was a clear moment that Ignited the fire in me. I told my inner self never to back down and to keep pushing through, to persevere. I remember feeling that I had no choice but to move forward. That wasn't true; I *made* the choice.

That one teacher was nothing more than a temporary fixture in my life, although he taught me a very important lesson: I could do anything I set my mind to, but I had to believe in myself first.

I graduated dental school in the top 20 of my class. Then, I dabbled in general dentistry for a few years, but I kept thinking about that endodontist who had saved my tooth and relieved my pain. I felt called to specialize in the field of endodontics… my life had come full circle. There was this energetic pull, seemingly from birth that I was born to do this; it was my destiny.

Shortly after I graduated, the United States economy tanked and I couldn't find a job. I had two choices: be unemployed or build my own practice. For me, the only option was to open my own dental office. Terrified and excited, I had no clue how to go about doing that. I basically had to learn how to do it on the fly. I needed to put my big girl panties on and make some big changes.

I became the first female endodontist in Charlotte, North Carolina and being a woman in that role had its share of struggles. I looked like a little girl and nobody would take me seriously. I didn't quite fit into the 'old boys club' and had very little in common with them. Once again, I had that same feeling as when my teacher had told me to give up. I questioned the bold move of starting my own practice. But what had I learned from before? Not to give up.

Building my practice was my biggest challenge. I could complete a mean root canal, but I didn't know how to be an entrepreneur. They don't teach you how to run a business in dental school. You never learn how to have a good bedside manner, lead a team, or balance your life as a working mom — it's no wonder most dentists suffer from burnout. I had so many moments where it almost broke me. I had times when my team walked out on me or I had to deal with a disgruntled patient. I had a high rate of staff turnover and I couldn't communicate properly. I always knew what I wanted to say and had the best of intentions, but it would come out all wrong. Every time someone would leave, I'd find someone new, train them, and keep running around the hamster wheel I couldn't escape from.

I had days and weeks where all I could do was cry. I couldn't believe I studied my butt off my entire life to get to THIS!!! I spent almost $1 million between my dental school tuition and a construction loan for my practice — just to end up feeling like a failure, to feel broken.

I was dying on the inside. I couldn't lead a team, I couldn't be a boss, I couldn't be a good mom, and especially NOT all at the same time. I hit rock bottom again; I was burnt out. And I knew I needed to make a change.

And the craziest thing was, amidst all of this madness, my practice had still managed to grow. I knew in my core that I was doing something right, but I couldn't bring it all together. No amount of new hires could keep me from drowning every day and putting out fires. That's not how you want your dentist to feel, when you're under their drill!

If I wanted to see any real *change*, I had to start working on myself. I didn't know what I wanted in life because I had never taken the time to understand my wants and needs. I had neglected myself for nearly a decade.

I chose to go inward. I started listening to podcasts that fueled my soul. I began going to events that taught me to be a better version of me. I got a coach and started taking time off to work ON my practice instead of IN it. Eventually, I had clarity because I started to take time for myself. I realized I could be a better mom, a better wife, a better dentist. I found a better way.

After being in my practice for 10 years and becoming an expert in my field, I took a look around and asked, "What else can I do? What will be my legacy?" I knew I needed to share my impact with the world. I felt I had more to give than what was within the four walls of my practice. But what?

When I took a step back, I realized that everyday I saw my own story in my patient's stories. I couldn't believe that, 25 years later, the profession had not gotten any better at figuring out what was really going on in a patient's mouth and fixing it quickly and inexpensively. We're being sent on a merry-go-round ride of medical visits, multiple procedures, and all at so much expense. It was obvious to me the dental education system was fundamentally broken.

I knew I could help people save their time, their money, and their teeth. I believed I could change dental education for the better. So, I created my own endodontic education platform to help dentists truly understand how to diagnose and handle these types of cases in their practices.

Through my blogs, tooth stories, and endodontic course for general dentists, I now teach dentists all over the world tips and tricks that I learned after a decade of being in practice. This empowers them to help their patients receive the treatment that they deserve. I feel as though now, I am in the midst of my calling. My education resources have already impacted thousands of dentists worldwide. I am the first to do this in my field; I am a Change Maker!

I'm determined to be a Change Maker for patients, too. To help patients be better advocates for their oral health. I want to eradicate the phrase 'the pain is all in your head.' I want to prevent dentists from advocating for a procedure that isn't in the patient's best interest. I want my story to help others.

Over the past few years of self awareness, I have come to learn that I am capable of great things. If you asked me 20 years ago what the future would hold, I would never have imagined anything this incredible. From burnout came such beauty, so when *you* are feeling burned out, exhausted, and ready to throw in the towel, remember… things can *change*. You will not always be that scared little girl. Life will give you scars and make you tough, give you lessons that you will initially view as the end of the world, and it is your job to find the beauty in them. Burning out and hitting rock bottom is just what I needed to happen to me; it brought me to my passion. It can do the same for you, if you allow it.

Change yourself… and you can change the lives of others.

Ignite Action Steps

Change requires you to zoom out and then go inward.

The first step is stepping back and taking care of yourSELF. Instead of looking at your life as if you do not have time, start putting time back into your life. Be intentional and schedule it. As a busy mom of three with her own business, I realized that I gave everyone time but myself. By scheduling unconditional 'me' time into my life, it allowed me to gain clarity into what I really wanted. I finally had time to dream.

Write down what you love to do and what you don't love to do. Once you figure that out, stop doing the things that don't bring you joy and find someone else to do them for you. Find space for the things that bring you joy.

Be creative with your time. I realized that my car was really the only place that I was alone. So, I made my car my personal university. I listened to podcasts and books that inspired me and made me feel good inside.

When you are in the middle of a storm, take a deep breath, see what you can learn from it, and behold the beauty that awaits for you on the other side.

Sonia Chopra, DDS - United States
Board Certified Endodontist
www.soniachopradds.com

CLAUDIA CHAVEZ GORDOA

"Being number one for others pleases your ego;
being number one for yourself pleases your soul."

Why do we do what we do? There have been many times where I have pretended to be someone I was not because I wanted to be liked, not realizing I could be loved for who I am. If you have ever felt this way, I hope my story gives you the awareness that you don't have to continue feeling this way. I want to share with you that when you follow the things you are passionate about, you will be true to yourself. You do not need to please others or look for their approval to validate who you are.

BE THE NUMBER ONE

It was early one Saturday and I was standing outside in the competitors' tent, cheering one of my friends who was competing in that morning's triathlon. I had just gotten myself a cup of tea, hot and steaming, and I wanted a moment of peace to drink it. A competitor I knew from past meets approached and I had to struggle to keep the smile bright on my face as he asked, "Are you coming back to defend your title?" I hadn't competed for a while, and he was curious about my return. I opened my mouth to tell him a glib answer, but then I stopped, frozen, thinking, "Did I still want to compete?"

I honestly didn't know what to answer. Would I be doing it for myself or to impress others? What had driven me to compete in the past? To go beyond just competing for fun and chase the titles, *earn* the medals, and then defend them at all costs? Was it the ego boost I got from winning or the sheer joy of participating? His question, while seemingly innocent and easy, had unleashed a whole storm of emotions inside of me and I wondered if I was doing things to be liked, to gain approval from others, or if I was doing things to improve myself and for my own personal enjoyment.

Part of me wanted to say yes, but another part of me knew the real answer to that question was "No! I won't do it until I can participate in a race *and* have fun, letting go of needing to be number one." I had done the competitive circuit of swimming, biking and running many times before. The last time, participating in the World Cup Triathlon, I hated that I had to wake up so early, eat healthy ALL the time, and do all the training and exercising day after day after day. Although my true passion in life is sport, I had lost my desire and motivation.

In addition, as a woman, I had to face the challenges of growing up in a country with a high unemployment rate, unforgiving class system, and old-fashioned male dominance. In my job, to grow professionally and advance my career, I also had to go above and beyond. I had to break through the societal and cultural norms in my country to be accepted as successful. That made a Change Maker and this is my story...

I was born in one of the biggest cities in the world, Mexico City, with more than 25 million people. I didn't come from a very big family, just my lovely parents, a younger brother and myself. I had the good fortune to have both of my grandparents nearby and when our families and cousins got together, we visited, played and laughed often and loudly. My grandfather, known as the 'Colonel,' due to the fact he was in the military all his life, was a prominent figure to everyone. It looked like we had a very nice family, but for me, it was not so. My brother and I were the ugly ducklings. The 'Colonel' never took us into consideration and I watched my cousins receive a lot of attention and love while my brother and I felt rejected; it was very painful for me.

When I was eleven, my parents divorced. I suffered a lot because I adored my father; he was my hero, my confidant, and when he moved out, I didn't see him often. This was a big change for me, not having a close relationship with him anymore, and it broke my heart. I felt he abandoned me. I didn't have anyone who I could trust or talk to about my problems anymore. Later, my father met another woman, moved four hours from me, and adopted her kids. Our communication became less and less and our relationship drifted further and further apart, leaving me feeling small and insignificant. In my eyes, I saw him giving more attention to *her* children than to my brother and me. That made me feel I was no longer important to him and he did not care about us anymore. Unable to share these thoughts with my mother, I used to go outside and wrap my arms around the jacaranda tree behind the house, drawing what strength I could as I shed my tears.

At that time, I attended one of the most prestigious Catholic girls' schools in the city. I should have felt very fortunate, but it was one of my biggest nightmares. Going there every day was like punishment. I was often rejected and bullied because I was not of the same social status as most of the kids. I was miserable at school until I finally moved to a new school close to my neighborhood. It was life changing. I went from being a very shy, sad person with low self-esteem receiving poor report cards to being one of the top three students in the school and a leader with lots of friends. The change in my environment truly changed who I was becoming.

As I reflect on all that happened in my early life, I see that it made me very determined to demonstrate to my extended family, my dad, and everyone else that I could be the perfect girl who everyone could admire and love.

At university, I studied Business Administration and had remarkable grades. I joined many social and sports groups, and started others, becoming captain of the female soccer team which made it to the National finals in the first year. Not only was I succeeding on the soccer pitch, my career took off. Even before completing my degree, I was hired by one of the biggest multinational companies, Coca-Cola FEMSA™.

My successful marketing career continued to rise and I was invited to move to Nestle™, another big multinational. I learned a lot there and my career climbed rapidly, yet it wasn't enough for me. I may have been the only one on my father's side of the family to earn a university degree, to have a great job, to purchase her own apartment, but I still craved *more* — I craved my family's attention; their recognition of my achievements. But no matter what I accomplished, my other cousins still had the attention of our family, and I felt ignored and unloved.

Although I had so much success in my life professionally, personally I felt unfulfilled. I decided to make a huge change in my life. I left everything behind and arrived in a small city in Australia. I stepped off the plane with two suitcases, my golf clubs, no house, no job, no friends, and no family. It was a huge change, but it was one I had been dreaming of since I was a little girl. I remember telling my mother I wanted to move to Australia and compete on their Olympic team after watching the Australian team winning medals in the

Olympics on TV. It was not an achievable dream for a girl of my background, but I wanted it desperately and always told myself I would get there one day.

After arriving in Australia, it took me several months before I could find a job. I discovered that in Australia it doesn't mean a lot if you have an impressive resume or if you worked for a global corporation. They wanted you to understand the Australian culture first, before you started work for them. Initially, it was not easy, and at every single service job (bartender, waitress, sandwich or coffee making), I was rejected. The only options were working as a cleaner or to keep searching for a better opportunity.

I never gave up. I was convinced I could find a position worthy of my skills and education. Finally, advancing my career through a series of opportunities, I got a sales position in another multinational company and I had resumed the same quality of life that I had in Mexico. It was only then, on the other side of the world, that I started to get attention from my family. But I still didn't have the attention of my father.

I didn't want to wait any longer for other people's approval. I wanted to follow my own passions. Sometimes we wait and wait for the best time to do something. There is no perfect time to start a business, quit your job, take the trip of your life, have enough money to buy something that you want or do something you have always wanted to do. I have learned that NOW is always the right time. If you really want to do it, just take action! If you have the intention and a strong desire to just do it, all of your desires will come true.

I had within me the desire to compete in sports at an international level. I discovered this by doing triathlons, because it meant I could participate in an international championship competition, like being in the Olympics, but in an amateur way so I could achieve my dream. I started to learn the three sports: swimming, riding and running, and practiced, practiced, practiced until I mastered them. I trained hard during my first season with a lot of discipline and determination, and to my surprise, I attained the 'State Champion' title for my age group. This gave me a lot of motivation to train harder at full capacity for the next season. I was very focused and strong-minded… determined to be number one in every single race, to get the points to qualify for the World Championship Triathlon and be part of the Australian Team — and I made it! The first race was in Chicago where I would compete with the number one women from all over the world. To my surprise and elation, I finished in one of the top five. Never underestimate what you can achieve!

Before going to the World Championships in Chicago, someone asked me a great question, "Why are you doing this? Why do you want to go to Chicago?"

I couldn't respond to this question. At the time, I thought I was pursuing my childhood dream, but when I tried to answer, the words turned sour in my mouth and wouldn't come out.

I went on to be the State Champion three years in a row, competed in five world championships, raced all around the world getting numerous medals and trophies, and being number one in every single race. My level of competition was the highest it could be. All that effort and training paid off!

I shared my racing journey, highs and lows, with people through Facebook videos. The overwhelming feedback I received made me feel I could Ignite my career, not in marketing, but as a coach and motivational speaker. I could influence people and change their lives, competing all the while. However, I started to sense emptiness, lack of motivation, questioning myself... was this really what I wanted to do? I felt there was no balance in my life, just sports and training.

I decided to complete my studies with one of the world's elite international speakers. This led to the opportunity to become part of his team. I was stunned and delighted! It was the opportunity of a lifetime. And I realized it was time to make another change. I quit triathlons, left Australia, and moved to Arizona, USA.

Arizona brought other new changes as well. My new friends in America introduced me to canyoneering and mountain climbing. I crossed the Grand Canyon rim to rim in one day. Then, I climbed Mount Kilimanjaro, the third highest mountain in the world. I started planning a climb to Mt. Everest, but the guide suggested I first do Aconcagua, the second highest mountain, to see how my body would respond. I was excited, as this was another opportunity to be noticed once again.

I started making arrangements to climb Aconcagua, but a few weeks before the trip a friend asked me a great question, "Claudia, why are you doing this?" That was the second time someone asked me that and I stood there unable to respond. After my silence, he said to me, "You have already achieved so much; you don't need one more achievement, medal, or reward in your life. *Why* are you doing this?"

Wow! It felt like a bucket of cold water had been thrown over me. I shivered head to toe with the realization that all my life, I have been trying very hard to be 'Number One' in *everything*: school, work, sports... I did crazy things like diving with sharks, jumping from airplanes, bullfighting, trips in the jungle, climbing mountains, traveling the world and living in different countries... I thought I had done everything to be successful, so why was I still striving to achieve more?

Through my experience, I became conscious of how I was operating in my life.

I would ask myself if I was doing things to be a better person, better partner, best friend, best daughter... or was I just doing things to seek approval from others and be accepted? I had gained the admiration of all my family, friends, colleagues and people who knew me, but I was still looking for more. And, I had been doing this for a long time. I realized in that moment that I wanted to demonstrate to my father and grandfather that I was good enough, just like my cousins.

Finally, I decided to ask my father why he never called me, why didn't he care about me. He answered, "I thought you didn't need me, you're a very strong and independent woman who has achieved it all. I felt you didn't need anything from me."

But I did. I realized that I created a lot of stories in my mind. I'm the only one who tells myself that I am not good enough. I do things for others, seeking their approval, when they don't really care. My EGO is what makes me do things like win medals, just to be recognized, to gain attention. But in reality, people who love me don't care if I win or lose, if I am number one or the last one. They are just happy for me, for who I am.

We all have different stories, unique childhood memories that affect us in our lives. The only thing we can do is to have an open heart, communicate with those who affect us, talk about what we feel, instead of creating stories that are not real and yet profoundly affect our lives. We can then change our future by leaving that all in the past. We can observe and be conscious of our feelings, thoughts, and the reality we create through our self-told stories.

I realized, I need to be able to pause, observe my story, listen, and be open to the situation from the other person's point of view, honestly evaluating without reacting. If I can understand why the other person acts the way they do, I can avoid a lot of conflict, problems, and unreal stories that affect my life.

We all have the capacity to erase the past by creating new stories of love and happiness. Sometimes we don't understand a situation because we were children, immature, and lacking all the information. We need to ask, to clarify, and confirm. We need to be able to listen and be open, observe, to be non-judgmental. We all need to avoid making decisions in anger, or like me, think my father didn't love me based on the actions of the past.

I accomplished a lot of things in my life to gain my father's and family's love and approval, but in the end, none of that matters. What I really gained through my journey was that I became a better person, woman, daughter, friend, partner and colleague. I changed my perspective and everything around me changed with it.

I don't need someone else's approval in order to BE someone. I can still perform at a high level and DO things that feel good to me, that motivate me and give me passion, love, and fulfillment. The only thing I need to be or do, is be the best person I can be — always. Not for others, just for me. I am who I am and I just want to be the BEST VERSION OF MYSELF!!! You don't need someone else's approval in order to be you. You can perform at any level by doing things that feel good and create passion, love, and fulfillment. The only thing you need to be is be the best person you can — not for others but for yourself. You are who you are… so, just *be* the BEST VERSION OF YOU!

IGNITE ACTION STEPS

- You cannot give what you don't have. You first need to generate inside of you the thing you want, so you can later give it to others. If you want love, you need first to love yourself.

- When you are doing something in your life, ask yourself: Are you doing this for yourself or because it makes you feel good? Or are you doing to gain the approval and recognition from others?

- It's not bad to be Number One or the best version of yourself. You do not need to win all the time, you can have fun, just enjoy, help and support others in winning big. You do not have to prove anything to anyone else.

- Be the best human being in your different roles in life. Love your mistakes, your qualities and defects.

- Surround yourself with positive people who support, motivate and empower you. Eliminate negative people who can destroy your dreams and goals. Remember you are the average of the five people who you spend the most time with.

Claudia Chavez Gordoa - Mexico & Australia
"NEXT STEP" Health - Image Consultant, Trainer & Coach
www.Presens.com.au
www.ClaudiaChavezG.com

JENNIFER WOOTTON

"Justice can only be achieved when all perspectives are treated fairly."

I want you to see that challenges in your life can be gifts. Look at those challenges from all perspectives and be mindful of how quick you are to judge. It may take time to discover the gift and it may not take the sting out of the pain, but when you examine your life's trials through a lens of compassion — for yourself and others — only then will you find justice. I hope you can find the gifts in your experiences and are motivated to make positive change in your life and in the lives of others.

FAIRNESS FOR ALL

Let me take you back to those heady and hormonal days of high school. I was sitting on the bench in the locker room after volleyball practice, peeling off my knee pads and chatting with the two remaining teammates who were still changing out of their sweaty gym clothes.

"Hey Woo, wouldn't it be funny if I put acid in your drink one night" one of them said with that funny half laugh that makes you wonder whether they are serious or not. Thirty-eight years later, I can't remember which one of my two teammates uttered those words to me. I knew they were experimenting with drugs, but I thought I could trust them. I thought they were my friends. I also thought — or chose to believe — they were kidding. In 1981, LSD was still popular, but it held no allure for me. I wanted no part of their suggested prank. I thought that my super sarcastic response, "What? Ya, that would be pretty hilarious." eliminated even the slightest possibility that they would ever do something so heinous.

That same insane comment surfaced again a couple of months later. In hindsight, it's obvious that I should have taken it more seriously. But if I had, I might have missed out on the gift they ultimately gave me.

It was the night of the Sadie Hawkins dance at school, that old tradition when girls ask the boys to the dance. Lucky for me I had a boyfriend, sparing me that particular teenage girl terror. Our small-town school dances were a big deal and we prepared for weeks in advance. And my friends and I had a plan.

"Mom, will you drive me to Sarah's house? We're all meeting there and going to the dance as a group." I neglected to mention Sarah's parents were out. That was, after all, the point of meeting there; it was a place to gather and drink some alcohol before the dance. We thought this would make the evening more fun. I knew drinking underage was breaking the rules, but I threw caution to the wind that night with my 'friends.'

One of us — I never knew who — convinced a guy in Grade 13 to buy us a bottle of whiskey. When Mom dropped me off, the alcohol was already waiting. "Throw in your cash," Sarah said, and we all pitched in to pay for it. My boyfriend Peter brought the newly released Foreigner album "4" on cassette. We cranked it up, and like magic, someone put a drink in my hand. I grabbed sips of the drink as we danced to "Urgent" and "Juke Box Hero." I felt rebellious and grown up. It never occurred to me to watch who poured the drinks — the pouring happened in the kitchen while I was rocking in the living room. These were the days before Rohypnol, and I'd forgotten Sarah's locker room comment from weeks before. I danced, we laughed, and when Mary handed me a second drink, I finished it.

"That's it" I declared, "Time to get to the dance!" I was a little tipsy and enjoying the feeling. We called cabs and within ten minutes arrived at the dance together. Walking into the school's gymnasium, my curly hair bouncing around my shoulders, I felt cool to be arriving as part of 'the' group — I belonged. The gym was dark, the music loud, and we danced. But I started to feel a little weird and I didn't know why; I'd only had two drinks.

When I told Peter I was going to the washroom, his only comment was, "Jenn, you're so pale." He kept a lookout for teachers as I made my way to the girls' washroom, but inside I ran smack dab into my volleyball coach. "Are you okay Jennifer? You look a little pale," she inquired, then rapid-fire asked me who I was at the dance with, even though it was obvious to her. Squirming, under her scrutiny, I ended the interrogation as quickly as possible and beelined it back to my boyfriend outside.

"Coach just quizzed me. Let's get out of here." The school had a new zero-tolerance alcohol policy and we didn't want to get nabbed. We quickly said goodbye to the gang and walked the 20-minute trek to my house. By the time we got there, I wasn't even tipsy anymore.

My parents were home and, predictable as ever, were waiting up to subject me to Janet and Frank's 'kiss and sniff' test. I leaned in to kiss them on the cheek while they sniffed deeply to detect whether there was any alcohol on my breath. They always tried to sniff discreetly, but never succeeded. Even though I had to run their gauntlet, I always appreciated how much they cared. That night, I passed the test. Peter and I headed to the basement, leaving my parents upstairs.

The phone rang about a half hour later. I surreptitiously listened in on the basement extension and heard my coach, "Hi Frank, Jennifer was here at the dance tonight and I think she's been drinking." "Oh-oh," I whispered to Peter with my hand over the receiver, "It's Coach, I'm busted!" Feeling guilty, I listened while Dad defended me, telling Coach that he didn't think so, that I was at home and he didn't see any signs that I'd been drinking.

After they hung up, I knew it wasn't going to be long before an interrogation began. Sure enough, "Jennifer!" my mom called out. Upstairs we went. Dad asked again if I'd been drinking. "No," I lied, and blew directly into his face. Dad turned to Peter, who looked a little green since my Dad, who was a high school vice principal at another school, could be a little intimidating. "Peter, has Jennifer been drinking?" "No sir," came his meek-ish reply. My parents questioned me a little while longer and, in the end, I convinced them Coach was wrong.

Then I woke up. I was in my bed. I had no idea how I got there. I was wearing my jammies and my hair was still damp. Snippets of memories from the rest of the night before swirled in my head; me thrashing about in the shower with hands holding me up, me slumped in the back of the car, my Dad driving in the dark, colored lights and nothing more. I was confused. I went to my parents' room. When she saw me, my mom started crying. They looked like they hadn't slept a wink.

They talked me through the parts of the night that were lost to me. I learned that I suddenly didn't know who I was and when they asked me my name, ironically, I told them I was Sarah. I told them they were Mr. and Mrs. Wootton, as though I had no idea they were my parents. Dad had driven me back to the school, looking for answers. He also drove me to Sarah's house to speak to her mom. It's fair to say they had been frantically worried, and thankfully their worry turned to relief rather than anger. Shame took hold of me. I'd put my parents through so much.

Though confused, I started examining the evidence. I calculated the amount of alcohol I drank — it simply wasn't enough to cause my black out. I was tipsy, but not drunk, and wasn't showing any signs of the alcohol by the time I got home from the dance — and I'd passed the kiss and sniff test. And then I remembered… Sarah and Mary's comment in the locker room weeks earlier flooded back to me, "Hey Woo, would it ever be funny if I put acid in your drink one night." I thought about how they handed me the drinks — I never saw them poured. A wave rushed over me as something else that didn't make sense at the time popped into my head... after I finished my first drink, Sarah and Mary suddenly burst into an uncontrolled fit of laughter. They laughed hard as they rolled on the ground. Nobody else knew why. I blew it off at the time but the morning after, I put all the evidence together and came up with my own conclusion, but not before the disbelief and the shock settled in. My shame deepened. Why would they do that to me? How could I have been so dumb?

When the Monday morning announcements were over, my homeroom teacher beckoned to me and said, "Jennifer, Vice Principal Donnelly is expecting you." I lowered my head. Everybody watched me as I walked quickly out of the classroom. More shame. The Vice Principal was surprisingly kind to me as he suspended me for two days for being under the influence of alcohol at the dance. He explained that the suspension would go on my student record. I just sat there, took it in, and eventually cried. I was so ashamed. It never even occurred to me to tell him the full story — about Sarah and Mary. I kept that to myself. I still don't fully know why. I knew that I had broken the rules and there was a price to pay for that — I just didn't realize the price would be so high.

I later learned that while I was on suspension, one by one the gang was called into the Vice Principal's office. Nobody else got suspended, but each of them was read the riot act. The Vice Principal also reprimanded the guy who bought us the alcohol because someone gave the VP his name. It wasn't me — I was never even asked the question. In my absence though, I was fingered as the snitch.

Like an uncontrollable virus, news of my bad deeds — one true (that I had a couple of drinks before the dance) and the rest false — my fall from grace, my supposed snitching all spread, intensified, multiplied, and the rumors ultimately took on a life of their own. I was vilified, isolated and shunned. When

I walked back into the school after serving my suspension, I was *persona non grata*; people either turned away when they saw me or stared and shot daggers with their eyes. I was falsely labelled a rat and a snitch, and everyone seemed furious with me. My 'friends' thought I squealed on them to the VP and all but two of them disowned me — even Sarah and Mary. In solidarity with the senior I supposedly had ratted out for supplying us with alcohol, the senior students were especially mean. I was not the betrayer they thought I was, though I was found guilty in the court of public opinion and punished harshly.

All along I remained quiet about what Sarah and Mary had done. Who would believe me? I figured I had already embarrassed my parents. I had scared them and broken their trust, become the subject of intense gossip in a small community where gossip was invited in like a dear friend, and was alienated from most of my friends and the entire school community. I thought I might not go to university, thinking I would be untouchable with the incident on my record. I was scared about the long-term effects of LSD as well. I had heard stories about teens experiencing psychosis from a single bad trip, and about people having terrible flashbacks years later.

High school kids can be mean and have long memories in some ways. Between my fears and my acute shame at the social isolation, rightly or wrongly, I never fully recovered socially from the incident while I was still in high school. It took a very long time before I felt secure, like I belonged and could trust again.

In addition to the ability to stand up for myself, what I lacked at the time was perspective. In particular, the perspective that things were not as bad as they seemed, that all those challenges would pass, or at least the importance of them would diminish, or new pathways would open. This was my Ignite moment, the moment that would drive me to become a Change Maker.

Though I didn't know it at the time, the betrayal, shame, confusion, and isolation I experienced at fifteen fueled my passion for the workplace human rights work I've focused on for the last 20 years as a human rights lawyer. I'm brought in when one employee alleges they have been harassed or bullied by another. I'm the one who investigates and decides what happened. I take my role very seriously. People's lives are deeply affected by it. The stakes are high and the health and well-being, reputations and livelihoods of the individuals involved often hang in the balance. The lessons I learned at fifteen have served me well in this work.

Recognizing the many gifts that came from this experience took a long time, but eventually I saw that there were many of them. I was reminded that my parents loved me unconditionally. I learned that people who have been harmed do not always speak up and it's essential to create safety to allow them to do so. I understood the destructive power of shame and the affirming power of validation. I experienced the importance of treating every person accused of wrongdoing with unwavering fairness as well as close and compassionate listening. I appreciated that when we seek justice for those who have been harmed, we equally have an obligation to ensure fairness to those who have been accused. I witnessed that there are many sides to every story and justice demands careful attention to each one of them.

I also experienced the importance of taking responsibility for one's own bad behavior — as difficult as that may be. I learned that the best person to stand up for you... is you! I found that I could benefit from coaching myself to find my own voice and exercise my own agency. I appreciated the necessity of proportionality when someone does behave badly. And, consistent with that proportionality, I gained the clear perspective that forgiveness is a powerful force for the forgiver and the forgiven. I've long since forgiven Sarah and Mary for their betrayal and the harm they did to me. It took much longer though to shake the pain of the isolation.

T.D. Jakes once wrote "Your ministry is where your misery lies." I read that years ago and it has stuck with me ever since. The misery of my worst high school experience led me to the unwavering principles that I bring to bear as a Change Maker conducting independent and neutral investigations of workplace harassment for over 20 years.

Before every investigation interview, I work hard to set aside any of my own biases. When I'm reaching findings of fact, assessing people's credibility, and deciding whether workplace harassment or bullying have occurred in each case, I am acutely aware that it is a privilege to investigate... and a heavy responsibility. At the end of each case, after agonizing over the details of the different versions of events, drawing my conclusions and submitting my results, my inner fifteen-year-old allows me to sleep well knowing my work has passed her test; that I've treated every person involved in the investigation with fairness and compassion, listened empathetically, examined closely, and impartially considered all scenarios offered to me.

You may have suffered betrayals. You may have hurts and injuries from your past that still haunt you in some way or cause you pain or that you have had trouble letting go of. If so, you may be very well served to resolve them by examining them and looking for the gifts within. Instead of pushing them away, look at them closely and consider all perspectives. If you examine your life's trials through a lens of compassion — for yourself and others — if you can see everyone in their full humanity, it can dissipate the power these memories have over your present. Justice is a gift that only comes when a safe space is made for all perspectives.

IGNITE ACTION STEPS:

Fairness is for everybody. In the heat of the moment: stop, look, and listen. Empathetic listening is something that takes a lot of practice. Practicing listening to the words being spoken instead of preparing what you're going to say next when the other person stops talking is the first step in fairness.

Pair up with a partner. Come up with a subject matter that's personal in nature. While one partner speaks for three minutes, just listen. Don't compose a reply or a rebuttal in your head. Don't plan what you're going to say next. Focus on projecting understanding, empathy, encouragement, and positive support as they speak. When they are finished, simply thank them for sharing. When you're holding space for them in this positive way, you just might be providing a safe space for them to share something deeply important.

Jennifer Wootton - Canada
Workplace Human Rights Lawyer
www.workplaceresolutions.com
www.optimalresolution.com
@jennifer-wootton-264b064b/

JB OWEN

"Incredible is just waiting for you!"

It is my intention that you see the Change Maker in you. That you awaken to the power you have inside. Your drive, determination, and destiny are all interwoven. The steps you take to discover and uncover them will be your greatest journey. Find what you love, go after it and embrace the gifts you have to give. Your talents are exactly what the world is waiting to see.

FINDING YOUR OWN INCREDIBLE

There I was... in a dark soundstage, standing at the top of a platform, waiting for my cue. I had just come out of hair and make-up. I had a microphone clipped to the back of my waistband and had just completed a three-second soundcheck in the small entrance between two sets of steel doors that lead from one cavernous television set to the next. A young production assistant with curly baby-fine hair and thick glasses welcomed me in a whisper. They were filming in the distance and we all needed to be quiet: myself, the assistant, and the eager cameraman who was following me, getting the behind-the-scenes action with his assistant coupled beside him carrying umbilical-like power cords to the portable battery pack.

It was all overly intimidating: the darkness, the need to step over cables that lay strewn across the floor like anacondas on a jungle path. The scaffolding and raw set design that looked good from the front, yet from behind had jutting two-by-fours that could knock you in the head and sandbags as counterweights that might cause you to trip. People scurried past with headsets plugged onto their ears, rushing to perform the task that had been requested on the in-house walkie-talkies. A few glanced at me but said nothing. To me, there was a slight look in their eyes that made me feel like I was the new lamb to the slaughter.

I had been on television sets before. In fact, I had spent 15 years of my career working in film as a set supervisor in the costume department. I had seen hundreds of star-struck extras, new up-and-coming actors, and even executive producers who flew in and showed up on set big-eyed and nervous. Between the twenty-foot ceilings and the expansiveness of the studios, the make-believe creation of a different world inside a massive building is both wondrous and mind-blowing at the same time. I had often been the one to guide people to their spot, talking them through their 30 seconds of instructions, and then leaving them to do their thing. Now, I was the one being herded to my spot… amidst a swirl of instructions... to the top of a wooden platform… a camera in my face… smiled at like a Cheshire cat by the baby blonde assistant… shown yellow tape on the floor as my endpoint… told to go out there and give it my all.

I am not normally a nervous person. Things don't really rattle me. I have spoken on stages in numerous different countries. I have been in front of audiences both receptive and not. I have met A-list celebrities and 'important' people. Years before that, I spoke in front of the camera on a news program and interview show. This was not my first time on a soundstage, nor the first time I was going to talk about my product. But being rushed into an unknown space and given an exact spot to walk to and an exact amount of time to speak in had my mind whirling. The cameraman asked me how I was feeling while thrusting his wide-lens camera a mere four inches from my face. It was unnerving. Knowing I was about to face six "Dragons" with only 90 seconds to give my pitch had my heart pounding, my ears ringing, and my mouth dry as dust.

"Go!" The assistant said, louder than expected. Just seconds before, she had given me my instructions in a rapid whisper and now her loud voice startled me like a young colt hearing the starting gun before its first derby race. "Walk close to the wall, but not too close. Don't walk too fast but don't go slow. Smile, but not too much. Look happy, but not overly. Try not to look down when you are going down the stairs. Don't take too long, but don't rush. You'll see yellow tape on the floor, but don't look at it! Go right to it and start talking. Be natural, but get to the point. Be excited, but not animated. The cameras will be all around, but don't look at them, just talk. You'll be fine."

Her instructions were a topsy-turvy Willy Wonka array of contractions, but it was the ominous foreshadowing of her saying, "You'll be fine" that felt like a clamp around my throat. They could see it. *I* had seen it. Pupils that dilate when the fight-or-flight response kicks in. The tips of the ears that turn slightly red from rapid blood flow, or the moving of a pasty tongue around in the mouth like a fish gasping for air on a wooden dock. I had witnessed those sensations in others many times throughout my career and now I was the one grabbing the plastic cup of water the camera assistant so magically thrust toward me. The one whose heart was pounding so loud it drowned out any other sounds. I had a fake smile pasted on my lips, nodding in agreement, when in truth my stomach was a fisherman's knot and my feet felt like Goliath's stones.

I was a bit surprised by my body's reactions. I remember feeling amused at my flush of nerves and humored that I, someone who seldom felt stagefright, was getting a full dose of it right then. I laughed at myself internally, embracing the full gambit of light-headedness and nervous laughter. It was as if I was observing myself from the outside in, sympathetic and yet chuckling that something quite harmless was brewing a plethora of internal, yet fearful responses.

I had been quite calm since finding out I was going to be on the show. Months had passed since my audition and back-and-forth phone calls with the producers had made it seem exciting yet completely harmless. Getting on the hit show, Dragon's Den™, Canada's version of Shark Tank™ and pitching my product for investment had been a strategic decision on my vision board for almost two years.

I had mapped out much of the process with wit and precision not emotion or nerves. I had purposely driven four hours to a smaller city for my audition rather than going to the big city with its thousands of hopefuls an hour away. I was up at 5 AM, arriving four hours before the 9 AM call time to make sure I was number one in line. And I was well prepared. I had a glossy packet of my company's information and had rehearsed my audition speech numerous times in the mirror, on the treadmill (so I could do it with an elevated heart rate), and in front of friends.

When the call came that I had made it and would be filming in three months, I watched every season of the show. I analyzed the other contestants, calculated their deals, and looked for recurring patterns in the pitches, offers, and handshakes. I planned every nuance of my pitch, every design element of my presentation down to the smallest detail. I researched each of the Dragons, their histories, their business styles, and their preferences to products, people, and even the temperament of those giving the pitch. It was a fact-finding endeavor that allowed me to be methodical and practical about the formula one must adopt to be successful on the show.

After a 5-hour flight, I arrived at the Canadian Broadcast Corporation building in Toronto and, before any of the other contestants showed up, systematically practiced my speech in the acoustic emptiness of the hallway. The security guard was reluctant to let me in as the doors were still locked and I was incredibly early, but my eager grin and two oversized suitcases won him over and he admitted me into the inner sanctum of the Candian film corporation's award-winning show. I knew it was vital to be early. I needed to acclimate myself to the space and take in all the details, the newness, so I wouldn't be distracted when I needed to be on. I read all the plaques on the wall, looking at the old pictures of past productions and celebrities who had graced the building. I acted as if it was a history tour, soaking in the bravado and braveness each one of those people had mustered in their quest to be the successes that they were.

I had come alone to the filming. I didn't want the distraction of any family. As others started arriving, I cringed at their entourage of spouses, parents, and kids; all there to support them, but in truth, only adding more stress. I felt bad for one contestant who was holding a baby in one arm, the hand of a toddler in the other, and ordering her star-struck husband to stop ogling over the hockey memorabilia and help her with their oversized display. I didn't want anyone or anything distracting me from my purpose. I was laser-focused on delivering my proposal; graciously asking for 140 thousand dollars in exchange for 18 percent of my company. A big ask for a product that was both ahead of its time and slightly controversial.

For more than four years, I had been advocating a new product I created that would revolutionize the feminine hygiene industry. *Lotus Liners — the most comfortable, reliable, fashionable, washable panty liners on the planet.* I had traveled to China to design and manufacture them and had been selling them successfully in over 140 stores across the country, but I wanted an influx of capital to expand the concept. I felt the capital was necessary to educate women of the importance of washable menstrual options on a *global* scale. Being on the show, gaining exposure, and getting a deal would allow me to expand my reach, sharing with women all over the world the negative impact disposables have on both the body and the environment,

Blood and urine are not your average topic for television entertainment and the producers loved the shock appeal such a product would create. It would make for great groundbreaking, chair-squirming television. I knew every woman from ages 12 to 55 needed to know an alternative to disposable menstrual products was available that was 10 times more absorbent, 100 times healthier, ⅛ the cost, and would significantly reduce the amount of waste in the landfills.

I also knew I had a great business concept with plush margins, proper distribution streams, and global fulfillment structures in place. Of course, I knew it was awkward to talk about periods and piddles. Most people get squeamish if you mention menstruation and incontinence.

Yet, despite the questionable subject matter, I arrived at the studio confident, practiced, and prepared. I set up my display proudly, ignoring the snickering and raised eyebrows. I brazenly delivered my pitch when the crew came by to do a mini run-through and let me practice the big reveal. If you haven't seen the show, I'll share that they like to surprise the Dragons with a dramatic 'ta-da.' Mine was lifting a five-foot, black, foam-core screen off the front of the table to unveil my colorful menstrual pads displayed beautifully for millions of viewers to see.

Everything had gone according to plan, so when it was my moment to walk out on stage, I was both miffed and entertained by my body's bubbling palpitations. But go meant go! And go I did… down the fake wooden corridor… past the row of frosted windows… to the top of the stairs… down to the yellow tape on the floor… in front of a dozen blaring lights… and six semi-scowling, confidently-sitting investors whom everyone calls THE DRAGONS!

Seeing them in person was admittedly daunting and my nerves caused me to do a little hop before I landed on my mark. If you watch the show you will see me gleefully arriving at the *spot* I was *told* to be on with a joyous skip of excitement. With the lights nearly blinding me, I took a pause to absorb the moment. I breathed in all that it meant to be there. Not standing there potentially getting money, but on that spot because I had made it… to that moment in my life… where I had pushed past the impossibility of going to Asia alone to invent a new product… where I had disregarded the naysayers and dejectors who said Lotus Liners were stupid, ridiculous, and gross. Where I had formed a desire to be on the show, pasted it on my vision board, and then step by step, failure, after failure, achievement after achievement, struggle after struggle followed the wish, knowing, and dream that was rooted in my soul. I did everything I needed to get there. From idea to completion, from crazy dream to fruition. That was the moment where working toward something and achieving it converged… and I had to take a moment to take it all in.

Sometimes in life, we set a goal far out in the distance and we make changes… adjustments… and alter our life in such a way that the dream is the only thing we focus on. Change Makers are known for this. We are driven to set an ambitious desire that seems impossible, outlandish, and even *unnecessary* to others. Change Makers see their purpose differently. They see the good it will do. They see how it will benefit others. Any self discrimination, rejection, or struggles appear small in comparison to the gain it will bring. Makers of change push past the obstacles and focus on the outcome they envision. They put it all on the line because they see that the change they are fighting for is worth far more than the recognition, wealth, and accolades that might come. They know that change means improvement and a better life for others. These unrelenting individuals stay the course to reach their desired outcome. I was no different and for many weeks, months, and years I had been moving in that trajectory: the one that required me to be more of who I was and go after the change I wanted to see.

Standing there was exhilarating, but it wasn't quite my Ignite moment.

Yes, it was filled with accomplishment and pride, but that moment didn't change me so much that I walked off the stage a transformed individual. I did feel proud of myself and the rewarding exhale that comes from reaching a goal. But I noticed how the Dragons were sitting on a raised stage to give them a more dominant appearance. I saw the ricketiness of the set, the false walls, the black heavy curtains to cover the open areas, and the unused equipment stashed to the side. I observed the massive amounts of makeup the Dragons all wore on their face, camera make-up that looks good through a lens but artificial and somewhat comical when seen from up close. I noticed how their discerning looks and color-coordinated outfits were strategically planned and how the look of surprise from my reveal was overly rehearsed. It was then that I remembered that it was all for the audience and the anxious worry and heightened trepidation I had felt suddenly left me like water pouring from a bucket. It was a show for mass entertainment and hopeful consumption. I was there to please the viewers, impress the investors, and talk about something few want to mention; especially to a nation of followers. I moved from wanting it so badly to seeing that just being there proved I could do it. That I *had* it done it. That in itself was the prize.

In perfect Dragon's Den fashion, I was questioned, quizzed, and 'raked over the coals' by the six multi-millionaires. One by one they mocked, teased, inquired, joked, investigated, and probed me, my business, and my projected ROI. One by one they said, "No thank you, not for me," and "Not interested." My favorite was when one of the male judges said, "I consider myself to know a lot of things about a lot of things, but this is one thing I don't want to know anything about." After what seemed like forever and at the same time mere moments, my 50-minute interview was coming to an end. I felt like I had done my best, stood my ground to their slights, and demonstrated with integrity the benefits of my product and my devotion to the vision.

I was getting ready to walk out. I had surrendered to all the rejections and thanked the judges for their time and feedback. I began to say my goodbyes when the judge on the far right spoke up that she had not yet had her turn. I immediately felt like a fool and apologized profusely for forgetting she had not yet given her judgment. Like the other Dragons, I was expecting a logical business criticism and a polite refusal wishing me luck with my endeavor. Instead, she asked a few more questions, made a couple of comments, and took a long pause to look down at her notebook. That riled up the judge who was the first to reject my offer. A couple of curt, cross of words ensued as I stood cemented to the yellow tape beneath me. Suddenly, all of the Dragons began adding in their opinions. Some for, some against. Some encouraged her, others tried to dissuade her. Before I knew what happened, I was offered a deal.... 150 thousand dollars for 30 percent of my company.

Contrary to the rush of emotional glee, I played coy for a nano-second. I had pre-planned a delayed reaction in hopes of drawing out viewer anticipation. I wanted to pretend I needed to think about saying yes. In truth, I had gone in knowing I would take *any* deal as I wanted so much to use that injection to widen my distribution, expand to Europe, and educate women on a much larger scale. Following my preconceived plan, I dramatically rubbed my chin in contemplation even though I was bursting internally with excitement. Then I clapped my hands, skipped again in delight, and joyously rushed over to hug the judge who believed in me enough to make such an offer. Our hug felt like hugging my future. I was elated and had a deep sense of appreciation for the entire process.

I walked off the set feeling a combination of super sassy and at the same time sliced to ribbons by the entire interrogative affair. Within seconds a camera was again four inches from my face and the same assistant was shaking my hand in congratulations. My adrenaline was high and this time I playfully showed my excitement for them to record. I hammed it up for the camera because I know what a network wants: big reactions, super doses of appreciation, and incentive to get others to apply for the show. Happy inside on one level, judging my performance on the other, we celebrated in whispers as the next contestant was up and I was escorted off of the soundstage.

I walked back into the holding room feeling a mix of emotions. Yes, I had just landed a deal. Yes, someone believed in my dream. But the scrutiny and barrage of questions had taken a toll on my veneer. I was whisked into a small room to sign papers, confidentiality agreements, and read a long list of rules that included the fact that I was to tell NO ONE about my deal until the show aired in five to six months. Revealing the results could jeopardize my deal, so I had to sign documents to guarantee my silence until the episode officially aired.

Robotically I packed up my display and went to my hotel, awaiting my flight the next day. Finally alone and in the darkness of my room, I cried. It had been endless hours of waiting then rushing, going through each hoop of the process before finally standing before six very opinionated, very brilliant people as they judged me, my invention, and the depth of my financial understanding. I felt my performance had been good but not great. I was mad that I had been tripped up by their imposing analysis of my industry. I regretted that I didn't push back harder when they quizzed me. I rehashed the entire interaction word for word and was ashamed at my lack of witty answers, my failure to contradict their barrage, and how I fumbled when they tried to confuse me. I wanted to do better. I saw myself being smarter than I was, faster with my numbers, and more jovial when they made jokes about menstruation. I felt disappointed in myself and, to be truthful, I cried each time I evaluated my performance once I returned home. Since I couldn't reveal what had happened, everyone thought I had lost and spent time consoling me. I was melancholy inside because I knew deep down I should have been more prepared. I could have been tougher and I felt embarrassed because, while I did well at some things, I felt like I dropped the ball on others.

I know it sounds ungrateful to be moping over *getting* a six-figure deal, but my performance had spotlighted some of my shortcomings and deep down I knew I could have done better. It Ignited a fire in me to do more from then on and never *ever* allow myself to be in that position with my business again. I was a changed, Change Maker. I vowed to make sure that when it came to my company and my holdings, I was going to be fully knowledgeable and always prepared.

Yet, this was also not my full Ignite moment.

It was, though, the catalyst to cataclysmic change. I tripled my efforts and expanded my thinking. I dove headfirst into learning *everything* I could about my market, the trends, the business, and what my long term projections were. My Dragon had sent me a long list of requirements to solidify our deal. Each month I was required to provide a full report of profits and losses, income and projections, sales, shorts, new clients, targeted clients, and a dozen other business-related data points that would help her decide if Lotus Liners was worth investing in. I spent eight months religiously submitting my president's report and summarizing my accounts on our monthly one-on-one calls. After half a year the negations stagnated, but I preserved like I always do. Believing that dedication pays off and my Dragon would sign the check the next month, or after that next hurdle, or once I reached that next percentage increase we had agreed to.

Once the show aired to the public I was certain the money would arrive. Everyone now knew the deal that had been struck and I was convinced the transaction would go through. But the months went on and the calls from my Dragon became less frequent. I was doing my utmost in submitting my brief, streamlining my procedures, increasing my online presence, and shaving costs to raise my margins. I intimately knew every aspect of my operation. I took all those previous negative feelings and funneled them into new goals and doing more good than ever before. It was the best business training I could have asked for.

Still believing my deal was to happen, I flew back to Toronto nine months after the taping of the show. This time I was there as one of the finalists in a nationwide award for female entrepreneurs. And at the evening's gala... *my* Dragon was the keynote speaker. I sat in the front row looking up at her during her speech and tried to envision us working together, ploughing through the stigmas and redefining the norms. She was brilliant in her industry, but I realized quickly, she didn't know much about mine. She was younger than me and outspoken in ways that were not fully in alignment with where I was headed. As I listened to her share her corporate dealings and shrewd business tactics, I questioned if that's what I wanted in a partner. As she spoke about the other people she had invested in, those who had let her down, those who had been a disappointment, I wondered how it must feel to give money away to people who don't invest in themselves.

Suddenly the padded seat under my chair felt very uncomfortable. I had to ask myself what made me want a complete stranger to give me money? What made me believe that she knew more about my business when I was fully immersed in it? Why was I looking for an outside injection when I had proven from the conception of my product that I knew my business, could grow it, and was highly successful in doing so?

That was my Ignite moment.

I awoke to the realization that she had her ways and I had mine. She knew what she knew, but over the last year, I had learned how to take my business to new heights all on my own. I had tripled our profits, I had expanded our distribution, and I had stepped into my own arena of success. Maybe not to the same level as her bank balance, but I was making strides in my own way and I was doing it all while maintaining 100 percent ownership of my company. I was successful, I was profitable, and if I stayed on target — focused on what I was good at — and maintained my vision, I would reach the same amount of money in the business as what I was asking for from her.

Suddenly the thrill of getting a check from her was cast into the shadows of all the work I had accomplished in my own right. As soon as I realized I was on track to make that money on my own, needing it from her felt unnecessary. In fact, a huge well of ownership fell over me. My company was *my* responsibility. Once I embraced my own capacity to earn those funds independently and stopped looking anywhere else but at me, her *lack* of investment actually became evident. My company was my heart and soul, she merely saw the profits and loss. My success hinged on me, not anyone else!

Later that night, I approached my Dragon as she was mingling in the crowd. She recognized me and we hugged in a welcoming way. Nine months prior I had embraced her with so much thankfulness for what she *might give* me, yet that evening I felt different. I was grateful for what she *had given* me. I stepped back, out of our clasped arms, and knew *my* future was in my *own* hands. As I listened to her, socializing politely, a voice inside me said, "You don't need anyone to make you a Change Maker. You are already one."

I had learned a great deal from my Dragon in providing those statements, concentrating on my business, and I used the entire situation to step into the next version of me. I let go of wanting funds from investors and focused on being my own investor. I became eager to formulate what business news I would tell myself at the end of the month and what financial summary I would report to the CEO in me. I looked at myself as *the* investor and made making the money *as an independently owned company* my only financial option.

As soon as that thought took form in my consciousness, everything changed. Less than five months later, I *earned* the full amount of my deal. I didn't have to give up 30 percent of my company; instead, I started another new company and made the same amount as my deal in less than six months. I saw that I could do it. The changes I made in my business practices surmounted into tremendous business strides. Incremental moves, slight pivots, and consistent, repetitive work yielded consistent, productive results. That's the essence of becoming a Change Maker: making a significant change.

The icing on the cake is the lives of the people who have been changed by me stepping into the grace and magic of my gifts. When I embraced what I was doing, and what I was doing well, the way before me was revealed. The Universe opened more doors and introduced me to the right people. Trusting in my own ability gave me a greater ability. My change inspired others to change and a chain reaction of Change Makers began happily changing their own lives.

They say that going all-out allows others to do the same. We each have talents. We each have something powerful to offer the world. Some days we know it beyond conviction; other times our hearts pound with unsureness and fear. Many times we look for approval from those who we *assume* know more when the truth is we have all we need to know within ourselves. The abilities and possibilities are right in front of us; all we have to do is change the way we see ourselves and become the Change Makers we were born to be.

Your gifts, strengths, and aspirations are the gems in the journey. You can have all that you believe in when you begin believing in yourself. It may sound too simple and even cliche to 'believe in yourself,' but I assure you it isn't. When you know that you have the ability to accomplish something, your abilities grow. How you get those abilities is by doing it; by learning it step by step; and by teaching yourself through hard work, investigation, curiosity, and the wisdom of a few good mentors. You don't have to do it alone, but *you* have to *do* it. Your success comes directly in proportion to the amount of effort you put in, so put in massive amounts of effort and you will get massive amounts of results. Incredible is just waiting for you!

IGNITE ACTION STEPS

- **Be your biggest investor.** Too often we want someone to invest in our projects more than we want to ourselves. We look for others to do the work and complain that the mundane things are boring and useless. Get deeply interested in every aspect of you. From your health to your relationship... in your words, actions, and activities... be the one who injects more into it than anyone else. No one is going to care as much as you and no one is going to work as hard for your success as you should. Taking the easy route does not teach you more. Learning everything you have to in order to achieve success *will* get you there.

- **Know your business inside and out.** Knowing everything about your business puts you in the success bracket. You don't have to execute everything, but you need to know the systematic workings of every aspect of your business. Before you farm things out, learn how they work. Understand the fundamentals so you can make good decisions that benefit and profit you. Not knowing how to do something is disempowering. Educate yourself so you know how to make the right choices that lead to more business and more beneficial choices.

- **Have a clear vision of what you want.** When you know EXACTLY what it is you want, you'll get it. Look at your goals from every angle. Envision every aspect of them in your mind from start to finish. Know them intimately. See them happening in the greatest detail and tell yourself exactly what the outcome will be. The brain does not know the difference between what it sees with the eyes and what it sees in the mind's eye, so fill your mind with scenes of the life you choose to create.

- **Get ready for incredible!** Incredible is just waiting to happen to you. The Universe is working with you, *for* you, and in harmony with all that you say and do. Know that your greatness is already assigned to take place. Your gifts are eagerly awaiting and what you bring to the world, others want! Embrace it, love it, and be all in it.

JB Owen - Canada
Founder and CEO of Ignite, Lotus Liners and JB Global Incorporated
www.igniteyou.life
www.lotusliners.com
www.thepinkbillionaire.com
🔲 *@ThePinkBillionaire*
🔲 *Ignitewithjb*
🔲 *thepinkbillionaire*

WE HOPE THIS BOOK TOUCHES YOUR HEART,
MOTIVATES YOUR SPIRIT, AND AWAKENS YOUR
SOUL TO GO OUT AND BE AN AMAZING

Change Maker

IN YOUR OWN LIFE, RIGHT NOW!

Thank you

A tremendous thank you goes to those who are working in the background, editing, supporting and encouraging the authors. They are some of the most genuine and heart-centered people I know. Their devotion to the vision of IGNITE, their integrity and the message they aspire to convey is of the highest possible caliber. They, all, want you to find your IGNITE moment and flourish. They each believe in you and that's what makes them so outstanding. Their dream is for your dreams to come true.

Editing Team: Alex Blake, Andrea Drajewicz, Jock Mackenzie, Wendy Albrecht, and Chloe Marie

Production Team: Dania Zafar, Peter Giesin & JB Owen

A special thanks and gratitude to the project leaders: Marnie Tarzia, Alex Jarvis, and Ana Sofia Orozco for their support behind the scenes and for going 'above and beyond' to make this a wonderful experience, ensuring everything ran smoothly and with elegance.

A deep appreciation goes to each and every author who made Ignite Female Change Makers possible — with all your exciting stories embracing this amazing idea of making change across the globe.

To all our readers, we thank you for reading and loving the stories, for opening your hearts and minds to the idea of Igniting your own lives. We welcome you to share your story and become a new author in one of our upcoming books. Sharing your message and Ignite moments may be exactly what someone needs to hear.

Join us on this magical Ignite journey!

IGNITE

Leading the industry in Empowerment Publishing,
IGNITE transforms individuals into
INTERNATIONAL BESTSELLING AUTHORS.

WRITE YOUR STORY IN AN IGNITE BOOK!!

With over 400 amazing individuals to date writing their stories and sharing their Ignite moments, we are positively impacting the planet and raising the vibration of HUMANITY. Our stories inspire and empower others and we want to add your story to one of our upcoming books!

If you have a story of perseverance, determination, growth, awakening and change... and you've felt the power of your Ignite moment, we'd love to hear from you.

Go to our website, click APPLY and share a bit of your Ignite transformation.

We are always looking for motivating stories that will make a difference in someone's life. Our fun, enjoyable, four-month writing process is like no other — and the best thing about Ignite is the community of outstanding, like-minded individuals dedicated to helping others.

Our road to sharing your message and becoming a bestselling author begins right here.

YOU CAN IGNITE ANOTHER SO JOIN US TO
IGNITE A BILLION LIVES WITH A BILLION WORDS.

Apply at: www.igniteyou.life
Inquire at: info@igniteyou.life

Find out more at: www.igniteyou.life

Anne Catherine Færgemann
www.nordicclinic.com

Asifa Akbar
shineyourbestlight@gmail.com

Beejal Coulson
www.quantumlifetechnique.com

Chrissy Levett - From a Place of Despair to Purpose
- *Drawdown* by Paul Hawken
- *https://www.creative-conscience.org.uk*
- *https://www.forumforthefuture.org*
- *https://bcorporation.net*

Christy Parker - Escape Your Cage and Learn to Soar
- *The Code of the Extraordinary Mind* by Vishen Lakhiani
- *https://www.myss.com/*

Diana Borges - Acknowledging the Power Within
Diana Borges, Heart Access/Tuning Forks healing sessions ~ BorgesExperience.com

Elena Harder - The Deep End of Mom Guilt
ElenaHarderR.com/nomad for a video walkthrough of the action steps

Holly Olp - Running Up the Down Escalator
www.hollyolp.com

Jennifer Newton - Co-creating the New Earth
www.worlddharma.com (Alan Clements)

Katarina Amadora - Cultivating Change
- *Food Fix* by Dr. Mark Hyman

- *Grain Brain* by David Perlmutter
- *The Doctor's Farmacy Podcast with Dr. Mark Hyman*
- *https://americanpromise.net/blog/2019/06/18/ big-money-the-farm-bill-and-family-farms-vs-industrial-agriculture/*
- *https://www.earthconsciouslife.org/theneedtogrow*
- *https://regenitech.com/*

María Eugenia Anés Draegert - Getting to Know Vulnerability
- *Measuring Women's Economic Empowerment: Critical Lessons* Edit by Susana Martínez Restrepo and Laura Ramos Jaimes
- *Ask For It* by Linda Babcock and Sara Laschver
- *Playing Big* by Tara Mohr
- *What Works. Gender Equality* by design by Iris Bohnet
- *Opcion B by Sheryl Sandberg and Adam Grant*
- *https://www.corewoman.org*

Mindy Stern - I'll show them who's irresponsible!
www.healthyfinancesglobal.com

Priya Lakhi - The Wild Art of Unbecoming
- *The Artist's Way* by Julia Cameron
- *Autobiography of a Yogi* by Paramhansa Yogaananda
- *First, We Make the Beast Beautiful* by Sarah Wilson
- *Rising Strong* by Brené Brown
- *A Thousand Names For Joy* by Byron Katie
- *Untie The Strong Woman* by Clarissa Pinkola Estes
- *Vipassana, which means to see things as they really are, is one of India's most ancient techniques of meditation ~ www.dhamma.org/en-US/index*

Stephanie Barros - Igniting Your SPARK
- *The Six Pillars of Self-Esteem: The Definitive Work on Self-Esteem by the Leading Pioneer in the Field* by Nathaniel Branden
- *Team Code of Honor: The Secrets of Champions in Business and in Life* by Blair Singer
- *A Woman's Self-Esteem - Struggles and Triumphs in the Search for Identity* by Nathaniel Branden
- *https://www.success.com/the-business-of-self-esteem/*
- *https://www.highperformanceinstitute.com/*

Vivien Hunt - Being OK with Uncertainty

www.gumboots.org.uk - The Gumboots Foundation supports community grassroots projects for children and education in South Africa (UK Registered Charity number 1123418). In partnership with Gumboots South Africa and its sister organization Kidlinks World in the USA.

PHOTO CREDITS

Ana Sofía Orozco - *Shirley Salvatore @rishphotostudio*
Andrea Drajewicz - *John Drajewicz*
Andrea Szücs - *Nonoka Judit Sipos*
Asifa Akbar - *Bill Meachem, Artistic Creations Photography*
Beejal Coulson - *Cat Lane*
Chrissy Levett - *Kersti Niglas*
Christy Parker - *Nikki Incandela*
Claudia Chavez Gordoa - *Dora Basaca*
Diana Borges - *Star Shots Photography*
Diana Lockett - *www.lostboyfindings.com/*
Elena Harder - *Alexander Harder*
Holly Olp - *13 Snaps Photography*
J Meehan - *Evolved Imagery*
JB Owen - *Kersti Niglas*
Jennifer Newton - *Heather Holt Photography*
Karima Nadine Stein - *Wencke Lieber Photography*
Katarina Amadora - *Karen Harms*
María Eugenia Anés Draegert - *Edward Jiménez*
Melissa Elevey - *Bethany Tara Photography*
Nicole Stoker Evans - *Cydney Luks Photography*
Priya Lakhi - *Rupa Kapoor*
Rosalyn Palmer - *Kersit Niglas*
Vivien Hunt - *Manuela Fraioli*